BY ANY MEANS NECESSARY

BY ANY MEANS NECESSARY

Malcolm X: Real, Not Reinvented

Critical Conversations on Manning Marable's
Biography of Malcolm X

Edited by Herb Boyd, Ron Daniels, Maulana Karenga and
Haki R. Madhubuti

Chicago

Third World Press
Publishers since 1967
Chicago

© 2012 by Herb Boyd, Ron Daniels, Maulana Karenga and
Haki R. Madhubuti

All rights reserved. No part of the material protected by this copyright
notice may be reproduced, stored in a retrieval system, or transmitted
in any form by any means, electronic mechanical, photocopying,
recording or otherwise without prior written permission, except in
the case of brief quotations embodied in critical articles and reviews.
Queries should be addressed to Third World Press, P.O. Box 19730,
Chicago, IL 60619.

First Edition
Printed in the United States of America

Generously supported by the Lomax Companies of Philadelphia

Library of Congress Control Number: 2011943075

ISBN 13: 978-0-88378-336-8
16 15 14 13 12   6 5 4 3 2 1

Cover and Interior layout: Relana Johnson
Photos courtesy of: Malcolm X Estate and Library of Congress
Malcolm X at Queens Court | 1964. | 1 photographic print. | Hiller, Herman | LC-USZ62-119478
New York World-Telegram and the Sun Newspaper Photograph Collection (Library of Congress)

Dedication

For Minister Malcolm X, El Hajj Malik El-Shabazz, whose message and meaning are uniquely uplifting and eternal and whose life models and mirrors the dignity-affirming way we should walk and work in the world, seeking and speaking truth, doing and demanding justice, and striving constantly for the good world we all want and deserve.

For Dr. Betty Shabazz, resilient and resourceful wife and co-worker, who added her knowledge, strength and contribution to that of her husband's, lifted up his legacy and raised their children in his name and honor.

For Attallah, Qubilah, Ilyasah, Gamilah, Malaak and Malikah, his beloved children, who embody another important legacy he left us and who have borne a great burden of history, given their father's mission, martyrdom and transition at such an early age.

And for his people, us, Africans everywhere, for whom he prophesied liberation, sacrificed his life in striving and struggle, and lifted up the light of our history that pointed toward the unlimited possibilities we possess and are compelled to pursue.

Contents

Opening Words
Malcolm | Sonia Sanchez xi
Publisher's Statement: Actually an Obligation | Haki R. Madhubuti xiii
Introduction | Herb Boyd..xxv

Laying the Groundwork
When All is Said . . . Malcolm's Legacy is Secure | Ron Daniels................3
The Meaning and Measure of Malcolm X: Critical Remembrance and Rightful
    Reading | Maulana Karenga..10

Response, Message and Meaning
The Meaning of Manning Marable's Biography of Malcolm X |
    Imam Talib Abdur-Rashid 29
On Manning's Malcolm X | Mumia Abu-Jamal 34
Rethinking Malcolm Means First Learning how to Think: What was Marable
    Thinking? And Why? | Abdul Alkalimat...36
An Afrocentric Take on Manning Marable's *Malcolm X: A Life of Reinvention* |
    Molefi Kete Asante..51
Malcolm X Still Inspires Today | Rick Ayers 60
Manning Marable's Malcolm X Book | Amiri Baraka................................68
Malcolm X: A Life of Reinvention by Manning Marable, A Look at the Book |
    Amir Bey 76
The Fault Lies not in our Stars, But in our Biographers: Minutes to Midnight,
    Manning Marable Succumbs | Todd Steven Burroughs 81
The Legacy of Malcolm X | Ta-Nehisi Coates..87
Marable, Redefining Biography | Jelani Cobb.......................................97
Paper Tiger | Karl Evanzz..101
Evolution of a Black Nationalist Revolutionary | Iyaluua and Herman Ferguson..107
Manning Marable and the Malcolm X Biography Controversy: A Response to Critics
    African World | Bill Fletcher Jr. 121
Dragging Malcolm X to Obamaland | Glen Ford....................................136

CONTENTS

Marable's Revolutionary Malcolm | Rhone Fraser 142
Manning Marable: Humanizing Malcolm or Denigrating Legacies? |
    Kelly Harris 149
Manning Marable's Malcolm X | Wil Haygood 159
A Toothless Pursuit of a Revolutionary's Truths:
    Marable's *Malcolm X: A Life of Reinvention* | Errol Henderson 163
Malcolm X: The Man and Our Times | Fred Hord 178
Unearthing Meaning in Marable's Malcolm X | Peter James Hudson 188
Manning Marable's Regurgitation on the Life and Memory of Malcolm X |
    Ezra Hyland 191
Is Imitation Truly the Mother of Invention? | Regina Jennings 200
Rescuing Malcolm X From His Calculated Myths | Peniel E. Joseph 207
Malcolm, Charisma and Ancestry | Clyde Ledbetter Jr. 217
Reinforcing Barricades | Fred Logan 224
On Malcolm, Ourselves | Kevin McGruder 230
A Response | Starla Muhammad 235
Revising Perspectives on Malcolm X | Nell Irvin Painter 238
A Review of Manning Marable's *Malcolm X* | Imani Perry 241
By Any Means | Gregory J. Reed and Bryonn Bain 244
We Declare Our Right to be a Human Being: Malcolm X, "A Life of
    Reclamation" | Michael Simanga 257
Malcolm X: Reinvention or African-centered Service and Sacrifice |
    Diane D. Turner and Aslaku Berhanu 263

Last Word

On My Father | Ilyasah Shabazz 275

Contributors 278

OPENING WORDS

Malcolm
Sonia Sanchez

do not speak to me of martyrdom
of men who die to be remembered
on some parish day.
i don't believe in dying
though i too shall die
and violets like castanets
will echo me.

yet this man
this dreamer,
thick-lipped with words
will never speak again
and in each winter
when the cold air cracks
with frost, i'll breathe
his breath and mourn
my gun-filled nights.
he was the sun that tagged
the western sky and
melted tiger-scholars
while they searched for stripes.
he said, "forget you white
man. we have been
curled too long. nothing
is sacred now. not your
white faces nor any
land that separates
until some voices
squat with spasms."

do not speak to me of living.
life is obscene with crowds
of white on black.
death is my pulse.
what might have been
is not for him/or me
but what could have been
floods the womb until i drown.

Publisher's Statement: Actually an Obligation

Haki R. Madhubuti

Original.
Ragged-round,
Rich-robust.

He had the hawk-man's eyes.
We gasped. We saw the maleness.
The maleness raking out and making guttural the air
and pushing us to walls.

And in a soft and fundamental hour
a sorcery devout and vertical
beguiled the world.

He opened us—
who was a key,

who was a man.
—Gwendolyn Brooks

Gwendolyn Brooks' poem "Malcolm X" clearly defines without ambiguity the mission and mettle of our fallen leader. "Original" he was from his military-like stature and manner, rhythm-cadenced speech, eye-glassed enclosed eyes that could detect smiling liars, and an all-encompassing mind quicker than today's Internet search. He did open us a door and remained the key that redefined Black manhood while urgently issuing in a call for a richer personal creditability and a placing of the Black family into the center of our lives, deep learning, cultural and economic responsibility, self-definition and self-discipline, demanding organization and Black institutional development. He was the key that opened a Black world door for me.

My intention here is not to supply deep discussion on the pros and cons of Professor Marable's book, *Malcolm X: A Life of Reinvention*. All of the contributors to this volume, *By Any Means Necessary: Malcolm X, Real, Not Reinvented*, have done a marvelous job of discussing his text. As the publisher of this critical response and review collection, my goal is to bring clarity to the significance and importance of Malcolm X to me, our people, the Black Arts Movement, Pan-African and human rights movements and to thank him for putting me (us) in a position to respond to this attack on him, his family and by extension all conscious Black people. It is my responsibility as a cultural son of Minister Malcolm not to stand on street corners throwing invectives at Professor Marable, but to use the tools of my profession (poet, publisher, editor, educator, cultural intellectual and Black man) to fight all white supremacist slander even if produced by Black people.

I am serious as a first love. I am here, able, ready and have never detoured from the Pan-African path that Margaret and Charles Burroughs, Dudley Randall, Hoyt W. Fuller, Barbara Ann Sizemore, Gwendolyn Brooks and Malcolm X prepared me to undertake. As a dear friend of Dr. Betty Shabazz and their family,* I have always been in consultation with her, a first responder to the Shabazz family needs as best as I am capable of doing. Along with supporters like Ossie Davis and Ruby Dee, Susan L. Taylor and Khephra Burns, Maya Angelou, Coretta Scott King, Myrlie Evers (Williams) and others. I was always a phone call away.

Third World Press, The Institute of Positive Education, our four schools—The Betty Shabazz International Charter School, Barbara Ann Sizemore Academy, New Concept School, DuSable Leadership Academy, and Third World Press Foundation would not exist if Malcolm X (El Hajj Malik El Shabazz) in 1962 had not entered my young life like a runaway train picking up inquiring and angry Black men and women ready for battle and ready to explode. I was then known as Don L. Lee, serving in the United States Army stationed outside of Chicago. I read any Black literature I could get my hands on. By the age of 18, I had devoured the works of

---

* In 1992, Betty Shabazz came to my 50th birthday celebration, which was a fundraiser for our schools; she made a major donation at that time. During the decade of the 1980s she would regularly attend the National Black Wholistic retreats at the National Black Wholistic Society sponsored each year in upstate New York. I brokered the public meeting between Dr. Betty Shabazz and Minister Farrakhan at the Apollo Theatre in New York City and was the Pan-African-Nationalist family supporter who spoke at her last rites.

Richard Wright, W.E.B. Du Bois, Langston Hughes, Rayford T. Logan, E. Franklin Frazier, Carter G. Woodson, Paul Robeson, Marcus Garvey, Sterling A. Brown, Alain Locke and most of the Black poets, experimenting with the language at that time, including Gwendolyn Brooks, Melvin B. Tolson, Frank Horne, Margaret Walker, Robert E. Hayden, Frank Marshall Davis, Countee Cullen, Arna Bontemps, Jean Toomer, Paul Laurence Dunbar, James Weldon Johnson and others. In fact, in October of 1960 on the bus going to basic training at Fort Leonard Wood, Missouri, I was reading Paul Robeson's *Here I Stand.* I share this only to note that I was intellectually ready, culturally sensitive, economically destitute (the U.S. Army was the poor boy's answer to unemployment—as it is today) and politically motivated for direct involvement in the struggle and ready for a new Black voice.

Malcolm X was the first Black man who had a national reputation that I saw and heard speaking truth to his people and to power. Before I heard Malcolm X, I was literally suffocating in a room full of "white" air. Malcolm X helped to shape my young voice. His articulations were the immediate call, an S.O.S. to young Black men and women who felt deeply that we needed a Black leader that would push our agenda via direct action rather than always reacting to white world supremacy. His vision was one of a liberated African people functioning pro-actively, always in their best interest worldwide.

Therefore, I do not come to this issue as a non-participatory observer. Most people who know me and/or my work understand the significant influence that Malcolm X has had on my life. I've dedicated many of my books and published poems and essays in respect to his life. I have said many times in public and in private that of the men who emerged in the 1960s, I credit Malcolm X with liberating my voice and planting the seed of commitment to building independent Black institutions in me. Malcolm X's foresight regarding the need to internationalize the Black condition in the United States helped me in my later choices to become directly involved with the African liberation struggle.

However, it was Malcolm's personal demeanor: his intelligence, self-discipline, study habits, seriousness, respect for family, political and cultural awareness, frugality, honesty, strength in the face of evil fire, work ethic, boldness, humility, trustworthiness, preparedness, selflessness, and most of all, winning attitude and integrity that attracted me to him and his ideas. Most importantly, he came from the same street I came from and did not remain a victim.

The distinguished historian John Henrik Clarke, a personal friend, supporter and co-worker in building The Organization of Afro-American Unity (OAAU) gives of greater insight into Malcolm X in his influential book *Who Betrayed The African World Revolution?* He writes:

> He was a man, one of the fastest learners that I have ever met in my life. You could give him information and he would read this information back to you teaching you lessons over and above your instructions to him without offending you...He could speak to the reader and the non-reader, the college professor and the illiterate, simultaneously and the message would get across to them... Malcolm X is too big to fit into any kind of bowl...marked communism, socialism or capitalism. He was a believer in the ultimate destiny of his people.

Professor Clarke also states that Malcolm X's most revolutionary statements are in "Ballot or the Bullet" and "Message to the Grassroots" where Malcolm X specifically dealt with political power and the "land question as the basis of the Nation." Professor Clarke's criticism of the political left as "a bunch of opportunists" who were able to gain the rights to Malcolm X's speeches, he writes, "They began to publish his speeches and interpret them, trying to prove that he was what they decided him to be." If one reads Professor Marable's books carefully, as noted by several of the contributors, it too is a "left" critique.

It was Malcolm's influence and his practice of Islam that helped to push me to visit Africa in 1969 to see the religion in practice and to see how it served our people at the "source." Three weeks among Africans who viewed Islam as blood and oxygen itself was not enough to convert me, but my investigations in Africa (multiple visits) and continuing study of Islam and other world religions have helped to prepare me to be the man I am today. The spiritual core that Islam embraces—along with all great religions—is that of the moral and ethical person, the good, giving, and serving individual. The selfless individual in the midst of sacred and secular corruption crying against hellish odds to return the masses of people to good work and good life is what Malcolm X was about. However, he never lost his Black political and cultural mindset; he expanded it.

Deep in the pit of my stomach, I knew that when Malcolm broke with the Nation of Islam he also signed his death certificate; he knew this too. He could have had a life with his wife and children, an honored position in international struggle, and a materially comfortable life if he had remained silent. However, there is something inside men and women of honest conscience that will not allow them to take the easy and safe compromise. There is something about being able to live with one's self and daily look your spouse, children, family, friends, and co-workers in the face and tell them lie after lie after lie. For Malcolm there was always the question of moral authenticity, the going sub-surface to live one's words, always an honest search.

The principles, values, ideas, and the Islamic lifestyle that Malcolm was taught and that he taught others was more than foundational theory; they were life itself. The source was the *Holy Qur'an*—the book that represents each Muslim's personal connection to Allah and the Prophet Muhammad. Far from being a perfect man, Malcolm X was a man seeking perfection. His separation from the Nation of Islam (NOI) marked a period of rapid reformation, growth, and much mental pain for Malcolm. Very few of us understand the hourly effects of fear and terror that constantly and persistently plagued Malcolm's physic during his last two years. In choosing the truth, he assigned his loyalty to a higher power (as he was taught). In doing so, he came up against all the fury and anger of the most military-minded and organized group of Black men in America at that time. Also he was considered an enemy of the state and was under a constant surveillance and monitoring by state and federal agencies. Malcolm X understood the gravity of his decision. From that day on, he knew that his time was limited. He had trained many of the men himself. He knew that to speak ill against Elijah Muhammad, the "father," was, in their eyes—regardless of the truth—blasphemy.

Malcolm X's assassination on 21 February 1965 sent young brothers like me (I was 22) back to tears and weapons. His assassination stopped an important part of the movement. Many in the Black Nationalist community separated themselves from the NOI and even refused to buy its newspaper. We could not prove it, but we knew deep in our hearts that Malcolm was murdered by members of the NOI with full knowledge of federal, state and local law enforcement agencies. Dr. Clarke made this observation:

> Some will argue about who assassinated him and why. But Malcolm X learned something on his way home from Africa, after he arrived in Paris and was barred from entering, after that he knew that the plan to destroy him was not designed by his own people. He knew that the apparatus was bigger than anything controlled by his own people...He knew that master murderers were out to get him and no matter whose hand pulled the trigger, that was not the planning and design of Black people.

We live in a short memory culture. White supremacy is the system that dominates Black life from cradle to grave. Therefore, Black life is seldom formally taught in our institutions and even less discussed informally. Malcolm X told our stories over and over again. Each telling gained substance and nuance as he grew, studied, struggled, traveled, dialogued with heads of state and others, debated with family, friends and foes all making a statement on his ever expanding maturity. His storytelling, especially his analyses of white supremacy, enabled us to tell our own stories without the customary editing by enemies and cowards. The moral and cultural imagination of Malcolm X transitioned into our own lives producing generations of cultural sons and daughters who do not tap dance to the latest feel good tunes provided by government or corporate America. He arrived during a time of deep winter and it is still cold, with snow falling during the summer months.

Charles W. Mills writes the following in his book *The Racial Contract*:

> White supremacy is the unnamed political system that has made the modern world what it is today. You will not find this term in introductory, or even advanced texts in political theory. A standard under-graduate philosophy course will start off with Plato and Aristotle, perhaps saying something about Augustine, Aquinas, and Machiavelli, moves on to Hobbes, Locke, Mill, and Marx, and then wind up with Rawls and Nozick....And this omission is not accidental. Rather, it reflects the fact that standard textbooks and courses have for the most part been written and designed by whites, who take their racial privilege so much for granted that they do not even see it as *political*, as a form of domination. Ironically, the most important political system of recent global history—the system of domination by which white people have historically ruled over and, in certain important ways, continue to rule over nonwhite people—is not seen as a political system at all. It is just taken for granted, it is the background against which other systems, which we are to see as political are highlighted.

The culture of white supremacy is pernicious and all encompassing in most if not all of the institutional structures of the United States, including the Black family and church. The political, historical, commercial, legal and educational institutions that nurture, guide, inform, employ, entertain, educate and define Black life and development in America represent the front line of white supremacist thought, theory, and practice. Malcolm X understood this fact, yet soldiered on.

Malcolm X was not perfect; he made mistakes and on many occasions to friend and foe, admitted error. But, who among us during the difficult sixties and the decades to follow did not error? The Malcolm X difference was that he did not allow his mistakes to destroy him. He learned from them and took succeeding steps with careful deliberation. No, he was not perfect, but he was moving toward a kind of working perfection, whether or not he would have arrived we do not know. However, the odds are it would have been a well-fought battle.

The short life of El-Hajj Malik El-Shabazz is without parallel in African American struggle. His impact is immeasurable, his message undying, his integrity legendary, his commitment unquestioned and his significance and contribution are still growing. In fact, it was Malcolm X and the Nation of Islam that first popularized the using of Black as the correct designation for people of African ancestry in America. It was also Malcolm's Organization of Afro- American Unity that made the ultimate connection between Black people here and Black people in Africa, Asia, the Americas and elsewhere. Somehow I don't feel that the ongoing debate over what we should call ourselves would have taken up too much of his time, Black and African American had entered his lexicon already married, and a divorce seemed unnecessary. Ossie Davis, a man who was usually careful with his adjectives, called him our "Black Shining Prince." He did shine, as in illuminate, and the light that glowed behind his ever present glasses should always burn in us, our children and their children until the evil that killed him and continues to kill millions of our people yearly is plowed into the earth never to rise again.

Malcolm X, the name most people remember him by, was the complex, serious, multifaceted, quick-smiling man who doubted and questioned, doubted and questioned until inaction would have been viewed as endorsement of the hypocrisy with which he could no longer live. He tried in his own unique way to give answers to those difficult and murderous times. To forget and not honor his contribution is to give quarter to the enemies of Black people and, in effect, bury memory and history in an unmarked grave.

Malcolm X understood that America was built, economically, politically and culturally on the backs and bodies of African people. His unrelenting attacks and deconstruction of white supremacist history and politics in a language and style that influenced millions of people will forever be his calling card. The novelist Russell Banks in his book *Dreaming Up America* writes:

> The narrative of race began when the first European arrived off the shores of the Caribbean Islands and Florida... where they met dark-skinned people who happened to reside here already, people whom the Europeans chose to deal with in the majority of cases as less than human, treating them instead as human chattel, as being less worthy of natural respect and kind treatment than draft animals like horses or cattle. The rationale was twofold: first, that the economic usage or exploitation of them wouldn't have made sense unless they could be seen as lesser creatures, and second, because they were not Christians...so from the very beginning, racial difference was situated at the hot center of the American imagination. And it is still there. It's still control.

Russell Banks goes on to note that race is at the core of most of America's wars, political conflicts and political campaigns, the issue that shapes "our economic lives, views of the world and "how we are dealing today with the Arab world, how we treat Africans—it all comes down to race." Malcolm X, as was Du Bois, Delany, Robeson, Garvey, Padmore, Nkrumah, Wells-Barnett and countless others understood America's central narrative and metaphor and took appropriate actions.

Our commitment to Black world struggle, and African American struggle in particular, ideally should be no less than his. To not try and reach his level of seriousness is to acknowledge our own failure and, just as important, would be a confirmation of Black impotence. Such inaction will confirm us to the garbage bins of history, and people worldwide will continue to use Black people as the catch-line in their jokes. If anything can be said about Malcolm X, it is that he was not a comedian and he did not sell "wolf tickets." This too should be our call.

In Houston A. Baker's very important book *Betrayal,* he writes of Black intellectuals who have worked incessantly against the legacy of Dr. Martin Luther King Jr. He names names and rises above any "ad hominem sensationalism, generalized condemnation, and scintillating innuendo." Yet, Dr. Baker is very serious in his analyses of their intent and outright betrayal of Dr. King's legacy, he writes:

> It is, I think, time they were "ousted" as nostalgic, black,

money-hungry reactionaries who are fully allied with the worst offices of white American power brokers, publishers, newspapers, media moguls, Internet magnates, and Ivy League universities that are, in any cultural capital and economics of the public sphere models of analysis, principally responsible for such intellectuals' esteem, wealth, and harm to the black majority.

Much of *Malcolm X: A Life of Reinvention*, the biography of Malcolm X is more about the worldview and character of Professor Manning Marable than that of Malcolm X. Marable's criticism of Alex Haley can also be explained in this light—that it was more of an Alex Haley book—in terms of politics, than Malcolm's. Professor Marable's politics, historical influences, intellectual guidance, economic support, and total disregard for Malcolm's and Betty Shabazz' six daughters and grandchildren are on grand display in his book.

Since 1971, I have been a close friend to the Shabazz family, first meeting Betty Shabazz on a plane between Chicago and New York. The Shabazz daughters have suffered in unbelievable ways having lived through the tragic death of both parents—a story worthy of a Toni Morrison novel—yet this is not fiction. Professor Marable has accepted the culture of "say or write anything and prove me wrong" with total disregard for the political and cultural affect his words and accusations would have on anyone, especially the family.

The Black creative and academic community responded quickly with deep affection to our call for this volume. It is common knowledge of the influence that Malcolm X had on members of SNCC, RAM, The Black Panther Party, Us Organization, Congress of African People, African Liberation Day Committee, and other formations. He was one of the first Black activists to raise the question of our human rights as a political strategy. However, one of the largest and most active and influential movements to hit America as a result of his assassination was The Black Arts Movement (1965-1975). Amiri Baraka, Sonia Sanchez, Larry Neal, Askia Toure, Maulana Karenga, Kalamu ya Salaam, Jon Onye Lockard, Audre Lorde, Eugene Redmond, Murray DePillars, Hoyt W. Fuller, Lucille Clifton, Mari Evans, Dudley Randall, Barbara Ann Teer, Abena Joan Brown, Gil Scott-Heron, Woodie King, Jr. Gwendolyn Brooks, Don L. Lee, and countless others were the movers and shakers of that historical period.

We must never forget that Medgar Evers, Malcolm X and Betty Shabazz, Martin Luther and Coretta Scott King are not only honored ancestors, but represent Black America's first families of the last half of the

20th century. They lived and gave their lives in a struggle that is ongoing but has advanced to a state that we their political sons and daughters can now answer lies, innuendoes and outright defamation of character quickly without fear or favor from the institutions that we own and do such liberating work.

As history would have it, this collection is edited by four men who have been influenced and critically impacted by the life and work of Malcolm X. All of the contributors also have felt and benefited in unknown ways from the presence of our beloved brother and carefully composed their essays as a contribution to the wonderful legacy of Minister Malcolm. Therefore, the royalties from the sale of *By Any Means Necessary: Malcolm X: Real, Not Reinvented* will be donated to four not-for-profit institutions designated by the editors with the greater portion going to the Malcolm X and Dr. Betty Shabazz Foundation in New York City.

Our work is not done. With over 2.5 million incarcerated Black and brown men and women in America's prisons, over 50 percent of Black and brown high school students not completing their studies, with the Black unemployment rate hitting over 50 percent in some areas, as Black home ownership is becoming a nightmare in the international corrupt money game, the "New Jim Crow" as Michelle Alexander writes in her major work is more subtle, yet ten times more effective in the dismantling and negation of Black communities. Yet, we still keep getting up, walking taller, breathing deeper as Isabel Wilkerson recounts in her marvelous epic of our great migration, *The Warmth of Other Suns*. Malcolm X taught us to confront our worst fears whether it's Wall Street, the corporate state, the small monied elite represented by the likes of Goldman Sachs, Bank of America, Citicorp, The Supreme Court and its Citizen United ruling and other legal gangsters. We must remember that pre-Malcolm X most Black people or people of African ancestry grew up hating themselves. Our ultimate mission as Malcolm X would have it is to build and resist, resist and build, and in the middle of such struggle never forget who we are and to love whom we are and pass it on. If I were to suggest one book to keep us on the right path of history and politics it would be *The Destruction of Black Civilization* by Chancellor Williams.

The documents and essays in this collection represent the first critical assessment of Professor Marable's book and I am sure that it will not be the last. In America most of us grew up running from ourselves because we did not know who we were. Malcolm X played a significant role in stopping that. He knew that more than anything else that self-knowledge was the beginning of self-empowerment. I'll end as I began with powerful words of Gwendolyn Brooks, now writing about Paul Robeson:

> *Warning, in music-words*
> *devout and large,*
> *that we are each other's*
> *harvest:*
> *we are each other's*
> *business:*
> *we are each other's*
> *magnitude and bond.*

Introduction
Herb Boyd

> This book is particularly significant for the generation who grew up after the Civil Rights Movement and the Black Studies revolution because the crisis in literature and history concerning the Black man as hero is even more critical now.
>
> —John Henrik Clarke, *The Second Crucifixion of Nat Turner*

The above quote is taken from John Henrik Clarke's introduction written some forty-three years ago in a book he edited of ten Black writers responding to William Styron's *Confessions of Nat Turner*. Styron, the writers concluded, had grossly distorted the revolutionary's true character, and they felt compelled to offer their own interpretation of this historic figure. What Dr. Clarke said about his book then and the importance it had for that generation can be applied to *By Any Means Necessary: Malcolm X: Real, Not Reinvented: Critical Conversations on Manning Marable's Biography of Malcolm X*.

This is not to compare Styron's "meditations on history" with the late Manning Marable's biography. They differ in several critical ways, most noticeably in that one is clearly fictional and the other an attempt to capture as factually as possible the life and legacy of an African American hero. While the general reaction to Styron's book was opprobrium, notwithstanding James Baldwin's endorsement, Marable's tome has created a wave of mixed reviews, practically dividing some families. And it is the plethora of diverse opinions that form the heart of this conversation, and that gives renewed impetus to Malcolm's most famous quote, "By Any Means Necessary."

Our purpose here with this collection is to continue, and to expand, the debate arising from Marable's biography. It is tragically ironic that neither Marable nor Malcolm lived long enough to enjoy the fruits of their labor. But both leave behind a number of significant issues that even the editors here have discussed, debated, and struggled for consensus. Taken together, we represent nearly two hundred years of teaching, writing, and activism. And, as a matter of full disclosure, each of us attributes our political and intellectual development to the revolutionary path forged by Malcolm X (El-Hajj Malik El-Shabazz). Thus, as we avow Malcolm's revolutionary Black Nationalist, Pan-Africanist ideology, we are ever mindful of other political and philosophical outlooks in our determination to be as even-handed as possible.

Much of our concern about publishing a book that reflects a universe of critiques—and there must be more than a hundred reviews of Marable's book—is contained in Dr. Haki Madhubuti's statement. "Our ultimate mission as Malcolm X would have it is to build and resist, resist and build, and in the middle of such struggle to never forget who we are and to love who we are and pass it on," Madhubuti charges. "The documents and essays in this collection represent the first critical assessment of Professor Marable's book and I am sure that it will not be the last." The editors are in concert with this perspective and what he proposes is in keeping with that premise of "unity without uniformity."

One of our editors, Dr. Maulana Karenga, provides an opening salvo, observing that "Marable embraced a deconstructionist approach to the life of Malcolm X as one of repeated reinvention as the title of his book, *Malcolm X: A Life of Reinvention*, indicates. It is this academically faddish and popular culture category that informs and problematizes Marable's work, for it can be understood as an expression of agency or indictment. Thus, it can reflect creative and constructive change or manipulative masking and shape-shifting of the most indictable kind."

Dr. Ron Daniels, another one of the book's editors, believes that after all is said and done about Marable's book, Malcolm's legacy is secure. He recalled the firestorm that erupted when Spike Lee's film *Malcolm X* hit the big screens, "it was also the subject of controversy because of what critics felt was a superficial treatment of the life and legacy of an iconic figure," Daniels relates in his essay. "I took the position that for whatever its shortcomings, the film exposed more people to Malcolm than any event in recent history, creating an opportunity for Malcolm devotees to set the record straight and fill in the blanks by seizing the moment to teach about one of the most remarkable African leaders of all time. I feel exactly the same way about the frenzy of concern and debate precipitated by Marable's volume. Those of us who are Malcolm devotees must utilize the increased scrutiny of Malcolm as a teachable moment."

For Imam Talib Abdur-Rashid, the book though flawed, is not without "teachable moments." He posits his overall impression at the end of his review, noting that "I believe it to be worthy of reading by a wide audience, and even more worthy of vigorous critique—praise what is good, and denounce its flaws. I'm only sorry that the professor is no longer here, so that we could challenge him in person." Although Mumia Abu-Jamal, for the most part, praises Marable's research, deeming him a "master historian," he feels there are some serious shortcomings, some issues he could have addressed with greater care and substance. For example, Abu-Jamal opines, Marable "treats the COINTELPRO-type files and FBI interest and actions regarding Black groups as givens, normalized and to be expected instead of the unconstitutional and indeed, criminal race police that they functioned as, against Malcolm, the Nation of Islam, and even the pacifist movement led by Dr. Martin L. King Jr. (whom the FBI regarded as 'the most dangerous man in America!'). Nor does he note how laughably unreliable many of these files were."

In his thoroughgoing analysis of Marable's book, Abdul Alkalimat cites 15 points in which there is insubstantial documentation or wrong conclusions, all of which indicate "that this is a poor job of empirical scholarship. Moreover, only about 20 percent of the 63 pages of footnotes come from primary sources. The rest of the footnotes come from published work based on other peoples' research. And Marable hardly ever engages the serious scholarship of others, and fails to give any credit to his first project director who guided the day-to-day research effort, Cheryll Greene—not even a mention in the acknowledgments."

The late Preston Wilcox, Black theologian James Cone, and Bill Sales are others mentioned by Alkalimat who Marable failed to include among his interviewees. Molefi Kete Asante is another notable authority on Malcolm X who could have enhanced Marable's perspective. "After reading the book, actually after locating it as is the method of Afrocentricity," Asante writes, "I determined that the flaws in Marable's work were not simply errors of references, innuendoes, and narrow flights off into squeaky sexual matters, but rather that the writer, despite his notoriety, was deeply dislocated politically. Consequently his analysis of Malcolm X was fundamentally off-center. Every space where Malcolm X could have been viewed as having taken agency was locked down, filled with unsanitary speculation, and hurriedly dismissed as being something other than the powerful assertion of African will. This is the style of the deconstructionists and post modernists who see cracks in every wall where power is amassed by blacks and who believe that to humanize a figure, especially a favored personality esteemed by blacks, one must kill the iconic image in a way that destroys it forever."

Of central importance to Rick Ayers is Malcolm's core vision, his fundamental significance and in the final analysis he feels Marable dropped the ball on this and gets it all wrong. "In the midst of his detailed research, he swipes at the philosophy of Black Nationalism and anti-colonial internationalism," Ayers contends. "In describing Malcolm X's historic 1960 debate with civil rights leader Bayard Rustin, he asserts that Rustin won hands down because he proved the 'practical impossibility' of setting up a Black state, exposing the 'essential weakness' of the nationalist line. It is one thing to be opposed to Black Nationalism, but to suggest that it is simply an illusory idea with no possible way of being pursued is to mislead." Ayers recommends that readers consult Malcolm's speeches in order to gather a fuller appreciation and understanding of the man and his legacy. "Malcolm X understood and pursued the implications of the earth-shaking revolutions going on and his words continue to capture the radical imagination of freedom lovers around the world today precisely because he stood for international solidarity and a restructuring of power. It is a vision that still inspires," he writes.

If there is one good thing about Marable's book in the estimation of Amiri Baraka it's the extent to which it revives a discussion about Malcolm X. But Baraka takes exception to Marable's political line which, as he relates, weakens the book, particularly as it "attempts to 'reduce' Malcolm's known qualities and status with many largely unsubstantiated injections, many described by Marable himself as 'rumors.' Is there, for instance, any real evidence of Malcolm's or Betty's sexual trysts? People who knew Charles Kenyatta, for example, in Harlem, will quickly recall a vainglorious fool and liar. Could much of this rumor material actually have come from Marable's 'official' sources, the FBI, CIA, BOSS, NYPD, as well as those in the NOI who hated him? About Malcolm, a sentence like Marable's 'that evening Sharon 6X may have joined him in his hotel' is inexcusable."

Essential to Amir Bey's take on Marable's work is his insightful probe of Malcolm's last years, most notably his travels abroad and the extensive diary he kept. "By viewing Malcolm's diary that documented his travels, combined with media and government accounts of them, we can see his international threat to the NOI: he was developing ties with Muslim countries and institutions that had long had trouble with the Nation's brand of Islam, and were offended by Elijah's claim to be 'The Messenger,'" Bey asserts. "They accepted Malcolm as a true Muslim, and gave recognition to the MMI (Muslim Mosque, Inc.) granting 20 scholarships to members of his organization to study Islam in those countries. For the NOI this was another reason why Malcolm had to go, because he was acquiring the legitimacy from the countries and religious institutions that they were seeking. Another sore point was Malcolm's perceived influence and bonding with Elijah's sons Wallace D. Muhammad and Akbar, who also practiced orthodox Islam, and who had troubles with their father's affairs and children by young girls."

There is very little of merit in Marable's biography for Dr. Todd Steven Burroughs. He contends that the author was bereft of sources, relied too much on graduate students, and was ultimately seduced by the siren call of celebrity. Most telling are his comments on the nature of biography, which he writes, "is a hard game to play and an easy one to lose, although only other historians and some well-read journalists will ever see the losing score. First, the biographer must choose a person he or she wants to spend years of life living with, thinking about and, most importantly, thinking *through*. Second, the author must learn all he or she can about the subject, literally tracing his or her life from the first day to the last. Significantly, while doing the first two tasks, the biographer must learn the differences between his or her views and the subject's views, but at the same time learn about himself through his subject. Exploring the subject's world gives the biographer insight into his or her own. Marable only succeeds in the first of the three tasks and even then only partially."

Ta-Nehisi Coates frames his discussion on Marable and Malcolm within a very rewarding personal context before submitting his assessment of the book. "To Marable's credit," he writes, "he does not judge Malcolm's significance by his seeming failure to forge a coherent philosophy. As Malcolm traveled to Africa and the Middle East, as he debated at Oxford and Harvard, he encountered a torrent of new ideas—new ways of thinking that batted him back and forth. He never fully gave up his cynical take on white Americans, but he did broaden his views, endorsing interracial marriage and ruing the personal coldness he'd shown toward whites. Yet Malcolm's political vision was never complete like that of Martin Luther King, who hewed faithfully to his central principle, the one he is known for today—his commitment to nonviolence."

Dr. King and Malcolm are also invoked by Jelani Cobb who finds common ground in their furious passage among us. "On some level, the resurrection of Malcolm X began with a generation that was drawing its first breaths that day," Cobb begins. "Raised outside the veil of segregation, we imbibed the freedom songs and King's speeches, recognized the achievements of the civil rights era yet also knew ourselves as heirs to some lesser freedom, one perforated by AIDS and crack, homicide and unemployment. For many these ills were an indictment not against a system whose racism and inhumanity was a foregone conclusion but against the naïveté of those who thought it could ever be anything else. And in Malcolm we found our prosecutor."

Karl Evanzz unleashes a fusillade of denunciation on Marable and his method of research; charging that much of it was lifted without attribution from his own work. According to Evanzz, when summarizing Malcolm's assassination, "Marable has two primary arguments: (1) the intelligence community and the New York Police Department deliberately ignored serious threats against Malcolm's X life, and (2) there is overwhelming evidence that the five assassins came from the Nation of Islam's Newark mosque. That's it." His first argument, Evanzz continues, "is based upon research in my first book, *The Judas Factor: The Plot to Kill Malcolm X*, published in November 1992. His second argument—and the one that the media chose to ignore for the past two decades—is based upon the research of Zak Kondo of Baltimore City Community College. *Conspiracys: Unraveling the Assassination of Malcolm X* (1993) [Kondo's book] is without question the most authoritative examination of the mechanics of the assassination. Marable had hundreds of thousands of dollars at his disposal for more than a decade. He had over twenty researchers at his disposal. Given far less capital and manpower, both David J. Garrow and Taylor Branch separately produced three-volume works of encyclopedic detail on Malcolm's contemporary, Dr. Martin Luther King Jr. Despite his acknowledgments of gratitude to other prominent researchers and benefactors, Marable's book is a single volume with questionable documentation. Poor exposition and inexcusable typographical errors taint the book."

None of these miscues can be blamed on Herman Ferguson, who was among Malcolm's closest associates toward the end of his life and certainly within the Organization of Afro-American Unity. Ferguson, now 90 years old, with the help of his wife, Iyaluua, has completed his autobiography and while he shared many of his memories with Marable, he apparently kept a lot of new information for his own book, or Marable chose not to use it. In this excerpt from his book, Ferguson recalls the scene of the assassination. "As I stood amidst this scene of carnage and terror, I began to sift through what I had just observed over the past few minutes," he remembered. "It began to occur to me that during the entire episode I had remained rooted to my seat and had only taken refuge under my seat after the second series of shots had rung out. I recall that while the firing was going on, there was a series of flashing yellow bulbs like the kind used to focus light on a scene that was being filmed. These flashing yellow lights were flickering off and on rapidly one after the other, and seemed to be coming directly over the Audubon stage area. It dawned on me that the entire scene of Malcolm's assassination was being filmed. Son of a bitch, I thought, they filmed the whole horrible event! Only governmental intelligence agencies have such a capability. This certainly lends credence to Malcolm's claim that Washington was the area from which his problems were coming. Not Chicago."

Malcolm's assassination is also a riveting part of Bill Fletcher's assessment of Marable's biography, and for the most part he defends his friend, though not without raising some poignant concerns. Nevertheless, he believes what Marable had to say about the assassination is noteworthy. "There are many points of controversy surrounding the assassination," Fletcher cites, "but what is especially worth noting is that Marable's investigation identified three forces that had an interest in Malcolm's death: the State; the NOI; and some of Malcolm's own supporters. This is not the first time that history has demonstrated that an assassination or otherwise criminal action had multiple players, each with their own interest in the success of the operation even if they may not have been actively collaborating or have consciously conspired. In this case, the curious actions of the police on the day of the murder; the faulty security (by Malcolm's own people); and the identification of the assailants, point to multiple perpetrators, each with its own set of objectives. The problem of Malcolm's followers seems to have been a matter—never publicly discussed—revolving around some of them feeling betrayed by Malcolm's own evolution, an evolution which was moving at the speed of light compared with their own changes."

A direct outgrowth of Malcolm's militancy was the Black Panther Party, at least that's the position fostered here by Glen Ford. "It is nearly impossible to conceive of a Black Panther Party had there not been a Malcolm X," he avers. "Marable insults a generation of Blacks who came into political consciousness in the Sixties—a cohort to which he chronologically belonged. He substitutes his imagined, inferred, reinterpreted Malcolm for the man whose words and bearing called forth and virtually sculpted the youthful Party that debuted in the year following his death. Marable projects Malcolm as if he would be a stranger to the Panthers, with whom he would have to 'negotiate,' when Malcolm's life tells us it is far more likely that the emergence of a militant revolutionary nationalist youth movement that spoke his language—because they learned it largely from him—would compel Malcolm to take the struggle to an even 'higher level.'"

A possible route to this "higher level" may entail a few of the steps Rhone Fraser offers in his estimation of Marable's biography, especially for politically conscious revolutionaries. These revolutionaries, Fraser contends, "must fearlessly confront white supremacy at a personal level;...develop a hatred of the colonial relationship between Blacks and whites in the U.S. and abroad;...work with radicals within as well as outside the electoral system;...be personally dedicated;...have a more democratic organizational structure that is prepared to continue revolutionary work despite any member's removal...perceive women as equals who are more than capable of wielding ideological influence; and be careful about what they tell the mainstream media."

Kelly Harris finds several unfulfilled promises in Marable's book, few more egregious than his failure to provide a full exegesis on the missing chapters from Malcolm's autobiography. "The selling point for Marable in his 'Democracy Now!' interviews and in *Living Black History* is that the autobiography is in fact three books," Harris explains. "In contrast he claimed his project would detail the 'missing chapters' that Haley described as 'lava-like.' While Marable is very provocative concerning the missing chapters in the interviews, he ultimately fails with his treatment of the same in his book. To be fair, this has more to do with Detroit attorney Gregory Reed (owner of the chapters). Reed only allowed Marable to peruse the chapters for fifteen minutes. That clearly is not enough time for Marable (or anyone else) to fill in the blanks. As a result Marable is virtually silent on the contents of the missing chapters—a promise unfulfilled."

At the peak of his tenure with the Nation of Islam, Malcolm was known to excoriate the mainstream black leaders, then putatively known as the "Big Six"—Roy Wilkins, A. Philip Randolph, James Farmer, John Lewis, Whitney Young, and the Rev. Dr. Martin Luther King. Even so, if Wil Haygood is right, "Marable persuasively shows us the tightrope that Malcolm walked in the early 1960s. He would belittle civil rights leaders but also, after breaking with the Nation, would seek common ground with them. Marable does not shy away from Malcolm X's repugnant statements and actions, such as dismissing well-meaning whites who wanted to join his non-violent, Muslim-led crusade for equality; and his bizarre negotiations with the Ku Klux Klan, in 1961, to buy land for blacks to live on."

Errol Henderson goes to great and compelling length to show how derivative Marable's research is, his predilection to offer unsubstantiated conclusions, and the tendency to impose on Malcolm his own political orientation. However, he summarizes, "there are some laudable aspects of the book, such as the attempt to engage the historical development of Islam in the U.S., the impact of Garveyism on Malcolm's parents, and the general discussion of Malcolm's family; there are many more areas of the book that are poorly thought out, lacking in evidentiary support, and generally unpersuasive. But, in this brief essay, I want to emphasize that it is

Marable's neglect of these inherently political issues of Malcolm's important theorizing and advocacy of black nationalism and cultural revolution in the U.S. that undermine the work. These factors reflect the core of the politics of such an important political leader; and as such they deserve a much more serious and rigorous examination than what Marable—an often politically astute biographer—chose to or was able to provide."

In his essay, Fred Hord chooses to accentuate the positive, winnowing Marable's text for Malcolm's ideas that might be useful in today's struggle for liberation. "African Americans must not only free their people from economic slavery by, in part, maintaining a technical pool and technical bank," Hord believes, "but also defend themselves physically by any means necessary. Those five practical pillars of strategy for the future Black Freedom Movement (restoration, reorientation, education, economic security, and self-defense) point yet today in real ways to institutional solutions for the malaise and confusion that have proceeded inherently from neither fully understanding nor practicing the ultimate extension of Malcolm X's legacy: resisting the Whiteness of culture and painfully, doggedly, systematically recovering the best of a Black value system."

One of the interesting themes evoked by Errol Henderson, dualism, is touched on by Peter James Hudson, who also broaches the ideological trajectory of the lives of Malcolm and Dr. King. "One of the great shibboleths of American thought puts Martin Luther King and Malcolm X as reconciling opposites: Martin vs. Malcolm, the integrationist apostle of non-violence versus the separatist demagogue, coming to a dialectical synthesis near the end of their lives," he proposes. "Marable evokes this dualism while implicitly rejecting it. Malcolm X demonstrated that mere reconciliation would not suffice, especially within the insular political and spiritual worlds of the U.S. By showing how Malcolm X had to look abroad fully to apprehend the condition of blacks in the States, Marable suggests that American redemption may only come through the path that Malcolm took: through the political philosophy of pan-Africanism and the theological ambit of pan-Islam. It is, on Marable's part, a bold and radical move, but one of critical importance. 'Malcolm X,' Marable writes, 'represented the most important bridge between the American people and more than one billion Muslims throughout the world.'"

In the deft hands of Ezra Hyland, elements of myth, mysticism, linguistics and various psychological terms are given relevance when applied to the life and legacy of Malcolm X. But he also sheds considerable light on Marable's failure to offer a full explanation of his allegation of William Bradley as one of the assassins, an accusation that may lead to a lawsuit by the accused. Among the goals Marable listed, according to Hyland, was his intention to identify those responsible for Malcolm's assassination. But he was scooped again, Hyland charges. "In 1977, Talmadge Hayer gave the first of several detailed confessions naming his fellow killers and details of the plan that differed from the official governmental story," he observes. "Marable writes on May 2010, Abdur-Rahman Muhammad directly accused William Bradley as the man who "delivered the first and deadliest shot" in an "Internet publication." (p. 476) Marable does not even bother to give the link to the article in the notes. It is inconceivable that Marable could claim one of his chief aims was to identify the killers of Malcolm X, and then cite the Internet as the support for his claims is pitiful at best. At worse, to accuse someone of murder and expose that person and his family to harm based on an Internet publication is criminal."

But even with its flaws and inconsistencies, Hyland concluded, "hopefully this biography will inspire new efforts to interrogate and make meaning of Malcolm's life and in reexamining his life cause us to reexamine ours. If we allow anger, fear and shame to cause us to shun the book and not reexamine our beliefs, to not become reacquainted with Malcolm or meet him for the first time, then the fault will be our own. Then and only then, when we transform Malcolm from a living force to an idol, will he die, and this time the blood will be on our hands."

Regina Jennings takes Marable to task on several critical points, including her wish that he would have spent more time discussing the class backgrounds of Elijah Muhammad and Malcolm X, in effect, how a ex-sharecropper and an ex-prisoner were able to build one of the most powerful organizations in African American history. "What were the economic factors that Elijah mastered that enabled him to build an enterprise that employed thousands?" Jennings asks. "How did he become first a small businessman and then CEO without a hedge fund? How did Elijah Muhammad create independent schools that taught the next generation from his perspective, not school board selected texts? How did this man layout a platform that encouraged maleness to soar independently from White America? Neither Malcolm nor Farrakhan had to submit to a company or corporation for a job. Marable judges Malcolm and Muhammad by a set of Christian rules and values based on and biased to Black revolutionaries."

Malcolm X has been dead for more than 45 years, Peniel Joseph laments, but with the publication of Marable's book he insists, "We now have a historical portrait of Malcolm X that goes beyond literary clichés and autobiographical fictions to reveal an all-too human man beset by personal trials and political tribulations that would have felled the less courageous. Stripped from the cocoon of his posthumous aura of invincibility, Malcolm X emerges from these pages an endlessly fascinating and protean figure whose shortcomings make his political accomplishments all the more remarkable. Against the backdrop of private disappointments and embarrassingly public betrayals, Marable reminds us that Malcolm X still managed to transform "the discourse and politics of race internationally," a final enduring reinvention that continues long after his death.

From Clyde Ledbetter Jr.'s viewpoint, Marable launched an unprovoked attack on a charismatic ancestor. Charisma isn't a subject that Marable engaged in a direct way, but Ledbetter devotes considerable space to defining the concept and applying it to Malcolm and to Elijah Muhammad, and the degree to which their charisma differed. "Pure charisma is what differentiated Malcolm's authority ultimately from that of Elijah Muhammad whose charisma was more traditional as the source of his authority rested in his position as prophet to Allah who members of the Nation believed came in the form of W.D. Fard," Ledbetter explains. "Malcolm's pure, and in relation to Elijah Muhammad, greater charisma would ultimately lead to his break with the Nation. His charismatic authority was so strong that even without a well-defined program he was followed out of the Nation by large numbers of the faithful who had hitherto structured their lives on the teachings of Elijah Muhammad. It was this pure charisma that made Malcolm's split from the Nation so dangerous for so many different groups. For those in leadership positions inside the Nation, Malcolm's charismatic authority would in all likelihood continue to lead people both away from and out of the organization. For the reactionaries of America, Malcolm's charismatic authority would influence a much larger audience and be coupled with an ever sharpening revolutionary Pan-African political and economic ideology."

By far the most controversial aspect of Marable's book, the issue that has aroused the most discussion is the allegation that Malcolm had a homosexual relationship. It's a disquieting charge and one that Kevin McGruder handles delicately, comparing it to the "one-drop theory" in the context of race. "The use of the term sexual orientation over the last thirty years was meant to acknowledge the gender to which a person's attraction is primarily oriented regardless of the behavior that person might engage in at a given time," McGruder argues. "Sex research has concluded that there is a spectrum of sexual orientations ranging from people who are only attracted to the opposite sex, people who are predominantly attracted to the opposite sex, people who are attracted to both sexes, people who are predominantly attracted to the same sex, and people who are only attracted to the same sex. Even given this spectrum, people may occasionally or frequently engage in sexual activity with someone of the gender different from their sexual orientation, often motivated by what is sometimes called 'situational sex.' A heterosexually oriented man engaging in homosexual activity in prison because he does not have access to women is an example of situational sex. A homosexually oriented man engaging in sex with a woman in order to maintain a marriage is another example. In this construct the homosexual activity that Manning Marable suggests that Malcolm X engaged in during his years of criminal activity would be described as situational sex, in this case for pay, by a person whose previous and later known sexual activities suggest that he was predominantly heterosexual."

And while Marable cites only one incident based on a questionable source with perhaps less than honorable intentions, really amounting to hearsay, the salaciousness of the assertion provides the fodder to garner public attention. Moreover, to be gay does not obviate one's contribution, lest we would have to repudiate James Baldwin's books and essays, and the tireless advocacy of Bayard Rustin, just to mention two gay men of incomparable achievements and civil and human rights credibility.

The hope to have more women involved in this conversation was not realized, but Starla Muhammad brings a special and important angle, particularly in providing us with some impressions from two key figures in the Nation of Islam. "The Honorable Minister Louis Farrakhan has repeatedly called for reopening and investigating the case and releasing government files," Muhammad writes, referring to the reopening of the case which civil rights activist Alvin Sykes has already initiated. "On May 6, 1995 at Harlem's legendary Apollo Theatre, Min. Farrakhan along with Malcolm's widow, the late Dr. Betty Shabazz met publicly to begin a process of healing and reconciliation between the Nation of Islam and Malcolm's family." Haki Madhubuti played a critical role in orchestrating the meeting.

Starla appends these comments from Akbar Muhammad who has been a member of the NOI for over 50 years and is often cited in Marable's book. Though there are aspects of the book he does not agree with and differs with, he said he can appreciate the tremendous research that went into the book. "I would hope, agree or disagree with Dr. Manning Marable that Muslims who want an insight to this period, you know Malcolm is an enigma and in the American landscape especially in the Black American community, people want to know and this book gives them a base of knowledge about Malcolm," he told Starla.

"With the publication of *Malcolm X: A Life of Reinvention*, Manning Marable offers a fuller portrait of the minister, the activist, and the man, beautifully advancing our understanding of the accomplishments of this pioneering leader within his own time," writes Nell Irvin Painter. She feels the book supersedes Malcolm's autobiography and...helps us understand the development of a leading American struck down before he could help us understand our world in which Islam plays so crucial a role."

Imani Perry is in accord with many of Painter's conclusions, and sees how Malcolm's life exemplifies the struggle of Afro-Americans. "Although the conflict over the content has probably driven sales and attention to the book, the brilliance of this biography has little if anything to do with its apparently shocking revelations," Perry declares. "Marable has crafted an extraordinary portrait of a man and his time. Malcolm moves through the social and intellectual history of mid-20th century Black America, and his periods of growth and stagnation mirror the tides of black life."

Marable's book, Perry extols, "arrives in a moment of petty partisan politics and a sound-bite-driven culture, and gives us a glimpse into a past of rich debate and impassioned struggle. Marable's Malcolm assists us in understanding the current wildfire of resistance and revolution through Africa, the Midwest and the Middle East. Most of all, in this book, Malcolm is re-imagined as an intellectual and political role model for us all, a man who possessed the courage to put himself at risk consistently in order to better understand the world, in order to make the world better."

That world Malcolm X sought to traverse and to understand was as boundless as his imagination. Gregory Reed and Bryonn Bain underscores Malcolm's international quest during their interview. Reed, it should be noted, possesses the three missing chapters of Malcolm's autobiography and a trove of other valuables related to Malcolm. "Malcolm saw things from a global perspective," Reed proclaims. "Along with Dr. King, he was one of the first African Americans of his time to travel internationally and develop this ability to relate to all persons. This has helped many of us to recognize that we have the ability to relate to all persons from a global perspective. If you look at Nelson Mandela, he set the example for South Africa to seek freedom and self-determination on various levels internally. We can credit Malcolm with waking us up on an international plane to see that we are all connected. We are still struggling with that today, but he set the foundation for what is yet to come. This is why he was seeking to take the African American plight to the United Nations—which is still overdue."

Michael Simanga with his essay makes a salient point and offers another iteration of this book's overall intention while recalling the differing views among our thinkers and activists of Marable's conclusions. "As it should be, there are occasions where the community of liberation fighters and scholars disagreed with some of his ideas and conclusions," he observes. "That disagreement is not a bad thing; it is an important part of our struggle. We must be able to disagree and have open discussion and critique of our ideas and our work in order to come to greater theoretical knowledge and practical unity. Again, that is part of the how, but we must not lose sight of the what. The open debate must not prevent us from finding common ground for organizing together to fight our enemies and continue to move our struggle forward. The discussion cannot deteriorate into destructive and paralyzing posturing and personal attacks."

Nor should the discussion be devoid of a serious inclusion of the gender issue, if Diane Turner and Aslaku Berhanu have a say. They conclude that Malcolm's views on women were like his overall political development, constantly evolving. "During his last year, Malcolm's views were changing with regards to the role and place of women," they state. "He also said in the Paris interview that, 'one of the things I became thoroughly convinced of in my recent travel is the importance of giving freedom to the woman, giving her education, and giving her the incentive to get out there and put that same spirit and understanding in her children' (179). This is a different Malcolm than the minister controlled by Elijah Muhammad in the Nation of Islam. Malcolm concludes by stating that, 'And I frankly am proud of the contributions that our women have made in the struggle for freedom and I'm one person who's for giving them all the leeway possible because they've made a greater contribution than many of us men' (179). What might have Marable revealed to readers by investigating Malcolm's changing views on questions of gender?"

The Last Word

It is fitting and proper that Malcolm's daughter, Ilyasah Shabazz, has the last word in this book. Her admonition has universal portent and should be heeded by all who dare to tell someone's story. "This topic of discussion should teach all of us that we must be consistently diligent in our demands that any historian not be allowed to reduce 'history' to speculation," she advises. "I believe that, at this juncture, our purpose has been defined for us, and I am encouraged by all of you who have...the knowledge that this is not a dilemma, predicament or difficulty that we can afford to ignore. All history must be as factual, as humanly possible. Truth must always prevail and we must be able to separate truth from sensationalism.

"I do not stand in defense of my father. El Hajj Malik El Shabazz...stands on his own! It was Brother Malcolm's personal journey and self-discovery that led him towards peace. His short life was a continuous search for truth—for us! And the least we can do for our beloved Malcolm is to demand that those who claim to define him bring us his truths," she concludes.

LAYING THE GROUNDWORK

When All Is Said...
Malcolm's Legacy is Secure
Ron Daniels

The late Dr. Manning Marable's biography *Malcolm X: A Life of Reinvention* produced a firestorm of controversy in Black America. For many Malcolm devotees Dr. Marable's "revelations" about Malcolm's alleged homosexual activities and infidelities in his marriage with Dr. Betty Shabazz are sensationalized information, which only serves to needlessly smear the legacy of the man Ossie Davis eulogized as our "Black Shining Prince." Others contend that as a scholar and academician, Dr. Marable had every right, an obligation even, to provide an unvarnished picture of Malcolm X based on his research. From my perspective, it is understandable that family members, friends and supporters of Malcolm would be upset by any information that might tarnish the legacy of one of the most revered leaders in the history of Africans in America. Accordingly, one of the most important challenges facing scholars, commentators and activists is to separate fact from fiction in Dr. Marable's book. Indeed, there are already a number of scholars who suggest that the most explosive allegations in his volume are largely unsubstantiated or based on less than stellar research. In due course, I have no doubt that the numerous scholarly investigations and critiques of Dr. Marable's biography will shed definitive light on these questions.

Beyond the controversial discussion of Malcolm's personal life, an equally important question is whether Dr. Marable's book breaks any new ground or adds to our knowledge about the era in which Malcolm lived, his contribution as a Nationalist, Pan-Africanist and internationalist leader and the circumstances of his assassination. Frankly, controversy sells books, particularly in a Capitalist political-economy. Therefore, there is a tendency for publishers to push authors to include "juicy" tidbits that will create a buzz to induce consumers to buy their books. Who can forget Michael Eric Dyson's *I May Not Get There with You* in which he discusses aspects of Dr. Martin Luther King's personal life, particularly his extramarital affairs? The book contains important chapters, which cast Dr. King as a progressive reformer in the Democratic Socialist tradition. Yet, initially much of the public controversy and conversation focused on the revelations about King's personal life—and anger by some toward Dyson for including these aspects in his book. It may well be that there are times when flaws and failings in the personal lives of leaders outweigh their contributions. But, what the controversy surrounding Dyson's book revealed is that when the dust settled Martin Luther King's legacy was unaffected. In fact, Dyson's examination and presentation of Martin Luther King as a committed progressive reformer no doubt enhanced his legacy in some circles.

I suspect the same will be true as it relates to the current controversy over Dr. Marable's biography. Though I am obviously concerned that the most controversial revelations be substantiated, no doubt there is much more to chew on in Dr. Marable's book than issues surrounding Malcolm's personal life. Moreover, my admiration for Martin and Malcolm is not because I view them as "St. Martin" or "St. Malcolm." I am acutely aware that as human beings leaders are subject to failings and may have some knots and warts. Indeed, I believe we make a serious mistake when we attempt to canonize our leaders. To do so is to set ourselves up for disappointment when we discover they were really human after all. This is not to ignore or condone personal failings or misconduct, which is properly substantiated. However, unless such behavior is so egregious that it significantly impacts or overshadows the work and accomplishments of a leader then the personal is best viewed as private to be addressed by those within the leader's life who are affected. I am most interested in the contributions of our leaders: the lessons to be learned from their work, and how we might best preserve their legacies as templates for teaching future generations. In this regard, I am convinced when all is said regarding the controversial aspects and other sections of Dr. Marable's book, the legacy of El Hajj Malik El Shabazz will be secure.

Indeed, as an organizer, I tend to look for teachable moments when events can be utilized to advance our struggle for full freedom. The firestorm of controversy over Dr. Marable's book may just be such an occasion. When Spike Lee's film *Malcolm X* hit the big screens, it was also the subject of controversy because of what critics felt was a superficial treatment of the life and legacy of an iconic figure. I took the position that for whatever its shortcomings, the film exposed more people to Malcolm than any event in recent history, creating an opportunity for Malcolm devotees to set the record straight and fill in the blanks by seizing the moment to teach about one of the most remarkable African leaders of all time. I feel exactly the same way about the frenzy of concern and debate precipitated by Marable's volume. Those of us who are Malcolm devotees must utilize the increased scrutiny of Malcolm as a teachable moment.

In that regard, it occurs to me that one of the greatest lessons to be learned and transmitted to this generation about Malcolm X is not "a life of reinvention," but a life of "transformation." The term "reinvention" suggests a conscious effort to remake oneself, like an artist, entertainer or performer eager to maintain one's marketability. This was never the case with Malcolm. Rather what we see in tracing Malcolm's life from Malcolm Little, to Detroit Red, to Malcolm X and El Hajj Malik El Shabazz is a gifted human being adversely impacted by circumstances in a white supremacist/racist society who eventually breaks the psycho-cultural, material chains that bound him to become a leading voice and force for the liberation of Black people! His is the story of a troubled young man who turned a jail cell into a library and prison into a university! At a time when millions of young Black men have been criminalized and marked for prison, death or a life of misery on the margins of society, there is no better example or model of hope and transformation for our young brothers (and sisters as well) in America's "dark ghettos" than the life of Malcolm X.

If Malcolm, with the burden of internal and external oppression on his shoulders, could emerge as a "manchild in the promised land" to become one of the most knowledgeable, skillful, dynamic, inspiring and beloved leaders the Black world has ever known, then every "gangsta," wannabe gangsta and gangsta rapper has the potential to overcome the "realness" of their circumstances to become a force for change at some level in Black America and the Pan African World. That's why, whatever the flaws in Alex Haley's *The Autobiography of Malcolm X*, it is one of the most powerful teaching tools available to us for the cultural, educational, political offensive which must be waged to rescue millions of Black youth/young people from the self-destructive fratricide devastating urban inner-city neighborhoods across this country.

Accordingly, it is imperative that Malcolm devotees view the widespread controversy, discussion and debate surrounding Dr. Marable's book as an opportunity not only to defend Malcolm's legacy but to explore a variety of avenues to utilize the lessons of his life to educate and inspire legions of youth/young people to embrace his mission of liberation in these difficult times. As I remarked at the Institute of the Black World 21st Century's Public Conversation on "The Meaning of Manning Marable's Biography of Malcolm X," the enormous concern, passion and outrage many Malcolm lovers feel regarding Marable's book must be converted into an action agenda to make the life, legacy and lessons of Malcolm a living, breathing part of the Black community again! Otherwise it's just momentary outrage, which will soon subside with no constructive outcome.

In an article I wrote for Black History Month, I noted that in one of my classes at York College City University of New York, not a single student was aware that February 21 was the date of the commemoration of the assassination of Malcolm X. In fact when one reflects on the media coverage or public awareness of the significance of February 21 or May 19 (his birth date), beyond the true believers in the Black community, the memorial of the assassination of Malcolm X and celebration of his birthday pass with little notice in the Black community at-large. This was not the case twenty or thirty years ago. For a period of time highly publicized memorials of the assassination of Malcolm X were common, including an annual observance at the Abyssinian Baptist Church in Harlem. For years on May 19, thousands used to converge on Anacostia Park in Washington, D.C. for a daylong celebration of Malcolm's birthday. In New York, Professor James Small would lead annual pilgrimages of hundreds of community people to Malcolm's gravesite. Annual celebrations were also held in Pittsburgh, Chicago, Philadelphia, Detroit, Los Angeles, Omaha and numerous cities across the country. These commemorations and celebrations notwithstanding, a group of scholars and activists felt that even more should be done to enhance the standing and broaden the appeal of Malcolm in the Black Nation.

To intensify the uplift of Malcolm and create greater public awareness and observance of the memorial of Malcolm's assassination and celebration of his birthday, in 1989 the African American Progressive Action Network (AAPAN) declared 1990, the 25th anniversary of Malcolm's assassination and his 65th birthday, *The Year of Malcolm X*. The idea was to gain media attention to expose Malcolm to an even wider audience in the Black community and the nation, particularly young people. Though the organizers did not undertake the effort as an anti-Martin Luther King initiative, the objective was to elevate Malcolm to his proper place as an iconic fountainhead of Black Power, Nationalism, Pan-Africanism, internationalism and human rights as vital dimensions of the Black freedom struggle in the U.S. and globally.

Toward that end, AAPAN created the National Malcolm X Commemoration Commission (NMXCC). Chaired by Dr. James Turner, Director of the famed Africana Studies and Research Center at Cornell University, and with me as Co-Chair, Convener of AAPAN, NMXCC included notable leaders like Sonia Sanchez, Preston Wilcox and Haki Madhubuti. With administrative/coordinative support from Jill Soffiyah Elijah and Junette Pinkney, the Commission devised plans for a massive Memorial Observance at the Abyssinian Baptist Church, February 21, 1990 and a National Day of Commemoration in Omaha May 19. To ensure a grassroots character to the campaign, the Commission launched a petition drive to secure hundreds of thousands of signatures nationwide to declare May 19 a National African American Day of Commemoration as an act of self-determination. In addition, the Commission asked local Malcolm X Committees around the country to hold Memorial Observances on February 21 and celebratory events on May 19.

In 1990, it was a huge success for Malcolm X. With the support of columnists from the National Association of Black Journalists, the Initiative generated articles about the two major events in Black newspapers and mainstream press across the nation. In addition, Black talk radio precipitated tremendous buzz in the Black community, all of which added to the mounting momentum. By the time February 21 arrived, Black people were on fire with anticipation of memorial observances in countless communities throughout the Black Nation, most notably the flagship event sponsored by NMXCC at the Abyssinian Baptist Church in Harlem. On the occasion of the 25th anniversary of the assassination of our "Black Shining Prince," more than 3,500 people jammed the sanctuary and fellowship hall of the church with more than 1,000 people filling the street outside. Spike Lee, whom the Commission had unsuccessfully attempted to contact to be on the program, arrived late and elected to join the multitude in the streets to participate in the Memorial. Rev. Dr. Calvin Butts, Pastor of Abyssinian Baptist Church and host of the Memorial, directed his staff to put T.V. monitors in the windows so the audience in the streets could witness the proceedings.

Inside Dr. Betty Shabazz, who came out for the first time ever for an event on February 21, sat with obvious satisfaction among family members and friends as an exhilarating program unfolded. Testimonials were presented by the Honorable Percy Sutton, attorney for the family; Councilman Al Vann; and leading community activists. The program concluded with an absolutely electrifying speech by NMXCC Chairman Dr. James Turner who stepped to the podium to proclaim to Dr. Shabazz, the family and the adoring audience, "we will never forget Malcolm." The audience exploded with applause. It was one of the most memorable moments of my life, and it was captured live and broadcast nationwide on C-SPAN!

February 21 was the predicate for the celebration of Malcolm's 65th birthday May 19 in Omaha, the city where he was born. Prior to the Memorial Observance, the NMXCC circulated petitions around the country for local organizations and organizers to gather signatures to proclaim May

19 a National African American Day of Commemoration. If memory serves me correctly, Drs. Ronald Walters and Haki Madhubuti were asked to draft the Proclamation. The highly acclaimed actor Avery Brooks agreed to read the Proclamation at the Ceremony in Omaha. There was a sense of intense excitement in the air in the Black Nation as we approached the day of the Commemoration. Dick Gregory, Dr. Maulana Karenga, Sonia Sanchez, Dr. Haki Madhubuti and scores of activists from local committees around the country joined Dr. Betty Shabazz, family members and the NMXCC for the historic celebration of the 65th birthday of El Hajj Malik El Shabazz. Obviously pleased with the national spotlight on their native son, hundreds of sisters and brothers from Omaha, Lincoln and Black communities from Nebraska turned out for the celebration. With some of the most notable Nationalist and Pan Africanist leaders, teachers and artists in the Black world assembled in one place, the program was powerful and inspirational. The highlight, however, was the reading of the document proclaiming May 19 a National African American Day of Commemoration, a Black Holiday! With a firm, resolute and resonate voice, the words of Avery Brooks reverberated throughout the auditorium and indeed across the Black Nation. It was a fitting climax to an Initiative which achieved its objective in its time of elevating Malcolm to his proper place as a man and human being whose life mattered and had meaning for the era in which he lived and for generations to come, including the present.

I cite this history not out of a sense of nostalgia but because there is an urgent need to replicate an informational, educational, public awareness and mobilizing/organizing process like 1990 the Year of Malcolm X today. As noted earlier, there is far too little acknowledgement of the contribution of Malcolm X in our community today and insufficient use of the lessons of his life, philosophy of liberation and legacy as a servant-leader to guide Black people, particularly this generation's "Malcolm Littles," "Detroit Reds" and aspiring leaders. This is why it is imperative that Malcolm lovers/devotees see this moment, when Dr. Marable's volume is generating so much discussion and debate, as an opportunity to educate and organize!

Therefore, I announced at the Forum in New York that IBW seeks to revive and reconstitute the National Malcolm X Commemoration Commission as a key programmatic and coordinative mechanism, charged with dramatically and substantively raising the profile/presence of Malcolm X in Black America and the Pan African World. Hopefully, Dr. James Turner, who is retiring as a Professor from the Africana Studies and Research Center at Cornell, will agree to continue to serve as Chairman of the Commission for a period of time. As a matter of principle, the Commission should forge a collaborative relationship with the Malcolm X and Dr. Betty Shabazz Memorial and Education Center (the old Audubon Ballroom) to maximize efforts to elevate the profile of Malcolm. The most immediate task will be to identify a core group of scholars and activists with the interest, resources and capacity to function as effective members of the Commission. Once the Commission is comprised, a national survey should be conducted to determine where local organizations and/or commemoration committees exist that conduct programs or action-oriented projects/initiatives in the spirit of Malcolm.

At a minimum, beginning in 2012 each year the Commission should suggest a theme for commemorations, celebrations and action-oriented initiatives and plan national activities on February 21 and May 19 (such activities could be in conjunction with local committees or organizations). The Commission should also convene periodic local, state and national workshops, symposia and conferences designed to deepen the knowledge and awareness of the philosophy and work of Malcolm among potential devotees, advocates and organizers. Similarly, the Commission could publish a range of educational materials to empower more and more of our people with the knowledge of our "Black Shining Prince." To ensure the Commission has minimal staffing, I have recommended that IBW create a Malcolm X Fellow to be occupied on an annual basis by a skilled graduate or undergraduate student recruited from the City University of New York (CUNY). In the spirit of Malcolm, the Fellowship would be funded by contributions from the Black community.

When all is said regarding the controversy over Dr. Manning Marable's *Malcolm X: A Life of Reinvention*, the legacy is El Hajj Malik El Shabazz will be secure. However, our task as scholars, activists, organizers, Malcolm devotees is to make certain that the lessons of his life and legacy are instructive for the Black freedom struggle in our time. To achieve this task, we must work to make Malcolm's name, image, words, and deeds a matter of widespread awareness, deliberation and action again. The State of Emergency gripping Black America demands nothing less. The National Malcolm X Commemoration Commission is one of the mechanisms, which we must revive to meet this challenge. Let the work begin!

The Meaning and Measure of Malcolm X: Critical Remembrance and Rightful Reading
Maulana Karenga

The life and legacy of Minister Malcolm X, El-Hajj Malik El-Shabazz, weighs heavy in the scales of African and human history, measuring as a mountain's weight against the leaf-light and less-notable lives of his would-be detractors (Malcolm X, 1965a, 1965b, 1970, 1989, 1992). As I (1979) have written elsewhere, Malcolm is an Imhotepian man i.e., multidimensional; offering a series of models and messages of rich and timeless value, as a model master teacher, student, organizer, critical thinker, and revolutionary, and as a model of Black manhood in the most moral, mental, and cooperatively practiced ways. Moreover, he is rightly conceived of and honored as a soldier/servant of the people and a moral teacher. Thus, his measure and meaning lie in his written and oral teachings, as well as his living-practice texts which provide us numerous models and messages of infinite and enduring value of which only a few can be identified and discussed here.

Malcolm comes into consciousness and active commitment at a fundamental time of turning for our people, this country and indeed the world. This is that awesome decade of the 60s in which liberation struggles reached around and engulfed the world. Malcolm (1971:130), reading the signs of the times, says, "We are living in a world where great changes are taking place." Moreover, "our present generation is witnessing the end of colonialism, Europeanism, Westernism or whitism . . . the end of white supremacy."

In other words, he (1965b: 217) tells and teaches us, "we are living in an era of revolution, and the revolt of the (African American) is part of the rebellion against oppression and colonialism which has characterized this era." And though this process is still unfolding with bumps, bad faith, betrayals, diversions and setbacks, the struggles continue.

Mary McLeod Bethune (1974:16) taught us that, "the measure of our progress as a race is in precise relation to the depth of faith in our people held by our leaders." Therefore, she says, "we must never forget their sufferings and their sacrifices, for they were the foundations of the progress of our people." Such is the status and contribution, and the remembrance, respect and rightful reading of Malcolm. For Malcolm begins his project and practice with love of and faith in his people. He will not confuse individual ascension or personal success or respect with justice, respect and success for the people. He says, "No matter how much respect, no matter how much recognition whites show towards me, as far as I'm concerned, as long as it's not shown to every one of our people...it doesn't exist for me."

The measure and meaning of Malcolm is rooted first and foremost, then, in his conception of and commitment to his people, to Africans at home and abroad, here, in the larger Diaspora and on the continent (Asante, 1995; Clarke, 1969; Conyers and Smallwood, 2008; Sales, 1994;). He wants them to learn their history, question their religion for its relevance to lived life, and to view and value themselves as possessors of dignity and divinity, worthy of ultimate respect and having within themselves the capacity and courage to examine and alter their lives in productive, progressive and promising ways (Karenga, 2009).

It is important to note that in his commitment to Third World alliance and struggle, and to the human project of freedom and flourishing, he argues that within our concern for the world, one must always and rightly start with one's own people and develop from that a world-encompassing conception of one's obligations and practice. "I can state in all sincerity that I wish nothing but freedom, justice, equality, life, liberty and the pursuit of happiness for all people," he (1969a: 303) writes in the *Egyptian Gazette*. "However, the first law of nature is self-preservation; so my first concern is the oppressed group of people to which I belong, the 22 million Afro-Americans...."

Malcolm is concerned that we understand ourselves and our humanity in expansive ways, not only as part of the rising, rebellious and revolutionary tide of history, but also as bearers of dignity and divinity, worthy of the highest respect and equal and inalienable rights, and to fight fiercely and uncompromisingly for them. And "We are fighting for the right to live as free human beings," he (1965b: 51) states. And "We declare our right on this earth to be a man, to be a human being, to be respected as a human being, to be given rights as a human being in this society, on this earth, in this day, which we intend to bring into existence by any means necessary" (1970:56).

Malcolm, as a moral teacher also taught us also to think deeply and to think in self-determined ways as an ethical obligation. He (1965b: 137; 1991:49) tells an audience of African American college students, "one of the first things I think young people nowadays should learn is how to see for yourself, listen for yourself and think for yourself." Ever mindful of the awesome burden of history placed on each generation and the critical juncture, which they stood, he continues saying, "this generation, especially of our people, has a burden, more so than any other time in history." Thus, he concludes re-emphasizing "the most important thing that we can do is think for ourselves." Indeed, like Frantz Fanon (1968) and Sekou Toure (1976), he knew that the decolonized mind precedes and makes possible political decolonization, even if the process continues after liberation.

Finally, Malcolm stresses the cultural return to Africa and a pan-Africanism that reflects cultural and political consciousness and active commitment (1970:54-56). And it will mean, Malcolm (1970:146) argues, returning to the source, Africa, in culturally-grounded ways, and linking together in common and urgent work and struggle for liberation. Malcolm's (1971:136) call was for Africans to "wake up, clean up and stand up" and when he was asked, "wake up to what?" He (1965b: 198) answered, "wake up...to their humanity, to their worth and to their heritage," that equally valid and valuable way of being African and human in and for ourselves and the world.

For, again, we must free the heart and mind and imagine and create new ways of being African and human in the world. In sum, then, he offers us a model and message of *jihad*, that righteous internal and external struggle, reflected in his own self-sacrificing life which has become a sacred text and testimony of our capacity and obligation to constantly struggle to transform, repair and remake the world in the process of transforming, repairing and remaking ourselves in the most laudable and liberational ways (Karenga, 2008b).

I met Malcolm in the summer of '61 at Mosque 27 in Los Angeles where I had gone with friends to hear him lecture. Afterwards, he invited us to come to the Muslim restaurant to talk and we talked at length on a host of religious, social, political and cultural issues. Realizing I was going to catch the bus, he drove me home, himself, and we continued our wide-ranging conversation. From this time on, I tried to come to hear him lecture whenever he came to town, followed closely his work and press coverage, and thought deeply about his teachings taught to him, he would always affirm, by the Hon. Elijah Muhammad. Also, working within the Black Student Union, we had brought Malcolm to UCLA to speak in 1962. Moreover, when the Mosque was raided and Bro. Ronald 26X (Stokes) was killed and several Muslims were wounded by the LAPD, Malcolm invited me to emcee a memorial and resistance rally in a united front initiative at the Garden of Prayer Baptist church, one of the few Christian venues open to Muslims at that time. He was for our generation already a luminous sign and symbol of an emerging new consciousness and confrontational struggle, which would define and mark off the field of our focus and efforts.

Malcolm's suspension from the Nation of Islam and the hatred and hostility directed against him by the NOI after his suspension was both surprising and saddening and his assassination was clearly a devastating blow. However, I also understood his assassination as martyrdom, a courageous sacrifice of self for the life and liberation of our people. He could have withdrawn, retired or gone to Africa to stay and work. But he returned to resume his work in spite of the real, numerous and consistent threats to his life.

It was for me and my colleagues a model and message of struggle and sacrifice that was central to his legacy, and thus, in founding our organization Us in the wake of his martyrdom and the Watts Revolt, September 7, 1965, we dedicated ourselves to lifting up, teaching and continuing his legacy as a living practice. In fact, one writer, noting this, wrote that "Mr. Karenga often refers to the (teachings) of the late black nationalist Malcolm X, in much the same way Malcolm X had quoted the Black Muslim leader Elijah Muhammad" (*New York Times*, 9/27/66). Indeed, we of Us were among the first to boldly stand up and bear witness to Malcolm's legacy in the midst of the silence and fear engendered by internal and external forces that surrounded his assassination and martyrdom. Our first major public event was a memorial service for Malcolm at which we declared the day of his martyrdom a holiday called *Dhabihu* (Day of Sacrifice) in homage to his service and sacrifice for our people and the struggle for liberation (*Los Angeles Sentinel*, 3/3/66: p.A-11). Pan-Africanist and anti-imperialist in its thrust in reaffirmation of Malcolm's and our own political teachings, the commemoration also paid homage to the martyred Congolese Premier Patrice Lumumba and we denounced the Vietnam War as racist, immoral and illegal, and called for resistance to the war and the draft.

Us also celebrated Malcolm's birthday and established another holiday in his honor called *Kuzaliwa* (The Day of Birth) the same year in May, bringing his widow and co-worker, Betty Shabazz to Los Angeles to give the inaugural lecture, her first public address since Malcolm's martyrdom. The following year we called for students not to attend schools on Kuzaliwa and to come to celebrate Malcolm's birth and life at Us' headquarters and they responded in great numbers.

Since the Sixties, then, we of the organization Us have seen ourselves as heirs and custodians of Malcolm's legacy, not only in the general way that all Black Power advocates lay rightful claim to his legacy, but also in a more comprehensive, depthful and sustained way through the study, teaching and application of his most central ideas, embracing them as an expansive Black cultural nationalism that was revolutionary because of its commitment to radical self- and social transformation, the overturning of self and society, and because it was what Malcolm rightly called a rational and compelling response to our oppression and the demands of liberation (Karenga, 1967; 1969).

Indeed, we took seriously in both principle and practice, Malcolm's teachings on self-transformation in and for the liberation struggle, i.e.: "wake up, clean up and stand up;" the indispensability of culture and cultural revolution as a weapon and emancipatory process to prepare, aid and sustain the liberation struggle; the return to the source, Africa, culturally, psychologically and spiritually; the right and responsibility of self-defense, resistance and the struggle for "freedom by any means necessary," armed and otherwise; pan-Africanism; a religion with a God in our own image and interests and which is committed to justice, liberation and the liberation struggle; Black united front strategies; and Third World solidarity. It is this context and from this standpoint that we engage in critical remembrance of Malcolm; and try as best as we can to live his legacy, to offer a rightful reading of this legacy, and to challenge those interpretations that miss the mark, falsify, trivialize or in any other way tend to reinvent and render less meaningful this awesome legacy and shared African heritage (1965a; 1965b; 1970). And thus, it is within this framework of history and practice, intellectual grounding and critical concern for keeping and expanding Malcolm's legacy that a critique of Manning Marable's new book on Malcolm becomes imperative.

Every work reflects, consciously or unconsciously, a philosophical framework within which it is rooted, conceived and carried out, no matter what claims are made about objectivity and detached critical analysis, and Manning Marable's recent, posthumously published and problematic book on the life of Min. Malcolm X, El-Hajj Malik El-Shabazz, is not exempt from this rule or reality. Indeed, Marable's work and the subsequent controversy of denunciation and praise which surrounds it, raises larger questions beyond the book about how we understand, interpret and write history. It also raises interrelated questions of how we address the tendency of so many Black intellectuals to embrace the deconstructionist approach to history and humanities writing, pursuing criticism as an act of faith, and revelation of the unseemly as proof of progress toward "humanizing" persons thought to be in need of it.

Clearly, deconstructive writing as critical analysis is to be embraced and encouraged, but deconstructionism in its most negative forms can easily degenerate into collecting and musing over trivia, trash and other extraneous information whose sensationalist character becomes a substitute for things relevant and more intellectually rewarding. Indeed, it becomes little more than the passionate pursuit of racialized pathology by another name. And, at its worst, it takes the form of *scavenger history*, the constant search for stench and stain, bottom feeding on the salacious, unseemly and sensational. This leads to pretensions and claims of revealing new material and offering original insights into things found earlier by others but were rejected as uninstructive and unuseful to a more disciplined and rigorous scholarship.

It is Malcolm (1965b:8), himself, who affirmed that, "of all our studies, history is best qualified to reward our research." But this, in the Malcolmian critical thinking tradition, assumes a mind receptive to discovery, not one determined to prove preconceptions (Karenga, 1993). And it presupposes an emancipatory intent in pursuit of knowledge, not one that binds the mind in ever-tighter conceptual chains forged and offered as liberational tools by the established order. As Malcolm noted in a lecture at Harvard, the logic of the oppressed cannot be the logic of the oppressor, if they seek liberation. He (1969b:133) states that "there just has to be "a new system of reason and logic devised by us. . ." if we seek liberation.

Marable embraced a deconstructionist approach to the life of Malcolm X as one of repeated re-invention as the title of his book, *Malcolm X: A Life of Reinvention*, indicates. It is this academically faddish and popular culture category that informs and problematizes Marable's work, for it can be understood as an expression of *agency* or *indictment*. Thus, it can reflect creative and constructive change or manipulative masking and shape-shifting of the most indictable kind.

It is also Malcolm (1965a: 344) in his *Autobiography* who defined the positive self-constructive changes of his life saying, "my whole life had been a chronology of—*changes*." Moreover, he (Ibid: 315) states that "Despite my firm convictions, I have been always a man who tries to face facts and to accept the reality of life as new experiences and new knowledge unfolds it. I have always kept an open mind which is necessary to the flexibility that must go hand and hand with every intelligent search for truth."

This is salutary change and self-transformation that the *Odu Ifa*

(245:1) teaches when it says, "If we are given birth, we should bring ourselves into being again" (Karenga, 1999: 403). This is self-creation in the most positive sense, not the negative deconstructionist conception of invention as a deliberate disguising, a constant change of costumes and character in manipulative ways. Unfortunately, Marable's reinvention of Malcolm is too often portrayed in negative and diminishing ways, depriving Malcolm of one of his most definitive characteristics, an audacious agency reflective of the awesome history and expansive humanity of his people.

Conceptually imprisoned by the philosophical framework he has chosen and the presuppositions it invites and imposes, Malcolm is portrayed as a wily wearer of "multiple masks" with an astute ability "to package himself" (10-11). Moreover, it is said he lined his life with "layers of personality," "manipulated" his voice, told tales and was "consciously a performer" (480).

Pursuing the deconstructionist popular culture path, Marable situates Malcolm in "the folk tradition of Black outlaws and dissidents," not the Black cultural tradition of master teacher and moral leader. He assigns to this list Gabriel Prosser, Nat Turner, Stagger Lee, blues guitarist Robert Johnson, and catering to the hip-hop constituency, rapper Tupac Shakur. A few lines down we discover he is not talking about Malcolm, but rather Detroit Red. This, too, is a problem of his portrayal of Malcolm, the collapsing of Detroit Red with Malcolm X, refusing to accept the radical rupture Malcolm makes to reconstruct himself as a more worthy and world-historical person and a continuously unfolding human possibility. This is the audacious agency that appealed even to President Obama (2006) in his search for an African anchor for his identity, purpose and direction, and is the basis of Malcolm's durability as a model of African and human excellence and achievement among his people.

Marable tells us that he and his researchers and perhaps, co-writers of sections, wanted to "humanize" Malcolm, a kind of saving him from his "manufactured" self and from the alleged mythological conceptions of him hosted and harbored by those too appreciative of Malcolm to see his flaws. But it is important to know what these "humanizers" really mean by this self-assigned and sanctimonious sounding mission of "humanizing" Malcolm. In such a conception, the flaws are the defining feature of Malcolm's being human and his excellence assumes a secondary role and relevance.

Malcolm, himself, expressed a myriad of flaws, but Marable believes he exaggerated some and left out others, and he must set the historical record straight, assigning Malcolm flaws which cater to or coincide with current tastes and talk, disrobing and redressing him in costumes of assumed and anticipated audiences, publisher and PR preference. Thus, Marable dismisses Malcolm's pre-Muslim serious juvenile and adult lumpen life, downgrading it as a kind of *lumpen lite*. He pursues his deconstructive argument against available evidence by characterizing Malcolm's pre-Muslim life of crime as a thief, robber, numbers runner, dope-dealer, pimp, panderer and burglar as "amateurish," "clumsy," and "ridiculous," and calling his crime partners "a motley crew " (pp. 65, 67).

In addition, he tells us that pre-Muslim Malcolm's efforts to shield his younger brother from lumpen life, "suggests he was never himself a hardened criminal" (p. 62). It's like arguing a mafia member, shielding his son from his business or a pimp protecting his daughter from prostitution makes them less lumpen, i.e., less committed to crime. It is such specious speculation and repeated misreading of Malcolm in too many places that calls to mind a diligent but mistaken scholar trying to translate a Swahili text with a Zulu dictionary.

Marable's re-invented Malcolm is deconstructed and pieced back together in such problematic and unproductive ways, the project clearly falls short of his goal to provide a corrective or even reliable supplement to Malcolm's original narrative told to Alex Haley. However, Malcolm's *Autobiography* is not as flawed as Marable wishes to make it in order to augment the importance of his own work. In fact, its reliable reflection of Malcolm's thinking and work is revealed through a comparative reading of Malcolm's *Autobiography* and lectures in and after the Nation of Islam (NOI) (Malcolm, 1965b, 1970, 1989 1992). Concluding his *Autobiography*, Malcolm (1965a: 385) expressed the hope that his "life's account, read objectively. . . might prove to be a testimony of some social value." Indeed, Malcolm is a world historical figure whose life and struggle, rightly read, offers an invaluable resource and legacy and Marable's book in no way alters this firmly grounded fact or diminishes the enduring relevance of Malcolm's own account.

Marable's book does have additional material, but critical analysis is not always evident and its quality is attenuated and often tainted by its mixture with trivia, trash and material extraneous to the political mission and meaning of Malcolm X. One could argue "the personal is political" and that all related can be used in political discourse. But what kind of personal and related material is to be sought after and used? Certainly, we could in the midst of discussing Martin Luther's central role in the Protestant Reformation raise questions about reports of his chronic constipation and speculate on its effect on his work, but to what useful or scholarly ends?

Likewise, with Malcolm, a major figure in the Black Freedom Movement, what counts as truly useful in understanding him and the Movement? And when does the pursuit of the insignificant and uninstructive, the petty, rumored, and imaginary and anecdotal sexual material become little more than *sensationalist tales from supermarket tabloids with numerous footnotes*?

Lacking a self-regulating rationale, the deconstructionist project, in its pursuit of things to criticize, easily moves from trying to find meaning in things to finding things out of which to make meaning. Likewise, it moves from finding meaning in things that are actually there to putting things there to find meaning in them. It clearly contrasts with the *sankofa* project of recovery and reconstruction of African history in the most intellectually disciplined, depthful, and dignity-affirming ways possible (Malcolm X, 1967; Keto, 1991; Karenga, 2008a: 65).

Marable's deconstructionist impulses led him to repeat and pursue lurid and baseless rumors and specious speculations concerning Detroit Red's possible sexuality and sexual practice. His decision reflects a growing tendency to try to *dress-the-hero-in-drag* or otherwise expressed, to discover and disrobe the Marlboro Man, believed to be concealed under the covers of questionable conceptions of masculinity. It is also an attempt to be current and correct, a concession to an insistent constituency; gays and lesbians, concerned with discovering and identifying unrecognized, disguised and distinguished members of their community.

There is no way or need to discuss the *concrete evidence* for Marable's make-believe claims, for there is none and Marable admits it. Indeed, they are neither real, nor relevant, to Malcolm's life and work. Thus, a question could be raised about Marable's intended message and motive in cobbling together and presenting this sordid assembly of rumor, innuendo, insinuations and unfounded assumptions. Other questions can also be raised, but to do so would prolong the discussion and give it more attention than it deserves. After all, we could discuss the presence of leprechauns and elves in Ireland, but lack of evidence and the demands of scholarship direct us away from this and toward that which is more thoughtful, relevant and real. Such a propensity for sallying forth with rumor rather than real evidence and specious speculation rather than reasoning rooted in solid evidence-based findings are also reflected in the problematic portrayals of the weak, wild and wanton women that populate his text.

Marable's attempt to convince us Malcolm's life as Detroit Red was not as degraded and desperate as his *Autobiography* leads us to believe is a deconstructionist thrust directed against Malcolm, the NOI and its leader, Messenger Elijah Muhammad. He speculates that Malcolm presented his pre-conversion life in such low-life and lumpen terms to better praise Messenger Muhammad and the NOI for lifting him up from the "grave of ignorance," immorality and self- and community destructive activity. Thus, Marable did not critically engage the Nation's complex theology and ethics of knowledge acquisition, agency and self-transformation, and instead contented himself with repeated references to the Yakub narrative (Muhammad, 1965; 1973).

But Malcolm is justified in giving due and lavish praise to his God, leader, religion and organization. It is what is done every day and certainly on every Sunday by Christians who bear witness to wondrous things that their Savior God, pastor/bishop, religion and church have done for them. It is an expression of the religious experience, a normal practice, not the pretension or less than honest activity Marable's deconstructionist project depicts it to be.

Moreover, for those who appreciate the rich resource of Black cultural and religious practices, bearing witness is a beautiful poetic expression and experience. Therefore, Marable missed a chance to critically explore the meaning of Malcolm's conversion and his description of it, as he did with the meaning of his break with the NOI, trying instead to direct the latter toward speculation about imagined sexual jealousies and related irrelevant anecdotes (Karenga, 1982). Clearly, there is both literary and historical value in Malcolm's looking at his old lumpen hideout from a window at the Harvard Law School Forum and musing over his rise from such a low level of life and the old hustler's fate that was waiting for him if Islam had not enabled and elevated him. Indeed, he (1965a: 291) says, "But Allah had blessed me to learn about the religion of Islam, which had enabled me to lift myself up from the muck and mire of this rotting world."

An even more poetic and powerful window into his thought and commitment is a quote from a university lecture, recorded by Louis Lomax, which points to the sense of agency, possibility and promise Islam, its Messenger here in the wilderness of North America and the NOI gave him. He (Lomax, 1963:170) says, "I myself, being one who was lost, dead, buried here in the rubbish of the West, in the sick darkness of sin and ignorance, hoodwinked completely by the false teachings of the slave master am able to stand upright today, perpendicular, on the square with my God, Allah, and my own kind . . . able for the first time in 400 years to see and hear." I see no reason to suspect Malcolm's motives in bearing such witness. It is part of the moral anthropology he taught, i.e., the capacity of human beings for *audacious agency*, self-transformation and liberational struggle, while recognizing the awesome conditions under which they labor and rightly praising the source of their insight, grounding and achievement.

Regardless of all the other philosophical and factual flaws that weaken and undermine the structural and intellectual integrity of Marable's work, the reef and rock on which his deconstructionist project flounders and is ultimately wrecked is his limited and less than expansive and thus, inadequate conception of Blackness and Black Nationalism. He wants to portray Blackness and Black Nationalism as narrow notions needing repair and rehabilitation, if not outright rejection. This is one of the reasons he portrays Malcolm as reaching out to the Civil Rights leaders as a repentant and reformed petitioner rather than a colleague and ally, pursuing a politics of united front as a self-conscious and carefully conceived strategy rooted in long-held nationalist views and values.

But Black Nationalism is not the reactive practice born of the belief in the impossible assimilation of Blacks that Marable suggests (p. 485). On the contrary, nationalism is profound commitment to community, to peoplehood and the *right* and *responsibility* of a people to exist, to be self-determining, and to define, develop and defend its members and interests (Karenga, 1976). Malcolm is renamed an internationalist, as if nationalism in its expansive and progressive form does not include and require a world-encompassing understanding and ethic, and as if there can be an internationalism without the distinct and numerous nations that embrace and practice it.

It is Malcolm, himself, who teaches this expansive conception of Black Nationalism, not only in his NOI, early Third World and Bandung period, but also in his last lectures (1965b, 1971, 1989, 1992). Praising the global thinking that characterizes the new Black consciousness of the Movement, Malcolm (1989:45) states that one of its defining features is that "the thinking ... is broad. It's more international." He goes on to say that, "you find the masses of Black people today think in terms of Black. And this enables them to think beyond the confines of America. And they look all over the world. They look at the happenings of the international context."

Indeed, Marable's "reinvention" of Malcolm has him constantly whittling down Malcolm's feet to fit Marable's deconstructionist shoes, and desperately and repeatedly trying to reshape Malcolm's head to fit the various hats he's chosen for him to wear. Thus, Marable (p.479) claims that "Malcolm's strength was his ability to reinvent himself," not his brilliant mind, his incisive analysis, his ethics of liberation, his organizing skill or his personal discipline, dedication and courage. Also, he claims Malcolm becomes "less intolerant and more open to multiethnic and interfaith coalitions" (p. 485). But Malcolm was, since the NOI, committed to Third World alliances and Black united fronts on the model of Bandung (1965a, 1965b, 1970, 1971).

He also wants us to believe Malcolm "resisted identification as a Black nationalist, seeking ideological shelter under the race-neutral concepts of Pan-Africanism and Third World revolution," a possible concession to post-racial fantasy discourse (p. 485). But Malcolm is clear about the racial bases of pan-Africanism—defining it as a project of "peoples of African heritage" and the Third World was always defined as the dark peoples of the world, those oppressed and exploited by the White imperialist West (1965a, 1965b, 1971, etc. In his last speeches, he talks of "we nationalists," defines the OAAU as nationalist, and in his travel diaries, he wrote that "our success in America will involve two circles: Black Nationalism and Islam" as Marable notes (p. 311).

If we want to advance beyond the philosophical and factual flaws of Marable's attempt to reinvent Malcolm and understand Malcolm in the most expansive, productive and promising sense, we must read and study him and his ideas as they evolved and developed in processes of both *change* and *continuity*. Clearly what is called for here is a critical practice that is emancipatory and inclusive, rather than narrowly focused and faddish, and self-determining and constructive, rather than deconstructionist and derived from the established order.

As Malcolm (1992:148) says, it begins with forming "the habit of seeing for ourselves, hearing for ourselves, thinking for ourselves, and then we can come to an intelligent judgment for ourselves." It requires also the development of "a new system of reason and logic," a liberational logic, both oppositional and affirmative, and rooted in our own culture (1969b: 133; Karenga, 1993). Indeed, Malcolm (1970:54-56), asserting a central cultural nationalist tenet, says "we must recapture our heritage and our identity if we are to liberate ourselves from the bonds of White supremacy." "We must launch a cultural revolution to unbrainwash an entire people," one that frees our hearts and minds and prepares us for and sustains us in the larger liberation struggle. This cultural revolution, he says, will not only enable us to recapture our heritage, but also serve as "the means of bringing us closer to our African brothers and sisters," and "be a journey to our rediscovery of ourselves." The recapturing of heritage and return to the source are in the interest of building and strengthening a revolutionary culture, Malcolm argues, for "culture is an indispensable weapon in the freedom struggle."

Following Malcolm (1965b: 10) we linked the love of nationalism and love of revolution and accepted his position that by definition and the demands of the historical moment, "a revolutionary is a Black nationalist" and vice versa. Thus, as both revolutionaries and cultural nationalists, we said in the Sixties "nationalism today by its very nature has to be revolutionary if it is for liberation..." (Karenga, 1969:14). And cultural grounding and cultural revolution are indispensable, for "culture provides the bases for revolution and recovery (Karenga, 1967:14). Indeed, we say "culture is the basis for all ideas, images and action (and thus) to move is to move culturally, i.e., by a set of values given to you by your culture" (Ibid: 14).

Therefore, it is culture that gives us the vision and values for the will and way to wage the liberation struggle. And again, for us, as both Toure (1976:77) and Cabral (1973:43) contend, "the national liberation struggle is an expression and 'act of culture'." Given this, Kawaida contends, a critical and rightful reading of Malcolm, as well as Toure and Cabral, leads us to conclude that "the problems of the liberation of the national community (or nation), then is a problem of culture and the problem of culture is a problem of liberation. Without a cultural revolution, there can be no real liberation of the people. But without the struggle for total liberation, a dynamic, self-affirming, self-developing past-and-future-facing culture cannot be created" (Karenga, 2008a: 5).

Malcolm (1965:345) taught that we should keep "an open mind which is necessary to the flexibility which must go hand in hand with every form of intelligent search for truth." This in no way suggests one should not be anchored in a definite philosophy that is life-enhancing, dignity-affirming and rooted in one's own culture and history. It simply means being open to expansion without self-erasure, change without self-negation, and liberation without the loss of one's cultural self. Malcolm, by his own self-definition, was "a Black nationalist freedom fighter." And his nationalism, Kawaida teaches, is defined by three major principles and practices: self-determination, self-respect and self-defense. This means control of our space, destiny and daily life in this country and the world African community; cultural grounding which affirms our identity and dignity as persons and a people; and the right and responsibility to defend ourselves against systemic and social violence and oppression by any means necessary, including armed struggle.

These are the concentric circles, the hinge and hub on which his thought and practice turn as interpreted by Kawaida philosophy. And it is these three principles and practices that we of the organization Us

It is this expansive conception of cultural revolution and cultural nationalism by Malcolm as well as the writings of Sekou Toure (1976), Frantz Fanon (1965), Amilcar Cabral (1973), Julius Nyerere (1974) and others which formed the basis of the revolutionary cultural nationalism of Us as expressed in the philosophy and practice of *Kawaida* (Karenga, 2008a, 1998). It is not the simplistic and ideologically contrived limited definition of cultural nationalism Marable offers, i.e., "a deep pride in African antiquity, history and culture together with rituals and aesthetics of drawing from Africa and the Black Diaspora" (p. 81). No honest and critical reading of Kawaida, a paradigmatic cultural nationalist philosophy and practice, could miss its central focus on cultural revolution; self-determination; armed self-defense and resistance; communitarian African socialism; pan-Africanism; social revolution; and Third World solidarity among other essentials.

Thus, a more accurate and expansive definition is in order, eliminating the artificial, ideologically-driven and falsified distinction between cultural nationalism and revolutionary nationalism, between areas of social emphasis, i.e., culture, religion, economics and politics, and qualities of social thought and practice, i.e., revolutionary, radical, progressive, reformist, conservative, reactionary, etc. (Karenga, 1976:124-127). Malcolm made no such distinction stressing revolution and nationalism as interrelated and interdependent (1965b: 10). Kawaida defines culture in the most inclusive sense, i.e., as the totality of thought and practice by which a people creates itself, celebrates, develops and sustains itself and introduces itself to history and humanity. Thus, Kawaida defines resistance, revolution and liberation along with Toure and Cabral as "an act of culture." For it presupposes and requires a *culture* of *struggle* which prepares aids and sustains it and brings it to successful conclusion. Therefore, within Kawaida philosophy, which evolved and was self-consciously shaped and forged in the furnace of the Black liberation struggle, cultural nationalism is thought and practice organized around the fundamental understanding that the defining feature of a nation or people is its culture; that for a people to be itself and free itself, it must be self-conscious, self-determining, and rooted in its own culture; and that the quality of its life and the success of its liberation depend on its waging cultural revolution within and political revolution without, producing a radical transformation of both self and society (Karenga, 2011:7).

Again, Us saw and sees its cultural nationalism as revolutionary and like Malcolm saw culture and cultural revolution as an indispensable weapon and process for the liberation struggle.

embraced and used to define and struggle for Black Power (Karenga, 1967:26). As I (Karenga, 2008a: 17) stated elsewhere, "In the Sixties we had stood up seeing ourselves as descendents of Malcolm with an awesome obligation to wage the revolution he had conceived and called for,"–both the cultural and political revolution. Thus, following Malcolm, "we declared revolution the answer and ourselves the agents of this radical change." Indeed, we saw ourselves as servants and soldiers of our people and keepers of his legacy and we have not abandoned or budged from this position or project.

Having met and talked with Malcolm, I have studied, written and lectured on his thought and work and that of the Nation since the Sixties. As a Malcolm scholar in the process of writing a book on his ethics of liberation which has a complex, personal and social transformative dimension, I do not dare assume to "humanize" Malcolm, but rather seek to understand and interpret his humanity in its most profound and expansive form. And I explore, not paths to imagined or possible pathology or flaw, but the ground and applicability of his excellence, as expressed in his intellectual and social practice. For in the final analysis, we engage him, even in criticism, not as a model of flaws and failure, but as a model of excellence achieved against the heavy odds of a history of savage and sustained oppression and in the radical and relentless struggle for liberation which forms and grounds his enduring legacy.

References

Asante, Molefi. (1995) *Malcolm X as Cultural Hero and other Afrocentric Essays*, Trenton, NJ: Africa World Press.

Bethune, Mary. (1974) *The Legacy of Mary McLeod Bethune*, Washington, D.C.: National Education Association.

Cabral, Amilcar. (1973) *Return to the Source*, New York: African Information Service and PAIGC.

Clarke, John Henrik. (ed.) (1969) *Malcolm X: The Man and His Times*, New York: Macmillan Co.

Conyers, Jr. James L. and Andrew P. Smallwood. (eds.) (2008) *Malcolm X: A Historical Reader*, Durham, NC: Carolina Academic Press.

Fanon, Frantz. (1968) *The Wretched of the Earth*, New York: Grove Press, Inc.

Karenga, Maulana. (1976) *Afro-American Nationalism: Social Strategy and*

Struggle for Community, unpublished dissertation, United States International University, San Diego.

——. (2008a) *Kawaida and Questions of Life and Struggle*, Los Angeles: University of Sankore Press.

——. (2011) "Malcolm and Kawaida on Culture: Recovery, Revolution and Resistance," *Los Angeles Sentinel*, 9/1/11, p. A7.

——. (2008b) "Malcolm, Liberation, Jihad and Justice: Righteous Warrior and Witness to the World," *Los Angeles Sentinel*, (May 15), p. A-7.

——. (1982) "Malcolm and Muhammad: Beyond Psychological Assumptions to Political Analysis," *Western Journal of Black Studies*, 6, 4 (Winter) 193-210.

——. (2008a) "Malcolm X, History and Struggle: Grounding, Insight and Action," *Los Angeles Sentinel* (February 21) p. A-7.

——. (1999) *Odu Ifa: The Ethical Teachings*, Los Angeles: University of Sankore Press.

——. (1993) "The Oppositional Logic of Malcolm X: Differentiation, Engagement and Resistance, *Western Journal of Black Studies*, 17, 1 (Spring) 6-16.

——. (1967) *The Quotable Karenga*, Los Angeles: Us Organization.

——. (2009) "Remembering Malcolm: Becoming and Being Ourselves," *Los Angeles Sentinel* (May 14) p. A-7.

——. (1969) "Revolution Must Wait for the People," *Los Angeles Free Press*, May 16, 1969, p. 14.

——. (1979) "The Sociopolitical Thought of Malcolm X," *Western Journal of Black Studies*, 3, 4 (Winter) 251-262.

Keto, C. Tsehloane. (1991) *The African Centered Perspective of History: An Introduction*, Laurel Springs, NJ: K. A. Publishers.

Lomax, Louis. (1963). *When the Word Is Given*, Cleveland, OH: World Publishing Co.

Malcolm X. (1965a) *The Autobiography of Malcolm X*, New York: Grove Press.

——. (1970) *By Any Means Necessary*, New York: Pathfinder Press.

——. (1971) *The End of White Supremacy*, New York: Seaver Books.

——. (1992) *February 1965: The Final Speeches*, New York: Pathfinder Press.

——. (1967) *Malcolm X on Afro American History*, New York: Pathfinder Press.

——. (1989) *Malcolm X: The Last Speeches*, New York: Pathfinder Press.

——. (1965b) *Malcolm X Speaks*, New York: Grove Press

——. (1991) *Malcolm X Talks to Young People*, New York: Pathfinder Press.
——. (1969a) "Racism: The Cancer that is Destroying America" in John Henrik Clarke, *Malcolm X: The Man and His Times*, New York: Macmillan Co., pp. 302-306.
——. (1969b) *The Speeches of Malcolm X at Harvard*, New York: William Morrow & Co., Inc.
Marable, Manning. (2011) *Malcolm X: A Life of Reinvention*, New York: Viking.
Muhammad, Elijah. (1973) *The Fall of America*, Chicago: Muhammad's Islamic Temple No. 2
——. (1965) *Message to the Black Man in America*, Chicago: Muhammad's Islamic Temple No. 2.
Nyerere, Julius. (1974) *Freedom and Development*, New York: Oxford University Press.
Obama, Barack. (2006) *The Audacity of Hope: Thoughts on Reclaiming the American Dream*, New York: Crown Publishing.
Sales, William. (1994) *From Civil Rights to Black Liberation*, Boston: South End Press.
Toure, Sekou. (1976) *Revolution. Culture et Panafricanisme*, 3ème edition, Conakry: RDA, Revue du Parti-Etat de Guinée.

The Meaning of Manning Marable's Biography of Malcolm X
Imam Al-Hajj Talib 'Abdur-Rashid

Institute of the Black World 21st Century Forum, Saturday, May 7, 2011

Thanks and honor to IBW and my friend and respected colleague, Dr. Ron Daniels. The late Professor Marable is someone whom I have respected over the years for his scholarship and activism in African American studies, the labor and anti-war movements, and especially for his scholarship on Malcolm X. I had been aware over the years of Dr. Marable's work on Malik Shabazz's biography, so it was with great interest that I anticipated the release of his book.

I believe that accurate and detailed accounts of the character and deeds of great men and women illuminate their greatness, and the greatness of the causes to which they have dedicated their lives. As such, while reading *Malcolm X: A Life of Reinvention*, I was thrilled, inspired, stunned, energized, and empowered, by what I read in detail of general events and occurrences that I have been aware of my entire adult life. I have many, many books written about Malcolm X.

Forty-four years ago in 1967, the Mosque of Islamic Brotherhood Inc. (MIB) was incorporated. This was two years after the martyrdom, of El-Hajj Malik El-Shabazz. The MIB is the lineal descendant of the Muslim Mosque Inc. (MMI). As such, it has its own institutional memory of events written about and not written about in Professor Marable's book. I am in my 23rd year as the imam of that congregation, having succeeded my late teacher, our founding imam of the MIB—Ash-Shaykhul-'Allama Al-Hajj K. Ahmad Tawfiq.

The Shaykh is mentioned in Dr. Marable 's book, as a "...furious MMI member named Talfiq" who advocated to brother James 67x (Abdur Razzaq) on behalf of the brothers and sisters of the MMI, during moments of friction with members of the OAAU, he is also mentioned in sister Ilyasah Shabazz 's book, *Growing Up X*.

Not only have I inherited aspects of the MMI's institutional memory from Shaykh Tawfiq, but from MMI members who are mostly not mentioned by name in Dr. Marable's book, but with whom I developed a relationship with over the years. We of the MIB have buried several of them as they have grown elderly, including Brother Bilal Abdullah (Brother Gladstone), Sister Catherine Crum, Salahuddin "Bullet" Abdullah, Atallah Muhammad Ayyubi, Taha Muhammad Abdullahi, and others. Former MMI members still worship at the MIB even now. All of these folks add to my own institutionally inherited memory, which I utilized to cross-reference and cross check some of Dr. Marable's assertions.

As I read *Malcolm X: A Life of Reinvention*, I found myself loving our brother even more as a leader and an inspiration than I already have, during my life for more than four decades, as I have grown from a teen-ager to a grandfather.

A couple of weeks ago, I was carrying Dr. Marable's book while walking across 125th Street and I ran into a young man, an African American Muslim, who asked me: "Imam why are you reading *that* book? I heard that Marable said this and that about Brother Malcolm. I would *never* read that trash!" he exclaimed, or something very close to it. I explained to him that I intended to critique the book in detail, and cannot do so if I have not read it. He understood and said that he would be waiting to hear my evaluation.

"Are there positives about the book?" Without a doubt, there are many. Dr. Marable's grasp of African American History and his activist rootedness serve him well as the biography's first major contribution to the legacy of El-Hajj Malik El-Shabazz. This is particularly, so I think, for the present and future generations of youth in America.

It does so by establishing in clear and detailed descriptive terms, the social, political, economic and cultural *context,* into which Shabazz was born, grew up, and lived his life. One cannot really understand him without understanding those critical factors. We, who lived through that era unto this one, know and understand that context. Those who do not will not grasp the full significance of Shabazz. The depth of his significance must be fully grasped by us as individuals and as a people.

Looking at the names on this esteemed panel I'm sure there will be much qualitative exposition on the illumination of the political dimensions of Malcolm X's mission. Dr. Marable's detailed account of the last year or so of our extraordinary leader's life makes it clear what *really* caused him to be considered a threat to national security by the government sponsors of boss and COINTELPRO. A*ny*one moving as he moved *then* or *now,* not only Pan-African wise, but *Pan-Islamic-wise,* would be targeted for neutralization or elimination by Uncle Sam's allied forces of oppression and repression. There can be no doubt about this. But the fact is that there has been no one who moved as Shabazz did—before or since.

Until now, the presentation of Brother Malik El-Shabazz's conflicts within and without the Nation of Islam (NOI) has been presented in either social or political terms. The causative factors being identified as:

1. Jealousy within NOI ranks (as noted publicly by the late Imam W.D. Mohammed, who is confirmed in Dr. Marable's book as having been very close to Minister Malcolm);

2. COINTELPRO and other-wise government instigated subterfuge; and

3. The actions of Malik Shabazz himself (i.e., his quiet investigation, and later public airing of Elijah Muhammad's sins, etc.).

But I want to add another dimension to consideration of those causative factors leading to the NOI conflict. I will identify them as being of a religious and spiritual nature, rooted in the difference between a narrow, proto-Islamic understanding, and one increasingly rooted in the Qur'an, and the prophetic tradition of the last and final messenger of Allah, Muhammad Ibn Abdullah, to whom the Qur'an was revealed (peace be upon him).

The prophetic value of justice was a major motivating force in Malik Shabazz's life. Once he became incarcerated, the seeds of righteousness and justice rooted in the teachings and legacy of the honorable Marcus Garvey, and planted not only in Shabazz, but *all* members of his family, emerged from their dormant state.

His January 1951 declaration, written while he was still a prison inmate, expresses a commitment to "love and justice" in thought and deed, rather than "hate and revenge." This speaks volumes as to the spiritual, prophetic values intrinsic to faith that were reawakened and re-embraced by him. Shabazz lived out those values until the day that he died.

Malcolm X's mission within the NOI and without was rooted in those spiritual, prophetic values. He was a deeply religious man who while a member of the NOI viewed himself as being on a divinely decreed mission of upliftment, under the guidance of a divinely selected leader. His personal and public life was consumed by that belief.

However once Shabazz came to realize that for the Muslim there is no substitute for Prophet Muhammad (peace be upon him) insofar as the "excellent exemplar" of righteousness is concerned, Shabazz shifted his allegiance from an exclusively particular one, to one that was both universal and particular. Thus he became even more consumed by a faith centered on love and justice.

Malcolm X's urgency to confront injustice rather than wait for divine intervention in the last days is a value deeply rooted in the Qur'an, and prophetic tradition of Islam. (The Prophet Muhammad, peace be upon him, said "when you see an evil, change it with your hand. If you can't do that, then speak out against it." He called the speaking of truth in the face of a tyrant "the greatest jihad." "If you can't speak out" he said, "then hate it in your heart. But that is the weakest of faith.")

The same applies to Malcolm X's willingness to tell the truth no matter who or what, even against him. His quiet investigation of an allegation of grave religious and spiritual impact at the highest level, his abstention for so long from broadcasting the sins of others, but rather covering their faults until they became a source of injustice that had to be aired—all of these are deep values in Islam. I could go on at length, but time is limited. But I will say that these Islamic values, and the young warrior-leader's dedication to them, are on full display in Dr. Marable's book.

"Are there issues of concern about the book?" Certainly. I was and am outraged that the same attention to detail and certainty that dominates the primary text of the book is abandoned by Marable in his quest to present the great leader as a flawed human being rather than as an icon.

Marable's *curious mathematics,* wherein 1 + 1= 5, is disgraceful. His accusations of an immoral nature against both Malcolm and Betty Shabazz, two moral young people, while offering almost no concrete proof of anything, his repeating of gossip, innuendo, back-biting, and slander—calling these things circumstantial evidence in one paragraph, yet referring to them in the next as if they were facts, is irresponsible, and slanderous. It detracts from the brilliance of the book. It is the biography's most serious flaw.

This sickness, wherein African American writers broadcast the sins or moral short-comings, or in this case the unproven allegations of sins or moral shortcomings of our people's great leaders, after their deaths when they can't defend themselves, is so-called "yellow journalism" or sensationalism at its worse. It is something that other people don't do, especially when their leader's sins or alleged sins have no bearing on the leader's mission, and do not create an injustice to others.

Novelist John Williams seems to have opened this Pandora's Box in 1970, when he wrote the book, *The King God Didn't Save*. The book has been described as containing "sordid depictions" of Dr. Martin Luther King Jr.'s "sexual indulgencies." Once trusted King aide, Ralph Abernathy, reopened the box in 1989, with his own book.

Three years later in 1992, Bruce Perry ventured into the same territory with his book *Malcolm—The Man Who Changed Black America*, described as a "psychological portrait." however Perry's musings were speculative and unpopular among the people, as Marable admits.

Lastly (because of time), unknown to most readers is Professor Marable's use of a Muslim blogger, Abdur-Rahman Muhammad, as a source of verification of various allegations or theories. Last year Abdur-Rahman Muhammad uncovered a current living-a-low-key-life-in-Newark, New Jersey, William Bradley—an unprosecuted authentic assassin of Malik Shabazz. Muhammad broadcast his discovery on the Internet, via his blog.

However, notwithstanding his discovery, Abdur-Rahman Muhammad is otherwise widely known in the Muslim community as an Internet gossiper, a cyber-slanderer who for years has broadcast innuendos as facts after failing to carefully check the authenticity of allegations.

The blogger is known as a basher of Muslim leaders and organizations. Last year in 2010, he became a low-level media-darling, openly admired by people like Sean Hannity, Glenn Beck, and the NYC-based, anti-Muslim bigot, Pamela Geller. Yet, Marable uses this guy as an authenticator of facts in his biography of Malik El-Shabazz. I say again, that to do so was irresponsible and disgraceful.

Marable's flaw in this area marks him as guilty of *character assassination* of the honest and upright Muslim leader.

"What is your assessment of the overall value of the book?" Contrary to Karl Evanzz's brilliant put-down of Marables's book, I believe it to be worthy of reading by a wide audience, and even more worthy of vigorous critique—praise what is good, denounce its flaws. I'm only sorry that the professor is no longer here, so that we could challenge him in person.

On Manning's Malcolm X
Mumia Abu-Jamal

For master historian, Professor Manning Marable of Columbia University, a book on the life of Malcolm X could only be a challenge that would daunt the faint-hearted.

Dr. Marable, founder of nearly half a dozen Black studies programs at colleges and universities across the country, would meet that challenge which demanded decades of study, reflection and writing to produce *Malcolm X: A Life of Reinvention* (Viking Press, 2011). Published at nearly 600 pages in length, it will stand as his masterwork, for Marable, who died, at 60, mere days before its release.

It captures the tone and tenor of the time, the quiescent '50s, the rolling '60s, and the equally turbulent, never resting spirit of Malcolm X (years before his "X"), as a hustler, prisoner, convert, minister, activist, exile, revolutionary organizer and martyr.

Marable questions large parts of the classical texts drawn from the *Autobiography of Malcolm X*, (which, in retrospect, appears more biography than autobiography), and seems more the result of Haley's craft than the subject, as shown by much of the internal correspondence between Haley and his editors, shaping the form, tone and context of the book.

Marable's book, however, is not free of critique. It opines that both Malcolm and Dr. Betty Shabazz (his wife) had sexual dalliances that may stain their memory. Moreover, he suggests Malcolm may've been involved in a homosexual affair in his youth. These seem more speculation, rumor and innuendo than proof, however.

Finally, Dr. Marable treats the COINTELPRO-type files and FBI interest and actions regarding Black groups as givens, normalized and to be expected instead of the unconstitutional and indeed, criminal race police that they functioned as, against Malcolm, the Nation of Islam, and even the pacifist movement led by Dr. Martin L. King Jr. (whom the FBI regarded as "the most dangerous man in America!"). Nor does he note how laughably unreliable many of these files were.

There is much here that is new; Malcolm's teenage fascination with white women (and their real names and identities); police tracking of

Malcolm since the mid '50s; the treacherous internal dynamics of the Nation of Islam; and Malcolm's courting of the Muslim Brotherhood (of Egypt).

There is too, the tragedy of its writer who, if in better health and perhaps with more time, could have devoted more of his energies and prodigious intellect to polish a work of such length and complexity.

That said, the work, *Malcolm X*, shines because of the brilliance not only of its author, but of its principal subject—Malcolm X. For his life was one constant reinvention in an age when the nation itself—and Black Americans—were in the process of transformation. America was trying to shed its apartheid past, and Negroes were becoming Black people, and African-Americans—and some (like Malcolm) citizens of an emerging (largely non white) international community.

Dr. Marable has made, virtually with his last breath, a bold and mammoth addition to our storehouse of knowledge.

Of that, we, and he, should be proud, for by painting Malcolm thusly, he makes him more human—more like us.

Rethinking Malcolm Means First Learning How to Think: What was Marable Thinking? And How?

Abdul Alkalimat

The new book by Manning Marable, *Malcolm X: A Life of Reinvention*, will help us get to a deeper understanding of Malcolm X and the times we're living in now. This will not be a direct result of what Marable has done, but rather what needs to be done because of what he has done. We can advance our thinking through deep and thorough criticism of this book.* We are facing a challenge to our perspective, our philosophy and our politics for Black liberation. We respect Manning Marable and ourselves by taking him seriously and raising our critique to the highest level. Many will oppose and even resent this review, but I write for the brothers and sisters who will dare to struggle, to take the hardcore stance we need for victory.

First came the book days after Marable's death, and then an avalanche of praise and polemic vaulting Marable into the esteemed ranks of ruling class darling public intellectuals. I collected and sent to the H-AFRO-AM e-list nearly 100 reviews and commentaries on this Marable book. They range from "magnificent," "magisterial," and "a magnum opus of a life's work based on 20 years of research," to "sloppy," "unprofessional," and "speculative based on logical fallacy." Why such extremely opposite views of this book?

Of course, we have been here before, with a book trying to redefine a major historical figure under the pretext of making him or her more human. This is usually done with innuendo, hearsay, and gossip supported

---

* This is an Anti-Duhring moment for the Black liberation and social revolution forces, as it's a matter of fundamental issues. Eugen Duhring was a leading German academic who published more than 10 books from the 1860s to the 1880s. He promoted a version of socialism while attacking Karl Marx. (see http://en.wikipedia.org/wiki/Anti-D%C3%BChring) Marable is a leading academic who has published many texts, while following social democracy toward a reformist path and not the Marxist-Leninist tradition for social revolution. Past his book on Malcolm X, we need a review of Marable's entire body of work.

by state surveillance reports, all amounting to nothing that can be supported with responsibly sourced data, meaning what would stand academic peer review. The main trend uniting these books is their focus on redirecting the force of revolutionary nationalism toward reform, toward the kind of social democracy that finds its home in the capitalist Democratic Party or toward the personal (sexual identity) being as important as the political. Such work has been done on, among others, Nat Turner (Styron 1976), Paul Robeson (Duberman, 1989), Martin Luther King (Garrow 1987 and Dyson 2000) and Malcolm X (Perry 1991, Lee 1992). As a generational deviation, this trend is exposed in the book *Betrayal* by Houston Baker (2008). Marable's book is somewhat different from this trend, but nevertheless fits the genre.

It is necessary to critique this book for at least three reasons. First: Marable speaks from within the movement with the legitimacy of being a Black Studies professor at an Ivy League school. This reverses the "street cred" marshaled by Spike Lee for his 1992 film *Malcolm X*. Many have learned from Marable and, given his recent death, are not open to deep and revealing criticism. But this cannot serve our movement. Silence never trumps critique. As on Malcolm, so on Marable on Malcolm.

Second: The rulers are making the Marable argument their own, as are the reigning Black public intellectuals, namely Henry Louis Gates, Mike Dyson, Cornel West, Peniel Joseph, Nell Painter, etc. It is unprecedented for a book on a leading revolutionary nationalist to be positively reviewed in the main English language capitalist media in the world—*New York Times, Washington Post, Wall Street Journal, Guardian* (UK), *Financial Times* (UK), and so on. Reviews are in all the major European languages as well. They hyped the book into the *New York Times* hardback non-fiction bestseller list for five weeks: April 24, number 3 on the list; May 1, number 6; May 8, number 13; May 15, number 16; and May 22, number 34.

But third and most important of all is the fact that the issues are fundamental and involve both what we think and how we think. This is my main concern. Elijah Muhammad wrote several books on "How to Eat to Live." Now we need to focus on "How to think to Live!" And by live, I mean to affirm our radical Black tradition, to critique and resist all forms of oppression and exploitation, and to chart a path of social justice toward social transformation.

We need to consider perspective, philosophy, and politics in critiquing *Malcolm X: A Life of Reinvention*. Our concern is to probe past the specific inaccuracies, innuendos, and judgmental conclusions to get at the basics of how to think to live.

Perspective

First, the question of perspective: Whose eyes do we use to see? Whom do we intend to hear us? One of the great paradigm shifts of Black Studies is to reclaim and reorient the relationship between Black intellectuals and their community. We began to speak to and with each other without necessarily seeking the approval of white authority. We sought peer review from each other and the brothers and sisters off campus. We wanted to understand each other and map our agreements and disagreements, find the intertextuality of our traditions (meaning Black Liberation Theology, Womanism, Nationalism, Pan-Africanism, and Socialism), and base our understanding on the dogmas and debate of these traditions.

Marable says this of his collaboration with his Viking editor: "Kevin and I communicated almost daily, discussing various versions of chapters, in the effort to build a narrative to reach the broadest possible audience" (Marable 2011 p. 492; unless otherwise noted all page numbers are from this book).

This explains why he regards the Organization of African American Unity (OAAU) as "controversial" (p. 2) and not merely what it was, an attempt to bring the united front strategy of the Organization of African Unity to the Black liberation movement. Who considered it controversial? He refers to alleged "anti-Semitic slurs" (p. 246) without putting this in the context of a necessary struggle against Zionism and the relative power of Black and Jews in New York City. He regards the surveillance of the state as legitimate rather than as flawed disinformation spread to discredit and disorient. No serious Black liberation perspective would allow this.

On the one hand, Marable contributes interesting summations of Harlem (p. 51-64) and Islam (p. 79-86), but he is noteworthy for not engaging any of the major writers who have done serious research, which has resulted in viewpoints different from his own. A good example of this is Bill Sales' work on the OAAU, listed in the bibliography but not engaged in the text. Nor does Marable engage the primary references used by Sales, notably the main state surveillance of the OAAU. And the same goes for James Cone and his definitive comparison of Malcolm X and Martin Luther King. Both Sales and Cone were members of the Malcolm X Work Group, a collective of intellectual activists working collaboratively on research about Malcolm X and holding important symposia in 1987, 1988, and 1989.

Perhaps the most cold-blooded negation is his statement that Malcolm has to be resurrected for Black people, where most certainly he should have said most white people. Black people have never forgotten

Malcolm X, and certainly the state and white intellectuals haven't either. He was more of an icon in the Black radical tradition than even Martin Luther King, Jr. The primary reference for this can be found in the website BrotherMalcolm.net, where there are lists of schools, parks, cultural events, academic lectures and many other things named after Malcolm in communities all over the world. Included are the proceedings of the historic 1990 international conference on Malcolm X, "Radical Tradition and Legacy of Struggle."

Perhaps the most egregious omission in this regard is the failure to mention Preston Wilcox. Not only had Preston been a professor at Columbia University, but he was the founder of the Malcolm X Lovers Network. As a community-based archivist, for decades he sent out mailings of the news clippings and ephemera he collected at the community level, flyers of events, petitions, documentation of naming ceremonies, debates and lectures, conferences, etc. He was a long time resident of Harlem and left his papers to the Schomburg Center. To ignore Preston Wilcox is to show no respect for the Black community and its community-based intellectuals who have always kept the memory of Malcolm alive.

The perspective of Marable's book is not the Black studies approach of respecting our own tradition. Instead it gives credence to such as the Bruce Perry book on Malcolm (1991), which was written as a police agent's attack filled with lies and innuendo. What was Marable thinking? Or not thinking?

Philosophy

Now let us take up issues of philosophy. Here I want to focus on two questions: what is real? And how does reality change? In other words, this is an investigation as to whether Marable uses a dialectical materialist philosophy in this book. How was Marable thinking?

First, what is dialectical materialism? Materialism is a philosophical position that affirms the existence of the material world outside of and independent of our consciousness, hence we must be in the world and engage it in order to come to any understanding of it. This means that when you want to speak about the world you have to provide material evidence so that others can evaluate whether and how your words correspond with material reality. Dialectics is about the nature of reality, that everything is in motion, and this motion reflects the conflicting tensions between contradictions. Most things have many contradictions, but in general there is always a principal contradiction that dominates the identity of that reality. External contradictions are the conditions for change, but internal contradictions are the basis for change. So to understand something we have to include both the external and the internal contradictions as part of our analysis. This is a philosophical approach that is essential for understanding the complexity of the world, human society, and of course important historical figures.

In sum, we can say that philosophy is not (and should not be portrayed as) a mystery but something that all of us can master. This is clearly a different approach to philosophy than the archaic approaches usually associated with philosophy as an academic discipline. For our purposes here, there are two fundamental philosophical questions:

> How do we know something? This gets at our grasp of material reality. We all think we know some things so how do we know what we think we know?
>
> And, so what? How does our understanding capture the nature of reality such that we understand the motion of how things change, how change comes about?

In this regard, Marable sets a high standard for this book:

> My primary purpose in this book is to go beyond the legend: to recount what actually occurred in Malcolm's life. I also present the facts that Malcolm himself could not know, such as the extent of illegal FBI and New York Police Department Surveillance and acts of disruptions against him, the truth about those among his supporters who betrayed him politically and personally, and the identification of those responsible for Malcolm's assassination. (p. 12)

First, when you apply the revolutionary mandate "no investigation, no right to speak," the book comes up short for a lack of evidence. Why not provide the source and let the reader be the judge? Here are some examples of statements with no evidence presented in the 63 pages of footnotes:

Page 12 – "55 year old audio tapes" are cited as having been reviewed by Marable but no additional information is given like number of tapes, dates, etc. Good scholarship requires documentation of evidence so it can be checked by others.

Page 22 – "Amy Jacques Garvey...may have been involved in Eason's assassination," a statement based on the conjecture in a secondary source

Page 36 – "He may have also believed that his mother's love affair [was] a betrayal of his father." Here Marable is practicing psychoanalysis without any data to back this conclusion.

Page 123 – He states of the Nation of Islam (NOI) membership, "until 1961, it would expand more than tenfold, to...seventy-five thousand members." Again no source (NOI? FBI?), so why should we consider this a fact?

Page 137 – "James Warden...son of a labor organizer who may once have been a member of the Communist Party." He interviewed Warden on three occasions, so why no indication of the source of this? Exactly what was said? James Warden, now Abdullah Abdur Razzaq, stated during the Malcolm X Museum forum on the book, held at the Schomburg Center on May 2011, that he was totally misquoted in the book, and he has the transcripts of his interview to prove it. Wassup?

Page 147 – Referring to his wife Betty: "Malcolm rarely, if ever, displayed affection toward her." But then on page 180 Marable writes: "Malcolm conveyed his love for her." Which is it? And without evidence, how can we believe the amateurish psychoanalysis he presents?

Pages 174-175 – "a fire broke out in Louis's home...most NOI members believed (Ella) Collins was responsible." Again, no evidence.

Page 247 – Elijah Muhammad "interpreted the [*Autobiography*] as evidence of Malcolm's vanity but [decided] at least temporarily, to cater to this." Here Marable's father-son Freudian analysis about Elijah Muhammad and Malcolm X remains speculative without even a footnote that exposes the intellectual framework for such an idea. This idea is at least more responsibly argued in Wolfenstein (1981).

Page 266 – Regarding the notion that Malcolm was romantically involved with a woman whom Elijah Muhammad got pregnant: "no one else—not even James 67X—has made such a claim." So why such a big deal out of this sexual controversy on at least five different places in the book?

Page 268 – "nearly every individual he trusted would betray that trust." Again, such a global statement without proof can only sow the seeds of distrust in the movement and go against those living who were close to Malcolm.

Page 284 – "There is evidence that Malcolm may have met with the leaders of the Communist Party's Harlem branch…" Now, while this is perfectly possible, why no documentation of the evidence? And what about Bill Epton?

Page 294 – "it is likely that no more than two hundred members in good standing quit the sect: less than 5 percent of all mosque congregants." Why use the pejorative word "sect" for the NOI? And, again, what is the source of these numbers?

Page 423 – "Sharon 6X may have joined [Malcolm] in his hotel room." Again, a damning statement with no evidence whatsoever.

Page 469 – "The organization's archival heritage…were [sic] largely destroyed, and a new memory, branded by orthodoxy, was imposed." What is the source for this? There are several organizations who claim to have the archives, so why does Marable think they are gone? And who imposed what new memory? While many may believe this, a serious work of scholarship would provide some kind of proof.

So the basic trend of these points tells us that this is a poor job of empirical scholarship. Moreover, only about 20 percent of the 63 pages of footnotes come from primary sources. The rest of the footnotes come from published work based on others peoples' research. And Marable hardly ever engages the serious scholarship of others, and fails to give any credit to his first project director who guided the day-to-day research effort, Cheryll Greene—not even a mention in the acknowledgments.

Marable states in the acknowledgments, "Elizabeth Mazucci was largely responsible for building the Malcolm X chronology…" In fact, the first chronology on his Columbia University website was lifted entirely from our BrotherMalcolm.net site without any attribution. I had to protest to Marable, and when I got no response from him I wrote to the Columbia administration. The page was taken down, but no one gave me the courtesy of a response. Marable then reposted the chronology with a new format and a couple of new dates added, but still with no acknowledgment of sources. Marable and I were among the five founders of the Black Radical Congress, but this was hardly the move of a comrade, or a brother, or an honest scholar.

The overarching philosophical error in this book is suggested by the title, *Malcolm X: A Life of Reinvention*. There are two incorrect aspects to this fundamental idealist error. First, Marable discounts Malcolm's own autobiography, writing, "In many ways, the book is more Haley's than its author's: because Malcolm died in February 1965, he had no opportunity to revise major elements of what would become known as his political testament" (p. 9).

I was at the 1992 Knoxville, Tennessee auction of the papers from the Haley estate and reviewed the documents such as the final copy edited by Malcolm, and the missing chapters. After but a quick scan I don't believe there is any basis for this authorial challenge, which seems like just another attack on Malcolm X. The *Autobiography* was not a life invented by Alex Haley. The documents in question were purchased by Detroit attorney Greg Reed, and we await their release for a closer examination. Reed also has obtained a trove of documents recovered from the papers of a former member of the NOI in Detroit that will increase the archives we have.

Second, Marable suggests that Malcolm opportunistically invented and re-invented himself as a form of self-promotion, "to package himself to maximum effect" (p. 10). He thinks the process was based on intentional agency by Malcolm X himself. Does consciousness determine being, or does being determine consciousness? Marable takes the first approach, while I suggest a materialist perspective that follows this observation by Karl Marx: "It is not the consciousness of men that determines their being, but, on the contrary, their social being that determines their consciousness." We must look to the concrete circumstances of Malcolm's life and how the interplay of external and internal forces played out in his dialectical transformations.

There is no evidence that Malcolm deliberately reinvented himself. Rather, as with anyone who matures, the stages of Malcolm's life can be understood as resulting from the dialectic of his consciousness and his concrete experiences. His ideas about himself and the world were negated by his experience, compelling him forward, even against his will at times. He was a youth believing in and wanting to be part of society, but the negation of dominant society by his father and his mother, and then the negations of Malcolm by his teachers and his foster home experience all made him reject mainstream aspirations and pulled him into the street and being an outlaw. As an outlaw, the state negated him and put him in the joint, where he continued being a satanic character. In opposition to this negation, his family and fellow prisoners then provided support and a path into a new form of consciousness and being. He cleaned up and began to recapture consciousness, to follow the path of his father and family. As Malcolm Little he was in small Midwestern towns (Omaha, Milwaukee, East Lansing). As Detroit Red, he was in large East Coast cities (Boston, New York,

Washington DC). What was a constant was his eagerness to learn and achieve, first as an affirmation of society, then when negated as a negative force in society.

Once Malcolm X joined the NOI, led by his family members, he combined the lessons of both earlier stages of his life and built its membership up by going among the gangsters, the negated and most oppressed, and raising them into the lifestyle that his parents taught him and Elijah Muhammad reaffirmed—all of them moral, disciplined, and proud people. And at least three more forces changed Malcolm X. First, he was appointed by the NOI to become National Minister and travel the county at the same time that the national freedom movement was reaching its peak in terms of consciousness and mobilization. He read and engaged with activists. While he changed many, he was also changed. Second, the police attacked and killed members of the NOI (especially in Los Angeles—see and Malcolm was ready for action that far exceeded what the NOI was prepared to do. Third, the world situation was ablaze with armed struggle for national liberation, from Vietnam to Africa, Cuba and Latin America. He followed these movements very closely. His three great Detroit speeches from 1963, 1964 and 1965 make this very clear.

His final break with the NOI was conditioned by these external factors and two more factors internal to the NOI. One was Elijah Muhammad violating his own moral teachings regarding adultery. Two was Malcolm's direct violation of the central leadership's order of silence on the Kennedy assassination. Elijah Muhammad negated himself; Malcolm, having internalized the external political forces acting on him, negated the order of silence.

Malcolm's new status free from the confines of the NOI was reinforced by his continued movement into Sunni Islam via his Hajj and his continued movement into world revolution by extensive trips abroad in Europe and Africa. My argument is that Malcolm's life is not a self-invention process intended through Malcolm's agency, but a global process that summed up the journey so many were to make from the oppressed, through the street, to Black self-determination, to revolutionary. This is the dialectical materialism of social change in the late 20th century, and on that basis people held and hold Malcolm in the highest regard and lived and are living the life he epitomized.

Politics

Now we come to politics, and the strategy and tactics advocated by Malcolm X. Strategy is the long term view of how to seize power and transform society, making clear what forces in society can be counted on and what forces one will have to fight. Strategy also focuses on the goals of a struggle. Tactics are the methods used in the day-to-day struggle in which a lot of flexibility and innovation is needed in the tit-for-tat encounters with the enemy and in mobilizing the masses of people. Tactics are subordinate to strategy, and can't be equated or one confuses the zigzag of the struggle with the goal and basic plan for mobilization, organization, and victory.

On a global level, Marable gives us a clue of how he invents his own Malcolm X. He states: "The United Nations World Conference Against Racism, held in Durban, South Africa in 2001, was in many ways a fulfillment of Malcolm's international vision" (p. 485). This is ridiculous. Malcolm X would have condemned the Durban meeting just as he did the 1963 March on Washington. Apparently the writer of the epilogue of Marable's book forgot what the writer of chapter four had written: "Black American leaders, Malcolm now urged must 'hold a Bandung Conference in Harlem'" (p. 120). Durban was a conference in which the imperialists were trying to assert their hegemony over anti-racism and decolonization. Bandung was a Third World gathering to plan unity and resistance in opposition to the imperialists. Malcolm X never believed an honest discussion could be held with imperialists. He would have predicted what actually happened in Durban: the U.S. imperialists blocked any open debate in order to defend their client state, Israel.

On Malcolm X's political thinking, Marable writes: "Despite his radical rhetoric, as 'The Ballot or the Bullet' makes clear, the mature Malcolm believed that African Americans could use the electoral system and voting rights to achieve meaningful change" (p. 484). Here Marable refuses to embrace the dialectical thinking of Malcolm X. First, Malcolm's thinking was grounded in the radical Black tradition. See what Frederick Douglass wrote 100 years earlier in an article titled "The Ballot and the Bullet":

> If speech alone could have abolished slavery, the work would have been done long ago. What we want is an anti-slavery government, in harmony with our anti-slavery speech, one which will give effect to our words, and translate them into acts. For this, the ballot is needed, and if this will not be heard and heeded, then the bullet. We have had cant enough, and are sick

of it. When anti-slavery laws are wanted, anti-slavery men should vote for them; and when a slave is to be snatched from the hand of a kidnapper, physical force is needed, and he who gives it proves himself a more useful anti-slavery man than he who refuses to give it, and contents himself by talking of a "sword of the spirit." (1859, reprinted in Douglass 1950, p. 457-458)

The ballot or bullet theme in Black radicalism is in fact a fundamental tenet of *American* politics. It was part of the ideological rationale for the American anti-colonial war of liberation from England. It was stated in the 1776 Declaration of Independence, 235 years ago. Read the full text if you want to understand the tradition on which Malcolm X stands—a radical American tradition.

Malcolm's "Ballot or the Bullet" speech was part of his spring 1964 offensive. It is important to be clear on the historical context in which he was giving political leadership. Forces that preceded and surrounded him undoubtedly impacted his thinking: The increasingly militant struggles in the South, especially those led by Medgar Evers after the brutal murder of Emmett Till in 1955.

Robert Williams and his Monroe, North Carolina armed self-defense strategy as summed up in his book *Negroes with Guns* (1962). The armed group Deacons for Defense and Justice formed in Louisiana in 1964. The Revolutionary Action Movement, a group led by Max Stanford, who went on to influence the development of the Black Panther Party. This was the only other organization that Malcolm X joined. (Stanford 1986)

President John F. Kennedy was assassinated in November 1963. Vice President and then President L. B Johnson consolidated his own leadership by staying the course and supporting major civil rights legislation, so the Civil Rights Act of 1964 was signed into law on July 2, 1964. During the summer of 1964 SNCC led the civil rights organizations that had formed into a coalition called COFO in 1962 for a major offensive in Mississippi. This was the Mississippi Summer Project. Hundreds of activists poured into the state and confronted the heart of racist state power. The House passed the bill in February 1965, but a Senate filibuster held it up. The Senate filibuster ended on June 19. Three movement activists (Goodman, Chaney and Schwerner) were martyred by assassination in Philadelphia, Mississippi on June 21. Out of the Mississippi Summer Project came a political party, the Mississippi Freedom Democratic Party (MFDP). (It was the MFDP that brought Fannie Lou Hamer to Harlem in 1964 where she appeared on a platform with Malcolm X.) From the local precinct level to a delegation going to the national convention, the MFDP fought the racist party organization that excluded Black people. The main civil rights leaders tried to get the MFDP to accept being seated at the convention without voice or vote. The MFDP, with SNCC, rejected this as a sellout. In the meantime, the bullets kept flying:

1963	June	Assassination of Medgar Evers
1964	Jul	Rebellion in Rochester, New York
	Aug	Rebellion in Philadelphia, Pennsylvania
1965	Feb 21	Assassination of Malcolm X
	Aug	Rebellion in Watts, Los Angeles
1966	Jun	Black Power slogan emerges in militant march in Mississippi
	Jul	Rebellions in Cleveland, Ohio, and Omaha, Nebraska
	Oct	Black Panther Party is organized in Oakland, California
1967	Jul	Rebellions in Newark and Plainfield, New Jersey Rebellion in Detroit
	Oct	Assassination of Che Guevara
1968	Apr	Assassinations of Black Panther Bobby Hutton and Martin Luther King, Jr., and Rebellions in Chicago and more than 100 other cities
1969	Dec	Assassination of Black Panther Fred Hampton
	Jun	League of Revolutionary Black Workers is organized in Detroit

In 1965-66, the struggle was developing. The defeat of the Watts rebellion led to the ideological advance of the Black Power slogan, and the new revolutionary organization called the Black Panther Party, followed two years later by workers throwing up a new revolutionary force on the factory floor called the League of Revolutionary Black Workers. The U.S. armed forces put down major urban rebellions, and assassination of Black radical leaders continued.

The 1964 presidential campaign brought forward the ultra-right in the form of Barry Goldwater. By 1966 Black Power emerged as a key ideological slogan. Electoral victories led to the first major Black Mayors of Cleveland, Ohio and Gary, Indiana. By 1968, things got even more extreme when Alabama governor George Wallace, the nation's leading segregationist politician, ran for president and won the Indiana primary! Richard Nixon was elected president in 1968 and 1972, but was run out of office in disgrace in 1974. A struggle for power was taking place.

Malcolm X laid the basis for understanding these events: the Senate filibuster and racist state power; the murders and the unity between the Klan and the government; and the emergence of Black Power in both electoral and more militant forms as well. This was indeed the ballot and the bullet, 20th century edition.

The analysis that Malcolm laid out in his spring 1964 speeches amounts to a theory of the U.S. racist capitalist state that is based on finding a strategy to fight against it. First, the power of the US ruling class as based on southern fascism, versus a Black united front. Then, armed self-defense for Black liberation as self-determination versus that racist state power.

Marable advances an argument that separates Malcolm from his legacy, a legacy that was in fact us, the Black liberation movement. But no activist in that movement who was in motion at the time will believe his argument. It flies in the face of our experience.

Why this book, at this time?

We have reviewed Manning Marable's book on Malcolm X as far as perspective, philosophy, and politics. But we still have an outstanding question: why *this* book, at *this* time? President George W. Bush was a right-wing standard bearer. We took to the streets to fight his policies. The resistance to the imperialist war on Iraq and then Afghanistan produced a major antiwar movement with heightened consciousness that developed faster and with a sharper focus than the movement against the Vietnam War. But now we have the Obama moment. Barack Obama is a Black face on US imperialism. While he has escalated Bush's war, and extended it into Libya, we have no antiwar movement challenging Obama's legitimacy. The ruling class is using a Black man to advance the cause of neo-liberalism. They are concerned more about banks "too big to fail" than unemployment and the suffering of the masses of people.

Maybe I should say Obama is our man doing their work. We voted for him but he lacks the guts to fight for us against the rulers and generals who govern. He seeks to compromise with right-wing Republicans and Democrats captured by the fascist Tea Party that holds 10 percent of the seats in Congress.

Rather than give us the Malcolm X of the Detroit speeches, the Malcolm X we love and respect, Marable tries to cut him down to size with unsubstantiated arguments under the guise of trying to humanize Malcolm

X. In summary, Marable gives us a perspective that is outside of the Black Studies tradition in his attempt to sell books to a wide American book-buying public. Marable gives us a philosophy that is mechanical and not dialectical, idealist and not materialist. And he attempts to turn Malcolm X into a social reformer rather than the revolutionary that he actually was. In short, Marable fabricates a Malcolm X who would not take militant and revolutionary action against the global war, poverty, and degradations of today. That's why we have to speak up: to respect our legacy and affirm our future.

References

Baker, Houston. *Betrayal: How Black Intellectuals have Abandoned the Ideals of the Civil Rights Era.* New York: Columbia University Press, 2008.

Clarke, John Henrik, ed. *William Styron's Nat Turner: Ten Black Writers Respond.* Boston: Beacon Press, 1968.

Cone, James. H. *Martin & Malcolm & America: A Dream or a Nightmare.* Maryknoll, NY: Orbis Books, 1991

Douglass, Frederick. *The Life and Writings of Frederick Douglass, Volume 2.* Philip S. Foner, ed. New York, International Publisher, 1950.

Duberman, Martin Bauml. *Paul Robeson.* New York: Alfred A. Knopf, 1988.

Dyson, Michael Eric. *I May Not Get There With You: The True Martin Luther King, Jr.* New York: Free Press, 2000.

Engels, Frederick. *Anti-Duhring (Herr Eugen Duhring's revolution in science).* Translated by Emile Burns. Moscow: Progress Publishers, 1947. Available at http://www.marxists.org/archive/marx/works/1877/anti-duhring/

Garrow, David J. *Bearing the Cross: Martin Luther King Jr., and the Southern Christian Leadership Conference.* New York: William Morrow & Company, 1986.

Lee, Spike. *Malcolm X* [movie], 1992.

Marable, Manning. *Malcolm X: A Life of Reinvention.* New York: Viking, 2011.

Muhammad, Elijah. *How to Eat to Live, Volume 1.* Chicago, Muhammad Mosque of Islam No. 2, 1967. Available at http://www.seventhfam.com/temple/books/eattolive_one/eat1index.htm

Muhammad, Elijah. *How to Eat to Live, Volume 2.* Chicago, Muhammad Mosque of Islam No. 2, 1972. Available at http://www.seventhfam.com/temple/books/eattolive_two/eat2index.htm

Perry, Bruce. *Malcolm: The Life of a Man Who Changed Black America.* Barrytown, NY: Station Hill Press, 1991.

Sales, William W. *From Civil Rights to Black Liberation: Malcolm X and the Organization of Afro-American Unity.* Boston: South End Press, 1994.

Stanford, Maxwell C. "Revolutionary Action Movement (RAM): A Case Study of an Urban Revolutionary Movement in Western Capitalist Society." Master's thesis. Atlanta University, 1986. Available at http://www.ulib.csuohio.edu/research/portals/blackpower/stanford.pdf

Styron, William. *The Confessions of Nat Turner: A Novel.* New York: Random House, 1967.

Williams, Robert F. *Negroes with Guns.* New York, Marzani & Munsell, 1962.

Wolfenstein, E. Victor. *The Victims of Democracy: Malcolm X and the Black Revolution.* Berkeley: University of California Press, 1981.

An Afrocentric Take on Manning Marable's *Malcolm X: A Life of Reinvention*
Molefi Kete Asante

I wanted to make sure that I had time to fully digest Manning Marable's "study" of Malcolm X before I commented, although I must confess that I wanted to speak immediately when I heard the praises the book was receiving from the Left and the Right. Furthermore, I knew something was amiss when the white mainstream began to push the work as a monumental analysis of the life of Malcolm X. I wondered, "When has the white mainstream press pushed works that were favorable to Nat Turner, Du Bois, Marcus Garvey, Assata Shakur, Robert Mugabe, Amiri Baraka, or Maulana Karenga?"

Isn't the politics, particularly, revolutionary politics that chastises oppression, racism, sexism, and nationally sanctioned attacks on freedom fighters normally considered anathema to the white mainstream press? What could bring Marable's *Malcolm X: A Life of Reinvention*, so much positive reaction? Obviously, there was something in Marable's work that tweaked the consciousness of the white media toward this portrait of Malcolm X. I think the initial reaction of the white Left was based on the perceived tarnishing of Malcolm's Black Nationalist and Pan African dimensions. No, I do not believe for one minute that the Left was looking to praise Malcolm, but to find favor in dishonoring him. The idea that someone could tarnish the image of Malcolm X was enough to make the living praise the dead. Yet for those others of us in the society who have seen, all this time, that Malcolm was our burning spear, a prince of time, nothing said about him would diminish his authenticity as a revolutionary icon.

After reading the book, actually after locating it as is the method of Afrocentricity, I determined that the flaws in Marable's work were not simply errors of references, innuendoes, and narrow flights off into squeaky sexual matters, but rather that the writer, despite his notoriety was deeply dislocated politically. Consequently his analysis of Malcolm X was fundamentally off-center. Every space where Malcolm X could have been viewed as having taken agency was locked down, filled with unsanitary speculation, and hurriedly dismissed as being something other than the powerful assertion of African will. This is the style of the deconstructionists and post modernists who see cracks in every wall where power is amassed by blacks and who believe that to humanize a figure, especially a favored personality esteemed by blacks, one must kill the iconic image in a way that destroys it forever.

There is a lot to respect in Marable's body of work and one should not measure his career's success or failure by one book, a work that he may have revised had it been read by some critical readers prior to the rush to publication. My last conversation with him took place at the University of Illinois where we were both speakers for the evening on theoretical and political issues in Africology. I found that evening the same thing I found in his work on Malcolm X and that is a tremendous reliance on class formation with less and less regard for operable racism, based on long years of brainwashing, in American society. While it is impossible to show all oppression as racial the existence of racism does pose special problems for black people. Consequently, Malcolm X represents for black people the great objection to place, problem, burden, and other terms of confinement in the American prison of race.

Now it is possible to ask, "So, why Malcolm X must be murdered twice?" Perhaps because he understood, as he said, we needed him. "I am the man you want to be, I am the one you wish you were," he once said. To deny Africans in America and elsewhere the standard bearer who carries the sword against the oppressor is to rob Africans of models who count their lives dear only if the collective wins. Here is a man who opposed in language and action the attitudes that had held us back for decades. He was the spirit of resistance and the persona of assertion.

I often tell my students that I can read the first five pages of a text and tell you precisely where the author is going. I can know the writer's location by the language she chooses. Thus, Marable's Malcolm defies the reinvention launched by the scholar. To say, however, that he succumbed to the temptation to woo the progressives is not exactly my reading. Marable was a journalist seeking to uncover the clay feet of an iconic figure and he found evidences in what he sees as Malcolm's sexual exploits, the crevices in Malcolm's attitude toward women, and Malcolm's love-hate relationship with Elijah Muhammad. The book shook the ground where African Americans stood their Malcolm X.

But one thing is clear: we are a resilient people, toughened by adversity and inspired by possibility. We do forget our heroes and we cannot be deterred by misunderstandings, petty jealousies, and class warfare. Malcolm X remains heroic despite the post-modern turn presented by Marable's socialist orientation. I am neither socialist nor capitalist, neither Christian nor Muslim; my allegiance is only to the liberation of African spaces intellectually, politically, and culturally. Narrow and provincial arguments over religion, class, and color can only bring confusion, distrust, and insanity.

There is much to admire in Marable's work, but it is not radical. I would never call Marable a radical although he liked being referred to as a Radical Democrat, much like my friends Cornel West and Michael Dyson, but I am not sure they are radical democrats either. Marable's notion of radical was to be Left because he did not properly appreciate the history of African nationalism or Pan Africanism; he was essentially an African Americanist with a strong sense of racial justice. One could just as well be a white liberal and come to the same conclusions. I do not disparage this position, but it was not Malcolm's position; it is not my position. In many ways I find Malcolm's response to the denial of space and place for Africans in this society the most logical answer to white racial nationalism. We are stuck perhaps with the term nationalism or Black Nationalism but in the end Malcolm X sought to undo the construction of race and racism in America; this was a revolutionary objective. However, if you can only think of revolution in a class-sense you will miss the fundamental role of Malcolm in our struggle. He never denied class contradictions; he responded to all oppressions concentrating primarily on racial oppression because that was the key to our historical experiences.

Malcolm X: A Life of Reinvention unfortunately becomes the work most closely identified with Manning Marable. Born in Dayton, Ohio, Marable attended Earlham and the University of Maryland and in some ways was never able to get the institutions or their training out of his mind. I am only able to say this after reading the full extent of his treatment of Malcolm X, including his ability to differentiate the significance of a white controlled and black controlled social and political groups, e.g., Nation of Islam and Socialist groups.

I always see texts in the context of struggle; I am a child of the

Sixties where the purpose of struggle was always to make the world better. To us, as members of the SNCC, Us Organization, Black Panthers, and other student activists, this meant to assert ourselves in the way that Malcolm asserted himself. He was the fiery example of our best hope, our most courageous symbol, and it is out of this cauldron that we understood what to make of Cabral, Fanon, and Fannie Lou Hamer. I could care less about the sexual proclivities of Cabral, Fanon, or Fannie Lou Hamer; I am interested, keenly so, in what they experienced and were able to say to change our objective locations. We believed that it would be university students with a sense of purpose tied to activism that would become the new hope of our generation. I mention this only to suggest that when younger people came along, such as Marable, the force of the movement had been dissipated by the COINTELPRO and other system machinations and they had to discover newer ways to maintain semblance of protest and activism and they often did this by seeking to discredit those who had established the models in the Sixties. Manning Marable was a mere child when blacks were in the streets for Black Studies and consequently he did not see the true character of Malcolm X. Learning it from the books is useful but nothing takes the place of actuality.

Here is what I think Marable missed in his portrait: Malcolm X was pre-eminently a cultural spokesperson, an analyst and theorist of culture, and a revolutionary cultural scientist. Thus, when he is examined within the context of his own community and within the framework of the African-American situation, he emerges as a concrete example of the cultural hero. Furthermore, Malcolm's identity as an intellectual, not a public intellectual, and an organizer must be seen in the light of his emphasis on people in transformation. He wanted to see Africans in America transformed, changed, and perfected in resistance to oppression. He expressed this in his concept of the radically different African person seeking to create a new type of African American who was not afraid to speak up and stand up for legitimate rights. This was the key to what Harold Cruse would see as the responsibility of the mature, independent thinking African American's response to the crisis in culture and leadership.

In my view *Reinvention* will only confuse those who did not see that Malcolm X radically changed the political discourse in the nation around African American rights in that he was not speaking merely a discourse of integration into the white society but rather demanding human rights as an African person. This was un-King like, unique, creative and yet so fundamentally authentic that the masses found his rhetoric compelling. Yet Malcolm was never a public intellectual in the sense that he was available to speak on every issue without participating in the resistance to oppression. His public stance was inevitably a very real demonstration of his passionate commitment to freedom. Thus, Malcolm's oratory was comprehensive, tight, sharp, unrehearsed, from the brain of an intellectual genius who felt one with his people in that his experiences had made him understand the self hatred, docility, and self degrading activities of many Africans. He rejected the condition of servitude and expressed himself as a conscious, historical being committed to the ultimate liberation of African people by any means necessary. This was a new status, in sharp contrast to the previous approaches of negotiation, petition, and prayer. Perhaps Marable's own location, stance, posture, was more Martin Luther King, Jr., than Malcolm X. There was always something frightening to careerists about Malcolm; he refused to sell out his people for material gain.

Malcolm taught that Africans in America had been badly educated. Most African Americans did not know their names and the names they wore were not their African names. Malcolm's idea was that Africans had allowed the white man to dictate terms of existence. Indeed, it was impossible for Africans to express concerns for liberation except on terms that had been determined by whites. Here was an example of blacks seeking freedom from oppression but going to whites to ask them to approve the rules of discussion or even more, in some cases, to provide the rules. Malcolm rejected this procedure and advanced what became a model for Afrocentric scholars who understood the dimensions of the servility and sought to assert political, economic, cultural, and moral authority based on a clear reading of African history, past and present.

It is this tendency toward seeming like a junior brother or sister that Malcolm struggled against and demonstrated in his public and private discourses a way to articulate new visions and new agendas. It is this juncture that was so productive and generative in the launching of youth movements and passionately cultural and political institutions such as the Black Panthers and the Us Organization and new philosophies like Kawaida and Afrocentricity. Each proponent of transformation saw in Malcolm's rhetoric and life a way to be; thus, it was his *being boldness* that alerted the white opposition that the reality of racism was doomed.

I am sure that Manning would have loved to have this conversation with me; he enjoyed differences of opinion, debate, and good argument, but in the end I believe that he would have to concur that while Malcolm was influenced by the Honorable Elijah Muhammad and held to the nationalist positions of the Minister of the Nation of Islam he emerged as a seminal thinker himself. The Malcolmian project, however, was never about human perfection or the idea that any human could be without blemish or sin; this is no mere Christian myth. So what is the point of Marable's deconstruction?

I sense in the *Reinvention* an attempt to claim, and this is without adequate proof because we are confronted with a preponderance of uncritically assessed references, that Malcolm's manliness and cultural nationalism were problematic given Malcolm's own digressions. Culture has the ability to assemble behaviors, symbols, customs, motifs, moods, and icons into a single comprehensive affirming presence. It is Malcolm's stance toward self-hatred, *culturicide,* and *menticide* that governs his political ideology. In fact, Malcolm could see that this new type of African rejected the white man's Christian religion, the notion of inferiority, and the imitation of whites. He recognized that the real enemy of the African in America is white racism and its attendant manifestations in the society's institutions. Malcolm explained it this way: when you are confused you can think that your friends are your enemies and your enemies are your friends.

If I could have wished for something more in Manning Marable's book it would have been an expose of Malcolm's political ideals. There seemed to be three overarching ideas that do not make the Reinvention but would have given the readers a much stronger idea of Malcolm's significance. Of course, I understand that this was not Marable's purpose. Nevertheless, Malcolm X suggested that there were three overarching political lessons that the African had to understand about America (1) American society could not be redeemed on the basis of its present institutions, (2) Whites would not agree to share power with Africans committed to social justice, and (3) Africans had to accept their Africanity as a basis for political, economic, and moral actions.

If Manning had concentrated on bringing to us the fundamental thought processes of Malcolm we would have gained immensely by this book, but alas, it is too late for Marable and a genuine study of Malcolm awaits to be done.

Marable was a keen observer but was probably a better observer than he was an analyst because to understand something you must have a consistent theoretical instrument as well as know what it is that you are evaluating. One could, as Marable did, take a Marxist approach to Malcolm but what is clear is that this approach in the hands of Marable was neither consistent nor did if allow him the opportunity to make good analysis of the entire Malcolmian Project. Actually one must be careful when listening to critics say that the book is highly referenced because there is always a difference between citations and analysis of the citations. To thoroughly document a book means that the writer must understand, and convey to the reader, the prejudices of the sources. For me, we have a feast of references but I am not able to see the broad outline of Marable's argument.

What would have been useful is for Marable to advance the idea that with the Age of Malcolm a new epoch began in the conception of a national culture causing a far-reaching revolution in the traditional views held by members of African-American institutions. Malcolm was not merely the African American's manhood, but the keeper of the ancestral flames of a proactive response to the human condition. His own life represented the rebirth of the extensive African commitments to cultural reconstruction, which would be seen in the extensive philosophical contours that came after him. You cannot write a biography of Malcolm X and not appreciate the revolutionary context of his work.

Malcolm saw that the adaptation of our ideas, attitudes, language and history to the social and cultural imperatives of the African people was the first requirement for a comprehensive transformation. There could be no other interface with our historical destiny; we had to center ourselves in our African reality. However much we search out the personal idiosyncrasies of Malcolm X or the petty discussions about his personal life we will learn nothing from him without a deep appreciation of his inherent commitment to overcome the conditions imposed by the doctrine of white racial domination. Our score sheets, without this understanding will amount to naught.

What may have been difficult for Manning Marable, although he recounted the impact of Marcus Garvey on the Little family, is the fact that Malcolm, in his maturity, was in the direct chain from Delany, Blyden, Garvey, and Robeson. They were, alongside the Honorable Elijah Muhammad, his intellectual progenitors. For the first time since Garvey and his express symbol of Africa as a powerful instrument in cultural awakening, Malcolm's rhetoric revived the cultural attitude. Here it came as a torrent, breaking the shackles of a genuflected people and announcing a new more aggressive approach to cultural "reconstruction." As we heard him and sat at his feet, it was inevitable that his knowledge and acceptance of duty would be reflected in numerous attempts to restructure our response to America. Thousands of urban Africans reached toward Malcolm's vision and when it was comprehended we preached in Shangoan voices the hard reality of self-determination.

I would loved to have seen a book by Manning that would have demonstrated how Malcolm brought discontent within the camp of the old order, creating by the power of his logic, schisms in the conservative body politic of African America. It is easy to understand the preeminent position of Malcolm as a cultural figure when in addition we consider the intense reaction of the white American establishment to his call for black cultural nationalism. Malcolm was considered an extremist and a militant by most of the white press. Of course, the African-American press, itself often tied to the white corporate structure, was hardly better on Malcolm. In fact the Black Church which had at moments seemed interested in Martin Luther King Jr.'s Movement found Malcolm too strong for its liking.

I would have preferred to see Manning Marable appreciate the fact that Malcolm was an end to the apologia of the Negro. He became in his life a figure transformed in the actuality of historical experiences, thus, to live Malcolm, is to see him as an *orisha* of power and purpose, a true aspect of Afrocentric culture. He is represented now by some with a string of solid black beads, an *aleke* of strength. Afrocentricity as an intellectual idea has the aim of fulfilling the Malcolmian project of removing African self-hatred and restoring African self-confidence even in the world of intellectual production. You cannot write of Malcolm as if you are afraid that someone is looking over your shoulder.

Now here is the thing about Marable's *Reinvention.* Manning seemed never to understand the nature of actual putting your career and your life on the line for the interest of oppressed people. This is what Malcolm did. While Marable may have become a member of the Democratic Socialists of America, even rising to become Vice Chairman of the organization, I am not aware of an African organization that Manning participated in as an active member. I am not making this a criterion of speaking, but it is an indication of how one postures career. Although some may criticize Marable for making his observations about the life of Malcolm from this or that political base, this has not been my objective. I simply believe that Malcolm's biography cannot be adequately written; in fact, it is possible that no biography can be adequately written. Thus, the problem here is that so many of us had wanted a massive work that situated Malcolm in his times as a force, a presence to be reckoned with intellectually and politically, rather than the portrait of a petty thug that Marable finally gave us or them. Who is this Malcolm that Marable has portrayed?

Perhaps the answer is that he is all of us and if that is the case then we, and Malcolm, deserve to be seen in the light of our own time for the higher purposes that constitute our trajectory, not for the pettiness and triviality that accompany our daily lives. As you can see I have not dealt with the truth or falsehood of "he said" or "she said" when it comes to the death of Malcolm; I guarantee you, however, that someone knows the answer to whodunit and I do not believe that it is found in Marable's book. What is found in Marable's book is a Social Democracy portrait of Malcolm using a deconstructionist methodology. Okay, now let us have a truly Afrocentric portrait of Malcolm that elevates his discourse and demonstrates the agency of African people fighting against oppressive conditions.

Malcolm X Still Inspires Today
Rick Ayers

Malcolm X was a towering figure of the 20th century, connecting the wave of Third World revolutions sweeping the globe with the Black Liberation Movement inside the US. While the ruling class seeks to domesticate the man and tame his legacy—a narrow self-help guide or high school lesson on pulling oneself up by the bootstraps—his deeper contribution to the central liberation struggles of our time continues to resonate.

Malcolm X's life and work were forged in the furnace of a specific historic moment: the old-style colonies were breaking up after the two devastating world wars; India won its independence; China overthrew a pro-western regime; revolutionary battles threw the French out of Algeria and Vietnam; and Cuban guerrillas evicted the U.S. supported dictator Batista. Vijay Prashad's powerful analysis of the period, *The Darker Nations*, documents the rise of the Non-Aligned Nations movement and the creation of the term "Third World" to describe the former colonial and neo-colonial regions which wanted to be in neither the Soviet nor the US camps—they wanted independence, freedom from nuclear threat, democratization of the United Nations, and their own locally-grown participatory democracies.

During this same time, the long struggle of African Americans against white supremacy and for basic Constitutional rights and fundamental recognition of their humanity was taking a more militant turn. Malcolm X, first from within the Nation of Islam and later from his own organization, pushed to redefine the terms of the movement—from a petition seeking a way into the U.S. mainstream to a liberation struggle demanding independent power and transformation of the political economy. Today we forget how far ahead of the wave Malcolm X was, how he created the wave. This is what made him so dangerous to those in power, what drew the attention of the FBI as well as the CIA and various military intelligence agencies.[1]

So many touchstone principles that would soon propel the Student Non-Violent Coordinating Committee (SNCC), the Black Panther Party, and dozens of other organizations and movements, were first given clear articulation in the early 60s by Malcolm X. These included:

- Black pride and "Black is beautiful."
- The move from a petition for rights to a demand for power.
- The change from seeing African Americans as a minority to recognizing them as part of a majority, the Third World majority, on a global scale.
- The identification of the conditions of African Americans as one of domestic colonialism as well as racial and ethnic discrimination.
- The questioning of the use of non-violence as the primary tactic for black liberation, encapsulated in the phrases "The ballot or the bullet" and "By any means necessary."
- The recognition that white people could be and often were a hindrance to the fullest development of Black leadership and the African American struggle in the South.
- The demand that white people work against racism in their own communities and build solidarity with the Black Liberation Struggle.
- The critique of the Black petty bourgeoisie, which seemed to be making it in America and leaving behind poor and working class African American communities.

The list goes on and on. While he did not invent or own each of these principles, Malcolm X was the most clear, consistent, and successful popularizer of these views.[2] African American insights, critique, and inventions have always been major drivers in politics and culture in the U.S.—whether it has been in music, theater, comedy, and literature or in the political struggles to enact democracy and change the power relations through elections, economic structures, or education. The reverberations of Malcolm X's leadership were felt everywhere, even penetrating the consciousness of this white liberal college student first getting involved and trying hard to understand the world.

I remember being in New York in the summer of 1966, a year after the assassination of Malcolm X. I lived with Charles, an old friend from prep school. We were exploring the city, taking classes, marveling at the explosion of arts, and following the various vibrant political battles everywhere. In mid-June the front page of the *New York Times* featured a story on the "March against Fear" in Mississippi, which SNCC had mobilized after James Meredith was shot at the beginning of his solo protest against the hatred and violence in Mississippi. Stokely Carmichael and Willie Ricks dropped a bombshell on the first evening rally, calling for something new to the Civil Rights Movement: Black Power! The marchers had responded with enthusiasm and Black Power became the chant punctuating the march and the Movement itself in that fateful summer.

Black Power had a resonance and meaning that was unmistakable, and it was not about "personal empowerment" or psychological states. It was an enunciation of the anti-colonial struggle of African Americans, a call for political power—by any means necessary. Everything Black activists said afterwards to elaborate and explain the idea was important, but the phrase was clear and people knew what it meant. It was Malcolm X's vision, come to life in the battles of the deep South.

My friend Charles and I diverged right then. He thought the Black Power turn was a disaster: it was reverse racism; it was going to isolate the movement. But I had already been drawn to Che and the Cuban revolution, to James Baldwin's *The Fire Next Time*, and to the Mississippi Freedom Democratic Party and Fannie Lou Hamer's articulation of the struggle in 1964. Many white activists agonized about what it would mean; some who risked their lives for the struggle for justice were hurt when they were asked to leave the South and organize against racism in their own communities. But many others got it, had even seen the truth of this analysis in the streets and the meetings. They were pleased, delighted, inspired by the powerful turn that the movement was taking.

Of course, the involvement of us white college kids was a matter of choice but also of privilege. It mainly consisted of reading and discussing. The challenge of the mid-1960s however plunged us into action. We were no longer just watching a movement; we started building a movement. We were pushed to drop our beneficent and patronizing charity ideas, to think in terms of solidarity. We began to fight as part of a strategy that recognized the leadership of the Black Liberation Movement and Vietnamese resistance, and the profound transformation of relationships around the world. Did the revolution of the late '60s and '70s win? No it did not. But the world would be a much better place if it had.

Dr. Manning Marable's new biography, *Malcolm X: A Life of Reinvention*,[3] does much to fill in and correct the historical record. Most agree that Malcolm X's autobiography, written with Alex Haley, is a powerful organizing document but leaves much out. Marable offers many beautiful and satisfying moments: the background on Malcolm X's family and upbringing, the story of the Garvey movement (the Universal Negro

Improvement Association—UNIA) and its strength throughout the U.S. in the teens and '20s, the descriptions of Malcolm X's trips to Africa and the Middle East which are much more detailed and impressive than earlier accounts, and the explication of the Muslim Mosque Inc. and the Organization of Afro-American Unity.

But on the fundamental significance of Malcolm X, on his core vision and contribution, Dr. Marable gets it wrong. In the midst of his detailed research, he swipes at the philosophy of Black Nationalism and anti-colonial internationalism. In describing Malcolm X's historic 1960 debate with civil rights leader Bayard Rustin,[4] he asserts that Rustin won hands down because he proved the "practical impossibility" of setting up a Black state, exposing the "essential weakness" of the nationalist line. It is one thing to be opposed to Black Nationalism, but to suggest that it is simply an illusory idea with no possible way of being pursued is to mislead. The long history of the struggle for Black Power goes back to Martin Delaney before the Civil War, through the UNIA of Marcus Garvey; it is seen in the work of W.E.B. Du Bois and Carter G. Woodson in education; and even in the position of the Communist Party in the '20s and '30s which defined a Black nation in the South; also critically important was the Négritude movement from the Caribbean and Harlem; and it includes many organizations in the '60s and later, such as the Student Nonviolent Coordinating Committee (SNCC) after they embraced Black Power, the Revolutionary Action Movement, the All African Peoples Revolutionary Party, the African People's Socialist Party, the Republic of New Afrika, the League of Revolutionary Black Workers, the Black Panther Party, DRUM, The Deacons for Defense and Justice, the Black Arts Movement, and the explosion of Black Student Unions. These movements had all kinds of proposals: some for territorial zones inside the U.S., some for reuniting with Africa, and some for independent political identity within an extended presence throughout the U.S. Malcolm X was neither confused nor stumped when confronted with anti-nationalist arguments. His was an internationalist, anti-colonial vision and politics. No one else in the U.S. during this historical period articulated and advanced this insight so powerfully.

Prof. Marable argues that reform was possible in the U.S. and that this fact undermined Malcolm X's position, suggesting that "perhaps blacks could some day become empowered within the existing system."[5] An example he cites to demonstrate that change can come without overthrowing the system is Nixon's introduction of affirmative action laws. A look at the condition of African American people today in relation to educational opportunities and meaningful schools suggests that Malcolm X's side of the argument was closer to the truth. Marable rejects Malcolm X's criticism of middle class Black leaders who had supported the election of Lyndon B. Johnson for president. "It apparently did not occur to [Malcolm X]," he asserts, "that great social change usually occurs through small transformations in individual behavior."[6] I'm sure the possibility occurred to him but he was part of a much more radical critique, a more far-reaching call for transformation of social relations.

Dr. Marable declares that, "'black nationalism' was highly problematic in a global context because it excluded too many 'true revolutionaries.'"[7] But it's not problematic at all, any more than Cuban nationalism, Latin American solidarity, Pan-Africanism, Vietnamese nationalism, or anything else that was shaking the world precluded relations between Third World movements.

As in all anti-colonial struggles, Malcolm X asserted the right of resistance and even the importance of African Americans arming themselves. Marable declares that such comments "alienated white and black alike."[8] But in reality, this is part of what made him so wildly popular. Marable claims that when Malcolm X said that African Americans should vote but not for Republicans and Democrats, he "was promoting electoralism but in practical terms gave blacks no effective means to exercise their power. Who were they supposed to vote for if no one on the ballot could bring any real relief?"[9] The answer is clear: Malcolm X advocated independent political action. That was the only place he believed African Americans could get relief.

The art of writing a political biography is tricky. Two examples that stand out as excellent are Barbara Ransby's *Ella Baker and the Black Freedom Movement: A Radical Democratic Vision*, and Henry Mayer's *All on Fire: William Lloyd Garrison and the Abolition of Slavery*. Each of these does something very important: they situate the focal lives within the movements that produced them and the movements they built. They explicate the positions of the protagonists and appreciate the evolution of their positions—including the debates, experiences, and commitments that made them. And they don't put themselves in the position of debating with the person they are profiling.[10]

While Manning Marable has opened up critical research with this biography, in some respects he misses the central significance of Malcolm X. The speeches of Malcolm X are available everywhere and should accompany this book, for they animate, explain and consolidate so many experiences and feelings that were boiling beneath the surface at the time.

Malcolm X understood and pursued the implications of the earth-shaking revolutions going on and his words continue to capture the radical imagination of freedom lovers around the world today precisely because he stood for international solidarity and a restructuring of power. It is a vision that still inspires.

Notes

1. The liberation struggles of the period were redrawing the political map and the rising of African Americans was a key challenge inside the US. J. Edgar Hoover of the FBI knew it as did the CIA and military intelligence agencies (p. 343). They all targeted Malcolm X from the time he was in prison. Malcolm X was an early and powerful advocate for Black community empowerment, for the right of self-defense, for mobilizing to speak to the interests of Black working class people. He was perhaps the first in the African American struggle to express solidarity with the Vietnamese (p. 411); he advocated the rights of Native American, Chicano, Latino, and other peoples. And, in the step that perhaps led to his assassination, he mobilized an international campaign to take the case for African American human rights to the United Nations.

2. The book does document the many powerful and deep connections Malcolm X made during his lifetime with leading activists and militants in the African American struggle—including Ossie Davis and Ruby Dee, James Baldwin, SNCC and CORE organizers, Grace Lee Boggs, and more. So when SNCC came out with the demand for Black Power two years after Malcolm's murder, it was not simply something they thought up. It was a continuation of the analysis and strategy that he had been developing when he was cut down.

3. The core organizing point of the book is in the subtitle, a life of reinvention. What is the insight Marable is proposing with this title? That Malcolm changed, he reinvented himself, as his life transitioned from one phase to another. Actually, everyone reinvents himself or herself. It's called growing, changing. So in that sense everyone reinvents himself or herself. But we begin to wonder about this subtitle when Marable comes back to again and again to a few assertions, for example that Malcolm's accounts of his crimes while he was hustling are inaccurate, amount to not much at all. Who would not, when talking to a writer in the process of creating an autobiography, disguise and change some of the facts? Does this point to some kind of terrible lie on Malcolm's part, an attempt to inflate his criminal past to make his redemption more dramatic? Hardly. But more importantly, the creeping sense in this talk about reinvention, which Marable never says but suggests each time he brings it up, is that Malcolm was an opportunist, reinventing himself to suit different moments, always to his own advantage. It suggests that Malcolm was always a hustler and the political and spiritual leadership

he exhibited was also a hustle.
   4. p. 176
   5. p. 298
   6. p. 406
   7. p. 406
   8. Malcolm X was clear on the role of white people: they could support, they could be in solidarity with, the African American struggle. And that was all. "When I say white man, I'm not saying all of you, because some of you might be all right. And whichever one of you acts all right with me, you're all right with me (p. 389)." This is exactly the view that SNCC adopted two years later.

   9. p. 307
   10. One of the disappointments of this biography is how narrowly Marable frames Malcolm X's motivations at key points of his life. He sets up Malcolm X as establishing his positions based on narrow self-interest rather than principle or conviction. Early on he suggests that Malcolm X was critical of Israel, not because of its suppression of the Palestinians, but because he sought financial support from Egypt which "may have made it necessary to adopt Nasser's political positions (p. 13)." There is really no justification for this supposition.

   Marable says that a primary concern of Malcolm X, as he was heading for a split with the Nation of Islam, was the control of the house he and his wife Betty lived in. When Malcolm X made public criticism of the NOI, Marable questions "whether (it was) motivated by strategy, expedience, or something deeper and more personal. . ." It seems odd that he would frame Malcolm X's historic break from the NOI as only one of these three choices, strategy, expedience, or something deeper and more personal. Here it seems he is saying that "personal" motivations are the deepest. But political and religious principle is a much clearer explanation of Malcolm X's motivation. While Malcolm's rift with the NOI grew, he continued to say that he respected the teachings of Elijah Muhammad. But Marable suggests that this was a matter of simple expedience, perhaps designed to keep his house, and not based on his own spiritual and social beliefs. Malcolm X is reduced to being a narrow schemer.

   Manning Marable relies too heavily on interviews he did with Louis Farrakhan to fill in details of Malcolm X's life in the Nation of Islam. Farrakhan, however, has his own complicated motivations for the comments he might make in an interview. As the head of the rebuilt NOI, as well as one of the main ministers implicated in calling for Malcolm X's assassination in 1965 (p. 398), he seeks to, on the one hand, suggest how close he was to Malcolm X and, on the other hand, denigrate Malcolm X's leadership and seriousness. One of the most unsubstantiated claims in the book, which comes only from Farrakhan, is that a main reason for Malcolm X's split from Elijah Muhammad had to do with jealousy over Evelyn Williams (p. 292). This not only diminishes the important difference over principles, it is really slander of Malcolm X.

   Marable's dismissal of Harold Cruse and George Padmore as anti-communists (pp. 158 and 368) fails to explain that both of these activists were revolutionaries but were highly critical of the Communist Party and the white-dominated left in the US and other parts of the world. The development of an independent, Third World, revolutionary movement placed many leading activists in conflict with the established left. Fidel Castro had fierce conflicts with the Cuban Communist Party in the 1950's and the Bolivian Communist Party was complicit in Che's capture in 1967. Many black intellectuals and revolutionaries, from Robert Allen to Ralph Ellison, made sharp and important criticism of the reformism, legalism, and go-slowism of the Communist Party. But it is a distortion to call these activists "anti-communist." Later, however, Marable speaks of Ghana as becoming a "Soviet client state on the model of Cuba." It's difficult to know where to start in unpacking that claim. Cuba was a Soviet client state? Ghana was? There are just too many assumptions here concerning political line as well as a lack of appreciation of the crucial struggles of the time.

Manning Marable's Malcolm X Book
Amiri Baraka

On March 30 I waited for a car that Manning Marable was supposed to send to pick me up at my house so that we could meet later that day in his office at Columbia University because he wanted to interview me as part of an oral history project. I had met with him two weeks before to discuss how Columbia would handle my papers, that is, when we scheduled this last project. But the car never came. I called another driver I knew, a friend of mine and we drove to Columbia, but Marable was not there. It seemed no one at the Africana Studies department knew where he was. Finally some word got to me that Manning had gone back into the hospital. I went back home, the next day I got the news on the Internet that he had died.

The strangeness of that missed appointment was weird enough, but the fact that his last work on Malcolm X was to be released three days later made the whole ending of our living relationship a frustrating incomplete denouement.

Initially, a friend of mine gave me a copy of the book at a happy discount. Taking it on one of my frequent trips out of town, I began to read. I gave that first copy to my wife when I returned because she had also, as many other people had, been clamoring to read it. As well as asking me relentlessly had I read it? I bought another copy of the book at the Chicago airport, and I guess started to get into the book seriously.

I have known Manning for a number of years. Actually I met him while he was still teaching in Colorado. I even worked under him, when I taught briefly at Columbia University, when he was chairman of the Africana Studies Department at Columbia. As well, I have appreciated one of his books, the Du Bois (*Black Radical Democrat*) work and at least appreciated the theme of *How Capitalism Underdeveloped Black America*, as well as the entire stance of his acknowledgment of the important aspects of American (Black American) history, which had to be grasped.

But as recently as a few weeks ago, ironically I had written him a letter about his journal *Souls* about an essay that quoted a man˚ who had been accused of participating in the assassination, making some demeaning remarks about Malcolm. My letter questioned the "intelligence" of including the quote since it offered nothing significant to the piece. This was not just loose criticism; I really wanted to know just what purpose the inclusion served.

But with the publication of what some have called "his magnum opus" *Malcolm X: A Life of Reinvention* it is not just Marable's inclusion of tidbits of presumed sexual scandal that should interest readers that I question, but more fundamentally, what was the consciousness that created this work?

First of all I don't think we can just bull's-eye the writer's intentions, we must include Marable's consciousness as the overall shaper of his intentions, as well as his method. Originally from Ohio, Marable was a freshman in college in 1969; he did not graduate until 1971. He has been attached to Academic institutions since 1974, Smith, Tuskegee, University of San Francisco, Cornell, Colgate, Purdue, Ohio State, University of Colorado, and Columbia. It is no denigration of his life to say that Manning was an academic, a well principled one, but an academic nevertheless.

But Marable did have a political aspect to his life, which I understood and why I think he was a very principled academic. He did understand that the "purely" academic was fabrication of the essentially unengaged. That whatever you might do, there was a conscious political stance that your political consciousness had to assume, even if you refused to take it. So his "membership" in the 1970's National Political Assembly chaired by Richard Hatcher, Mayor of Gary, Indiana, Rep. Charles Diggs, the congressman from Detroit and myself as chairman of the Congress of African Peoples, signified that he was aware and a partisan of that attempt to raise and institutionalize Black political consciousness as a way to organize Black people nationally to struggle for Black political power.

In 1974 Marable joined the Democratic Socialists of America [DSA], and for a time was even a Vice Chairman of that organization which is called "Left" but is not a Marxist and certainly not a Marxist-Leninist organization. It is one of those organizations like the group that split from Lenin's 2nd International, which he called socialists in word but chauvinists in reality. So that it is important that we recognize the specific political base upon which Manning's "observations" may be judged. He is not simply "observing." He is making judgments.

So, for instance, for Marable to consistently, throughout his book, call the Nation of Islam [NOI] a "sect" is a judgment not an observation.

---

* (This man Thomas 15X is the same one quoted by Marable as saying that it was the Nation of Islam that burned Malcolm's house down.)

The NOI certainly has and had more influence on society than the DSA, certainly on Black people. The meaning as a small breakaway group of a religious order only used now to connote a "jocular or illiterate" character (according to the Oxford University Dictionary) is spurious.

But then in relationship to revolutionary Marxism or Marxism-Leninism, DSA certainly fits the description. My point being that Marable must be judged by what he says not by what others say he "intended." The best thing about the book, of course, is that it raises Malcolm X to the height of our conversation again, and this is a very good thing in this Obama election period. (Post racial it ain't!)

The very profile of Malcolm's life, the outline of his life of struggle needs to be spread across the world again, if only to re-awaken the fiercest "blackness" in us to fight this newly packaged "same ol' same ol'" emergence of white supremacy and racism.

Whatever Marable is saying or pointing out, in the end, is to convince us of the superiority of social democracy which he refers to as "the Left," which is anything from DSA to the Trotskyists. The characterization of Bayard Rustin's "superior" reasoning in a debate with Malcolm or the response of James Farmer to Malcolm's bringing a "body guard" to Farmer's house, "Do you think I want to kill you?" tries to render Malcolm some paranoid case when indeed there were people plotting very actively to kill him.

Ultimately, it is Marable's own political line that renders the book weakened by his consistent attempts to "reduce" Malcolm's known qualities and status with many largely unsubstantiated injections, many described by Marable himself as "rumors." Is there, for instance, any real evidence of Malcolm's or Betty's sexual trysts. People who knew Charles Kenyatta, for example, in Harlem, will quickly recall a vainglorious fool & liar. Could much of this rumor material actually have come from Marable's "official" sources, the FBI, CIA, BOSS, NYPD, as well as those in the NOI who hated him? About Malcolm, a sentence like Marable's "That evening Sharon 6X may have joined him in his hotel" is inexcusable.

When I wrote the FBI asking them to release surveillance materials they had gathered on me, at first the director even denied such papers existed. It was Allen Ginsberg's lawyer who finally got an admission that such papers existed, and that I could get them for ten cents a page. But when I got the papers, it was my wife, Amina, who said how do we know that the information they haven't crossed out is stuff they want us to see and so confuse us about what was really going on.

I would submit that is exactly what those agencies would do in this case! To assume because you are given "access" to certain information, that that information is not "cooked," as people around law enforcement say, is to labor in deep naiveté as to whom you are dealing with!

Marable never made any pretensions about being a "revolutionary." His hookup with the DSA is open acknowledgment that he rejected Lenin's prescription for a revolutionary organization, or party of the advanced, or such concepts as "The Dictatorship of the Proletariat." In fact the DSA says they are not a party, aligning themselves very clearly with Lenin's opponents in the 2nd International.

Such people, social democrats, are open opponents of revolution, so that at base Marable was opposed to the political logic of Malcolm's efforts to make revolution. Marable is even more dismissive of the Nation of Islam which he brands a "cult" a "sect" dismissing the fact that even as a religious organization, the NOI had a distinct political message, and that it was this message, I think, more than the direct attraction of Islam, that drew the thousands to it.

If Marable was giving a deeper understanding of Elijah Muhammad's call for Five States in the South, he would have mentioned the relationship of this concept to Lenin's formulation of an Afro American Nation in the black belt South (called that because it was the largest single concentration of Afro Americans in the U.S.). It was not simply some Negro fantasy.

If Marable actually understood the political legitimacy of Malcolm's Black Nationalism and how Malcolm's constant exposure to the revolutionary aspects of the Civil Rights movement and the more militant Black Liberation Movement shaped his thinking and made his whole presentation more overtly political and that this was not only negative to the core of the NOI bureaucracy but certainly to the FBI, &c. They have even written Malcolm X was much safer to them in the Nation than as a loose cannon roaming the planet outside of it. They understood that what Malcolm was saying, even in "The Ballot or the Bullet" was dangerous stuff. That his admission that all white people might not be the Devil was not morphing into a Dr. King replica but an understanding, as he said at Oxford University, that when Black people made their revolution there would be some white people joining them.

The meeting with the Klan was not Malcolm's idea, certainly it was Elijah Muhammad's as it had been Marcus Garvey's idea before him. Malcolm's Black Nationalism became more deliberately Revolutionary Nationalism, such as Mao Tse Tsung (or Cabral or Nkrumah) spoke of, necessary to rally the nation's forces together to make first a national revolution to overthrow foreign domination and followed by a revolution to destroy capitalism.

Importantly, Marable does draw a clearer picture of Malcolm's childhood and early days, especially indicating the Garvey influence his parents taught him and how that would make him open to what Elijah Muhammad taught, unlike the obscure flashbacks of Spike Lee's version of Malcolm's early days. Though Marable ascribes some wholly political "defiance" to the conked hair and zoot suits of the '40s rather than understanding that there was also a deep organic cultural expression that is always evident in Black life. It is not just a formal reaction to white society. African pants are similarly draped. Access to straightening combs or conkolene are a product of the period, and certainly if any straight hair is gonna be imitated, there was some here before the Latinos.

The "antibourgeois" attitude of the Black youth culture is organic and an expression of the gestalt of black life in the U.S. and Marable seems not to wholly understand it. For instance his take on BeBop as the music of "the hepcats (sic) who broke mostly sharply from swing, developing a black oriented sound at the margins of musical taste and commercialism." BeBop was a revolutionary music, dismissing Tin Pan Alley commercialism and raising the blues and improvisation again as principal to black music.

The essential "disconnection" in the book is Marable's failure to understand the revolutionary aspects of Black Nationalism, as a struggle for "Self Determination, Self Respect and Self Defense." A struggle for equal democratic rights expressed on the sidewalks of an oppressor nation by an oppressed Afro American nationality.

What the book does is try to remove Malcolm from the context and character of an Afro American revolutionary and "make him more human," by dismantling that portrait by redrawing him with the rumors, assumptions, speculations, questionable guesses and the intentionally twisted seeing of the state and his enemies.

Was Captain Joseph (who later changed his name to Yusuf Shah) close to Malcolm? He appeared on television calling Malcolm "Benedict Arnold" and told Spike Lee that I had come up to the Mosque and stood up to question Malcolm and Malcolm told me to "sit down until you get rid of that white woman." I met Malcolm only once, the month before he was murdered. This was in Muhammad Babu's room at the Waldorf Astoria. Babu had just finished leading the revolution in Zanzibar, and would later become Minister of Economics for Tanzania (which was Zanzibar and Tanganyika).

At that meeting Malcolm responded to my demeaning of the

NAACP by saying I should be trying, instead, to join the NAACP, to make a point about Black people needing a "United Front." That idea was not an attempt at "trying to become respectable," to paraphrase Marable, Malcolm had come to realize that no sectarianism could make the revolution we needed. Interestingly, Stokely Carmichael (Kwame Ture) also called for the building of a Black United Front, and Martin Luther King, when he visited my house in Newark, a week before he was murdered, called for the same political strategy. It was such a front that was a major part of the national democratic coalition that elected Obama.

As for Yusuf Shah, when Spike Lee repeated Shah's wild allegations about me in his book *How I Made The Movie X [By Any Means Necessary]*, I asked a college friend of mine, who had become my part time lawyer, Hudson Reed, to file a suit against Shah demanding he be questioned in court for any "exculpatory" evidence relating to the murder of Malcolm X, particularly as to the involvement of himself and organized crime. A short time later, Shah, who had moved to Massachusetts, died in his sleep. Marable reports that Captain Joseph/Yusuf Shah's FBI file was "empty"!

It is Marable's misunderstanding of the revolutionary aspect of Black Nationalism that challenges the portrait not only of Malcolm but of the period and its organizations as well. He treats the split between Malcolm X and the NOI much like he assumes the police did. (Though this is patently false.) As a struggle between "two warring black gangs," a sect splitting from the main.

So that there is much more from Marable framing Malcolm's murder as directed by the NOI, rather than the state. Marable's general portrait of Malcolm is as doomed and confused individual about whom he could say that "Malcolm extensively read history but he was not a historian." As if the academic title "HISTORIAN" conferred a more scientific understanding of history than any grassroots' scholar might have. Simple class bias.

To say of the NOI that it was not a radical organization obscures the Black Nationalist confrontation with the white racist oppressor nation. Marable thinks that the Trots of the SWP [Socialist Workers Party] or the members of the CP [Communist Party] or the Committees of Correspondence are more radical. That means he has not even understood Lenin's directive as pointed out in Stalin's *Foundations of Leninism*, in "The National Question,"

> ... *The revolutionary character of a national movement under the conditions of imperialist oppression does not necessarily*

> *presuppose the existence of proletarian elements in the movement, the existence of a revolutionary or a republican programme of the movement, the existence of a democratic basis of the movement. The struggle that the Emir of Afghanistan is waging for the independence of Afghanistan is objectively a revolutionary struggle, despite the monarchist view of the Emir and his associates, for it weakens, disintegrates and undermines imperialism; whereas the struggle waged by such 'desperate' democrats and 'socialists', 'revolutionaries' and republicans...was a reactionary struggle. ...Lenin was right in saying that the national movement of the oppressed countries should be appraised not from the point of view of formal democracy but from the point of view of the actual results, as shown by the general balance sheet of struggle against imperialism. (Foundations of Leninism, p.77.)*

Marable thinks that the Trots like the SWP or the soi-disant Marxists in CPUSA or the Committees of Correspondence (a breakaway from the CPUSA) or the DSA are more radical than the NOI or Malcolm X. Perhaps on paper. But not in the real world of the Harlem streets. Malcolm came out of the NOI, Dr. King from the reformist SCLC. But both men were more objectively revolutionary on those Harlem streets or in those southern marches than any of the social democratic formations and the social democrats ought to face this.

Marable spends most of his time trying to make the NOI Malcolm's murderers. Information from FBI, BOSS, CIA, NYPD, would tend to push this view, for obvious reasons. In this vein Marable says that Malcolm's Africa trips "made his murder all the more necessary from an institutional standpoint." That Malcolm's actions "had been all too provocative" to Elijah Muhammad and the NOI. But what about the Imperialist U.S. state and its agencies of detection and murder? They would be more provoked and better able to end such provocation. If there's a well-known murderer of Malcolm X still running loose as Marable and others have pointed out, how is it he remains free and we must presume that those agencies of the state know this as well as Marable and the others!

But even as he keeps hammering away that it was the Nation of Islam, he still says contradictorily "The fatwa, or death warrant, may or may not have been signed by Elijah Muhammad, there is no way of knowing." Many of Marable's claims fall under the same category.

He even quotes Malcolm after he was refused entrance into France that he had been making a "serious mistake" by focusing attention on the NOI Chicago headquarters "thinking all my problems were coming from Chicago and they're not." Asked then from where, Malcolm said "From Washington."

Marable also tells us that even today the FBI refuses to release its reports on Malcolm's assassination. Yet he will quote one of those agencies without question. Of Betty Shabazz' death Marable says flatly, of Malcolm's daughter Qubilah. . ."her disturbed twelve-year old son set fire one night to his grandmother's apartment." How does he know this? Is an official government "information" release that impressive? There are many doubts about that murder; shouldn't some of them have been investigated?

Some of the characterizations in the book are simply incorrect and suffer from only knowing about the movement on paper. Marable saying about Stokely Carmichael, after splitting with "pacifist" Bob Moses and SNCC that he would subsequently join the Black Panthers is such an example. Carmichael didn't join the Panthers; he was "drafted" along with Rap Brown.

Marable says in effect that Malcolm misunderstood Martin Luther King's influence on Black people. He didn't misunderstand that influence: he was trying to provide an alternative to it. Though ultimately I believe both leaders later conclusion that a United Front would be the most formidable instrument to achieve equal rights and self-determination for the Afro American people, I would have liked to see Malcolm and Martin in the same organization, and for that matter Garvey & Du Bois. They could argue all day and all night and in the end some of us might not agree on the majority's decision, but like the Congress of the United States we'd have to say, "I don't even agree with that. . .but that's what we voted to do!"

Interestingly, on the back of the book are three academics, who represent the same social democratic thought as Prof Marable. [Skip] Gates who disparages Africa, looks for racism in Cuba not Cambridge, and says the Harvard Yard is his nation.

My friend Cornel West who in response to me calling out at the Left Forum, "Where are the socialists, where are the communists" shouts "I'm a Christian!" And Michael Eric Dyson who wrote a book on Dr. King calling it the "True Dr. King" somewhat like Marable's approach to Malcolm. But who and what else in the paper "Garden of Even" of "Post Racial America"? So it is necessary that we rid ourselves of the real leaders of our struggle, in favor of Academics who want to tell us we were following flawed leaders with flawed ideas. We don't need equal rights and self-determination, an appointment to an Ivy League school will do just fine.

Malcolm X: A Life of Reinvention by Manning Marable, A Look at the Book
Amir Bey

Manning Marable's *Malcolm X: A Life of Reinvention* stands to be the most thoroughly researched book on Malcolm now written. Marable began his twenty-year endeavor when he felt that Malcolm's Autobiography had inconsistencies and parts that Malcolm may have fictionalized to illustrate certain points.

  He felt that it lacked an adequate account of Malcolm's rapid evolution in the last few years of his life, particularly the foundation of his two groups after splitting with Muhammad: the MMI (Muslim Mosque Incorporated) and the OAAU (Organization of Afro-American Unity). Marable also felt that Alex Haley, who by his own admission was less a collaborator and more a recorder and editor for the *Autobiography*, may have influenced its slant after Malcolm's death by being a Republican integrationist.

  Other than addressing the perceived shortcomings of the *Autobiography*, what makes *Reinvention* a more complete study of Malcolm than previous ones is the source materials and the time that was invested in its making. The bibliography is huge, including Malcolm's detailed diaries, which were not available to scholars until 2008; letters to Elijah Muhammad, some of them deeply personal, where he discusses tensions with his wife Betty; interviews and oral histories with former close aides, and FBI and New York City police intelligence (Bureau of Special Services and Investigations (BOSS) agents and documents; letters and statements from his brothers, Farrakhan, court documents, and many other sources.

  Marable passed away from a chronic pulmonary ailment days before *Reinvention* was released. This is a well-crafted oeuvre from a prolific historian. The *Autobiography* will remain a classic of African American literature; *Reinvention* will become an important reference to the life of one of the most complex individuals of 20th century America. Not only that: it is also a well-structured testimony of the complex group of forces arrayed against him, the NOI (Nation of Islam); FBI; CIA; BOSS; and other government agencies and interests who through lack of a true understanding of Malcolm, as well as real fear would not be comfortable until he was dead.

Reinvention causes one to ask whether *any* autobiography could be honest or truly objective. An autobiography is like an individual's signature: it indicates the way its writer presents an idea of who they are, and how they would like other's to see them. The *Autobiography* chose certain aspects of Malcolm's life, emphasizing some, obscuring or slanting others. According to Marable, he exaggerated his hustler period, and when he and his crew were finally arrested, it was due to his negligence. *Reinvention's* view of his early years emphasizes his instability and selfishness, creating a stronger contrast than the *Autobiography* does concerning his transformation after joining the Nation. Malcolm was a disaffected, essentially orphaned youth who was denied opportunities (he was told there are no nigger lawyers when he expressed an interest in being one) who became a petty hustler.

Malcolm always had a "gift of gab"; he was blessed with verbal ability. He developed his Lindy Hop skills and sometimes danced under the name Jack Carleton. He created a false worldliness to impress his siblings, stole from them, was not to be trusted. He was a dramatically different person than the profoundly dedicated self-sacrificing minister he came to be. Until he was incarcerated, he explored quick ways to attain an easy manhood, like many rootless young men-children. After his incarceration, he focused on developing his gift of gab into a powerful tool that was fashioned by a disciplined mind.

Marable makes a key observation about Malcolm's character and sets the stage for his split with NOI by describing him as an artist who reinvented himself throughout his life. He cites some of Malcolm's various names: Detroit Red, Homeboy, Satan, Jack Carleton, and Malik Shabazz. Being an artist explains one aspect of the split: Malcolm was someone who had an acute need to express his individuality, to be active, to challenge. He was not a conformist, which was necessary in being a member of the NOI.

The NOI was not only too confining for him temperamentally: its responses to the abuses of black people's human rights were too "tepid," for Malcolm, in Marable's estimation. And he became aware that the NOI's practice of not being involved in demonstrations and voting put the Nation out of touch with the majority of blacks who wanted to directly confront issues. Marable shows how even though Malcolm had these frustrations, he was dedicated to the Nation, and always acknowledged his indebtedness to "The Messenger." He worked tirelessly for the Nation, and was the NOI's point man to the outside world. This kind of attention made Elijah's sons Herbert and Elijah Jr., and son-in-law Raymond Sharrieff nervous about whether Malcolm planned to succeed The Messenger after his passing. It can't be known if Malcolm ever entertained that idea; but after reading *Reinvention* one has the impression that initially Malcolm may not have fully recognized his personal ambitions, that he had the capability and the desire to lead. He was aware of the affect of his leadership to the benefit of the Nation: he energetically built new mosques in major cities around the US, and he spread the NOI's word in the media. It seems that he saw himself more as a faithful "son" to Elijah's father, and was highly motivated to dedicate himself to that entity and the Nation's cause.

Malcolm's flaws are honestly discussed, including those that were fatal: his honesty and the trust he placed in others who later became his rivals and who wanted his destruction. It was impossible for him to wage the kind of war that eventually was waged against him. In this there was ambivalence; he would make statements against the Nation then retract them; and such shifting of positions also occurred when he would attack Martin Luther King and other "Uncle Tom Leaders," then would appear to accept them at other times. In some instances, the split wasn't entirely the fault of those within the Nation who were envious of him.

When Elijah ordered all ministers not to comment on JFK's death, Malcolm not only commented, but pushed the envelope further, enraging the hierarchy. This conflicted tendency to exacerbate his troubles with the Nation showed itself many times during that period. He could not fully bite through the bond he was trying to break while attempting to create a new foundation to replace the Nation.

By viewing Malcolm's diaries that documented his travels, combined with media and government accounts of them, we can see his international threat to the NOI: he was developing ties with Muslim countries and institutions that had long had trouble with the Nation's brand of Islam, and were offended by Elijah's claim to be "The Messenger." They accepted Malcolm as a true Muslim, and gave recognition to the MMI, granting 20 scholarships to members of his organization to study Islam in those countries. For the NOI this was another reason why Malcolm had to go, because he was acquiring the legitimacy from the countries and religious institutions that they were seeking. Another sore point was Malcolm's perceived influence and bonding with Elijah's sons Wallace D. Muhammad and Akbar, who also practiced orthodox Islam, and who had troubles with their father's affairs and children by young girls.

The government was also threatened by Malcolm's call for taking the plight of African American people to the UN, calling for their plight to be addressed as a human rights issue instead of civil rights. *Reinvention* shows how the FBI was at first alarmed by the Nation's power, and how it gradually exploited the growing rift between Elijah, the NOI hierarchy and Malcolm. It describes how the Nation and Malcolm's organizations were compromised by being heavily infiltrated by the FBI, BOSS, the CIA, and other intelligence agencies.

Marable draws profound distinctions between King and Malcolm and cites those differences to illustrate why if Malcolm were alive today he would not seek office or have been an integrationist as some have speculated; instead he is viewed as becoming an internationalist who would have valued and maintained his identity "as a black man, a person of African descent who happened to be an American citizen." (Page 482)

Reinvention's weaving of the Malcolm's assassination, like all reconstructions of it, is difficult reading; one of its most tragic aspects was its being a filicide: the father killed his son. Malcolm was Elijah's heir, not because he would have inherited a throne, but because Elijah led him on the way to creating a great spiritual and secular institution. It can be argued that Elijah's legacy would have been greater if Malcolm had not been assassinated. In Marable's presentation, Malcolm again swung between fighting and at times, pleading blacks should not be killing each other. Several times he said he would be killed. The pressure of living under the near certainty of death by your "father" and the institution that Malcolm helped to build was overwhelming.

Marable leaves no doubt that the assassination was carried out by a NOI manipulated by various government agencies who had infiltrated key positions in the NOI, and Malcolm's organizations, the MMI and OAAU. These government agencies did not work together, and even mistrusted each other. Yet they had a common goal, and used the NOI as their weapon. If only... if only the father had protected his "wayward" son...

Marable describes how government agencies knew that Malcolm had decided not to frisk people on February 21, and that only two of his bodyguards would be armed. This information was passed onto his assassins, and was coordinated by individuals within his organization. And it is well known that the NYPD was understaffed for that day, and slow in getting to the crime scene. One act that would have been unconscionable if it wasn't deliberate, was the manager/owners of the Audubon Ballroom where he was killed, had booked the same room for a George Washington birthday dance. The police did not protect the crime scene, but allowed the celebration to be held. The custodians mopped up Malcolm's blood, moved the chairs, thus making any reconstruction of the assassination impossible.

It's unfortunate that Manning Marable did not live to see this important work published, and to respond to its detractors, some of whom feel that Malcolm's memory has been sullied by it, that this icon has been done a disservice by revealing his private, human side. This is not true; it humanizes the brother, and from what those who were close to him have said, he might have appreciated it.

While *Reinvention* strives to make Malcolm more human, he shall remain iconic nevertheless. It can be said that Malcolm's story is one of the most dramatic in American history: his is what myths are made of. To capture his life, careful research such as *Reinvention* is required along with the skills of a story-teller who can evoke the power, majesty and anguish of "Our Black Shining Prince." However, symbols speak louder than pictures: even detailed revelations will merely add to his mythos, and in time his story will become an (the?) American Passion Play. As with Anthony Davis's Operetta "X, The Life and Times of Malcolm X," classic elements of a great legend are in it: the early death and inspiring influence of his father, the institutionalization of his mother, and the resulting disintegration of his family; his life of petty crime, incarceration, and the salvation through a new spiritual father-king; his battle with American society at large as well as for the souls of black folk; the father-king's fear of him, and the envy of the father-king's princes; the plotting of the larger forces circling around him, tightening the noose closer; his death and powerful legacy. Our ideas of history and individuality ask us to go beyond idolizing him, but our wonder at his life and how he shook things up continue to strike us. To mythologize is to be human?

Editorial decisions by the publishers may be to blame, but the selected illustrations are not on the same level as the text. There are twelve pages of photos, yet these do not adequately portray or highlight many of the major individuals discussed, or they include images of people who had less relevance than others. A case in point is photographs of the two "assassins" who were said to be wrongly accused, but Talmadge Hayer, the one assassin who admitted being a conspirator, and who was wounded at the scene, was not included. Better selections would have helped this complex narrative.

The Fault Lies Not In Our Stars, But In Our Biographers: Minutes To Midnight, Manning Marable Succumbs
Todd Steven Burroughs

Manning Marable's *Malcolm X: A Life of Reinvention* is the example, unfortunately, of a serious Black Marxist activist-intellectual being seduced by 21st century celebrity academia in the last years of his extraordinarily productive life. Originally meant to be a work of scholarship, it devolved, for more than one reason, into a work of entrepreneurship, peppered with some author hubris.

This biography, hailed as a masterwork by those in journalism and academia who know better but don't want to spit on a great Black writer's grave, was researched by a assemblage of hand-picked graduate students for a decade while the author worked on at least two other books and battled the lung condition that, at one point, left him immobile and ultimately claimed him the weekend eve of publication. The back-cover author blurbs are not from Malcolm X scholars like Zak Kondo, William Sales and Paul Lee, but from celebrity talking-heads Michael Eric Dyson, Cornel West and Henry Louis Gates, an Ivy League-smothered trio who have done well in the last 20 years role-playing the progressive scribe for love and money.

This book is a breakthrough—if that word is defined as an accomplishment of well-written compilation and commentary. A reading of the footnotes shows that Marable's Malcolm is, in many ways, the product of four previous books—*The Autobiography of Malcolm X,* the 1978 updated version of Peter Goldman's *The Death and Life of Malcolm X,* Louis A. DeCaro's *On the Side of My People: A Religious Life of Malcolm X* and, to a lesser extent, DeCaro's *Malcolm and the Cross: The Nation of Islam, Malcolm X, and Christianity.*

What is new, then? First, the creation of a narrative using much of the new Malcolm scholarship since the publishing of Bruce Perry's much-maligned *Malcolm X: The Life of a Man Who Changed Black America* almost 20 years ago. Second, the painfully personal parts of Malcolm's life—

his sexual dysfunction, possible marital infidelity and, according to one main source and one third-hand source, a possible pay-for-play homosexual relationship he had with a rich white man while still the hustler Detroit Red. (The last item was in Perry's book, but that revelation failed to produce the international electric shock that this mass-marketed book is doing now.) Third, use of Malcolm's diary of his international travels. This feat is achieved, tragically, by interviewing fewer than 30 subjects using, apparently, a single grant from Columbia University, where Marable taught for about 20 years. So instead of interviewing 100 to 1,000 people, standard for A-1 biographers, Marable conducts his own orchestra without all of the instruments, filling gaps by whistling his own critiques of Malcolm's intellectual development.

The outline of the story is well-known and well told by Marable when he sticks to and adds to established scholarship. Detroit Red transformed himself, through discipline and faith, and turned his righteous wrath on the white world. He gains power and loses faith. He gains a new faith but at the cost of his life. He becomes almost a concept unto himself, cheering Pan-Africanism, Black Power and Black Consciousness from the Realm of the Ancestors as Afro-ed revolutionaries come forth, bringing into the daylight the ideas Malcolm told Alex Haley late at night. "He presented himself as an uncompromising man wholly dedicated to the empowerment of Black people, without regard for his own personal safety," writes Marable. Now he is a Hollywood film and a postage stamp, the other half of "Martin And" every February. Like Charlie Parker, Marilyn Monroe and Mickey Mantle, Malcolm is safely ensconced in the middle of the last century, a favorite selection in the historical Netflix of black-and-white documentary footage.

Malcolm's essence, however, still means power to those who seek that through him. Men and women in the nation's jails and prisons, studying for their GEDs and college degrees through correspondence courses, still hold on *The Autobiography* in the hopes of imitating it on some small level. For decades, young Blacks in college either attempted to imitate his voice and his style when they are trying to make a point, or just quote him directly, as if his declarations were Biblical scripture used by church leaders to instantly quell a theological argument: "Just like Brother Malcolm said..." That his spirit lives can be quantified: just find that one brother wearing horned-rimmed glasses and a goatee at any Black activist rally. El-Hajj Malik El-Shabazz's face, image and voice are all over YouTube, ever present, eternally alternating between that direct punch and that aside laughter.

And now, almost half a century after *The Autobiography's* publication, the story sees major-league print again. *Malcolm X: A Life of Reinvention* has created a conflagration of responses as the Old Guard gets older and grayer and the Young Lions, awash with electronic toys that supposedly empower them while tracking their every (consumer) move, are largely indifferent to any event or person no longer trending. The author's death early in the spring of 2011 was quickly followed by the transitions of master musician Gil Scott-Heron, former Black Panther Geronimo Ji Jaga Pratt, one of the nation's most prominent political prisoners, and Abdias do Nascimento, the renowned Afro-Brazilian activist, political leader and artist. That spring was a season of death for longtime national and international Black activist voices. The reality of Malcolm X has proven more than powerful enough to defeat any attempt at popular culture co-optation or liberal intellectual and historical isolation, but can it, will it, defeat time itself?

How will this book and its subject fall into the Wikipedia-ization of knowledge? Those Elders—who, like their role model Brother Malcolm, have used words to liberate—now have to compete not only with their own mortality, but with the technological reality that, by the age of 15, young people in 2011 have been hit with a bombardment of commercialized words and images that would put the Blitz to shame. Actually, the Black activist rage over *Reinvention* may delve deeper than a rushed, dying author making controversial claims using flimsy sources: it could be that the brouhaha over the telling of this particular story, a holy one among formerly young Black radicals internationally, is but another skirmish in a continuing mental war for, but unnoticed by, most of today's electronically-brainwashed Black young. The problem is that any victory might seem invisible as more Elders join the Ancestors, the villages in slow burn, their individual and collective stories fading whispers in the wind.

Biography is a hard game to play and an easy one to lose, although only other historians and some well-read journalists will ever see the losing score. First, the biographer must choose a person he or she wants to spend years of life living with, thinking about and, most importantly, thinking *through*. Second, the author must learn all he or she can about his subject, literally tracing his or her life from the first day to the last. Significantly, while doing the first two tasks, the biographer must learn the differences between his views and his subject's views, but at the same time learn about himself through his subject. Exploring the subject's world gives the biographer insight into his or her own.

Marable only succeeds in the first of the three tasks and even then, only partially. Malcolm X is profiled by Marable as a performance-loving street cat who grew into a religious zealot and demagogue, who then grew into a prophetic voice and then, ultimately, emerged as an ambassador representing Black America in the Middle East, what El-Hajj Malik El-Shabazz termed "The Muslim World." He gives an ongoing analysis of Malcolm's words that has him close to calling Malcolm an anti-Semite more than once. Marable claims that Malcolm twisted facts about the March on Washington and its leaders. (He seems to be the first author to do this; although I would assume he would say that he was the first Malcolm biographer to take Malcolm's speeches seriously enough to do this.) This point is even more interesting because Marable doesn't back up his assertion, but radical historian Howard Zinn, in his classic *A People's History of the United States,* backs up his (and Malcolm's): that the Movement leaders were meekly following the goals of the Kennedy administration, and using the March to that end. An epilogue that tries to tie Malcolm into the empty symbolism of the World Conferences Against Racism just tones down what Malcolm says and does elsewhere in the book.

What is most disturbing and disappointing is how Marable uses only one or two sources to make all manner of claims. For instance, Marable said that journalist A. Peter Bailey said he attended a meeting of what would become the Organization for Afro-American Unity before Malcolm broke with the Nation of Islam in March 1964. "If true, this would explain the highly secretive character of these clandestine meetings, suggesting that perhaps Malcolm was pursuing a dual-track strategy: continuing to appeal to rejoin the Nation while simultaneously building an independent base loyal to himself." Why couldn't Marable and/or the graduate students find the others who attended "the small gathering of about fifteen people" so this very important piece of information could be confirmed and pinned down? This is basic History 101 stuff, dodged in this book over and over again by too many perhaps, suggests and ifs. Woulda, coulda, shoulda.

The author does a good job in showing how first Malcolm X, and later El-Hajj Malik El-Shabazz, put real fear into America by upstaging it at home and abroad, dumbfounding those who started dumb. "At every step, Malcolm was treated like a visiting dignitary, and his prominence over the course of several days at social and public events must have stunned the CIA and FBI," Marable writes. "The Bureau had spent years trying to split Malcolm from Elijah Muhammad, with the expectation that the NOI schism would weaken the organization and its leaders...[W]ith each stop in his itinerary, the FBI received fresh reports about Malcolm's expansive social calendar and his growing credibility among African heads of state." Marable explains that Malcolm had specific goals, which included not just "forging a Pan-Africanist alliance between the newly independent African states and Black America," but also de-legitimizing the Nation of Islam in the Muslim World, with Mecca ever denied to heretics. Whether with Black nationalists in America, Kwame Nkrumah in Ghana or the Muslim Brotherhood in Lebanon, the man born Malcolm Little becomes a world leader, representing a nation that exists only in the decolonized mind.

The pyrrhic victories are Malcolm's, but to paraphrase the last line of *The Autobiography*, the mistakes have been Marable's. Illness and death, although unfortunate, are not sufficient excuses, particularly for an Ivy League university professor with extended resources and contacts. (With all the prominent, skilled Black writers Marable knew over decades of intellectual work and political struggle, why couldn't he have drafted a co-author to bat cleanup?)

For instance, Marable and his graduate students lean on Malcolm's diary and newspaper articles and books to document his travels abroad. Obtaining the use of Malcolm's travel diary is a significant accomplishment, but which resident of Marable's Camp Biography traveled to the places Malcolm went to, meeting with and interviewing those people still alive there? Apparently, no one. This is inexcusable. A book needs to be written just on Malcolm's trips to Africa and Saudi Arabia by scholars who care enough to actually go to those places for an extended length of time to get more than just Malcolm's account. That would require getting travel-research grants that Marable and his graduate students did not have. (In between first and final drafts of this essay, Marika Sherwood's Malcolm X Visits Abroad, which uses the diaries and interviews, had been released.)

Malcolm X deserves better—a full, rich biography that brings his life and work further. This book carries some understanding of Malcolm forward, but not definitively. It could have come close with much more time and primary source research, but time tragically ran out for its author. Ultimately he, like his subject, stood alone, facing the abyss with an almost-finished book and an unseen-but-hoped-for big mainstream payday.

It's not up to Marable's heirs or his graduate students to set up the next biography. It is up to those of Malcolm's soldiers still alive to tell the tale to set up a Malcolm X Oral History Project and keep the flame alive until more documents are released from offices and attics. More books, then, will be written and published by people physically able and mentally willing to do the hard, unglamorous, time-consuming work of a biographer, like a brilliant young scholar and Black press columnist named Manning Marable did once upon a time with the political life of W.E.B. Du Bois.

Ultimately, this flawed book does a dual service to African-American letters and history. It permanently blasts *The Autobiography* into the fictional realm of Spike Lee's epic and *begins* a new era of Malcolm X scholarship for those who seek competing truths from as many voices as possible, not (just) lucrative book contracts or top listings on Amazon.com.

The Legacy of Malcolm X
Ta-Nehisi Coates

When my mother was 12, she walked from the projects of West Baltimore to the beauty shop at North Avenue and Druid Hill, and for the first time in her life, was relaxed. It was 1962. Black, bespectacled, skinny, and bucktoothed, Ma was also considered to have the worst head of hair in her family. Her tales of home cosmetology are surreal. They feature a hot metal comb, the kitchen stove, my grandmother, much sizzling, the occasional nervous flinch, and screaming and scabbing.

In the ongoing quest for the locks of Lena Horne, a chemical relaxer was an agent of perfection. It held longer than hot combs, and with more aggression—virtually every strand could be subdued, and would remain so for weeks. Relying on chemistry instead of torque and heat, the relaxer seemed more worldly, more civilized and refined.

That day, the hairdresser donned rubber gloves, applied petroleum jelly to protect Ma's scalp, stroked in a clump of lye, and told my mother to hold on for as long as she could bear. Ma endured this ritual every three to four weeks for the rest of her childhood. Sometimes, the beautician would grow careless with the jelly, and Ma's scalp would simmer for days. But on the long walk home, black boys would turn, gawk, and smile at my mother's hair made good.

Ma went off to college, leaving the house of my grandmother, a onetime domestic from Maryland's Eastern Shore who had studied nursing in night school and owned her own home. This was 1969. Martin Luther King Jr. was dead. Baltimore had exploded in riots. Ma hung a poster of Huey Newton in her dorm room. She donated clothes at the Baltimore office of the Black Panthers. There, she met my father, a dissident of strong opinions, modest pedigree, and ill repute. In the eyes of my grandmother, their entanglement was heretical, a rejection of the workhorse ethos of colored people, which had lifted my grandmother out of the projects and delivered her kids to college. The impiety was summed up in a final preposterous act that a decade earlier would have been inconceivable—my mother, at 20, let her relaxer grow out, and cultivated her own natural, nappy hair.

The community of my youth was populated by women of similar ilk. They wore their hair in manifold ways—dreadlocks and Nubian twists, Afros as wide as planets or low and tapered from the temple. They braided it, invested it with beads and yarn, pulled the whole of it back into a crown, or wrapped it in yards of African fabric. But in a rejection aimed at something greater than follicles and roots, all of them repudiated straighteners.

The women belonged, as did I, to a particular tribe of America, one holding that we, as black people, were born to a country that hated us and that at all turns plotted our fall. A nation built on immigrants and a professed eclecticism made its views of us manifest through blackface, Little Black Sambo, and Tarzan of the Apes. Its historians held that Africa was a cannibal continent. Its pundits argued that we should be happy for our enslavement. Its uniformed thugs beat us in Selma and shot us down in northern streets. So potent was this hate that even we, the despised, were enlisted into its cause. So we bleached our skin, jobbed our noses, and relaxed our hair.

To reject hatred, to awaken to the ugly around us and the original beauty within, to be aware, to be "conscious," as we dubbed ourselves, was to reject the agents of deceit—their religion, their culture, their names. To be conscious was to celebrate the self, to cast blackness in all its manifestations as a blessing. Kinky hair and full lips were the height of beauty. Their bearers were the progeny, not of slaves, but of kidnapped kings of Africa, cradle of all humanity. Old customs were found, new ones pulled out of the air. *Kwanzaa* for "Christmas," *Kojo* for "Peter," and *jambo* for "hello." Conscious sects sprang up—some praising the creator sky god Damballah, some spouting Hebrew, and still others talking in Akan. Consciousness was inchoate and unorthodox—it made my father a vegetarian, but never moved him to wear dreadlocks or adopt an African name. What united us all was the hope of rebirth, of a serum to cure generational shame. What united us was our champion, who delivered us from self-hatred, who delivered my mother from burning lye, who was slaughtered high up in Washington Heights so that colored people could color themselves anew.

In his lifetime, Malcolm X covered so much ground that now, 46 years after his murder, cross-sections of this country—well beyond the conscious advocates of my youth—still fight over his footprints. What shall we make of a man who went from thoughtless criminal to militant ascetic; from indignant racist to insurgent humanist; who could be dogmatically religious one moment, and then broadly open-minded the next; who in the last year of his life espoused capitalism and socialism, leaving both conservatives and communists struggling to lay their claims?

Gripping and inconsistent myths swirl about him. In one telling, Malcolm is a hate-filled bigot, who through religion came to see the kinship of all. In another he is the self-redeemer, a lowly pimp become an exemplar of black chivalry. In still another he is an avatar of collective revenge, a gangster whose greatest insight lay in changing not his ways, but his targets. The layers, the contradictions, the sheer profusion of Malcolm X's public pronouncements have been a gift to seemingly every contemporary black artist and intellectual from Kanye to Cornel West.

For virtually all of my sentient life, I have carried some talisman of Malcolm—key chain, audiotape, or T-shirt. I came of age not just among the black and conscious, but among that slice of the hip-hop generation that witnessed Malcolm X's revival in the late 1980s and early '90s, bracketed by the rapper KRS-One's appropriation of Malcolm's famous pose by the window and Spike Lee's sprawling biopic. For those who'd grown up in hardscrabble inner cities, Malcolm X offered the promise of transcending the street. For those who'd been the only black kids in their classes, Malcolm's early and troubled interactions with his own white classmates provided comfort. For me, he embodied the notion of an individual made anew through his greater commitment to a broad black collective. When I first lived alone, at the age of 20, I purchased a giant black-and-white poster of Malcolm with the phrase *No Sellout!* scrawled at the top.

But my life grew in ways that did not adhere to slogans. Raised in de facto segregation, I was carried by my work into the mostly white world, and then to the blasphemies of having white friends and howling white music. In 2004, I moved to Malcolm's adopted home of Harlem, and though I occasionally marveled at Malcolm's old mosque at 116th and Lenox, or the YMCA where he roomed as an aspiring Harlem hustler, my years there passed without note. I declined to hang my giant Malcolm poster in my new digs, stuffing him and all my conscious days in the closet.

I spent Election Night 2008 with my partner and our son, at the home of two dear friends and their young son. That they were an interracial couple is both beside the point, and the point itself. By then, my friends were so varied in hue, and more varied still in their pairings, that I'd stopped thinking in ways I once took as elemental. I joined in the spectacle of America—a country that had incorporated the fact of African slavery into its Constitution—handing its standard to a black man of thin résumé and fantastical mien.

And the next day, I saw black people smiling. And some conscious part of me died with their smiles. I thought back on the debate running from Martin Delany and Frederick Douglass through Martin Luther King and Malcolm X, and I knew a final verdict had been reached. Who could look on a black family that had won the votes, if not the hearts, of Virginia, Colorado, and North Carolina, waving to their country and bounding for the White House, and seriously claim, as Malcolm once did, that blacks were not American?

The opportunity for crowing was not missed. Writing three weeks after the election in the New York *Daily News*, Stanley Crouch, the pugilist and contrarian who'd earlier argued that Obama was not black, dismissed Malcolm X as "one of the naysayers to American possibility whose vision was permanently crushed beneath the heel of Obama's victory on Nov. 4." Last year, offering up on *The New Republic*'s Web site a listicle of those whose impact on black people he wished he could erase, John McWhorter gave Malcolm X the top spot. But from the shadows, still he looms. Bull Connor's world fell as the fortunes of Barack Obama rose. Yet its collapse was not assured until November of 2008. Now I see its amazing doom in ways both absurd and replete—Will Smith's conquest of cinema, his son as the new Karate Kid, the wild utterings of Michael Steele, the kids holding out for Lauryn Hill's mythical return. As surely as 2008 was made possible by black people's long fight to be publicly American, it was also made possible by those same Americans' long fight to be publicly black. That latter fight belongs especially to one man, as does the sight of a first family bearing an African name. Barack Obama is the president. But it's Malcolm X's America.

In the spring of 1950, the *Springfield Union*, in Massachusetts, ran the following headline: "Local Criminals, in Prison, Claim Moslem Faith Now: Grow Beards, Won't Eat Pork, Demand East-Facing Cells to Facilitate 'Prayers to Allah.'" The leader of the protest was an incarcerated and recently converted Malcolm X. Having converted several other prisoners, Malcolm began lobbying the warden for cells and food befitting his band's religious beliefs. He threatened to write the Egyptian consulate in protest. Prison cooks retaliated by serving Malcolm's food with utensils they'd used to prepare pork. Malcolm countered by spending his last two years in prison on a diet of bread and cheese.

The incident, as recounted in Manning Marable's new biography, *Malcolm X: A Life of Reinvention*, set the stage for Malcolm's political career, his split from the Nation of Islam, and ultimately the course of action that led to his death. The goal of his prison protest was to advance the kind of inner reform that first drew Malcolm to the Nation, with thousands to follow. But Malcolm's methods were protest and agitation, tools that the

Nation rejected.

Unlike Bruce Perry's 1992 biography, *Malcolm,* which entertained the most outlandish stories in an attempt to present a comprehensive portrait, Marable's biography judiciously sifts fact from myth. Marable's Malcolm is trapped in an unhappy marriage, cuckolded by his wife and one of his lieutenants. His indignation at Elijah Muhammad's womanizing is fueled by his morals, and by his resentment that one of the women involved is an old flame. He can be impatient and petulant. And his behavior, in his last days, casts a shadow over his reputation as an ascetic. He is at times anti-Semitic, sexist, and, without the structure of the Nation, inefficient.

Still, the broad strokes of Malcolm's life—the family terrorized by white supremacists, the murdered father, the turn from criminal to race man—remain intact, and Marable's book is at its best in drawing out its subject's shifting politics. Marable reveals Malcolm to be, in many ways, an awkward fit for the Nation of Islam. Elijah Muhammad's Nation combined the black separatism of Marcus Garvey with Booker T. Washington's disdain for protest. In practice, its members were conservative, stressing moral reform, individual uplift, and entrepreneurship. Malcolm was equally devoted to reform, but he believed that true reform ultimately had radical implications.

Coming out of prison, Malcolm was shocked by the small membership of the Nation, which was seriously active only in Chicago and Detroit. He soon became the sect's most effective recruiter, organizing or reinvigorating mosques in Philadelphia, Boston, Atlanta, and New York. That dynamism was not confined to growing the Nation, but aimed to make it a force in the civil rights movement.

His energy left him with a sprawling web of ties, ranging from the deeply personal (Louis Farrakhan) to the deeply cynical (George Lincoln Rockwell). He allied with A. Philip Randolph and Fannie Lou Hamer, romanced the Saudi royal family, and effectively transformed himself into black America's ambassador to the developing world.

It is tempting to say that Malcolm's politics did not age particularly well. Even after rejecting black supremacy, Malcolm was deeply skeptical of white America and believed its intentions could best be divined from the actions of its zealots. Malcolm had little patience for the politicking of moderates and preferred stark choices. A Manichean worldview extends from his days denouncing whites as devils up through his more nuanced speeches like "The Ballot or the Bullet."

But Marable complicates the case for firmly fixing Malcolm's ideology, by recounting how, as Malcolm tried to move away from Nation dogma, the sect made a concerted effort to rein him in. Officials demanded that Malcolm and the other ministers tape all their lectures and submit them for approval, to make sure they were pushing Nation ideology as opposed to political appeals on behalf of a broader black America. They repeatedly reprimanded him for going off-script, including, finally, when he seemed to revel in John F. Kennedy's murder.

Muhammad's subsequent response suspending Malcolm reveals much about the group's aims and politics: "The president of the country is our president too."

To Marable's credit, he does not judge Malcolm's significance by his seeming failure to forge a coherent philosophy. As Malcolm traveled to Africa and the Middle East, as he debated at Oxford and Harvard, he encountered a torrent of new ideas, new ways of thinking that batted him back and forth. He never fully gave up his cynical take on white Americans, but he did broaden his views, endorsing interracial marriage and ruing the personal coldness he'd shown toward whites. Yet Malcolm's political vision was never complete like that of Martin Luther King, who hewed faithfully to his central principle, the one he is known for today—his commitment to nonviolence.

For all of Malcolm's prodigious intellect, he was ultimately more an expression of black America's heart than of its brain. Malcolm was the voice of a black America whose parents had borne the slights of second-class citizenship, who had seen protesters beaten by cops and bitten by dogs, and children bombed in churches, and could only sit at home and stew. He preferred to illuminate the bitter calculus of oppression, one in which a people had been forced to hand over their right to self-defense, a right enshrined in Western law and morality and taken as essential to American citizenship, in return for the civil rights that they had been promised a century earlier. The fact and wisdom of nonviolence may be beyond dispute—the civil rights movement profoundly transformed the country. Yet the movement demanded of African Americans a superhuman capacity for forgiveness. Dick Gregory summed up the dilemma well. "I committed to nonviolence," Marable quotes him as saying. "But I'm sort of embarrassed by it."

But the enduring appeal of Malcolm's message, the portion that reaches out from the Audubon Ballroom to the South Lawn, asserts the right of a people to protect and improve themselves by their own hand. In Malcolm's time, that message rejected the surrender of the right to secure your own body. But it also rejected black criminals' preying on black innocents. And, perhaps most significantly, it rejected the beauty standard of others and erected a new one. In a 1962 rally, Malcolm said: "Who taught you to hate the texture of your hair? Who taught you to hate the color of your skin? Who taught you to hate the shape of your nose and the shape of your lips? Who taught you to hate yourself from the top of your head to the soles of your feet? Who taught you to hate your own kind?"

The implicit jab was not at some specific white person, but at a systemic force that compelled black people toward self-loathing. To my mother, a poor black girl, Malcolm X said, "It's okay. And you're okay." To embrace Malcolm X was to be okay, it was to be relieved of the mythical curse of Ham, and reborn as a full human being.

Virtually all of black America has been, in some shape or form, touched by that rebirth. Before Malcolm X, the very handle we now embrace—*black*—was an insult. We were coloreds or Negroes, and to call someone "black" was to invite a fistfight. But Malcolm remade the menace inherent in that name into something mystical—*Black Power*; *Black Is Beautiful*; *It's a black thing, you wouldn't understand*.

Hip-hop, with its focus on the assertion of self, the freedom to be who you are, and entrepreneurship, is an obvious child of black consciousness. One of the most popular music forms today it is also the first form of pop music truly to bear the imprint of post-'60s America, with a fan base that is young and integrated. Indeed, the coalition of youth that helped Barack Obama ride to the presidency was first assembled by hip-hop record execs. And the stars that the music has produced wear their hair however they please.

For all of Malcolm's invective, his most seductive notion was that of collective self-creation: the idea that black people could, through force of will, remake themselves. Toward the end of his book, Marable tells the story of Gerry Fulcher, a white police officer, who—almost against his will—fell under Malcolm's sway. Assigned to wiretap Malcolm's phone, Fulcher believed Malcolm to be "one of the bad guys," interested in killing cops and overthrowing the government. But his views changed. "What I heard was nothing like I expected," said Fulcher. "I remember saying to myself, 'Let's see, he's right about that ... He wants [blacks] to get jobs. He wants them to get education. He wants them to get into the system. What's wrong with that?'" For black people who were never given much of an opportunity to create themselves apart from a mass image of shufflers and mammies, that vision had compelling appeal.

What gave it added valence was Malcolm's own story, his incandescent transformation from an amoral wanderer to a hyper-moral zealot. "He had a brilliant mind. He was disciplined," Louis Farrakhan said in a speech in 1990, and went on:

> *I never saw Malcolm smoke. I never saw Malcolm take a drink...He ate one meal a day. He got up at 5 o'clock in the morning to say his prayers...I never heard Malcolm cuss. I never saw Malcolm wink at a woman. Malcolm was like a clock.*

Farrakhan's sentiments are echoed by an FBI informant, one of many who, by the late 1950s, had infiltrated the Nation of Islam at the highest levels: Brother Malcolm...is an expert organizer and an untiring worker...He is fearless and cannot be intimidated...He has most of the answers at his fingertips and should be carefully dealt with. He is not likely to violate any ordinances or laws. He neither smokes nor drinks and is of high moral character.

In fact, Marable details how Malcolm was, by the end of his life, perhaps evolving away from his hyper-moral persona. He drinks a rum and Coke and allows himself a second meal a day. Marable suspects he carried out an affair or two, one with an 18-year-old convert to the Nation. But in the public mind, Malcolm rebirthed himself as a paragon of righteousness, and even in Marable's retelling he is obsessed with the pursuit of self-creation. That pursuit ended when Malcolm was killed by the very Muslims from whom he once demanded fealty.

But the self-created, martially disciplined Malcolm is the man who lives on. The past 40 years have presented black America through the distorting prism of crack, crime, unemployment, and skyrocketing rates of incarceration. Some of its most prominent public faces—Michael Jackson, Mike Tyson, Al Sharpton, Jesse Jackson, O. J. Simpson—have in varying degrees proved themselves all too human. Against that backdrop, there is Malcolm. Tall, gaunt, and handsome, clear and direct, Malcolm was who you wanted your son to be. Malcolm was, as Joe Biden would say, clean, and he took it as his solemn, unspoken duty never to embarrass you.

Among organic black conservatives, this moral leadership still gives Malcolm sway. It's his abiding advocacy for blackness, not as a reason for failure, but as a mandate for personal, and ultimately collective, improvement that makes him compelling. Always lurking among Malcolm's condemnations of white racism was a subtler, and more inspiring, notion—"You're better than you think you are," he seemed to say to us. "Now act like it."

Ossie Davis famously eulogized Malcolm X as "our living, black manhood" and "our own black shining prince." Only one man today could bear those twin honorifics: Barack Obama. Progressives who always enjoyed Malcolm's thundering denunciations more than his moral appeals are unimpressed by that message. But among blacks, Obama's moral appeals are warmly received, not because the listeners believe racism has been defeated, but because cutting off your son's PlayStation speaks to something deep and American in black people—a belief that, by their own hand, they can be made better, they can be made anew.

Like Malcolm, Obama was a wanderer who found himself in the politics of the black community, who was rooted in a nationalist church that he ultimately outgrew. Like Malcolm's, his speeches to black audiences are filled with exhortations to self-creation, and draw deeply from his own biography. In his memoir, Barack Obama cites Malcolm's influence on his own life: His repeated acts of self-creation spoke to me; the blunt poetry of his words, his unadorned insistence on respect, promised a new and uncompromising order, martial in its discipline, forged through sheer force of will. All the other stuff, the talk of blue-eyed devils and apocalypse, was incidental to that program, I decided, religious baggage that Malcolm himself seemed to have safely abandoned toward the end of his life.

Last summer, I moved from Harlem to Morningside Heights, a neighborhood around Columbia. It was the first neighborhood I'd ever lived in that was not majority black, and one of the few that could not properly be termed a "hood." It has bars and restaurants on every corner, two different farmers' markets, and a supermarket that's open 24 hours and stays stocked with fresh vegetables. The neighborhood represents my new, fully cosmopolitan life.

I had spent the past two years in voracious reading about the Civil War. Repeatedly, I found myself confronting the kind of white Americans—Abraham Lincoln, Ulysses Grant, Adelbert Ames—that black consciousness, with some merit, would have dismissed. And yet I found myself admiring Lincoln, despite his diatribes against Negro equality; respecting Grant, despite his once owning a slave and his advocacy of shipping African Americans out of the country. If I could see the complexity in Grant or Lincoln, what could I see in Malcolm X?

And then I thought about the luxuries that I, and black people writ large, today enjoy. In his *Autobiography,* Malcolm harks back to his time in middle school, when he was one of the top students in his school and made the mistake of telling his teacher he wanted to be a lawyer. "That's no realistic goal for a nigger," Malcolm's teacher told him. Thinking back on that, Malcolm says,

> My greatest lack has been, I believe, that I don't have

the kind of academic education I wish I had been able to get...I do believe that I might have made a good lawyer.

What animated Malcolm's rage was that for all his intellect, and all his ability, and all his reinventions, as a black man in America, he found his ambitions ultimately capped. The right of self-creation had its limits then. But not anymore. Obama became a lawyer, and created himself as president, out of a single-parent home and illicit drug use.

And so it is for the more modest of us. I am, at my heart, a college dropout, twice kicked out of high school. Born out of wedlock, I, in turn, had my own son out of wedlock. But my parents do not find me blasphemous, and my mother is the first image of beauty I ever knew. Now no one questions my dark partner's right to her natural hair. No one questions our right to self-creation. It takes a particular arrogance to fail to honor that, and instead to hold, as his most pertinent feature, the prejudices of a man whose earliest memories were of being terrorized by white supremacists, whose ambitions were dashed by actual racists, who was called "nigger" as a child so often that he thought it was his name.

When I finished unpacking my new apartment, I made one immediate change. I took my old Malcolm X poster out of the bubble wrap and affixed it to my living room's western wall.

Marable, Redefining Biography
Jelani Cobb

Long before the evil that transpired on February 21, 1965, the man known as Malcolm X had gone metaphorical. The facts of his life, already epic had taken on hues of the tragic. His biographer appeared to view his imminent death in primarily commercial terms. Three separate intelligence departments—in the State Department, the FBI and the NYPD—monitored his activities and maneuvered to curtail his effectiveness. His marriage was severely strained and factions within the Nation of Islam were openly calling for his assassination. Before the podium in the Audubon Ballroom that afternoon stood a single man besieged by titanic forces, none of which wanted him alive. That he was the architect of some of those forces made that unblessed afternoon all the more bitterly ironic.

In death, the X that once stood behind Malcolm's name became curiously apt. Always a complex figure, he became an enigma, a riddle whose answers lay interred beneath the silt of history, his self-created mythology and the diverse perspectives of those laying claim to his legacy. Manning Marable's *Malcolm X: A Life of Reinvention* is a brilliant, flawed indispensible effort to sift through those layers in pursuit of a truer Malcolm.

On some level, the resurrection of Malcolm X began with a generation that was drawing its first breaths that day. Raised outside the veil of segregation, we imbibed the freedom songs and King's speeches, recognized the achievements of the civil rights era yet also knew ourselves as heirs to some lesser freedom, one perforated by AIDS and crack, homicide and unemployment. For many these ills were an indictment not against a system whose racism and inhumanity was a foregone conclusion but against the naiveté of those who thought it could ever be anything else. And in Malcolm we found our prosecutor.

The common cornerstone for these perspectives—to the extent that one existed—was Malcolm's autobiography, co-authored with Alex Haley. Yet in Marable's assessment, the book is, in essence, an act of political ventriloquism in which Haley distorts Malcolm's life as a brief for his own moderate integrationist politics. Of particular concern is the fact Malcolm X was murdered before the book was completed and never had the opportunity to approve the final drafts.

The other central theme in Marable's biography is the idea that Malcolm's life was a series of self-inventions, that he was essentially a trickster figure authoring the most useful version of his past to meet the demands of his present. This is not a novel claim for a biographer to make. And in the era of social media and "reality" television the self-invented life has virtually become the norm, not the exception. Yet if the theme is less than original in its nature it remains striking in its implications.

That Marable himself died just a few days prior to publication was doubly tragic. He was a prolific scholar whose numerous contributions helped shape the way we understand African American history in the 20th century. More pressingly, his death meant that the book is literally left to speak for itself. The more controversial claims in this biography cannot be further explored or explained by the person who made them.

The most explosive of these is the allegations that Malcolm X engaged in same-sex experiences during his time as a hustler (page 65) and that his later marriage to Betty Shabazz was fraught with discord and marked by mutual infidelities. The outsized attention paid to the former claim is disturbing given that it occupies a minor portion of a massive work of reinterpretation.

Still this is a claim that the author should have reasonably expected to generate controversy (despite similar claims made in an earlier biography). For that reason the scantily sourced allegations were probably not worthy of inclusion. Marable makes reference to "uncertain particulars" (page 65) of Malcolm's relationship with a wealthy white male employer but confidently assumes there was a sexual component to their interaction a few paragraphs later. (page 66) The evidence Marable cites simply doesn't warrant the conclusion.

Still the public reaction to those concerns overshadowed the numerous other insights that Marable offers: that upon being arrested Malcolm gave up his entire burglary crew in hopes of saving himself from prison, (page 67) that he may have embellished the story of his life as a criminal, (pgs 60-61) that following the murder of an unarmed Muslim by LAPD, Malcolm began organizing a team to assassinate police officers as retribution (page 208).

Malcolm X: A Life of Reinvention excels in both the contextualization of Malcolm's life, (to be expected from a historian of Marable's standing) but more impressively in detailing the arcane philosophy and political inner workings of the Nation of Islam. Introduced to the teachings of Elijah Muhammad while incarcerated, Malcolm, more than any other figure, was responsible for the transformation of the group from a small mid-western sect into a national organization with branches in every major city in the country.

It also becomes apparent that the NOI's growth fostered a culture of strictly enforced discipline within the ranks. The result was a martial culture in which physical violence was a common resort. Mosque's organized "pipe squads" responsible for administering beatings and in some cases murders on behalf of the hierarchy. Malcolm, as Marable points out, was both an architect and, ultimately, a victim of this culture (pgs 243-44).

The NOI's increased membership not only generated revenue for their Chicago headquarters, it raised their national profile and made conflict with local law enforcement nearly unavoidable. Following the 1957 assault of a NOI member, Malcolm X assembled a regiment of the mosque's paramilitary wing, the Fruit of Islam outside a Harlem police precinct and essentially forced them to release the man to receive medical treatment. Five years later LAPD officers raided a mosque and fired upon its members, killing one man and paralyzing another.

Elijah Muhammad's refusal to allow Malcolm to retaliate forced him to confront the reality that while the NOI claimed whites were devils, the genetically ordained enemies of black people, they had never laid a finger on a white person, not even those who killed their own members. Yet their violence toward other blacks remained undiminished. Implicitly, Elijah Muhammad was less a critic of white supremacy than an adherent to it.

Malcolm's frequent public sparring with civil rights intellectuals like Bayard Rustin and James Farmer forced him to recognize the essentially apolitical nature of Elijah Muhammad's program. Heavy on economic independence and moral reform, the NOI officially had little to contribute to the escalating struggle for freedom and equality in the United States. Yet those matters were a vital concern to the NOI's individual members as the police harassment of the rank and file illustrated. By the time he discovered Elijah Muhammad's marital infidelities and his impregnation of several secretaries—including a woman who had a long romantic history with Malcolm—a split was all but inevitable.

Of the many evocative moments in this book, none resonates like the conversation an exiled Malcolm holds with a Muslim friend in a car late one night in Harlem. Malcolm clings to a tendril of faith that he can reconcile with Elijah Muhammad until the friend blankly informs him, "You're not going back into the Nation. They're talking about killing you" (page 290).

Manning Marable marshals impressive resources in this relentlessly interesting and fluidly written biography. Yet it must be noted that the book is at least somewhat guilty of the same offense he lodges at Haley. Marable's dismissive treatment of Black Nationalism in general and what he sees as Elijah Muhammad's superficial understanding of race necessarily raises another question: if this is the case, how could Malcolm X become a revered national figure on the basis of a philosophy so bankrupt? The Third World socialism espoused the final year of Malcolm X's life is much closer to Marable's own political views and there is a visible if not quite triumphal skew in this direction.

Yet for these shortcomings this is as close as we've come to a definitive treatment of Malcolm X's life. In place of the ionic Malcolm we are left with the human one. There are, no doubt, many who still prefer that Malcolm be rendered in granite, not flesh. And that, if nothing else, makes this book required reading.

Paper Tiger
Karl Evanzz

Malcolm X: A Life of Reinvention is an abomination. It is a cavalcade of innuendo and logical fallacy, and is largely "reinvented" from previous works on the subject.

It may serve as grounds for at least two defamation actions. The publisher would do well to consider recalling the book and issuing an apology for two reasons: a man labeled an "alleged murderer" has never been formally accused or convicted of that crime, and a woman mentioned by name is accused of committing adultery 46 years ago. As such, there is virtually no way to verify the allegation.

Marable, who died on April 1, takes cheap shots at Malcolm X, Malcolm's parents, Betty Shabazz, Malcolm's siblings, and almost anyone with a familial nexus to Malcolm X.

Its official release on the 43rd anniversary of the assassination of Dr. Martin Luther King Jr. is symbolic because this book amounts to an assassination of Malcolm X's character. Marable's friends dare to call this his "magnum opus." To use street vernacular, this ain't his magnum nothin.'

It is merely the logical culmination of a life spent in the ivory tower writing books of scant interest beyond the tower walls. If the so-called public intellectuals praising the book were Marable's true friends, they might have at least apprised him of the hostile tone and the lack of vetting on key allegations, the central one being Malcolm X's alleged homosexual affair. The media ran with this allegation without checking its validity.

Malcolm X, Marable claims, "falsely attributed" his own sexual encounters with an older white male to a friend named "Rudy" (p. 66).

"Based on circumstantial but strong evidence, Malcolm was *probably* [emphasis supplied] describing his own homosexual encounter with Paul Lennon. The revelations of his involvement with Lennon produced much speculation about Malcolm's sexual orientation."

Speculation by whom? Marable, that's who.

There are four footnotes for this page, but none substantiates this scurrilous assertion, one that would be grounds for libel were either party alive. The claim is juxtaposed by dozens of pages relating to Malcolm's maturation into selling drugs, pimping (including white women), burglary, and other crimes. If you look at the mug shot—the first in a pallid 16-page photo section—you see the face of a thug you do not want to tangle with.

Moreover, there is nothing in Malcolm X's far superior work to suggest that there was any touching of genitalia, let alone oral or anal sodomy. In fact, Malcolm X's autobiography clearly shows (in the chapter titled "Caught") how amusing he found the strange things that made white "johns" reach orgasm. One man, he wrote, ejaculated by sitting outside a bedroom door listening to a black couple making whoopee.

Nor does Marable offer proof that the employer was homosexual, bisexual, or asexual. The only logical conclusion from the facts is that the man had unusual recreational habits. Marable offers no proof that the man didn't pay women to pour powder on him from time to time, for example, or that anyone employed by the man was homosexual. His proffer is a want ad for a male secretary. The ad ran twice over a three-day period in one newspaper on one occasion.

Another example of logical fallacy here is the one used to denigrate Malcolm X's father, Earl Little Sr., who is accused of bigamy. "Earl abandoned his young wife and children . . . He did not bother to get a legal divorce," he writes (p. 16).

Marable cites other authors to support this claim, but none of them establishes that he checked court records to confirm this allegation. He offers nothing to show that he conducted a court search for the divorce record.

On the opening page of Chapter One, Marable writes: "In 1909, he married a local African-American woman, Daisy Mason, and in quick succession had three children: Ella, Mary, and Earl, Jr."

Notice the problem? Marable neglects to inform us of the exact date that the couple married in 1909 and whether the marriage was done legally or by common law. Again, his notes show no indication that he searched court records for a marriage license. Did Marable know the date of the marriage?

If they were not legally married, Earl had no legal obligation to file for divorce. As such, Marable's condescending tone—*he did not bother*—shows his contempt not only for Malcolm but for Malcolm's father as well. The real sin here is that Marable fails to show that he *bothered* to check for a marriage license or a divorce filing.

He uses similar tactics to malign Ella Little—the woman who fired one of his key sources—describing her as "belligerent," "paranoid" and "reckless." While he tries to countenance his charge by citing a psychiatric evaluation, Marable knows full well that psychiatrists routinely employed such terms to describe supporters of Marcus Garvey. Their reasoning was simple: any black person who rejects America has to be crazy.

In the preface, Marable boasts that his book will "reconstruct the full contours of his remarkable life" (p. 14), and proceeds to contrive the most mean-spirited biography of Malcolm X in two decades.

The footnotes reflect heavy reliance upon people who were known enemies of Malcolm X. An earlier biographer used anonymous sources for some of his controversial claims, which was bad. Marable gives no source for some of the tabloid-type allegations, which is a million times worse.

According to Marable, Malcolm was having an extramarital affair with one of his secretaries, an affair that lasted until his death. Keep in mind that Malcolm knew by early 1965 that he was under constant surveillance by the FBI as well as by members of the Nation of Islam. How do we know? Because Malcolm X said so repeatedly in speeches and his posthumous memoir: "Elijah seems to know every move I make," Haley quotes him (Epilogue) saying in the final days of his short life. On February 16, Malcolm X told Haley: "I have been marked for death in the next fives days. I have the names of five Black Muslims who have been chosen to kill me. I will announce them at the meeting."

On February 21, five Black Muslims killed him while his wife and four little girls watched in horror.

FBI files show that agents worked in eight-hour shifts to keep Malcolm under around-the-clock surveillance in weeks prior to his death. Malcolm told Haley and others that he would see them watching him as they took notes while he left his house, as he went to the drugstore to get a newspaper, and as he went to his office. FBI documents confirm his suspicions.

Note further that Black Muslims were threatening to kill him to prevent him from testifying in a Los Angeles paternity case filed against Elijah Muhammad by two of his teenage secretaries.

With those kinds of stressors, an extramarital affair the night before he died seems highly unlikely, and he certainly would not have chosen a teenage girl at a time when he was scheduled to testify against Black Muslim leader Elijah Muhammad for doing the same thing.

After claiming that Betty Shabazz had an affair with one of Malcolm's assistants guarding his family (p. 394), Marable alleges that Malcolm X pursued yet another extramarital relationship.

He also claims that Malcolm met with Alex Haley on February 20 to discuss their joint book project, took Betty to a friend's house for her to spend the night, and then rented a cheap hotel room where he "may have" had the teenage secretary as a bed-warmer (p 423).

By that logic, he *may have* met with Olive Oyl, Bluto, and Popeye that night as well.

There are numerous published accounts from those close to Malcolm that he was near his breaking point by then. Black Muslims had bombed his home on Valentine's Day because Malcolm refused to move out of the house pending a judgment over its ownership.

Marable claims that the same teenager who was romantically involved with Malcolm the night of February 20 showed up at the Audubon Ballroom the next day. She sat in the front row next to a man whose name would later appear in FBI documents related to the assassination.

The teenager, Marable writes, and the Newark mosque official now "live together in the same New Jersey residence, and [name deleted] has maintained absolute silence about her relationship with both Malcolm X and [name deleted]" (p. 452).

The source given for this allegation is Abdur-Rahman Muhammad. When I asked Muhammad for his sources, he declined comment. Despite the obvious lack of due diligence, Marable spares no opportunity to praise his own ingenuity and tenacity.

"*After years* [my emphasis] of research," he writes in *Life Beyond the Legend*, "I discovered that several chapters had been deleted [from the biography] prior to publication—chapters that envisioned the construction of a united front of Negroes led by the Black Muslims."

Yeah, and Columbus "discovered" America. The word "years" has to be a typographical error. Surely he means *after minutes* of research. This is from the front page of the Life section of *USA Today*:

> **MEMORIES FOR SALE**: A manuscript of Alex Haley's first book, *The Autobiography of Malcolm X*, sold for $ 100,000 at an auction to settle claims against the late author's estate. The buyer was Detroit entertainment lawyer Gregory Reed, who also paid $ 21,500 for *three deleted chapters of the book*. [my emphasis]

The date of the story? October 2, 1992. The story ran in practically every major newspaper and black magazine in the next two months. Any college student could have signed on to Nexis or other news databases and found that in five minutes or less. A Google search for "Malcolm X," "autobiography," and "missing chapters" generated more than 4,000 hits on April 5.

As a former professional researcher (I worked in the news research department of *The Washington Post* for more than a decade), I immediately recognized Marable's fraud, one of many in this pedestrian publication.

The late professor uncovers no significant new material, yet he has the chutzpah to dismiss with a flick of his wrist earlier books about Malcolm's life and assassination:

In reading "*all* [emphasis supplied] of the literature about Malcolm produced in the 1990s, I was struck by its shallow character and lack of original sources" (p. 490).

When I began reading Chapter 7, I felt like I was revisiting my biography of Elijah Muhammad. It deals with marital discord between Nation of Islam leader Elijah Muhammad and Clara Muhammad. The chapter's first four pages read like a "reinvention" of chapters from *The Messenger*, published by Pantheon Books in 1999. I checked the footnotes for those four pages and noticed that seven of the first ten cite *The Messenger* as the source (p. 521).

Why didn't Marable use the original source material? He makes no mention of the FBI's national and Chicago files on Clara Muhammad.

Marable has two primary arguments: (1) the intelligence community and the New York Police Department deliberately ignored serious threats against Malcolm's X life, and (2) there is overwhelming evidence that the five assassins came from the Nation of Islam's Newark mosque.

That's it.

His first argument is based upon research in my first book, *The Judas Factor: The Plot to Kill Malcolm X*, published in November 1992. His second argument—and the one that the media chose to ignore for the past two decades—is based upon the research of Zak Kondo of Baltimore City Community College. *Conspiracys: Unraveling the Assassination of Malcolm X* (1993) is without question the most authoritative examination of the mechanics of the assassination.

Marable had hundreds of thousands of dollars at his disposal for more than a decade. He had over twenty researchers at his disposal. Given far less capital and manpower, both David J. Garrow and Taylor Branch separately produced three-volume works of encyclopedic detail on Malcolm's contemporary, Dr. Martin Luther King Jr. Despite his acknowledgments of gratitude to other prominent researchers and benefactors, Marable's book is a single volume with questionable documentation.

Poor exposition and inexcusable typographical errors taint the book. When I communicated with Marable last June regarding a statement obtained from Linward X Cathcart by New York police after the assassination, his reply referred to "Linwood" Cathcart. I advised him of the misspelling and cautioned him to check his manuscript for the mistake.

One of his assistants replied under his name and told me that Marable dictated his responses for her to relay. She blamed herself for misspelling the name and assured me that the book had the proper spelling. There are two references to Cathcart's full name in the book, and both times the name is spelled Linwood (p. 5, 452). It is also misspelled in the index.

In the prologue, Marable describes Malcolm X's memoir as a "cautionary tale about human waste and the tragedies produced by racial segregation (p. 9)." Human waste? As in feces and urine? "No man has more accurately described and analyzed the existential, political, social, moral and spiritual plight of a victimized people than has Malcolm X in this book," an objective reviewer wrote about the *Autobiography of Malcolm X*.

A Life of Reinvention, by contrast, is immediately forgettable. It was written by a chronic pen pusher who lived a rather unremarkable middle class existence but nonetheless implies that Malcolm X was an amateur this or a mediocre that.

"I'm the man you think you are," Malcolm X said. Malcolm X was at the top of the class in school, on top of the hustling game during his hoodlum years, and a hell raiser in prison. He was national spokesman for a black organization that barely functioned before he joined in 1952. He was, finally, a revolutionary known and respected by other prominent revolutionaries—Fidel Castro, Ben Bella, and Che Guevara, to name a few.

He was, in short, a black panther of a man. By contrast, Marable was just another paper tiger.

Evolution of a Black Nationalist Revolutionary
(From: An Unlikely Warrior)

Iyaluua Ferguson with Herman Ferguson

The St. Albans Plaza in Queens, NY, was packed on Thanksgiving Day 1963 for Malcolm X's appearance. Black folks had forsaken their traditional holiday feasting to perhaps feast on the wisdom of Brother Malcolm. Over 2,000 Black folks ignored the warnings of conservative Negroes that association in any way with Brother Malcolm could well mean the loss of their Civil Service jobs. The rumor mill had been spreading the word that association with Malcolm X and the Black Muslims could mark an individual, target him for government reprisal, and stop or reverse any forward movement that he or she had made. Knowledge of the U.S. government's Counterintelligence Program was not widespread at that time, but the belief that 'Big Brother' was watching permeated not only the Black community, but prevailed throughout the country.

However the threat of government reprisal could not deter these citizens of Queens from taking the opportunity to see and hear Brother Malcolm for their selves. Herman's goal to change the direction of the Civil Rights movement appeared more reachable. It was obvious to him that the people were hungry for guidance that would lift the boot of oppression they experienced in their daily lives.

Herman could feel the spirits of the people being heightened and galvanized by the presence of Malcolm. Organizing and channeling this interest and passion into meaningful action remained uppermost in Herman's mind. He well understood that Jim Crow policies, *de facto* segregation, rampant police brutality and all the evils that beset the Black community could not prevail without the quiet acquiescence of the U.S. government. Educating, politicizing and organizing the Black community to resist oppression and find ways to express its will was for Herman the order of the day. The U.S. government must be made to enforce its own laws.

Minister Malcolm, when he addressed the crowd at the Plaza, endorsed the Rochdale Movement's boycott campaign against the Jamaica Avenue merchants. But he cautioned that the boycott was just a start. Next moves would be to refrain from buying "where you don't work" followed by refusal to buy "where you don't own." He said Black folk should build factories and supermarkets and provide jobs for themselves instead of asking white people for jobs.

Slightly less than a week after this historic appearance in Queens, on December 4, 1963, Malcolm spoke at the Manhattan Center Auditorium in New York City. He delivered a very powerful speech in which he delineated the historic, moral and religious rationale for the separation of the races. His message was smothered, however, by events that followed immediately after his speech. John F. Kennedy, the late president of the U.S. had been murdered by an assassin's bullet two weeks earlier, on November 22. During the question and answer period that followed Malcolm's speech, he was asked by a reporter to comment on the Kennedy assassination. Brother Malcolm remarked that he viewed it as a case of "chickens coming home to roost." Then he added, "Being an old farm boy myself, chickens coming home to roost never did make me sad; they've always made me glad."

The white mass media went wild. Malcolm was accused of calling the U.S. president a chicken. It was said that he had expressed pleasure at the president's murder. None of this was true, but when it came to reporting on Black folks, the white media never showed too much concern for the truth.

Elijah Muhammad, Malcolm's mentor and the leader of the Nation of Islam, was enraged by the negative publicity. Muhammad did not allow his followers to engage in any political activity, and he had specifically forbidden any comment on the Kennedy assassination. He, himself, as leader of the Nation of Islam had sent condolences to the Kennedy family on the death of the president. He ordered Malcolm to report to him in Chicago. There he removed Malcolm from his stewardship of Mosque #7 in Harlem. Malcolm received a 90-day suspension from the Nation, and he was barred from public speaking during the period of his suspension. No Muslim, except Malcolm's wife and children, could speak to him, nor could he speak to them.

"Chickens coming home to roost" is defined as saying that you will pay for the bad things, the sins, you have done. Chickens scratch around in the barnyard, in the fields and woods, during the day. But at night they come home to the henhouse to roost. This saying is comparing a person's evil or foolish deeds to chickens. If a person does wrong, the payback might not be immediate. But at some point, at the end of the day, those "chickens" will come home to roost.

Kennedy as president of the U.S. symbolically carries the sins of his country on his shoulders. And the payback, the consequences of the many evil deeds perpetrated by this country, fell to him. *The New York Times* wrote, "in further criticism of Mr. Kennedy, [Malcolm] cited the murders of Patrice Lumumba, Congo leader, of Medgar Evers, civil rights leader, and of the (four) Negro girls bombed earlier this year in a Birmingham church. These, he said, were instances of other 'chickens coming home to roost'."

Black folks were confused by the suspension. What had Malcolm said that was untrue? If anything, he said what everyone knew. The United States government was complicit in many evil deeds. There was a climate of hate in the country that was a result of the action and/or non-action of the U.S. government. President Kennedy had been shot and killed while on a triumphant visit to Dallas, Texas. The gun featured mightily in the history of the United States. The country was stolen from the indigenous people at the barrel of the gun. The gun settled the Wild West.

The gun was used to strip Africa of its most precious resource, fine young men and women taken to the American shores as prisoners of war. The gun and the whip were used to enslave these captives, using their forced free labor to help build this giant nation.

It was the gun that ended the life of Abraham Lincoln because it was perceived that he had betrayed his class by "freeing" the slaves.

Several hundred Black people were allegedly killed by the gun and bombs wielded by whites determined to demolish the self-sufficient community known as Black Wall Street in Tulsa, Oklahoma.

The United States was a gun-toting, warmongering nation. Ask the Puerto Ricans, the Mexicans—all subdued by American guns. Now President Kennedy had fallen victim to the gun.

Yes, the chickens had come home to roost. Malcolm had not lied.

On March 4, 1964, Malcolm announced he was leaving the Nation of Islam. He perceived that his suspension would not be lifted. He understood that his enemies within the Nation of Islam had poisoned Muhammad's mind against him. They twisted Malcolm's investigation into Elijah's adulteries into a move by Malcolm for supreme power for himself. Nothing was further from the truth, but Malcolm could no longer work under Elijah's tutelage.

Herman received the news of Malcolm's resignation from the NOI with hope and optimism. He had long felt that Malcolm should leave the

Nation. He regarded the NOI as too crippling. It limited Malcolm's ability to organize Black people.

In his speech "Message to the Grassroots," Malcolm had said, "Revolution is bloody, revolution is hostile, revolution knows no compromise, revolution overturns and destroys everything that gets in its way. And you, sitting around here like a knot on a log, saying, 'I'm going to love these folks no matter how much they hate me,' No, you need a revolution. Whoever heard of a revolution where they lock arms....singing 'We Shall Overcome?' You don't do that in a revolution. You don't do any singing, you're too busy swinging. It's based on land. A revolutionary wants land so he can set up his own nation, an independent nation. These Negroes aren't asking for any nation—they're trying to crawl back on the plantation."

It was the kind of message that Herman understood. Now perhaps Malcolm would be able to take that message to a larger audience. Perhaps now with Malcolm's leadership, Blacks could be organized into the united force that was needed for liberation.

Herman's memories of his work with Malcolm X are vivid. He recounts here his work with the OAAU and shares with us that very short time (from March 1964 through February 21, 1965) that was so fraught with hope and purpose and promise of a better world to come—a world created and molded by Black people.   [I. Ferguson]

* * *

Shortly after Malcolm's expulsion from the Nation of Islam he announced he was forming a new organization that would be known as The Muslim Mosque, Inc. (MMI). It was to be open to all. I was one of the early people to approach Malcolm and offer my membership. After he expressed some concerns about me losing my job with the NYC Board of Education, we agreed that I would join the MMI without any fuss or fanfare. Shortly after that, Malcolm left the country to go to Africa and the Middle East. He was gone for about five weeks. During that time, I remember attending some of the meetings, but mainly I waited for Malcolm's return.

I was very active in organizing work out in Queens at that time. One of the brothers who was active with my Queens group was Lez Edmonds. He kept me in touch with what was happening in the MMI. It was Lez who told me that Malcolm had returned from his overseas trip and was meeting with a small group of people who were planning to announce the formation of another organization under Malcolm's leadership. The MMI was to remain a religious organization where the Muslims could worship. The new organization was to be more secular oriented and was intended as a political/cultural type organization.

Lez told me the group was in the early stages of forming their organization and he told me he would keep me informed. Shortly after that he told me that Malcolm wanted me to start meeting with this group and I should come to the next meeting. Lez picked me up that Sunday and we drove to the Flash Inn, a well-known nightspot in Harlem.

I learned that this new organization would be named the Organization of Afro-American Unity (OAAU), and its goal was to bring all the many organizations that were struggling for human and civil rights under the umbrella of the OAAU. The OAAU would be responsible for presenting a unified front that would bring the United States before the United Nations charged with the crime of denying the human rights of 22 million Black people. While Malcolm would be at the head, he would not hold any formal office. We would be responsible for staffing the various committees that were to be set up. Malcolm would work with us to develop the organization and he was to serve as our principal speaker at the rallies, which would be the main approach to expanding our membership, and at the same time bringing the thoughts of Malcolm before the public. The Audubon Ballroom was the place where our Sunday rallies would be held.

We were all so young then—ready to take on any tasks Malcolm assigned to us. Many came from the Nation of Islam with Malcolm. Others came from among the radical elements of the civil rights movement, looking for more action than those leaders were offering—SNCC; CORE; SLCC; etc. We were all looking to Malcolm for a new kind of leadership. We were all ready to go wherever he took us.

Some of us were more politicized than others. Some were already Black Nationalists. Some were Pan-Africanists. A few considered themselves political radicals. Some were intellectuals. Others were cultural nationalists. Whatever we proclaimed ourselves to be, we were all believers to some extent or other in Malcolm's call for self-determination, self-reliance and self-defense for Black people. Malcolm was our new leader and we were going to build a movement based on his leadership. No turning the other cheek for us. No begging, praying, singing or pleading for our civil rights. Malcolm had already made it clear; our struggle was for human rights and not for civil rights. That was as true to me as that the sun rose in the east every day. And I think all who became followers of Malcolm believed the same thing.

We were meeting regularly, getting acquainted with each other and trying to bring some structure to the new organization. Lynne Shifflett was the Secretary of the Organization while Brother James continued to head the MMI. The OAAU was divided into committees and a Chairman headed each committee. Some that I can remember were the Cultural Committee chaired by Sister Muriel; Communications Committee chaired by Brother Peter; Education Committee chaired by me; and later on Brother Jim Campbell came on and helped me to develop our Liberation School.

The Education Committee focused its attention on establishing a Liberation School that would cover two sessions on Saturdays. The first session was devoted to school age youngsters. Sessions began at 9:00 a.m. and ended at 11:00 a.m. The second session, which was for adults, started at 11:00 a.m. and continued until about 1:00 p.m.

One of my most vivid memories is that the family of Yusef and Dara Iman were all members of the Liberation School and were our most consistent attendees. Yusef was a brilliant revolutionary poet and actor, a member of Amiri Baraka's Spirit House Movers. Tragically, he made his transition far too young, succumbing to cancer at the age of 52.

A reading list was developed and assignments were given from this list. We used many speakers who were qualified to lecture on African History, the Middle Passage, Slavery and Reconstruction, and many other topics that were relevant to the centuries of suffering of our people here in the U.S. The list of speakers was long, and it included such names as John Henrik Clarke, Dr. Yosef Ben-Jochannan, Queen Mother Moore, Richard Moore, Mr. Lewis Michaux, Pork Chop Davis, and on and on. All these speeches were taped for the purpose of putting together a spoken word library.

Those tapes seem to be lost forever. The police seized those that were in my keeping when they invaded my home and arrested me. I suppose the police considered them contraband.

I should mention here that I chose to call our school a Liberation School because there were a number of schools operated by civil rights groups who called them Freedom Schools. I explained to Brother Malcolm that the name Liberation School conveyed the idea that we were educating our students to take their liberation rather than begging someone to give them freedom. Freedom when given can be taken back, but liberation has to be fought for and once we reach that state, our former masters cannot take it back.

When Jim Campbell joined the Education Committee, he introduced the idea of developing a Leadership Training Course that was based on the thoughts and ideas of Brother Malcolm.

At the end of the course a diploma was signed by Brother Malcolm and given to each individual who completed the course. The student was then supposed to go back to his community with a kit of resource materials to begin to organize and provide leadership. Our first class was made up of ten students who studied over a period of several weeks. A graduation ceremony was held at one of the Sunday rallies at the Audubon Ballroom. It was a thrilling sight to watch those ten proud students come out on the stage as their names were called to shake Brother Malcolm's hand and to receive a specially designed certificate of graduation that had been signed by Brother Malcolm. I particularly recall the phenomenal Yuri Kochiyama being in that first graduating class. Yuri has been a consistent warrior in our liberation struggle for as long as I can remember and remains so today.

Unfortunately, we did not graduate another class. Malcolm's assassination ended the OAAU and all of our plans we had for that organization. Somewhere today there are ten certificates, signed by Brother Malcolm, declaring that the bearer completed the OAAU Leadership Training Course.

As I look back at those hectic times I am struck by a multitude of random memories that have stayed with me through these many years. I can see Peter on his hands and knees on the floor of the office agonizing over pasting up a copy of the OAAU newspaper while Malcolm hovered over him, saying, "Don't worry, brother. We'll find some way to get the money for this paper." And the night when Malcolm had called a meeting to inform the brothers that there was to be no more searching of people who came to our rallies; and that the security brothers were not to be armed because he thought the sight of armed security was turning off people we needed to join the OAAU. That night will always remain with me. Brothers complained loudly about these new restrictions. But Malcolm was firm. No searching. No weapons.

I have often wondered if Malcolm realized the dangerous position he was placing himself in by issuing such an order. I also think back to that night and try to recall the brothers who agreed with Malcolm and those who didn't. In retrospect, I think that meeting was one of the most intriguing and important meetings that I ever attended as a member of the OAAU.

There are other images that are etched on my mind about those days. Things were moving quickly towards a head. My concerns about the rumors circulating among the OAAU members grew stronger, along with increasing pressures that were being directed towards Malcolm by the press and the NOI. Later we were to learn that this campaign to smear Malcolm was the dirty work of the government's strategy to confuse the general public, and particularly those in the OAAU. There was a noticeable decline in the work of the organization as a result of the attempts to destabilize us. Attempts to sow seeds of distrust and confusion among those of us who were the founders of the organization were made continuously. I recall discussing with Jim Campbell my concerns about what was happening to the organization and my fears about what was happening to Malcolm. Jim agreed with me that the picture looked very gloomy. We decided to contact Malcolm and request a sit down between the three of us so we could inform him of our concerns and see what he thought.

Malcolm met with us on a Saturday afternoon in Jim's Harlem apartment. The apartment we were meeting Malcolm in was located on the fifth floor and gave us a clear view of the entire street. We were able to observe Malcolm's car when he pulled up across the street from the building. I was struck by the fact that Malcolm was traveling alone and by his casual manner as he crossed the street and entered the building.

Throughout the ensuing meeting with us, Malcolm maintained that casual attitude. He flipped a large coin absently through the fingers of one hand as our discussion ranged over a wide spectrum of subjects. Although he listened carefully as we talked, he expressed no concerns about his personal safety, but he did attempt to deal with our concerns about the OAAU and how it seemed to be floundering, Although we had asked Malcolm to meet with us for about an hour, it was many hours later before we ended our discussion and he left.

My last view of him that afternoon was as he descended the stairs, still casually flipping that same coin as he returned to his car.

Most Americans who were adults on December 7, 1941, can recall what they were doing when they heard the news that Japan had attacked Pearl Harbor and that America would likely be entering the war already in progress in Europe. Similarly, most Black people 16 years or older, alive and living in New York City on February 21, 1965, can tell you where they were and what they were doing when they heard the announcement that assassins had shot and killed Brother Malcolm X.   [H. Ferguson]

* * *

The voice of Brother Malcolm had brought a sense of liberation to so many. Even those who publicly denounced his teachings privately admitted the truth of what he was saying. Malcolm had articulated for the world so much of what Black folks were saying in the privacy of their living rooms, in their backyards, in barbershops and beauty salons, at neighborhood barbecues, wherever groups of Black folks gathered. Now the voice was silenced, and the grief and sorrow of the people were deep and real.

Herman was present at the Audubon Ballroom that day and witnessed that heinous and gut-wrenching scene. He had come alone as he had to all of the Sunday OAAU rallies. He had not brought his family into the organization. His wife had become fearful and somewhat resentful of his almost total absorption with his organizing work in Queens and his association with Malcolm X. She found the rhetoric of the revolutionary nationalists frightening. Rose was an intelligent woman, and foresaw increasing violence due to the schism between the Nation of Islam and Malcolm. She did not want that violence entering her home. She had worked hard alongside Herman building a stable and comfortable life for themselves and their children. Now Rose believed that that life was being threatened by Herman's determination to find a way to bring his people forward to freedom. This was not what she intended when she taunted Herman to join the demonstration at the Rochdale construction site.

When Rose heard the news of Malcolm's assassination, her heart sank, not only for grief at the loss of this great man, but for the knowledge of what this would mean to Herman. She knew the effect would be devastating.

Indeed the assassination was earth-shattering for Herman. The events of that day are burned into his brain. He can recall chapter and verse at will. Malcolm's legacy remains with Herman. He carries with him always the responsibility to keep that legacy alive, and help, if he can, to harvest the seeds Malcolm sowed.   [I. Ferguson]

* * *

February 21, 1965, was a bright, sunny, cold day. It was a Sunday, and we had scheduled a rally at the Audubon as usual. The situation was far from normal. Some of the committees of the OAAU seemed to have ceased functioning. Malcolm's home had been torched and he and his family had barely escaped with their lives. Speculation was rife about who had done this cowardly act. It was said the Nation of Islam had done the deed. The press hinted that Malcolm had set the fire himself.

Malcolm said that the circumstances surrounding the fire were outside the things the NOI could or would do. "They would certainly try to silence me," he said, "but they don't wage war on women and children, and my pregnant wife and my young children were in that house at the time." Malcolm had earlier told some of the brothers that he had mistakenly blamed the NOI for the problems that were happening to him. He did not believe the NOI had the resources to try to poison him in Egypt, and he knew for certain that the NOI had no influence on the French government. They could not persuade France to bar him from entering that country. These things had all happened to Malcolm on his trip abroad.

When asked where those problems were coming from, Malcolm pointed to the South and said, "They are coming from Washington."

Malcolm, for the first time, was shifting the blame for his problems away from the NOI and shifting them to a far more dangerous source—the United States government.

My mind was racing with thoughts of that nature as I drove towards the rally. Which way to turn? What to do?

As I turned off Broadway into W.166th Street, I noticed something strange. Usually when we held our rallies, the street in front of the Audubon Ballroom was teeming with NYC policemen who were detailed there to cover the event. This day, there wasn't a cop in sight!

As I drew up in front of the Audubon, I spotted a lone cop standing across the street in the small park that faced the building. "That's strange," I muttered to myself. "Where are the police today?" I knew that Malcolm had ordered that no police were to be allowed inside the auditorium, but always there was a large contingent of police outside the building. Their absence today was most unusual and very strange.

I continued to drive down the street, looking for a parking spot for my car. I found a spot a block or two from the Audubon Ballroom, locked the car and returned on foot to the building. The cop whom I had seen standing across the street in the park was nowhere in sight. I entered the building and noticed some of our security people manning the entrance door. We greeted each other as they waved me in.

It was obvious that a large crowd of people were assembled to hear Malcolm speak. Not noticing any people from the OAAU in the crowd, I took a seat about midway in the aisle just across from a row of semi-circular booth-like seats. As I glanced around, I noticed that one of the semi-circular booths across from me was almost filled by some members of the OAAU. They beckoned for me to join them and I did. I sat facing the stage where I would have a good view of the podium from which Malcolm would soon be speaking.

The murmuring from the crowd came to a halt as the brother who would address them prior to introducing Malcolm began to speak. Brother Benjamin was a good speaker and he soon had the crowd giving him its full attention. The stage was empty except for Benjamin. A row of empty chairs was placed side by side on the stage as though speakers were expected to fill them. (I learned later that Rev. Galamison, Mae Mallory and Ralph Cooper had been invited to speak. None of them were there.) I noticed Brother James peeking out of the door leading from the off-stage holding room, surveying the audience, and then withdrawing. Finally Malcolm walked out. He took a seat in one of the chairs just behind Benjamin.

When Benjamin noticed the appearance of Malcolm, he took that as his cue and began to introduce Malcolm to the crowd. Malcolm stood and began to walk toward the podium. Benjamin turned to yield the podium to him, and as their paths crossed, Malcolm was seen to pause and whisper something in Benjamin's ear. Benjamin nodded and walked off the stage, heading towards the rear of the auditorium. (Benjamin told me later that Malcolm had ordered him to go to a telephone and find out if Rev. Galamison was coming.) Malcolm continued forward until he was standing at the podium, facing the expectant crowd. Every eye in the audience was fixed on Malcolm, and a hush filled the room.

Malcolm began to speak, saying "A Salaamu Alaikum, Brothers and Sisters!" At that moment, as though by some pre-arranged signal, a loud commotion broke out in the audience. There was the sound of loud voices cursing and that was followed by the sound of a chair falling to the floor.

I immediately swung my head to follow the sound of this interruption and saw that the noise was coming from two men who were seated near where I had originally sat when I first entered the room. The two men had flung aside their chairs and one man was crouched over as he moved away from the other man. "Get your hand out of my f.....g pocket, n.....r!" came out of the mouth of the other man.

At this moment, I realized that something was drastically wrong. Never had I ever seen such a spectacle before. In all the times I had seen Malcolm speaking to all sorts of crowds, there was never any type of interruption. Such a thing was unthinkable. I felt a distinct feeing of unease as I quickly swung my head away from that scene and focused my attention back to Malcolm. Very calmly and without any sign of what was about to happen, Malcolm had stepped aside from the podium and leaned toward the crowd with his hand upraised as he uttered his last words, "Cool it, brothers and sisters!"   He began to lower his arm when a loud noise tore through the air. It was the sound of a sawed-off shotgun being fired into Malcolm's exposed body. The blast straightened Malcolm upright, and as he stood there for the next few seconds, pistol shots began to be heard as the killers continued their depraved work. Malcolm was held upright as the storm of pistol shots continued. There was a momentary pause in the shooting and Malcolm then toppled backwards, his head making an awful sound as he fell prone on the stage. There was a brief pause in the shooting, and then it continued with the sound of large and small caliber pistol shots filling Malcolm's fallen body for what seemed to be an eternity.

I remember thinking, "If they would stop shooting into his body, maybe he could survive." But I knew from experience that nothing could live through such a fusillade of pointblank bullets, fired at such close range. Whoever was responsible for this deed wanted to send a message to the

Malcolm followers in the hall, and by extension the entire Black Nationalist community, that a similar fate awaited anyone who desired to take on Malcolm's role.

When the shooting ended, I found myself under the seat I had been occupying, with my head and shoulders extending into the aisle. The sudden end to the loud noises and the screams of terrified people created a vast and eerie silence throughout the hall. Chairs were flung all over the room. People were still cowering from the recent noise and the confusion. As I looked out on this scene, I noticed three figures standing in the middle of the room. There were three men standing one behind the other as though they were uncertain as to what their next move should be. The man in front wore what looked like a knee-length coat. There was a gun of some sort in his hand. I knew these were some of the men who had taken part in the just-completed killing of Malcolm.

I watched closely as long as I could. The three men suddenly began to run towards the rear of the hall, towards the exit door. A few seconds passed as the men passed out of my sight. There was the sound of some scattered shots as the men disappeared. By this time I had crawled from under the chair and the adjoining table and had taken a look at the stage. People were crowded around Malcolm's fallen body. There was nothing I could do there. I decided to go outside to see what was happening out there. During all this time there were still no police to be seen.

As I stood amidst this scene of carnage and terror, I began to sift through what I had just observed over the past few minutes. It began to occur to me that during the entire episode I had remained rooted to my seat and had only taken refuge under my seat after the second series of shots had rung out. I recall that while the firing was going on, there was a series of flashing yellow bulbs like the kind used to focus light on a scene that was being filmed. These flashing yellow lights were flickering off and on rapidly one after the other, and seemed to be coming directly over the Audubon stage area. It dawned on me that the entire scene of Malcolm's assassination was being filmed. Sonofabitch, they filmed the whole horrible event! Only governmental intelligence agencies have such a capability. This certainly lends credence to Malcolm's claim that Washington was the area from which his problems were coming. Not Chicago.

I went downstairs and out the front door to confront an unforgettable sight. To my right there was a crowd of people who had obviously rushed out of the hall in pursuit of the fleeing assassins. They were holding one man. It was clear that they meant him no good. A couple of policemen were trying to rescue the man from the enraged people who were trying to pull their captive apart. They didn't seem to need my help and I turned and walked towards Broadway.

On the corner of Broadway and W.166 St. was a shop that sold prosthetic devices. I stood there pondering the events I had just witnessed and trying to fit all the pieces together. From the entrance on 166th St., Malcolm's security people emerged carrying Malcolm's bullet-ridden body on a gurney commandeered from the hospital across the street. A small group of policemen were trailing the brothers, offering no help at all. I looked down at the body of my slain leader. His tie had been ripped loose from his throat; his shirt had been pulled open; and his chest was exposed. I could see the pattern of bullet holes that encircled his left chest around his heart. Rage and sorrow competed for a space in my being as I fought to control my emotions and focus on what I had seen and what might lie ahead.

At that point a New York City police vehicle pulled up at the corner. There was a police officer driving and seated beside him was an officer wearing the scrambled-eggs cap of an officer of some senior rank. This officer got out of the vehicle and began walking towards the commotion farther down the block. Within a few minutes he returned assisting a civilian who was bent over in pain. The officer helped this civilian to the police car and carefully placed him in the rear seat.

By this time my curiosity had been completely aroused. I thought the civilian was probably one of our people who had been on duty at the door and had been injured as the killers escaped. I walked over to the car and poked my head through the open window and looked directly into this man's face. I had never seen this person before! He was bent over, clutching his abdomen, seemingly in great pain. The police brass, who by now had gotten back in his seat next to the driver, ordered the driver to get out of there right away. The car sped off, but to my surprise they drove straight down W.166th Street and sped out of sight. I thought the injured man would be taken immediately just across the street to the large hospital (Manhattan Presbyterian) where Malcolm had been taken by our security people.

Who was this mysterious stranger? Why were the police so anxious to get him off the scene so quickly? What was his role in the killing? Why has nothing been said by the media and the police about this second man?

The first man had been rescued from the enraged crowd and placed under arrest. His name was Talmadge Hayer. He served 25 years for his involvement in the crime. Two other men were later arrested and convicted of participation in the assassination. But who was the man I saw in the police car, wounded and being shielded by police brass? This and other questions still cast their shadow around the events of February 21, 1965.

Malcolm's brutal and untimely death spelled the end of both of his organizations—the Muslim Mosque Inc. and the Organization of Afro-American Unity. My short period of time working in those two organizations marked a turning point in my life. Malcolm's legacy still gives direction and meaning to the Black Liberation Struggle. Our fight to liberate our political prisoners and to give substance to our drive for self-determination is clearly reflected in our call for land and reparations.

It does not seem that we only had Malcolm with us for about thirteen months after he left the Nation of Islam. Yet in that short period of time, Brother Malcolm cast his shadow over our Movement in so many ways. He changed our focus from civil rights to human rights. He influenced the birth of many Black Nationalist organizations (the Black Panther Party, the Republic of New Afrika, the Black Liberation Army, to name just a few). People who fight for their freedom from oppression and for national liberation know his name worldwide.   [H. Ferguson]

* * *

Whatever was left of the reformist in Herman was killed in the Audubon Ballroom on that cold February Sunday. Only the revolutionary freedom fighter remained. He now understood clearly that Black folk, if they were to survive, had to separate from this racist system or destroy it. Herman was not now nor had he ever been a romantic. He was not now nor had he ever been an adventurist. He was fully cognizant of the enormity of the task he was committed to undertaking.   [I. Ferguson]

Manning Marable and the Malcolm X Biography Controversy: A Response to Critics African World
Bill Fletcher Jr.

On the day of Manning Marable's death, April 1, 2011, I received an additional piece of disturbing information. A friend of mine informed me of a discussion he had just had with a Black activist-writer who, in hearing about Marable's passing, went into what could only be described as a rant against Marable. Marable's body was hardly cold, and this individual, who knew Marable, was castigating him to my friend, claiming that Marable was everything but a child of God. It was at that moment that I knew that Marable's *Malcolm X: A Life of Reinvention (hereafter referred to as MX)* would ignite a firestorm in some quarters of the Black Freedom Movement. Within days, despite the overwhelmingly positive response to the book, this firestorm emerged.

In approaching the controversies that surround *MX* it is important to ask two questions prior to responding directly to critics: (1) What did Manning set out to do? (2) Did he succeed? We will take these one at a time before commenting on some of the issues raised by various critics and what lies beneath them.

What did Manning Set Out to Do?
MX is a blockbuster of enormous proportions. The mere act of writing a 500-plus page biography is a significant achievement on any scale. Yet Marable was not attempting to write *the* definitive biography when he first started out on this journey. As he himself noted, his first objective was to write what he called a "political biography" of Malcolm X. Over time the objectives shifted somewhat and became a bit more complex.

Much has been made of the biography "humanizing" Malcolm, a term which I have myself used. Yet that is not the starting point for understanding the objectives. A better starting point is perhaps derived from Marable's own statements on the matter, the gist of which begins with the fact that Malcolm X had been—and remained—a hero for Marable, who, in his opinion, had been the most significant Black activist figure of the mid- to-late 20th century. It was Marable's committed belief in Malcolm X's significance that moved him to dedicate the last decade of his life to chronicling Malcolm's life and legacy through the Malcolm X Project at Columbia University. And it is this same commitment to Malcolm X's and his family's legacy that caused Marable to utilize his institutional influence and resources to push Columbia University to make good on its promise to open the site of the former Audubon Ballroom as the Malcolm X & Dr. Betty Shabazz Memorial and Educational Center. *MX* is the product of a historian who cared deeply for his subject, who felt that his subject was deserving of a comprehensive examination of his life. Marable took this task seriously; grappling with aspects of Malcolm's life that he knew would challenge our iconic view of Malcolm but also do it in a way that would deepen our appreciation of his heroicism as human being to other human beings. Yet in trying to understand Malcolm's trajectory, not just when he left the Nation of Islam, but much earlier, there were curious features in the *Autobiography of Malcolm X* that were difficult to either understand or explain.

From my own discussions with Marable, as well as what is contained in *MX*, I know that Marable had been perplexed for years regarding what was missing from the *Autobiography*. Most people that I know who have read the *Autobiography* found the ending somewhat odd, i.e., that there is little discussion of Black freedom strategy and then, suddenly, we are into Alex Haley's final words! Like many other things in life, the tendency was just to chalk this up to circumstances, in this case, that the book was completed after Malcolm's assassination and that not everything could be wrapped together.

This explanation did not satisfy Marable. His conclusion, as he notes in the book and in numerous interviews he conducted prior to his death, was that Haley edited the book in such a way as to make it more acceptable for the audience that Haley wanted to reach (mainstream white America). Accordingly, sections of the *Autobiography*, such as that which covered Malcolm's proposed Black united front, were eliminated entirely. Haley, a Black Republican, had no interest in a Black Nationalist or Pan Africanist vision. This mere fact makes highly ironic some of the criticisms raised *of* Marable in connection with the book, specifically, that he was attempting to make Malcolm more acceptable to a liberal audience. The facts, simply put, demonstrate that such a conclusion is ridiculous. Why it is being offered, however, is something that will be discussed later.

The *Autobiography* contained some other issues for Marable, however. In the process of conducting his research he came across contradictions, or at least problems, that led him to understand that the *Autobiography* was a political testimony by Malcolm that, like most autobiographies, had specific contextual objectives. As such, Malcolm tended to exaggerate certain things, and in other cases, ignore significant facts altogether. This is not uncommon and not something for which Malcolm should be chastised. But it is the job of the historian and biographer to search beneath that which is acknowledged to ascertain accuracies, patterns, as well as other potential 'story lines,' for lack of a better term.

It is in this context that one can better understand the notion of "humanizing' Malcolm X. From the moment that Malcolm was killed there were efforts by the State and the Nation of Islam to demonize him. On the other hand, there was a largely grassroots move among many black nationalists, Pan Africanists and socialists, to uphold his memory and work. Within this last category there were those who tended toward canonizing Malcolm X, irrespective of any qualifiers issued at the time or since.

Malcolm became larger than life, and for an activist, black radical historian like Marable, this produced complications particularly when the complexities of Malcolm's experiences were not properly understood. Yes, Malcolm was a hero, but what was going on with him as a person? What were the questions that he had? Did he ever stumble? Was there a straight trajectory in his evolution? What constituted the nature of his politics, including as they and he evolved?

An additional objective for Marable was to explain Malcolm's evolution, particularly what took place while he was in the Nation of Islam as well as what took place in the aftermath of his leaving. Again, for many revolutionary black nationalists and other radical forces, at least at the time, there was this sense of a dramatic break in 1964 followed by a straight radical line. This notion dissatisfied Marable and he went to work to research what took place, particularly when Malcolm was in the Nation of Islam.

There is another part to his objective, however. What was going on in the period of the building of, first, the Muslim Mosque, Inc., and later the Organization of Afro-American Unity? What strategies were being unfolded? How was leadership being addressed? How was the role of women changing over time in these formations?

In *MX* Marable also set out to show that Malcolm was not another version of Martin Luther King. Again, Haley implied, and many others have tried to suggest more explicitly, that Malcolm and Martin Luther King were somehow converging. As Marable demonstrates, and clarifies quite explicitly in the final chapter, that was not the case at all. While there were points of agreement and while the record is clear that Malcolm envisioned the possibility of a united front with King, Malcolm represented a different political tendency. He was a revolutionary nationalist and Pan Africanist, but he was also someone who entertained the use of electoral politics for more than symbolic value. His post-NOI politics, in other words, was in flux, but in either case they were not King's.

But here is where things get complicated: Marable sought to establish to what extent Malcolm's politics was in line with those of people who claimed to follow him. This became an additional source of controversy.

Finally, Marable sought to determine who killed Malcolm X. This was certainly not an initial objective of his when he chose to write this book but as he became more absorbed in the story he was drawn to examine the facts and myths surrounding the murder. As with other portions of the book, Marable drew from original sources, secondary sources, witnesses, etc. His conclusions were, to some extent consistent with some earlier analyses, but startling in others, particularly in his examination of the dynamics within the MMI and OAAU that very likely contributed to the success of the assassination.

Did Marable Succeed in his Objectives?

This is what makes the controversy surrounding the book both fascinating and, often, distasteful at the same time. Through depthful research, Marable does succeed in his objectives. He uncovered the "hidden" chapters of the *Autobiography* and demonstrates to the reader their importance in understanding Malcolm's evolution. He provides the reader with a detailed understanding, not only of the Nation of Islam, but of other Muslim currents in the USA that influenced Black America generally, but also the NOI. He shows the struggles within the NOI that helped to shape Malcolm, but also helps the reader understand the frustrations that Malcolm increasingly felt within the NOI. Finally, Manning offered the social and historical context for understanding Malcolm, both within his time, but also in subsequent decades.

There are two specific features of *MX* I wish to focus on, however. One has to do with gender and the second concerns the assassination. But prior to that a word on methodology. Shortly after the publication of *MX*,

I had the opportunity to speak with a Black journalist about the book. He indicated that he did not care for the book. When I probed, it turned out that his major concern was that he did not believe that Marable should have offered any tentative conclusions about matters where he failed to have complete facts. One example of this was the matter of the same-sex encounter for pay in the Malcolm Little period and a second example was the possible affairs that Betty Shabazz may have had.

I was a bit stunned in hearing these concerns only later to recognize that this journalist was approaching this book as if it had been an article for a mainstream newspaper. In an article for a newspaper there is a certain approach that the writer must take. That is *never* the case with a historian or biographer, and as such there is a standard that Marable is being held to that is both unfair and disingenuous. A historian (and biographer) looks at all of the available evidence and draws a conclusion. By analogy it is along the lines of a civil trial vs. a criminal trial. In a civil trial the jury looks at the *preponderance of the evidence* in order to draw a conclusion. In a criminal action the jury, as we know, can only convict if there is NO shadow of a doubt.

Historians look at the evidence and draw conclusions. This is why history is never an exact science. While we can generally confirm specific facts, e.g., Napoleon was defeated at the Battle of Waterloo in 1815, the reasons for an action, event, etc., are always the subject of analysis and debate. New theories emerge to explain different developments. This is also the case when one is developing a biography.

Further, a genuine scholar, of Marable's caliber, in writing a biography cannot simply refuse to acknowledge important claims or uncomfortable facts. Such matters must be addressed, in which case the biographer can certainly take a pass if they have not arrived at any conclusion; they can challenge them; or they can affirm the earlier conclusions.

For a variety of reasons which we shall touch upon below, there are many critics who challenge this approach. They may mechanically look at this matter from the standpoint of journalistic standards or they may have other motives that hide behind a challenge to the methodology.

With regard to gender, Marable dared to touch on a piece of Malcolm that has largely been ignored by biographers, both friend and foe. The matter of a same-sex encounter for pay, though related to gender obviously, was useful more in understanding the criminal, parasitic life that Malcolm Little lived prior to prison. What was, however, more useful in terms of gender, was to understand Malcolm's misogyny. Marable raised some uncomfortable questions on this score, including the manner in which Malcolm discussed his mother and her eventual collapse, but also the conclusions that Malcolm drew when his female collaborators in crime turned against him in order to save themselves. There is a pattern that Marable identifies that lasts into the post-NOI period when it came to women. Once Malcolm broke with the NOI his views began to shift on matters of gender, and actually shift in such a way so as to unsettle some of his key male supporters in the MMI.

One can go deeper, however. Malcolm's relationship with Betty Shabazz was more complicated than either the *Autobiography* or many of Malcolm's uncritical supporters would make it out to be. Betty was a strong woman in her own right who sought security and sexual satisfaction, to name just two items, in her marriage to Malcolm. She also strongly supported him, often raising cautionary notes that were prescient. However, she did not have identical politics to Malcolm and certainly did not evolve further down the path of revolutionary nationalism and Pan Africanism. In other words, the relationship was complicated, and in order to address some of the challenges contained in this relationship Malcolm sought help from Elijah Muhammad, only to have that request for help turned into an instrument against him in the factional wars in the NOI.

The entire matter of gender has caused its own uproar and in so doing has betrayed an uncomfortable vein within Black America that has hemorrhaged in the past and could very well again. One need only remember the controversy surrounding the Clarence Thomas hearings and the allegations by Anita Hill to recognize the volatility of the issue.

A second matter of focus was the assassination. As noted earlier, Marable did not set out to uncover the full scope of the plot, but here he touched upon one matter that had received very little earlier attention: the tension within and among his supporters in the post-NOI period. First things first, however. Marable's research has already provided the impetus for a discussion regarding the need for a new examination of the circumstances surrounding the assassination. This includes the role of the police, FBI, as well as some elements of the NOI. The facts, as presented by Marable, and in some cases by earlier scholars and investigators, raise such serious questions regarding who was actually involved in the assassination that silence on this matter is simply unforgivable.

There are many points of controversy surrounding the assassination, but what is especially worth noting is that Marable's investigation identified three forces that had an interest in Malcolm's death: the State; the NOI; and some of Malcolm's own supporters. This is not the first time that history has demonstrated that an assassination or otherwise criminal action had multiple players, each with its own interest in the success of the operation even if they may not have been actively collaborating or have consciously conspired. In this case, the curious actions of the police on the day of the murder; the faulty security (by Malcolm's own people); and the identification of the assailants, points to multiple perpetrators, each with their own set of objectives. The problem of Malcolm's followers seems to have been a matter–never publicly discussed–revolving around some of them feeling betrayed by Malcolm's own evolution, an evolution, which was moving at the speed of light compared with their own changes.

The Critics and Their Discontent

When one listens to the critics of *MX* it is often difficult to ask anything other than, *what is "really" going on here?* In order to understand what is going on, one must identify multiple sources, much of which has almost nothing to do with the book itself. These include: the creation of Malcolm-as-icon; homophobia; personal jealousy targeted at Marable; New York chauvinism targeted at Marable; and on-going differences regarding strategy within the Black Freedom Movement. As the reader will notice, however, the debate has little to do with the facts as articulated in the book, despite the words of some of the critics. None of the challenges regarding alleged errors in fact that have been raised, irrespective of their relative validity, calls into question anything of significance in the book. In fact, a surprising number of the challenges to the book appear to have come from people who, at least at the time of their criticism, *had not even read the book or just read selective passages.* I have personally found myself in situations where individuals, in discussing the book, begin by saying something like: "I have not read the book but..." or "I have not finished reading the book but..." and then gone on to offer impassioned analyses with very little foundation. The fact that individuals believe that they do not have to do a real reading is a matter that could be the subject of an entirely separate essay!

Unfortunately, for too many followers of Malcolm–myself included–the *Autobiography* has been treated as the word of God. Rather than appreciating the politics that accompany all autobiographies, many of us have treated this book, along with Malcolm's speeches, as the final or near final word on Malcolm-the-person. The story is a magnificent story of redemption, but also of pride and revolutionary courage. Yet in our search for heroes, we often seek demigods. We seek a type of perfection that does not exist within humanity and wish to believe that the only way that a hero can be a hero (or heroine) is if they have reached that dimensional plateau of perfection. As one critic of Marable stated, quite unapologetically: *the people need icons.*

It is true that the people need heroes and heroines, particularly as a means of fighting despair. It is often the case that we shape or reshape those heroes or heroines in order to accomplish other political purposes. The State certainly understands that. As Lenin so aptly noted, upon the death of a people's hero, the capitalist State moves to alter society's understanding of said hero in order that the dead hero can become acceptable and advance the interests of the State.

The people can also reshape a hero in order to uphold the cause(s) advanced by the hero during their life. Malcolm's immense courage and defiance are legendary, but is that courage and defiance called into question if we find out that Malcolm vacillated about actually splitting with the NOI? Is it called into question if we know that he expressed misgivings? Is his manhood—however we happen to interpret that—challenged when we learn that there was a sexual/emotional disconnect between Betty and him?

When we demand that our heroes and heroines be perfect, then each human challenge, such as those noted earlier, calls into question whether our hero can be our hero. This is what lies beneath many of the criticisms of *MX* and of Marable.

When we turn heroes and heroines into demigods there is an additional problem that arises: we make it less possible, and in some cases even impossible, to emulate said hero. As political activists we should be utilizing the memory and practice of heroes—whether Martin Luther King, Fannie Lou Hamer, or Malcolm—not simply to inspire but as sources of wisdom. We should be learning from their practices, including how they confronted their challenges, and shaped who they were and who they became. We should be learning how to take from those experiences and apply to our own. To borrow from the late, great leader of the revolution in Guinea-Bissau/Cape Verde, Amilcar Cabral, we on the Left must *"tell no lies and claim no easy victories..."* including about our own great leaders. But once these individuals rise to the status of demigods that all becomes impossible. After all, how can we mere humans emulate Hercules?

While the fury over the challenge to Malcolm-as-demigod has been at the core of much of the uproar, some of the initial outrage resulted from the discussion of the possibility that Malcolm engaged in a same-sex encounter for pay prior to his going to prison. There are some interesting features to this outrage. This is not the first time that this matter has been raised. In fact, several authors have posed this issue. As such, it would have been highly questionable for Marable to have ignored the matter as if it were some imaginary issue. It is important to note that in Marable's treatment of this aspect of Malcolm's life, he used both primary sources (prison letters Malcolm wrote) as well as three secondary sources (including memoirs from Malcolm's nephew Rodnell Collins and his partner in crime Malcolm "Shorty" Jarvis) to corroborate his conclusion.

Methodology, however, is not the main issue here. What infuriates some critics is that the possibility of Malcolm engaging in a same-sex encounter raises questions as to his manhood. This assumption is based on the erroneous notion that one's sexuality is a fixed and determined category and that the positive aspects of Malcolm-the-revolutionary leader are somehow invalidated by what *at one moment* may have been sexual ambivalence.

The outrage expressed by some people at this 'revelation' is certainly tinged with homophobia, although I am not assuming that all of those who have reacted negatively to this segment of the book are automatically homophobic. Nevertheless, both the outrage and any homophobia associated with it does not withstand scrutiny when challenged, as it has been by Michael Eric Dyson, who has pointed out that the Malcolm who may have engaged in a same-sex encounter for pay was the Malcolm Little of the thug period. In that period he engaged in pimping, gambling and armed robbery. For many critics it appears to be completely acceptable that he engaged in these assorted activities but somehow same-sex encounters for pay are over the top.

What is shocking about this debate is how few pages it covers in the actual book (no more than two) and that Marable was very careful in his conclusions. As with any historian, he draws certain conclusions from the evidence he had but then goes on to make an interesting point: there were no subsequent examples or claims of either same-sex encounters for pay or homosexual activity period. While this should have calmed down the critics, the mere suggestion of such activity was enough to unsettle them.

Another feature of the criticism of *MX* is the allegation that it represents an attempt to portray Malcolm as having the same politics as Marable; liberalize Malcolm so that he is more acceptable to a mainstream audience; or turn Malcolm into some sort of social democrat. There is no foundation for these arguments. The closest thing to a legitimate issue was Marable's poor choice of words to describe Malcolm's evolution toward Pan Africanism (see below).

The final chapter of the book refutes the critics—hands down—on this matter of an attempt to liberalize Malcolm, etc. One need only review that chapter and consider the points that Marable raised. Not in order of importance, but:

> 1. Malcolm was not converging with King. [We discussed this point earlier.]
>
> 2. Malcolm saw the need for a complete restructuring of the USA in order for Black liberation to ever be achieved.
>
> 3. Malcolm would most likely have not been enthralled with affirmative action because he would have been looking for more structural solutions to our situation.
>
> 4. Malcolm would have engaged in a certain form of electoral politics.
>
> 5. Malcolm was trying to define his politics at the global level and situate the African American struggle within the global struggle against imperialism and racism.

There is nothing in this that sounds like liberalism or social democracy. Instead it more closely conforms to variants of anti-imperialist politics, in particular a form of anti-imperialist politics that was prevalent in the global South at that time.

Some critics, however, have raised Marable's use of the term "race neutral" in talking about the form of Pan Africanism and Third World solidarity Malcolm was advancing in order to allege that Marable was trying to water down Malcolm. Having known Marable for more than 25 years, I would attribute this to either a poor choice of words or a mistaken editing decision. Let's explore, however, what Marable was attempting to address.

There was a moment that *Malcolm himself described* when, during one of his trips, he encountered a North African revolutionary. The North African revolutionary questioned Malcolm about his use of the term "black nationalism." This North African revolutionary, being AFRICAN, was apparently also quite light-skinned and asked Malcolm where that put him in the context of Black Nationalism. Malcolm did not have a clear answer for this, but towards the end of his life appeared to have been grappling with this issue and what it meant for how he was to conceptualize and describe his politics.

Marable used the term "race neutral" to describe a set of anti-racist politics that were Pan African and Third Worldist, not in the sense that liberals or the right use the term "Race neutral." It would have been more akin to what the South African movement has called "non-racial" or "anti-racist." He was trying to describe this as something that was not about black as skin color but more akin to the manner in which "black," terminologically, came to be used in places such as Britain, South Africa and the Caribbean in the late 1960s and 1970s, i.e., as a political characterization (thus, South Asians often identified as "black" in each of those settings and did not reserve this designation to only those of direct African descent). What makes the criticism of Marable so patently disingenuous is that one need only consider the *body of Marable's works* to know that his usage of the tern "race neutral" was far from an example of liberalism, or other such disorders.

This all leads to a final point, i.e., that many of the criticism of *MX* have little to nothing to do with the book itself; they have to do with Manning. So, it is time to explore some of these in order to understand additional aspects of the temper associated with many of the responses.

I began this essay with a story concerning the response by one person of note to Manning's death. This story was in some ways a subplot in a larger story.

The larger story includes the matter of the legacy of Malcolm X and who can lay claim to it. There is an assortment of Black radicals, largely men, who believe that they carry Malcolm's torch. Whether due to conferences that they have held or books that they have written, they believe that only they are entitled to pontificate on the question of Malcolm X. Marable's book, and the largely positive response that it received (not to mention the thoroughness of its research) inflamed many of these individuals who seemed to have concluded that they had been eclipsed. Rather than welcoming Marable's contribution, they chose instead to smear it and him, as if that would somehow enhance their own stature.

Then there is the particular question of Manning Marable-the-person. Marable was an incredibly smart, dynamic, and prolific African American who gained significant attention. At a relatively early age he positioned himself through reaching out to the broader African American population via his columns. What Manning understood, and something that he explained to me a long time ago, was that Black newspapers are regularly looking for good material. What he chose to do, which many other Black radicals ignored, was reaching out to the Black press and inserting a left/progressive point of view. That meant winning over publishers, many of who were/are relatively conservative and do not spontaneously gravitate to radical ideas.

Marable followed three courses. One was to make a name for himself in the academy as an exceptional scholar. Second, he recognized the importance of and worked at the building a Left. He was never a Marxist-Leninist and, as such, was not involved in the revolutionary party-building efforts of the 1970s and 1980s. His politics were complicated, even when he was in the Democratic Socialists of America. In essence he was a Marxist looking to create a mass, left-wing formation that was thoroughly anti-racist and anti-sexist. He was concerned with and critical of *vanguard-ism*, as he saw it, among so many radicals, not only in the USA, but overseas. In fact, his book about African and Caribbean politics goes through an important analysis of the collapse of the Grenadian Revolution, the sources of which involved elements of what came to be known as the "crisis of socialism," including but not limited to vanguard-ism.

Marable was very influential in the early stages of the Committees of Correspondence for Democracy and Socialism, a formation that resulted from a split in the Communist Party, USA. Although Marable had never been a member of the Communist Party, he hoped that CCDS would become a mechanism for a Left realignment and the building of a mass, radical, transformative project.

This was also the same person who was at the core of initiating the Black Radical Congress, an effort to create a front or coalition of Black leftists ranging from left nationalists to non-nationalist communists. If anything could be said of Marable, it was that he approached this in a non-sectarian manner, even where he had differences with individuals (and groups) from other tendencies.

The final of the three courses was Marable's commitment to *entering into mainstream discourses from the Left.* Contrary to many leftists who are content to speak to themselves and their small groups, Marable sought to reach out to a broader range of the general public, from liberals on to the Left.

The intensity of the attacks on Marable, and particularly the personal nature of some of the attacks, actually represents a continuation of a struggle that took place in the Black Radical Congress (BRC) between 1998-2001. The BRC was a broad grouping of Black radicals that came together to engage in joint campaigns. Formed in June 1998, the BRC had a diverse leadership core that included Marable. Marable, one of the co-founders of the BRC, became one of the three co-chairs of the BRC. This leadership position meant that he was one of the spokespersons for the BRC but also one of its acknowledged leaders.

Within the BRC there were those who both disagreed with Marable but also resented him. The resentment may seem a bit strange to the reader, but that is why I began this essay with the story of the reaction of one person to Manning's death. The resentment appeared to have been rooted in a combination of factors that included the high visibility that Marable had achieved by the 1990s; his appointment to Columbia University and the fact that this raised his profile in New York City (and for some New Yorkers this is unpardonable if one is not from New York, a point I can make as someone born and raised in New York); and, even more ironically, that Manning refused to stay in the box of being a traditional academic but instead insisted on being directly involved with the construction of a movement.

In addition to resentment, there were strategic differences within the BRC. These differences were quite natural for an organization that had the ideological breath of the BRC. The BRC was not a cadre organization and membership included people with very divergent views. In and of itself, this should not have been a problem. The problem, however, lay in how differences were handled.

Manning came under assault for an orientation that was reflected in his writing. He was intent on making the BRC a politically relevant formation by which he and many others meant that it would be a recognizable force in the Black Freedom Movement and would represent a legitimate pole of Left opinion in Black America and beyond. Such an approach necessitated alliances with forces far broader than the traditional Left. It included outreach to more liberal forces as well as other social movements, including the NAACP and organized labor. It also meant connecting with progressive Black Democratic politicians.

Manning's view stood in contrast with an alternative approach, or approaches. One alternative view was that which saw the BRC as needing to be more purist in its left-wing politics. For this segment, it was enough for the BRC to articulate the 'correct line' but there was less interest in interacting with forces outside of the BRC who were not on the Left. Those articulating such a view did not come from one particular group or represent one particular tendency. On both sides of the divide there were nationalists, communists, socialists, liberation theologians, feminists, etc. What split these two tendencies revolved more around something that Rosa Luxemburg called "revolutionary Realpolitik." To what extent should a formation like the BRC, or for that matter any other mass Left-wing formation, attempt to be a real political force with clear leftist politics vs. remaining a refuge for the tried and true? To what extent would the BRC roll up its sleeves and get a bit dirty interacting with those with whom it had political differences but might share some agreement on a specific set of issues? Manning favored taking the risk of such an engagement, and for that reason—often combined with other sources (mentioned earlier)—he came under attack. The attacks became so personal that Manning ultimately decided that both due to his growing concerns with his health (the sarcoidosis) and his determination to write the Malcolm X biography, that it was no longer worth it to subject himself to such a barrage.

MX attempts to speak to a broad audience. It is not directed at the Black Left, though certainly many members of the Black Left have been reading it. It seeks an audience within Black America and beyond who are and have been trying to understand this remarkable historical figure, Malcolm X.

Yet there is another side to *MX* that relates to the strategic differences that emerged in the BRC (noted earlier). To some extent Marable was attempting to better understand the strategic challenges that Malcolm confronted in attempting to build a Black radical pole to lead the Black Freedom Movement. The lost pages from the *Autobiography*, Malcolm's interest in electoral politics; and, Malcolm's embrace of Pan Africanism were not isolated ideas or notions, but reflected an effort by Malcolm to fashion a strategic vision and direction that would root the Black radical movement he sought to build within the larger currents of Black America. His announced intention, for instance, of supporting Civil Rights workers in the South was a significant step taken to build a bridge in the Black Freedom Movement. Rather than castigating Black liberals and progressives who followed Dr. King, by 1964 Malcolm saw a chance for his brand of Black radicalism (with a nationalist bent, since it is important to note that there was Black radicalism already within the "King" camp of both similar and different bents) to directly link with and influence other tendencies within Black America. I believe that this is one thing that made Malcolm most intriguing for Marable.

How to use MX?

In the fall of 2010, as Manning was recovering from his lung transplant, we spoke about his forthcoming book. I suggested to him that the book could become an important instrument for advancing a discussion about the state of Black America, but more specifically, the future of Black radical politics. In that light, I went on to suggest that the book should not simply be promoted through personal appearances by him, but that there should be activists and scholars around the country who were enlisted in building events and studies, using the book to move a discussion that needs to happen. While Manning was intrigued with this approach, for a variety of reasons he was unable to do anything about it.

One of the best tributes to Manning, and for that matter one of the best ways of honoring the memory of Malcolm X, would be to use the book precisely for discussions about the future of Black radicalism; its relationship to other progressive movements in the USA; and the relationship of Black American radicalism to the domestic and global movements of the world's "colored peoples." This certainly does not mean that everyone has to agree with me that *MX* is a fabulous book. What it does entail, however, is stepping back from the innuendo, personal jealousies, and trivial pursuits, and focusing instead on the issues that the book raises. Here are a few issues that have preoccupied me since reading the manuscript and then the final book:

1. What is the balance between charismatic leadership and democratic organization?

2. What do we mean by "Black political power" in the era of Obama, racial backsliding, and right-wing populism?

3. What sort of alliances can be built both within Black America as well as within the USA that advance the interests of the majority of African Americans?

4. What does 21st century Pan Africanism look like? What is its relevance to the domestic Black Freedom struggle?

5. How should issues of gender be addressed in ways that are more than symbolic?

6. How do we understand the role of the State and what are the implications of that analysis for public, political activity?

7. How does Black radicalism come to, once again, resonate within the Black working class?

Discussing issues, such as these (and this is not an exclusive list), can advance our movement. *MX* can become an instrument to help us further our journey. Twisting words, ignoring the scope of Marable's works, and settling personal, private, and largely irrelevant accounts does nothing more than demonstrate that some critics have allowed themselves to ultimately become condemned to irrelevancy.

Dragging Malcolm X to Obamaland
Glen Ford

In packaging the life of Malcolm X for a wide audience, the late Dr. Manning Marable has presented us with an opportunity to reignite the debate over the meaning of Black self-determination, a discussion-through-struggle that effectively ended when the Black Freedom Movement became no longer worthy of the name. Unfortunately, it appears this was not Dr. Marable's intention, since *Malcolm X: A Life of Reinvention* is largely an attempt to render useless the vocabulary of Black struggle. Essential terms such as "self-determination," "Black nationalism," "revolutionary" and "empowerment" lose their meaning, abused and misused in order to portray the great Black Nationalist leader as inexorably evolving into a "race-neutral" reformer on the road to Obamaland.

This article does not address the complaints of those angered by Marable's insistence that Malcolm X had a youthful homosexual relationship with an affluent white man, although it is shocking that Marable would throw this in the mix based on wholly inferential evidence and the author's own psychological speculations. Our overarching concern is that Malcolm's politics has been distorted by often clumsy, sometimes clever manipulation of the language of struggle, so that the politics of today's left-reformers and Obama supporters, like Marable, appears vindicated.

Marable's interventions in Malcolm's mental processes begin in earnest on page 285, in the "Chickens Coming Home to Roost" chapter. It is early 1964, and Malcolm is contemplating a final break with the Nation of Islam. Marable takes over as the Black icon's muse, deconstructing Black Muslim theological doctrine, as he speculates Malcolm must have struggled to do, and concluding that "a new religious remapping of the world based on orthodox Islam would not necessarily stigmatize or isolate the United States because of its history of slavery and racial discrimination. Instead of a bloody jihad, a holy Armageddon, perhaps America could experience a nonviolent, bloodless revolution."

While Malcolm was certainly questioning the catechism of inevitable, white man-scorching, Allah-directed Armageddon, it is another thing entirely to have Malcolm pondering a "bloodless revolution" in America. Malcolm derided those who conceived of revolution as anything other than bloody, and he was speaking in secular, not religious, terms. His best-known speech on the subject is "Message to the Grassroots," November 10, 1963.

"There's no such thing as a nonviolent revolution. [The] only kind of revolution that's nonviolent is the Negro revolution. The only revolution based on loving your enemy is the Negro revolution. The only revolution in which the goal is a desegregated lunch counter, a desegregated theater, a desegregated park, and a desegregated public toilet; you can sit down next to white folks on the toilet. That's no revolution. Revolution is based on land. Land is the basis of all independence. Land is the basis of freedom, justice, and equality."

Malcolm never did accept the notion of revolution as bloodless, nor did he recognize the fight against segregated public accommodations as revolutionary. But Marable tries to convince us that Malcolm must have contemplated a reformist political path in his mind, if not in practice. This is William Styron-style biography, as Morgan State University's Dr. Jared Ball has suggested, with Malcolm forced to play Styron's Nat Turner.

By 1964 Malcolm had made a strategic decision to support Black integrationist efforts, at least rhetorically, but there is nothing that leads us to think that integration had become his end-goal, or that he believed integration was revolutionary. He had decided to become part of the broad "movement," in order to both influence and benefit from it. Marable would have us believe (page 298) that Malcolm's public endorsement of desegregation and voter drives signified that he had scaled down his liberationist aspirations, or that he thought voting equals or leads to African American self-determination—some very faulty logic. Revolutionary Marxists have also seen the value in electoral politics at certain junctures, but that didn't mean they stopped preparing for the forceful overthrow of the bourgeoisie. Nevertheless, Marable tells us that Malcolm's movement activities "marked an early, tentative concession to the idea that perhaps blacks could someday become empowered within the existing system."

The clear inference is that Malcolm was wilting in his desire to wipe "the existing system" off the map. What existing system does Marable refer to, precisely? White supremacy? Capitalism? Bourgeois electoral pay-for-play democracy? Marable keeps Malcolm's mind vague and cloudy, although in his actual historical voice the "evolving" Malcolm hates capitalism and U.S. imperialism more intensely than did the "old," Nation of Islam Malcolm. Marable also introduces his trick word "empowered," which he will use repeatedly in the book to confuse, rather than clarify. Blacks "could someday become empowered within the existing system"—to do what? To determine their collective destinies? To defy white majorities? To push aside the rule of capital? Marable tries to cage Malcolm, while assuring us that the revolutionary Black Nationalist was "tentatively" becoming a liberal reformer.

Gratuitous, non-defensive violence, in Malcolm's NOI talks, always came from the hand of Allah. Malcolm never rejected the right of self-defense; otherwise, he would not have become Malcolm the icon. Marable knew this, so he again invades Malcolm's mind (page 302). "By embracing the ballot, he was implicitly rejecting violence, even if this was at times difficult to discern in the heat of his rhetoric."

What kind of violence was Malcolm rejecting? Certainly not defensive violence. And Malcolm had never publicly urged Blacks to commit unprovoked aggressions against whites. The purpose of Marable's sentence can only be to show alleged movement by Malcolm toward some state of non-volatility, which we are expected to associate with political moderation: reform.

Marable grows so bold in pushing his back-to-the-future reformist fantasies, by page 333 he describes a Malcolm X who has become "race-neutral." On May 23, 1964 Malcolm spoke at Chicago's Civic Opera House, telling a crowd of 1,500 people, "Separation is not the goal of the Afro-American, nor is integration his goal. They are merely methods toward his real end—respect as a human being." Malcolm went on the say: "Unless the race issue is quickly settled, the 22 million American Negroes could easily adopt the guerilla tactics of other deprived revolutionaries." Not that he necessarily advocated that. (wink)

Three days before he was assassinated, Malcolm said, "I'm man enough to tell you that I can't put my finger on exactly what my philosophy is now." But, not to worry, Dr. Marable has the vision and the answer. He concluded that Malcolm had "made his race-neutral views clear in Chicago." There is no rational basis for Marable's amazing interpretation, other than he thought it moved his political story line on Malcolm's evolution (or race-neutralization) forward.

The opposite of race-neutral, Malcolm lived and died a Race-Man, meaning simply that he put the Race first. As he wrote to an Egyptian Muslim Brotherhood luminary who was disappointed that Malcolm was so decidedly non-race-neutral, "As a black American, I do feel that my first responsibility is to my twenty-two million fellow black Americans." (p. 368)

In the final "Reflections on a Revolutionary Vision" chapter,

Marable speaks for himself—in the process confirming that he has been sneaking his own words, thoughts and politics into Malcolm's head for four hundred pages. The Columbia University professor of African American Studies claims to know what Malcolm really, really wanted: "What Malcolm sought was a fundamental restructuring of wealth and power in the United States—not a violent social revolution, but radical and meaningful change nevertheless."

Although the description is so vague, wishy-washy and—damnit!!—so soft and noncommittal as to bear no resemblance to any incarnation or developmental stage of Malcolm X, it fits the self-image of Manning Marable and his circle perfectly. They are the left Black Obamites, purported radicals who have a perpetual love affair with power. Such people cannot imagine that others are not as enamored of power as they are, and are eager to graft their own vacillations and corruptions onto others, by rhetorical hook or literary crook.

If this assessment seems harsh, it is certainly not as outrageous as Marable's gall in superimposing his politics on Malcolm X. Even when Marable speaks in his own voice, he manages to intimate that Malcolm would agree with him. "If legal racial segregation was permanently in America's past," wrote Marable on page 486, "Malcolm's vision today would have to radically redefine self-determination and the meaning of black power in a political environment that appeared to many to be 'post-racial.'"

Marable appears to think these are heavy questions, but they're actually products of an unfocused, but deeply biased, mind. First of all, legal segregation was defeated before Malcolm's death, and no sane person at the time thought it would be brought back. Malcolm had time to find out what life was like for Black southerners without state-sanctioned Jim Crow. Marable's question is badly put. If he means, what would Malcolm think about today's levels of segregation? Then the answer would be that the northern cities would remain very familiar to him in their racial composition, and are in fact blacker than in Malcolm's day—which might tend to indicate to Malcolm that self-determination was an even more critical concern.

Still, Marable insists that Malcolm would be forced to redefine self-determination and its sibling, Black Power. But self-determination, as a foundational principle of relations among peoples, requires no redefinition. Marable understands it as "the right of oppressed nations or minorities to decide for themselves their own political futures," and he agrees that Malcolm "never abandoned" the "ideal." Why then, would Malcolm in 2011 have to "redefine" self-determination and the "meaning of black power?"

Because the political environment "appeared to many to be post-racial?" Who is it that thinks the environment appears post-racial? If Marable is speaking of white people, or any non-African American people, their opinions cannot be cause for "redefinition" of another people's right. If he meant that Black people in the mass believe we live in a post-racial nation, he was a damn fool. But even if such Black folks existed, that would not require a redefinition of self-determination. African Americans would simply "determine" that they love post-racialism and want to do nothing to change it, as is their self-determinationist right.

Marable risks looking stupid simply to make the intended point that Malcolm and his Black Nationalism and self-determination talk are passé and should be dismissed except as historical artifacts. For Marable and his Black left Obamites, Malcolm's only other use is to somehow authenticate today's reformers—and even President Obama!—as heirs to yesterday's revolutionary Black nationalists. This is the purpose put to Malcolm by Peniel Joseph, the Tufts University professor of history and author of *Dark Days, Bright Nights: From Black Power to Barack Obama*, which attempts to draw a straight-line historical connection between Malcolm X and the corporate politician in the White House.

Manning Marable was up to the same trick. "Given the election of Barack Obama," Marable writes on page 486, "it now raises the question of whether blacks have a separate political destiny from their white fellow citizens." He does not explain why Black destinies have changed just because a Black Democrat who raised more corporate money than the Republican won a presidential election. How did that electoral fact entwine Black/white destinies in ways that did not previously exist? How were the Black masses empowered by Obama's victory, and if they were somehow empowered, why would that draw them closer to whites?

It would have been better for Marable to have left out his last chapter of Reflections—it reflected badly on his powers of reasoning.

Finally, Marable attempts to create artificial space between Malcolm X and his direct political progeny, the Black Panther Party for Self Defense. On page 403 he wrote: "Had Malcolm continued to mainstream his views, it is unclear how he would have negotiated relations a few years later with the Black Panthers, a group born of much of the intellectual framework Malcolm had assembled in the early to mid-1960s."

It is nearly impossible to conceive of a Black Panther Party had there not been a Malcolm X. Marable insults a generation of Blacks who came into political consciousness in the Sixties—a cohort to which he chronologically belonged. He substitutes his imagined, inferred, reinterpreted Malcolm for the man whose words and bearing called forth and virtually sculpted the youthful Party that debuted in the year following his death. Marable projects Malcolm as if he would be a stranger to the Panthers, with whom he would have to "negotiate," when Malcolm's life tells us it is far more likely that the emergence of a militant revolutionary nationalist youth movement that spoke his language—because they learned it largely from him—would compel Malcolm to take the struggle to an even "higher level."

Marable's Revolutionary Malcolm
Rhone Fraser

Manning Marable said in his seminal biography *Malcolm X: A Life of Reinvention* that the view that Malcolm was evolving into an integrationist, liberal reformer is wrong (Marable, 482). His five hundred plus pages of meticulous scholarship and research that utilized qualitative and quantitative methods is a testament to Malcolm's revolutionary vision. By Charles V. Hamilton's definition, a "revolutionary" is one who believes that "progressive change can only come by the use of calculated acts of instrumental violence " (McCartney, 112). While Marable may not focus on all of the revolutionary aspects of Malcolm's life, his presentation and analysis of Malcolm's life provides a very important blueprint about how to live as a revolutionary that should not be disregarded.

First, they have to be raised in a politically conscious environment run by people that seek progressive change in American society. Marable writes how Malcolm was raised by a father who thought it necessary to write to his president when disagreeing with his policies. Marable writes that when Malcolm was barely two years old, Earl Little, his father, wrote to President Calvin Coolidge on June 8, 1927 asking for Marcus Garvey to be released. This environment allowed for a second important characteristic of a revolutionary, and that is a fearlessness in confronting those who run institutions of white supremacy directly. Marable shows us clearly how Earl Little confronted Coolidge. Little's letter to Coolidge had something to do with his son Malcolm's decision to write President Harry Truman in 1950, in a much more militant tone, critiquing his military invasion of Korea, as Marable writes (Marable, 95). He also shows us how one two occasions, Malcolm confronted white supremacist institutions, once before the local draft board on June 1, 1943, when he was only seventeen. Malcolm rejects the U.S. military's effort to draft him to fight World War II when he tells a psychiatrist mockingly: "I want to get sent down South. Organize them nigger soldiers, you dig? Steal us some guns and kill us some crackers!" (58). Marable writes how Malcolm, by letter writing, directly confronts white supremacist institutions by rejecting its efforts to deny him his religious and intellectual freedom. His bold activism came from his father's willingness to confront white supremacy. Malcolm's demand that the New York Police provide medical treatment to Johnson X Hinton is another significant example of confronting white supremacy on a personal level.

According to Marable's biography of Malcolm, revolutionaries, third, have to be able to notice and develop hatred of the colonial structure of American society. As Marable shows more of Malcolm's life after prison, he shows more and more how Malcolm looked at American society as a racist colony based on the oppression of African Americans. He was granted parole from Charlestown on the condition that he works with his brother Philbert at Cut Rate Department store. While at Cut Rate Malcolm is able to perceive how the relationship between the store owners and its customers is both racial and colonial: "it was a shame, the way they paid three and four times what the furniture had cost, because they could get credit from those Jews" (100). He also called the police in Harlem an "occupying army" (335). On May 12, 1961 Malcolm presents a critique of the mainstream two party system role in the U.S. colony. This critique is still true today, about the Democrats being foxes and the Republicans being wolves: "the only difference is that the fox will eat you with a smile instead of a scowl" (240). Marable writes later that Malcolm "sincerely believed that blacks and other oppressed Americans had to break from the existing two-party system" (405). Breaking from this two party system was based on hating the underlying colonial relationship that U.S. society depended on. He described the gains that Blacks made in acquiring higher education, positions in the U.S. Congress as evidence of a "Negro revolution" and not a real one, which was a Black revolution. His hatred of the colonial structure moved him to notice, "it was the U.S. government and white liberals that controlled the Negro revolution" (264, 272).

To oppose this colonial relationship, Marable quotes Malcolm on March 16, 1964 saying at Harvard that the Black man had to "control the politics in his own residential areas by voting...and investing in the businesses within the Negro areas" (299). Marable shows that, for Malcolm, the work of a revolutionary must include working within the electoral system as well as working outside of it. He did this also in Africa and the Middle East, when he was able to work with the politically conservative ruling class of Saudi Arabia as well as the Muslim Brotherhood in Egypt. The former was very much outside of the revolutionary stream, and to maintain positive relationships with both required exercising "considerable tact and political discretion" (368).

Marable presents a full spectrum of the Black freedom struggle from Malcolm to Bayard Rustin to Ella Baker and presents a fourth characteristic of a revolutionary and that is the importance of working with other reformists and radicals to work towards Black liberation. Marable writes that Malcolm made overtures "to Blacks outside the Nation...Malcolm made a consciously broad appeal, focusing not on the NOI, but on the Black people of Harlem, the Black people of America, and the Black people all over this earth" (160, 170). Malcolm debated and worked with Bayard Rustin, and did not ignore him or his work simply because his methods of achieving social change differed from his. Marable shows Malcolm's extraordinary interest in hosting Fidel Castro when he came to New York in 1960 and Che Guevara in 1964 (172, 394-5). This was the beginning of Malcolm's Pan Africanist practice of uniting all revolutionaries to reject colonial oppression by the United States and European nations.

Malcolm was also able to critique the colonial structure of African nations, particularly Congo, and how some African leaders friendly to Western interests would uncritically accept colonial society. He made sure his public statements and speeches sent the message, meant for Blacks, that collaboration with European or American colonists was not acceptable. He developed a hatred of the colonial system he observed not only in the United States, but also in Africa. Marable's unique look at Malcolm's travel diaries expose his important critique of the colonial relationship in Liberia and how the ruling class there held on to power. Malcolm writes, interestingly, from their perspective: "we don't want them [Black Americans like Malcolm] to interfere with our internal political structure. Our fear is that they may get into politics" (384). Marable was interested in showing Malcolm's hatred of the European colony in the U.S. and in Africa. He used the institution of the United Nations to try to achieve the revolutionary change that he saw in Africa in America. In a letter dated August 4, 1964, to his wife Betty Shabazz, Malcolm tells her to tell others to bring racial issues before the United Nations. He says he recognizes the difficulties in remaining abroad so long but "the gains outweigh the risks" (362). Marable implicitly, and necessarily I believe, critiques Malcolm's actions and how they were affecting his wife and his children. He presents a fifth characteristic of a revolutionary and that is the importance of personal dedication. While Marable is obviously not interested in questioning Malcolm's personal dedication to revolution, it is obvious that Malcolm's revolutionary work was divided by the expectations from his role as a father and husband. By showing this strain Marable shows that a personally dedicated revolutionary is one who should not let their revolutionary mission affect or be affected by their role as a husband and father. The strain made Malcolm more human. It also teaches me personally that giving one's life to the cause of revolution may disrupt meaningful family relationships. It shows that revolutionary work is serious and one should be prepared to relinquish relationships for it.

In describing Malcolm as a person, he shows how his revolutionary thought functioned within organizations. Within Marable's description of the organizations like the MMI and OAAU that Malcolm founded is an implicit critique of its organizational structure. Marable presents what I see as a sixth characteristic of a revolutionary, and that is one whose organizations are made of like-minded radicals and not only yes-men or yes-women. Marable writes that Malcolm would adopt "uncritically" A. Philip Randolph's model of top down leadership (193). We see the flaw in this approach, particularly when Marable later writes that following Malcolm's death, "neither the OAAU nor MMI had cultivated procedures of collective decision making and without Malcolm, the weak bonds that had held the groups together came apart (460). Marable shows us that revolutionaries need to work in an environment that will have a thorough contingency plan in the event that a designated leader is removed by murder as Malcolm was. Because he used a top-down leadership model, when the top failed, the entire group failed. Marable suggests that Malcolm's life teaches future revolutionaries to belong to groups that have a more democratic organizational structure that is prepared to continue revolutionary work despite any member's removal. Marable's biography also teaches future revolutionaries not to let revolution be sidetracked by internal dissension. This was evident in Marable's writing of the NYPD and the FBI who at one time "planted letters meant to corroborate Malcolm's supposed rumor mongering" about Elijah Muhammad (278). The NYPD and FBI also planted individuals in Malcolm's organizations, the NOI, MMI, and the OAAU, who would report back information that would be used to undermine the work of the MMI and the OAAU. They eventually succeeded, partly because of their aggressive violence, but also because of flaws in organizational structure that Marable as a biographer is able to present.

Marable's biography also, by his anti-sexist analysis of Malcolm's attitudes towards women, finally presents a seventh characteristic of revolutionary, as one that must work alongside women, perceiving them as equals, and not as foes only by virtue of them being women. Marable writes that Malcolm "viewed all women as inherently inferior and subordinate to males"(142). Marable shows how Malcolm was obviously ideologically influenced by Maya Angelou whom he met at the United Nations headquarters protesting the assassination of Patrice Lumumba (189-190). When he first met her he denounced her protest, yet within three years of meeting her, he adopted the same strategy she used of seeking rights for Blacks by appealing to the United Nations (383). Malcolm came to use this strategy of appealing to the United Nations yet neither he nor Marable engage the possibility that Angelou's strategy could have influenced Malcolm. Marable shows how ideological influence on revolutionaries is not limited by sex or gender.

Finally, by Marable's omission of Malcolm's important response to a South African reporter, he presents an eighth characteristic of a revolutionary: the importance of supplying the mainstream media with *limited* information about revolutionary work. While Marable quotes this interview with the *Johannesburg Sunday Express*, he does not mention Malcolm's revolutionary work in it. In it reporter Alan Scholefield asks Malcolm whether he's given moral or physical aid to African revolutionaries. Malcolm, now aware of the hostile U.S. presence to his work, replies: "I'd rather not answer that" (Clark, ed., 70). Malcolm gives Scholefield limited information about details of his revolutionary work so as not to give the political enemy ammunition to stop this work.

In summary, Marable's biography on Malcolm shows us that revolutionaries tend to be raised in a politically conscious environment; they must fearlessly confront white supremacy at a personal level; they develop a hatred of the colonial relationship between Blacks and whites in the U.S. and abroad; they have work with radicals within as well as outside the electoral system; they have to be personally dedicated; they have to have a more democratic organizational structure that is prepared to continue revolutionary work despite any member's removal; they have to perceive women as equals who are more than capable of wielding ideological influence; they have to be careful about what they tell the mainstream media.

All influential revolutionaries, including Malcolm X, were grounded and raised in some religious institution. For John Brown it was the Protestant church; for Harriet Tubman the church of liberation theology; for Malcolm it was Islam. What Marable shows in Malcolm's life is not to discard the role of institutionalized religion, but to understand and strengthen its role in revolutionizing society. While he eschewed their lukewarm politics, Malcolm still utilized the teachings he learned from the NOI relating to a sober diet and sober sexual life, and he practiced them.

Critics of Marable's book tend to want dismiss the whole book because Marable *did* not write a revolutionary the way they wanted him to write it, even if they did not muster the amount of research and energy that Marable put into Malcolm's life.

As a same-gender loving (SGL) Christian academic, I can appreciate what Marable presents on several levels. First, I appreciate the similarities Marable presents between Malcolm's life and the life of another significant revolutionary, Jesus Christ. Also like Jesus, Malcolm hated the system set up by the "moneychangers" who arbitrarily set the value of the currency in a way that would keep them rich. "Moneychangers" today represent the Federal Reserve, composed of privately owned banks that make record profits by stealing federal revenues. They do this by flooding congress with the lobbyists funded by the industries their monies support. These corporate lobbyists lobby Congress and the White House to prioritize corporate tax cuts over social programs. Like Jesus, Malcolm hated this kind of influence and worked to revolutionize it. Also like Jesus, Malcolm was betrayed by forces that were once close to him. I appreciate significant similarities between Judas' role in the death of Jesus by the Roman state and Elijah Muhammad's role in the death of Malcolm by the American state.

Malcolm also teaches me the importance of being a citizen lobbyist. His letters to Truman and to elected officials teaches me the importance of staying abreast of political issues and using my constitutional right of free speech to fight imperialism. On a personal level, I appreciate Marable's inclusion of Malcolm's relationship to Paul Lennon because it necessarily shows how Malcolm not only challenged European colonial empire, but its strictly proscribed heterosexual gender norms also. Because of our being historically denied a healthy wholesome heterosexual relationship for generations due to enslavement and Jim Crow, many Black men rightfully feel a burden to publicly proclaim themselves and our heroes like Malcolm as strictly heterosexual. However Marable suggests through his study of Malcolm's life that our most important struggle today is a revolutionary anti-imperialist struggle, regardless of our sexual orientation or preference. Marable seems to say that being preoccupied with others' sexuality, including Malcolm's, inhibits very necessary revolutionary work that the mainstream American system actively discourages. James Baldwin wrote that the American ideal of manhood is so "paralytically infantile" that it prevents boys from becoming men (Baldwin, 815). The Malcolm that Marable presents questions this American ideal of manhood that, ultimately, uncritically upholds American empire because it suggests that Malcolm was still influential even though he was not strictly heterosexual. Marable questions the notion that Malcolm was less of a man or a revolutionary because he had same sex relations. Marable thought it necessary to include mention of Lennon because he wanted to write as comprehensive a biography as possible about Malcolm. Marable's choice to include Malcolm's relationship with Paul Lennon however should never distract us from the more important blueprint Marable provides through Malcolm about how to live as a revolutionary.

References

Baldwin, James. *James Baldwin: Collected Essays.* New York: Library of America, 1998.

Clark, Steve, ed. *February 1965: The Final Speeches, Malcolm X.* New York: Pathfinder, 1992.

Marable, Manning. *Malcolm X: A Life of Reinvention.* New York: Viking, 2011.

McCartney, John T. *Black Power Ideologies: An Essay in African-American PoliticalThought.* Philadelphia: Temple, 1992.

Manning Marable: Humanizing Malcolm or Denigrating Legacies?
Kelly Harris

When you come for the king, you best not miss.
—Omar (The Wire)

One of the most recognized faces and voices in U.S. history is that of Malcolm X. Since his assassination on February 21, 1965 his stature has grown. Countless interviews with "friends" and enemies have been mined as scholars, activists, and family members have sought to capture the historical significance of Malcolm's life. Because Malcolm was killed before his autobiography hit the press, he was not afforded an opportunity to speak for himself with regard to filling the voids or addressing the piqued curiosities created by his autobiography. Questions about his life, the Nation of Islam (NOI), and his evolution were never asked of, or answered by him, directly. This created a void that scholars interminably attempt to fill with a combination of research and speculation on the life of Malcolm X.

With all that has been written and said about Malcolm X, there are a few grounded truths that have been deemed irrefutable. For years scholars of the Black Power Movement located the beginnings of Black Power with Malcolm X. The years between 1965 and 1972 are generally viewed as a reasonable estimate of the time period that marks the movement although recent work has challenged that assumption.[1] 1965 marks the death of Malcolm and the beginnings of urban unrest that could be relied on every summer as if it were its own season. Numerous local, national, and international organizations such as the Revolutionary Action Movement (RAM), African Liberation Support Committee (ALSC), the Republic of New Afrika, Us, and the Black Panther Party were created and committed to Black Nationalism and Pan-Africanism, and they all were inspired by the objectives of Malcolm X.

The groundswell of activism that coalesced around Black Nationalism became visible on college campuses as students demanded Black professors and classes that spoke to their issues. Black scholars challenged the status quo in education and many viewed their particular disciplines as incapable of providing the context to address the challenges Black people were confronted with, and to provide alternatives. The culmination of these forces resulted in the beginning of Black Studies as an academic discipline dedicated to the liberation of the global African community.[2] In addition to the Black Studies Movement, some Black scholars in other disciplines were trying to apply a Black or African centered framework.[3] These scholars sought to break the shackles of Eurocentric education and use their scholarship to solve the problems confronting Black people. The concepts they would use reflected an attempt to be revolutionary and not carry the water for the status quo. Liberation, Revolution, Black Power, White Supremacy, and African centered, et. al. became a part of the scholarly lexicon in an attempt to create a "Black Social Science" grounded in the African worldview.[4]

Black scholars understood very well the challenge posed by worldviews and paradigms.[5] However, the push for creating a "Black Social Science" had a brief shelf life as did the Black Power Movement. While Afrocentricity would grow to be a force in Black Studies, the whole notion of there being an African centered paradigm based on an African worldview has lost traction in academia. Post-Modernists, Neo-Marxists, and various iterations of feminism in many ways are viewed as more legitimate approaches to examining phenomena than models grounded in the African worldview.[6] The result is that the importance of worldview has been taken for granted and scholarship about the African Diaspora and its descendants is disconnected from an objective such as liberation. It is in this context of worldview that Marable's work must be situated. Marable's well-known ideological bent towards Democratic Socialism as a paradigm colors his rendering of Malcolm's "Reinvention" and his assessment of Black Nationalism. It also accounts for his unfulfilled promises, technical shortcomings, and gross errors in the book.

Scholarship on Malcolm

Once any new work is published on Malcolm X a fair and obvious question is "what's new?" When one takes into account the work of Peter Goldman, Louis DeCaro Jr., John Henrik Clarke, Zak Kondo, Karl Evanzz, and Rodnell Collins it is noted that an assortment of resources were tapped.[7] The following sources were utilized by one or all of the authors:

- Interviews with people who knew pre-NOI Malcolm
- Interviews with people who knew NOI and post-NOI Malcolm
- FBI files

- Bureau of Special Services (BOSS)
- Detroit Police department FOIA files
- Department of State files on Malcolm X
- Manuscript and Oral Histories collections
- Audio and video recordings
- Newspaper accounts
- Television and radio transcripts

Therefore, any new work on Malcolm would be expected to use the aforementioned resources in new ways and/or discover and make use of new, untapped sources, which in this case might include:

- Private Letters
- Newly released or previously unexamined FBI and/or BOSS files
- Archival footage
- Travel Diaries
- New interviews of NOI, MMI, and OAAU members
- Unpublished material (i.e. missing chapters)

Marable does provide new interviews of key actors (i.e. Farrakhan, James 67x Warden, Max Stanford, et. al.), the first detailed exposition of Malcolm's travel diaries (which is powerful and will be discussed later in the article), and he gives effort to provide some insight into the missing chapters. These things could arguably warrant a "new material" qualifier for Marable's work. However, the depth and potency of "new" that garnered the attention and anticipation given to Marable's book was based on promises and premises that were not fulfilled.

Unfulfilled Promises

Marable makes the case that the previous books on Malcolm, particularly the autobiography, fail to sufficiently interrogate the contours of Malcolm's evolution, hence, the title "Life of Reinvention." More to the point is that Marable indicts Haley's motives for writing the book by recasting Haley as being duplicitous, interjecting his integrationist and republican sentiments, and for leaving out three missing chapters. In an interview on Democracy Now! on May 21, 2007 Marable says that "Haley and white journalist Alfred Balk were approached by the Chicago office of the FBI to funnel misinformation that was critical of the nation." Marable however, is not convincing in his attempts to expose Haley. First Marable unambiguously points out that:

> By building up Malcolm's role at Muhammad's expense, and suggesting a possible internal conflict, "Black Merchants of Hate" fostered even greater jealousy and dissent within the NOI's ranks: exactly what the FBI had hoped for when it agreed to feed information to Balk.[8]

Earlier, on page 220, Marable states that "the Bureau agreed to funnel them selective information about the NOI, based on its years of covert surveillance, but none of it could be attributed." Interestingly, Marable cites his discussion from his work *Living Black History* as his source. In this work Marable goes into more detail yet, clearly argues that Balk contacted the FBI in October 1962. He cites an FBI memorandum but does not show any connection to Haley. If Haley did indeed know or encourage Balk's contacting the FBI, no corroborating evidence is provided by Marable. Marable also clearly states that Balk had been "recruited."[9] The reader is left to wonder by whom? Haley? The *Saturday Evening Post*? This is one of the many places where Marable speculates without any support. He also ignores Haley's own comments in the autobiography. Haley says it was the *Saturday Evening Post* that "teamed" him with Balk in 1961 and 1962.[10] It is quite possible that the *Saturday Evening Post* worked clandestinely with Balk and the FBI without Haley's knowledge. However, Marable does not consider this possibility.

The selling point for Marable in his Democracy Now! interviews and in *Living Black History* is that the autobiography is in fact three books. In contrast, he claimed his project would detail the "missing chapters" that Haley described as "lava-like." While Marable is very provocative concerning the missing chapters in the interviews, he ultimately fails with his treatment of the same in his book. To be fair, this has more to do with Detroit attorney Gregory Reed (owner of the chapters). Reed only allowed Marable to peruse the chapters for fifteen minutes. That clearly is not enough time for Marable (or anyone else) to fill in the blanks. As a result Marable is virtually silent on the contents of the missing chapters—promise unfulfilled.

Technical Shortcomings
While the strength of the work is with his usage of the travel diaries, Marable has a larger problem: the vast majority of the book rehashes what

we already know about Malcolm and shrinks from some topics, issues, and personalities where others have thrived. In constructing his narrative on the NOI history, Marable does not add anything to previous discussions by DeCaro or Evanzz. The strength of Evanzz's *The Messenger* was his documentation of Elijah's pre-NOI history. The NOI denies wholeheartedly any connection of Elijah with the Moorish Science Temple of America (MSTA), but Evanzz skillfully makes the case that Elijah Muhammad was indeed a member of the MSTA. While it is certainly understandable to limit the amount of time and attention given to Elijah's history, it makes just as much sense to probe his pre-NOI days and the constant scrutiny Elijah Muhammad was under from government agencies. Evanzz's work provides examples of Elijah's pre-incarceration discourse, which explicitly promised military attacks against the United States. While the fall of America continued to be a theme for the Nation, it seems that Elijah tweaked his discourse on America after his prison stint. In short, be sure to toe the line of radical discourse that is not seditious.[11] In this manner, the silencing of Malcolm within NOI becomes more nuanced than simply the personal ambitions and jealousies of NOI elite who surrounded Elijah. Here, the suggestion is that Malcolm's silencing certainly is connected to personal animosity toward Malcolm, but it may also be a reflection of Elijah's understanding the possible repercussions for the type of language Malcolm used. It can be added that Elijah's failure to allow the FOI to respond to attacks on NOI members by the police in NY and Los Angeles may also be reflective of his early NOI history.

There are other odd omissions by Marable. He clearly locates Joseph Gravitt-el (Captain Joseph and later Yusuf Shah) as an important figure in the Nation. Marable credits Gravitt as being a significant figure in helping Malcolm build new temples. More importantly he discusses seeds of Gravitt's later vitriol against Malcolm, stemming from Malcolm's suspension and public humiliation of Gravitt.[12] Marable fails to mention that Gravitt's father, Joseph Gravitt-el Sr. was a member of the MSTA and friend of Elijah Muhammad. Thus, Marable does not offer much insight into Gravitt's subsequent promotion as the authority over all NOI temples in the Northeast. It is from Evanzz that we learn the promotion is probably due to Elijah and Gravitt Sr.'s relationship. Marable only discusses Captain Joseph's animosity without providing a fuller context.

The other actors that Marable fails to properly contextualize may seem correct at face value. Ernest 2x McGhee, Jeremiah Shabazz (Jeremiah Pugh), and Herman Ferguson are all mentioned in the work, and Ferguson is interviewed by Marable. To be fair to Marable, each of the above are noted more for their actions after the death of Malcolm than anything they did while he was alive. However, more information about them would have provided more insight into the Nation and in Ferguson's case, more insight into the influence of Malcolm X.

Ernest 2x McGhee, as mentioned by Marable, was the national secretary in the NOI who was replaced by John Ali.[13] McGhee, later Hamaas Abdul Khaalis, was a member of the famous NY Mosque #7 and was ousted as national secretary for having the temerity to suggest the nation become more orthodox. Not long after his split from the nation, Khaalis led a sect of the Hanafi Muslims in Washington, D.C. Khaalis' criticism of Elijah and the NOI became more vocal after the 1960s. It is then that Jeremiah Pugh (Shabazz), while well-known and a part of the NOI leadership, plays a role in the most infamous killings in D.C. history.[14] When Malcolm first moved to Philadelphia he lived with Shabazz for a year. Shabazz would later become the Nation's point man in the southern region of the U.S. Shabazz and Captain Joseph were two of Malcolm's most outspoken critics in the Nation. Their animosity is on display in a lecture "Biography of a Hypocrite."[15] Shabazz returned to Mosque #12, and it was during this period that the "Black Mafia" in Philadelphia thrived, while many of its members were simultaneously members of the NOI Mosque #12. The "Black Mafia" Muslims would later be found responsible for the killing of Hanafi Muslims in 1973.

Herman Ferguson is interviewed by Marable and cited a few times. Marable's omission here concerns Ferguson's history. He fails to inform the reader that Herman Ferguson (MMI and OAAU member) became a well-known activist in Black Nationalist circles with the RAM and Republic of New Afrika (RNA). To be sure some would argue that Ferguson's life after Malcolm is immaterial. Yet, a part of Malcolm's legacy is inextricably linked to those who actually organized with him. Sundiata Cha Jua points out that Marable is equally silent on Milton Henry.[16] Marable mentions that Henry was "a good friend of Malcolm's" and "a leader of the Freedom Now Party in Michigan."[17] He does not mention that Henry, along with his brother Richard (Imari Obadele) would form the RNA, which became a significant Black Nationalist organization. But Marable organizes his narrative in such a way that connections of this sort are marginalized and viewed as unimportant. One might consider this to be a little strange, or at least irresponsible on Marable's part, considering Malcolm's influence on Black Nationalism.

Gross Errors

An example of this tendency to minimize Malcolm's Black Nationalism is none more evident than Marable's mention of Malcolm's speech before the

Militant Labor Forum. The speech (April 8, 1964), according to Marable, is when Malcolm "sharply broke with the NOI mold. The public lecture had been sponsored by the Militant Labor Forum, the nonpartisan outreach group of the SWP."[18] Marable writes no more about the speech, apparently satisfied with making his point that Malcolm makes a sharp break with the NOI in this speech. Interestingly, Louis DeCaro discusses the same speech, but provides a very different perspective. DeCaro explains that during the question and answer period, an elderly white man put forth a test of Malcolm's newfound humanism. He "suggest[ed] that, under Malcolm's direction, the entire audience should rise for one moment in honor of a white minister who had recently died...during a civil rights protest."[19] DeCaro provides Malcolm's response:

> We're not going to stand up and applaud any contribution made by some individual white person when 22 million black people are dying every day. What [the dead civil rights worker] did—good. Hooray, hooray, hooray. Now Lumumba was murdered, Medgar Evers was murdered, my own father was murdered. You tell that stuff to someone else. It's time that some white people started dying in this thing.[20]

Marable's willingness to describe this speech as marking a sharp break ignores that while Malcolm was developing new ideas, tactics, and strategies at a fast clip, he still held on to his Black Nationalist sensibilities.

Marable's most egregious errors are evident in his espousing of the more salacious parts of the book. This has raised questions for scholars and activists about what should or should not be off limits in a biography and what should be the threshold for proof. Unquestionably, Malcolm's iconic image of Black manhood is the source of the visceral reactions to Marable's claims.[21] Clearly, Marable is simultaneously on firm and shaky ground. Marable is on firm ground when discussing the marital problems between Malcolm and Betty insofar as his source is none other than Malcolm himself. Marable is on shaky ground when it comes to describing Malcolm's "relationship" to William Paul Lennon. His first problem is that he describes an "intimate relationship" between Malcolm and Lennon. What constitutes a relationship? Second, Marable claims that the evidence is "circumstantial but strong."[22] This circumstantial evidence is based on Malcolm "Shorty" Jarvis. Jarvis was Malcolm's partner in the burglary ring who was only caught because Malcolm gave the names of his accomplices. Jarvis was clearly upset at Malcolm and one has to at least question his forthrightness. Furthermore, Marable assumes that Malcolm was lying about the "Rudy" character in his autobiography and actually describing himself. DeCaro assumes that "Rudy" was Francis "Sonny" Brown, another partner in Malcolm's burglary ring. DeCaro adds that Bruce Perry, the author who first makes claims concerning Malcolm's sexuality, "presents many interviews, but it is clear that he weighed neither the integrity nor reliability of his interviewees and apparently used even the most controversial recollections without informing the reader of possible bias."[23] Amazingly, Marable thinks the same source is credible enough to call it convincing. Karl Evanzz included an episode in the *Judas Factor* where Malcolm was receiving fellatio from gay men during his Detroit Red days. However, Evanzz, in an interview with the author, states that he intends to take that part out of the next edition of the *Judas Factor*. According to Evanzz, his source was Rodnell Collins. After his book was published he found out that Collins was basing his information solely on the word of Malcolm Jarvis.[24]

In his zeal to "humanize" Malcolm, Marable utilizes an off the record source. On page 379 Marable states "According to Max Stanford...Betty charged in and accused Shifflett and an OAAU secretary of sleeping with Malcolm." Peculiarly Marable does not cite an interview for this source. Stanford, in an interview with this author, said that his comments to Marable were off the record. This makes sense when one considers Marable's discussion of RAM. Malcolm's revealing of NOI issues, ostensibly Elijah's dalliances, "threatened to destroy a potential relationship with Stanford's group."[25] It would then make no sense for Stanford to feel unease about Malcolm publically revealing salacious details, and then turn around and do the same.

The strength of Marable's work and where he flourishes is in his excellent job of creating a narrative based on Malcolm's travel diaries. The travel diaries, housed at the Malcolm X collection at the Schomburg Center, provide rare insight into Malcolm's thinking during his post-NOI life. In chapters 11-14, Marable uses the diaries and supplements them with interviews, private correspondence between Haley and Malcolm, and newspaper accounts of Malcolm's trips abroad. But, Marable does not provide much else to justify his implication that Haley was engaged in a duplicitous relationship with the FBI, nor does he support the sordid allegations about Malcolm's sex life, which only serve to denigrate his legacy. To make such bold claims, Marable needed more credible and reliable sources. In the final analysis, Marable adds little to the scholarly canon on Malcolm and raises more questions than he answers. Ultimately, the book fails to humanize Malcolm and denigrates the legacies of Malcolm X and Manning Marable.

Notes

1. Peniel Joseph, ed. *The Black Power Movement: Rethinking the Civil Rights- Black Power Era* (NY: Routledge, 2006); Timothy Tyson, *Radio Free Dixie: Robert F. Williams and the Roots of Black Power* (University of North Carolina Press, 1999); and William L. Van Deburg, *New Day in Babylon: The Black Power Movement and American Culture, 1965-1975* (Chicago: University of Chicago Press, 1992).

2. Nathaniel Norment, Jr., *The African American Studies Reader* (Durham, NC: Carolina Academic Press, 2001), introduction.

3. Joyce Ladner, ed. *The Death of White Sociology: Essays on Race and Culture* (Baltimore: Black Classic Press, 1998).

4. Claude Ake, *Social Science as Imperialism: A Theory of Political Development* (Ibadan, Nigeria: Ibadan University Press, 1979). This is an often overlooked work that provided a serious critique on the limitations of western social science.

5. Maulana Karenga addressed this issue in his 1988 essay "Black Studies and the problematic of Paradigm: The Philosophical Dimension." Karenga's discussion is rooted in the need for a paradigm specific to Black Studies and the world historical experience of African people.

6. Adolph Reed Jr. & Kenneth W. Warren, eds. *Renewing Black Intellectual History: The Ideological and Material Foundations of African American Thought* (Boulder: Paradigm Publishers, 2010). This work is the most recent challenge to the historic Black Studies paradigm. The editors argue that "much of the discursive strain associated with the frame of the African diaspora...relies on exceedingly thin intellectual or cultural history, naïve textual interpretations, nimble yet facile cultural analysis or other forms of metonymic fallacy to justify a claim that black Americans' beliefs and practices are most understood as nodes in a supraterritorial world of African descent."

7. Peter Goldman, *The Death and Life of Malcolm X* 2nd edition (Urbana: University of Illinois Press, 1979); Louis DeCaro Jr., *On the Side of My People: A Religious Life of Malcolm X* (New York: New York University Press, 1996); John Henrik Clarke, ed. *Malcolm X: The Man and His Times* (Africa World Press, 1991); Zak Kondo, *Conspiracys (Conspiracies): Unraveling the Assassination of Malcolm X* (Nubia Press, 1993); Karl Evanzz, *The Judas Factor: The Plot to Kill Malcolm X* (New York: Thunder's Mouth Press, 1992); Evanzz, *The Messenger: The Rise and Fall of Elijah Muhammad* (New York: Pantheon Books, 1999); Rodnell P. Collins and A. Peter Bailey, *Seventh Child: A Family Memoir of Malcolm X* (Kensington, 2002).

8 Manning Marable, *Malcolm X: A Life of Reinvention* (Viking, 2011), 231.

9. Manning Marable, *Living Black History* (New York: Basic *Civitas* Books, 2006), 150; and Marable, *Reinvention*, 220.

10. Malcolm X and Alex Haley, *The Autobiography of Malcolm X* (Ballentine Books, 1992), 443.

11. Evanzz, *The Messenger*, 93-145. The discourse I am discussing includes W. D. Fard.

12 Marable, *Reinvention*, 125-126.

13. Ali is the Judas mentioned by Louis Lomax in his work *When the Word is Given* and Karl Evanzz in *The Judas Factor*. While he is widely regarded as an agent, to date, there has been no evidence that he indeed was an agent. The case

against Ali, while convincing remains circumstantial. This probably explains Marable is careful not to indict Ali as an agent but does make clear Ali's animus towards Malcolm.

14. John King, The Breeding of Contempt: Account of the Largest Mass-Murder in Washington D.C. History (Xlibris Corp publisher, 2003); and Evanzz, *The Messenger*. King goes into great detail of the connection of Mosque #12 in Philadelphia, which at the time was under the leadership of Jeremiah Shabazz.

15. http://www.youtube.com/watch?v=Bqx7VErdjhs accessed on July 18, 2011.

16. Forum on *Malcolm X: A Life of Reinvention* at the Carter G. Woodson Library, Chicago, IL July 16, 2011.

17. Marable, *Reinvention*, 418.

18. Ibid., 305.

19. DeCaro, 283.

20. Ibid., 284.

21. What Marable tile "Reinvention" Wilson J. Moses in *Creative Conflict in African American Thought* views as a natural outgrowth of being a leader and public figure. Indeed, one might say simply being human. Moses argues that contradictions are bound to take place, particularly as the context changes. Reinventing oneself is thus inescapable and therefore not unique to Malcolm X.

22. Marable, *Reinvention*, 65-66.

23. DeCaro, 298. The reference to "Rudy" as possible "sonny" is on page 73.

24. Phone interview with Karl Evanzz on July 20, 2011.

25. Marable, *Reinvention*, 355; and Phone interview with Max Stanford, July 13, 2011.

Manning Marable's "Malcolm X"
Wil Haygood

Malcolm Little had a tragic childhood. His father, Earl, died in 1931 in a streetcar mishap that was quite possibly racially motivated. In 1939, when young Malcolm was 14, his mother, Louise, was taken away and confined to a mental hospital. The boy soon found himself in a foster home. By the time he had relocated to Massachusetts in 1941, his jagged spiral had begun. For several years he roamed, wolf-like, between Detroit, Washington, D.C., Harlem and Boston. His activities varied: selling dope, pimping, breaking into homes, hawking snacks on trains. In 1946, the doors of the Charlestown (Mass.) State Prison clanged behind Malcolm Little, putting an end to the foolishness. He would remain there for six years.

The reinvention of Malcolm Little—soon to become Malcolm X—began behind bars. "I don't think anybody ever got more out of going to prison than I did," he confided. Shortly after being freed, he became a rising star in the Nation of Islam, sent by its leader, Elijah Muhammad, up and down the East Coast to open mosques. Malcolm imbued Blacks with pride and offered an ultimatum to white America: Either "the ballot or the bullet" would transform American injustice. After hearing him, many Blacks, fed up with living under the American system of apartheid, joined the Nation.

But Malcolm X uncovered proof that Elijah Muhammad had impregnated at least half-a-dozen young Muslim women. Malcolm's decision to confront Muhammad set in motion their inevitable and dangerous split. Nation of Islam members believed Malcolm had been usurping Muhammad's popularity and plotting his own rise; Muhammad himself believed Malcolm was cozying up to mainstream civil rights leaders. Malcolm's celebrated visit to Mecca, which forced him to rethink his separatist leanings, further antagonized many Nation members. He had embarked on the path that led to his murder by Nation of Islam members on Feb. 21, 1965, at the Audubon Ballroom in Washington Heights.

Malcolm X's life has inspired filmmakers, writers, painters, rappers and dramatists, yet much about his murder has remained a mystery. Now we have Manning Marable's *Malcolm X*, a groundbreaking piece of work.

Marable, a historian who died three days before this book's publication, convinced people who had been silent for decades to sit for interviews. He also drew upon oral histories, dusty police reports and FBI and CIA documents. The result is not just a biography, but also a history of Muslims in America and a sweeping account of one man's transformation—and of the conspiracy, abetted by police inattention, that took his tumultuous life. The tension toward book's end—when Malcolm was trying to figure out who might murder him—is so gripping it nearly soaks through the pages.

At first, Elijah Muhammad saw Malcolm X as a gifted disciple with great potential and self-discipline. But Muhammad prided himself on getting the Nation to look inward; its followers would find love and attention inside the mosque. In contrast, political currents intrigued Malcolm, who particularly admired Harlem Congressman Adam Clayton Powell, Jr. "Elijah Muhammad," writes Marable, "could maintain his personal authority only by forcing followers away from the outside world; Malcolm knew that the Nation's future growth depended on its being immersed in the Black community's struggles of daily existence." Bypassing traditional civil rights leaders—Martin Luther King Jr., Whitney Young and Roy Wilkins—and often deriding them as "Uncle Toms," Malcolm appealed to urban Blacks in the ghetto. He warned in a 1957 speech that if the "Negro intelligentsia" didn't do something about Blacks being murdered in the South by white supremacists and discriminated against in the North by business owners, "the little man in the street will henceforth begin to take matters into his own hands." Soon the FBI and the New York police department were tracking Malcolm's movements and placing undercover agents inside the Nation.

Two incidents, in addition to Elijah Muhammad's infidelities, exacerbated the split between Malcolm X and Muhammad. The first came in 1962, when Ronald Stokes, an unarmed Muslim who was a friend of Malcolm's, was shot and killed by Los Angeles policemen in a parking lot. Malcolm wanted revenge, but Muhammad urged against it. Malcolm eventually joined with L.A. civil rights leaders to protest police brutality, a move that infuriated Muhammad. The second, more serious incident came in the aftermath of President Kennedy's assassination. Malcolm tried to blame the killing on U.S. military violence abroad; Kennedy's death, he said, was an example of "the chickens coming home to roost." Muhammad was livid. He believed that the authorities would strike back at Black Muslims, particularly those in prison, for Malcolm's words. He suspended Malcolm, and the suspension led to a convulsive split, with Malcolm eventually forming his own organizations.

Marable persuasively shows us the tightrope that Malcolm walked in the early 1960s. He would belittle civil rights leaders but also, after breaking with the Nation, would seek common ground with them. Marable does not shy away from Malcolm X's repugnant statements and actions, such as dismissing well-meaning whites who wanted to join his non-violent, Muslim-led crusade for equality; and his bizarre negotiations with the Ku Klux Klan, in 1961, to buy land for Blacks to live on.

Malcolm had also begun working on his autobiography with Alex Haley, one of the few Black writers able to get assignments from mainstream magazines. (One must not forget that at the time of Malcolm's struggles, the fields of law, medicine, journalism, university teaching, banking, finance and many others were difficult for American Blacks to penetrate.) The scenes of Haley and Malcolm sitting in Haley's New York apartment—two Black cats from different sides of the political divide—are priceless: Though glum about death threats and the safety of his family, Malcolm rises and jitterbugs to show Haley what he was like when he was known as Detroit Red. Marable challenges Malcolm's autobiography but offers no real surprises.

Marable works the reinvention motif into the book with authority. He accentuates Malcolm's fabled and life-changing journey to Mecca. "Malcolm was quick to credit Islam with the power to transform whites into nonracists," writes Marable. "This revelation reinforced Malcolm's new-found decision to separate himself completely from the Nation of Islam, not simply from its leadership, but from its theology."

Toward the end, many Nation of Islam members had ceased calling him "Brother Malcolm"; Malcolm X was now "a heretic." His house in Queens was firebombed—an event that Marable recreates with chilling effect. His murder was plotted—though not with the approval of Elijah Muhammad, Marable points out—a year in advance. Marable examines the evidence against a number of suspects and abettors, including informers, inefficient NYPD officials and the murderers themselves. This is tragic and shocking material: Some of the killers apparently remain at large while two of the convicted may have been innocent.

My only criticism of the book is that Marable did not tell us enough about Malcolm's family in the years following his death. That family has suffered much pain. In 1995, Qubilah, one of Malcolm's daughters, was charged with hiring a hit man to murder Louis Farrakhan, who had sided with Muhammad during the Malcolm contretemps. The case fell apart in court. Malcolm's widow, Betty Shabazz, died in 1997 from injuries suffered in a house fire set by her grandson Malcolm, Qubilah's son.

It will be difficult for anyone to better this book. It goes deeper and richer than a mere homage to Malcolm X. It is a work of art, a feast that combines genres skillfully: biography, true-crime, political commentary. It gives us Malcolm X in full gallop, a man who died for his belief in freedom, a man whom Marable calls the "fountainhead" of the Black power movement in America.

[First published in the *Washington Post*, 4/4/2011]

A Toothless Pursuit of A Revolutionary's Truths: Marable's *Malcolm X: A Life of Reinvention*
Errol A. Henderson

Manning Marable's *Malcolm X: A Life of Reinvention* is ostensibly intended to fill the biographical, philosophical and evidentiary chasm the author observes in much of the research on Malcolm X that has either singularly valorized or demonized him over the years since his death. He resisted what he saw as the construction on one hand of "a mythic legend to surround" Malcolm, which "erased all blemishes and any mistakes he had made"; and on the other hand, works that "simplistically equated" Malcolm with Martin Luther King, with "both advocating multicultural harmony and universal understanding."

The roots of the distortions of Malcolm's life and philosophy seem to lie in the duality and contradictions of Malcolm himself, which are myriad in Marable's telling and can only be briefly examined here. In one simplistic though innocuous dualism, Marable views Malcolm as "the embodiment of the two central figures of African American folk culture, simultaneously the hustler/trickster and the preacher/minister" (p. 11). In a less sanguine one, he views Malcolm as "a man who emphasized grassroots and participatory politics led by working-class and poor Blacks" (p. 9); but notes that "there was no tradition or practice of democratic decision making inside the MMI and OAAU." In a clearly pejorative example, Marable asserts that Malcolm develops a "commitment to gender equality" (p. 374); but is not committed to his wife (p. 423). The dualities that Marable observes inform and complicate Malcolm's life in ways that confound the simple trajectories of the narrative of Alex Haley's *Autobiography of Malcolm X* or popular conceptions that derive from it.

Depending on the observer, these dualities may be viewed as dialectical, developmental, disabling, or even destructive. But in large part, they are essential to the story of Malcolm X because for Marable they reflect, motivate, and reinforce Malcolm's tendency to "reinvent" himself both in his political and personal life. In fact, Marable projects "reinvention" as the central axis by which to interpret Malcolm's life given that Malcolm's life journey may be charted by his deliberate choices to "reinvent" himself.[1] Thus from orphaned child, to bright student, to hipster, to hustler, to petty criminal, to prisoner, to Black Nationalist, to NOI minister, to husband, to revolutionary leader, this "reinvention" is even manifest in his martyrdom and in the myriad representations of his life since his death.

But the difficulties in providing a more accurate assessment of Malcolm's life not only result from the dualisms of Malcolm, himself; for Marable, they are rooted in the persistence of prominent depictions of Malcolm epitomized in Haley's *Autobiography*. Marable views the celebrated work as more the product of Haley, "a liberal Republican" (p.9) who held the NOI's "racial separatism and religious extremism in contempt"; thus, he casts Malcolm's autobiography as "a cautionary tale about human waste and the tragedies produced by racial segregation" (p.9). Haley viewed "the transformed Malcolm" as "a pragmatic liberal, not a revolutionary," according to Marable, "which is why *The Autobiography* does not read like a manifesto for Black insurrection" (p. 466). For Marable, "Malcolm was unquestionably the most consummately 'political' activist" (p. 9); yet, "the autobiography is virtually silent about his primary organization, the OAAU," and "[n]owhere in the text does its agenda or its objectives appear" (p. 9). Marable also noted "numerous inconsistencies in names, dates, and facts" throughout the text.

Beyond Haley's work, Marable is critical of "nearly all of the literature about Malcolm produced in the 1990s," which he disparages as marked "by its shallow character and lack of original sources" (p. 490). Presumably these would include, but not be limited to, Perry (1991), Evanzz (1992), Karim (1992), Kondo (1993), Sales (1994), Strickland and Greene (1994), Dyson (1995), and Collins (1998).[2] The alleged limitations in earlier works as well as other factors set him upon a "search for historical evidence and factual truth" (p. 10), and led him "to write a full, comprehensive study of Malcolm's life" (p. 490).

Notwithstanding the vaunted purpose of Marable's project, the result is something less than what was seemingly intended. For example, critics have noted a range of historical errors, inconsistencies, and distortions in the work. These range from clear contradictions such as his assertion that "to Malcolm, armed self-defense was never equated with violence for its own sake," and on the same page: Malcolm "had come to reject violence for its own sake..." (p. 485); to the apparent reliance on rumor, innuendo, and a name redacted FBI file to suggest an adulterous relationship in anticipation of marriage between Malcolm's wife, Betty Shabazz, and MMI member Charles Kenyatta (p. 380).

One major problem is Marable's limited reliance on original sources, reputable eyewitnesses, and participants. For example, Marable lists less than thirty oral histories or actual individual interviews of friends, family, associates, contemporaries, and adversaries of Malcolm X (with a spattering of interviews listed in the footnotes) for a biography of a major historical figure, which the author maintains is a project that took some twenty years to complete—during the time when many notable friends and associates of Malcolm were readily accessible.[3] Among the prominent omissions are Maya Angelou, James Boggs, Grace Boggs, Albert Cleage, John Henrik Clarke, Harold Cruse, Vicki Garvin, Milton Henry, Benjamin Karim, Yuri Kochiyama, Warith Deen Muhammad, Gwen Patton, Alice Windom, and most glaringly, Betty Shabazz, among others. Instead, Marable's primary sources for some of the most contentious claims regarding Malcolm include some of his inveterate enemies such as Louis Farrakhan and his devotee Akbar Muhammad (Larry 4X Prescott); and sources such as Charles 37X Kenyatta whom the author himself acknowledges as an "opportunist" (p. 428) and a police informant (p. 467); as well as an insufficiently critical reliance on redacted FBI, CIA, U.S. State Department, Secret Service, and Bureau of Special Services (BOSS) files, interviews, and intelligence reports. Even more reputable sources such as Abdullah Abdur-Razzaq (James 67X Warden) have publicly stated that Marable misquoted and misrepresented important material attributed to him in the book.[4]

Ironically, much of Marable's work draws on second hand sources, among them, many of the studies of Malcolm X from the 1990s, which he disparaged as "shallow" and castigated for its failure to glean from primary sources. For example, Marable's discussion of the OAAU draws heavily on Sales (1994); his discussion of Elijah Muhammad's scandalous sexual affairs and his targeting of Malcolm draws on Evanzz (1992, 1999); his discussion of Malcolm's assassination—including the names and residences of the five likely assassins—draws heavily on Kondo (1993) and Evanzz (1992, 1999); and his allegations about Malcolm's sexuality draw on Perry (1991), Collins (1998), and are consistent with Evanzz (1992:8) as well. To be sure, this is quite a bit of reliance on works that are reputedly "shallow." Moreover, the book reflects less the historian's enterprise of meticulously distilling from the detail of an individual subject's experiences the prominent and specific contours of their life; and is more a synthesis of often thoughtful and informed reflections as well as extant arguments gleaned from previously published work and largely supplemented by two main sources: Malcolm's diary of his travels in Africa; and several reams of newly released government files. The result is a work that is (1) largely derivative; (2) one whose novel and forceful claims often rest on weak evidentiary support; (3) one which is largely colored by the author's own political orientations rather than those of his subject; and, (4) one that fails to appreciate the major political contribution of this exceptional political figure, Malcolm X. While various critics have proffered the first two critiques, in the limited space here I will discuss the last two.

To my mind, two things are unequivocal in a fair and accurate description of Malcolm X's ideology at the time of his death: he was a Black Nationalist, and he was a revolutionary. Marable equivocates on both. The ambiguity that Marable expresses with respect to these two aspects of Malcolm's political orientation primarily reflect Marable's limited conceptualization of both and advocacy of neither. As a result, Marable is guilty of the same tendency he excoriates Haley for in his writing of *The Autobiography*: shaping Malcolm's political orientation in such a way as to comport with his own political tendencies and in order to make his subject more palatable for a reading public to which he wants to sell his book. Thus, just as Haley's work "does not read like a manifesto for Black insurrection," neither does Marable's. Further, Marable's work "does not read like a manifesto for Black revolution" or "world-wide revolution" or "cultural revolution"; although these were political objectives Malcolm articulated up to the time of his death—the latter a centerpiece of Malcolm's OAAU and clearly annotated in its Charter.[5] But Marable does not develop a meaningful discussion of the OAAU Charter, Malcolm's thesis of Black cultural revolution embedded in it, its implications for 1960s activists or its relevance today. He opts, instead, to indulge the reader with salacious and largely unsubstantiated rumors about the sexual infidelity of Malcolm and Betty and the extent to which OAAU or MMI members were sexual partners. I am not making the case that it is irrelevant to examine the broad range of a person's experiences when composing a biography; but a biographer is clearly remiss if s/he fails to capture major political thrusts of an admittedly political figure, while seeking to capture even disparate remnants of rumor and innuendo regarding what are at best highly speculative conjectures regarding the largely non-political and intensely private aspects of the subject's life. For example, although Marable never mentions cultural revolution in his discussion of Malcolm X or the OAAU,[6] he does find time and space to provide this unsubstantiated speculation that on the night before his assassination "Sharon 6X may have joined him in his hotel room" (p. 423). Just five pages before discussing this possible tryst Marable is pointing out that "the themes of cultural identity...had recently traced its way through his speeches" (p. 418); and on the next page Marable discusses Malcolm's speech, "There's a Worldwide Revolution Going On," which he labels as "certainly the most significant of those he gave in the last two weeks of his life" (p. 419)—to which Marable devoted less than a paragraph. This lack of focus on and development of Malcolm's political ideology and theorizing in the last year of his life is doubly troubling in the case of Marable because he was an established political theorist, historian, and biographer who knew the importance of clearly articulating the political orientation of a man he correctly points out as a major political figure of the last half century.

Marable's lack of interest in offering a more thorough examination of Malcolm's political ideology may reflect the fact that he was an avowed Democratic Socialist and "New Leftist" whose particular brand of "radical integrationism" was not notable for its nuanced historical analyses of Black Nationalism.[7] Marable's approach to Malcolm's ideology may also have been hamstrung by his radical integrationist conception of revolution, which derided armed revolution in the United States for more gradualist approaches. While the former position is ahistorical and betrays a willful ignorance of one of the major theoretical orientations in African American politics (i.e. Black Nationalism), it is, nonetheless, a widely shared perspective in academia. The latter position (i.e. regarding opposition to armed revolution) is clearly the prerogative of those who espouse it. What is most important is that these orientations should not be substituted for Malcolm's perspective(s) since they were not central to Malcolm's ideology. Marable may choose to draw on them as a point of departure for relating Malcolm's actual political ideology to his readers; however, he does not have the license to present these as representative of Malcolm's actual ideology. Simply put, Marable has the right to interpret Malcolm's political orientation through the lens of his anti-nationalist, radical integrationism; but, he does not have the right to represent Malcolm's political orientation as if it were also anti-nationalist, radical integrationism. Nevertheless, I contend that Marable's work reflects such an imposition.

To be sure, since writing his relatively brief biography, *W.E.B Du Bois: Black Radical Democrat*, Marable has become more adept at the seamless weaving of a narrative, which is a hallmark of well-crafted biographies; but he has difficulty plaiting the threads of the tapestry of Malcolm X's Black Nationalist and revolutionary theses and programs. In the text, Marable views Black Nationalism, strangely, as the "unrealized dimension of Malcolm's racial vision." For Marable, Black Nationalism is "[a] political ideology that originated before the Civil War," which "was based on the assumption that racial pluralism leading to assimilation was impossible in the United States" (p. 485). He adds that "[s]o cynical were many nationalists about the incapacity of whites to overcome their own racism that they occasionally negotiated with white terrorist groups like the Ku Klux Klan..." (p. 485). In a more generous gesture he opines that Black Nationalism is based in the view "that the Black race possessed certain spiritual and cultural strengths, a collective personality, uniting Black humanity throughout the world" (p. 81); and that "Black cultural nationalism" reflects "a deep pride in African antiquity, history, and culture, together with the celebration of rituals and aesthetics drawing upon Africa and the Black Diaspora" (p. 81).

In less guarded moments, it is evident that for Marable, Black Nationalism is a rather narrow, inwardly focused, static, race-based ideology with few intrinsic valences (e.g. see Marable 1993: 93-128). But Malcolm viewed Black Nationalism as a broad, dynamic, and evolving ideology having political, economic, and social dimensions rooted in the conception that African Americans comprised a nation and that nation had the right of self-determination, which meant that it had the right and responsibility to determine the political entity that would govern it. Actually, Black Nationalism emerged from the national consciousness of a transnational enslaved society, whose members comprised diverse African peoples captured and transported to the United States. This Diaspora synthesized an amalgam of their African cultures into an African American culture whose remnants were manifest in such folk customs as the "ring shout," the "Buzzard Lope," "Pinkster festivals," trickster tales, burial practices, spiritually inspired water immersions (e.g. kalunga), and a host of other African retentions that ultimately were given American institutional forms (Stuckey 1987). These customs provided the bedrock of African American culture, which endured through slavery and both provided and reflected the commonalities that are the foundation of Black national consciousness.

This incipient national consciousness was reinforced by the commonality of Black racial oppression in terms of white exploitation of Black labor through racial slavery for the Black majority in the South and racist discrimination for the Black minority in the North. In addition, the galvanizing impact of the concerted effort of Blacks to fight to overthrow slavery during the Civil War, the reconstitution of Black familial based kin-groups after enslavement, and the institutionalization of prominent Black cultural practices ensured the enduring significance of racial identification for Black Americans. These factors combined to provide a sense of national identity among many African Americans and a framework for Black culture (Franklin 1984). Black Nationalism, which emerged from this original Diasporan sense of national identity, reflected, inter alia, "a spirit of Pan-African unity and an emotional sense of solidarity with the political and economic struggles of African peoples throughout the world" (Moses 1996: 20).

As opposed to the former conception, given his myopic view of Black Nationalism, not surprisingly, in Marable's telling Malcolm undergoes the obligatory "expansion" beyond the ostensibly narrow Black Nationalist frame as he incorporates more international dimensions into his ideology. For Marable, "as Malcolm's international experiences became more varied and extensive, his social vision expanded. He became less intolerant and more open to multiethnic and interfaith coalitions," such that "[b]y the final months of his life he resisted identification as a 'Black Nationalist,' seeking ideological shelter under the race-neutral concepts of Pan-Africanism and Third World revolution" (p. 485). Ignoring for the moment the counterintuitive construction of Pan-Africanism (and to a lesser extent "Third World") as a "race-neutral" concept since in its origin and development it was aimed at checking the power of European colonialists and their primarily Western collaborators who were not simply imperialists but white imperialists pursuing the "white man's burden," Marable's allegation that during the final months of his life Malcolm resisted identifying himself as a Black Nationalist is patently incorrect. In just one example, on a radio show in New York four days after his house was bombed, and three days before he was assassinated, Malcolm responded during an exchange: "...if you think that nationalism has no influence whatsoever, the nationalists, the Organization of Afro-American Unity, are having a rally at the Audubon Ballroom..." (Breitman 1990: 181). These are hardly the comments of—or the context for (i.e. a radio broadcast in New York)—someone reticent to associate himself, or his organization with Black Nationalism. Malcolm was not reticent about his Black Nationalism; Marable is.

Further, the suggestion that exposure to international politics compelled Malcolm to find a vocabulary for his political ideology outside of the limitations of Black Nationalism betrays Marable's myopic view of Black Nationalism. As any serious student of Black politics realizes, Black Nationalism has had an international dimension since its inception, rooted in its Pan-Africanism. Beyond the Pan-Africanist roots of its "internationalism," Black Nationalism had as its programmatic objectives several international goals. As early as the 18th century, Black Nationalism manifested a dual focus on territorial objectives abroad in Africa, North

America, and the Caribbean, as well as in the United States; and these are evident, for example, in Cuffee's request for both the establishment of a settlement in Africa as well as well as one on the frontiers of the incipient U.S. republic, while advancing a strategy to modernize Africa and to undermine U.S. slavery. These initiatives predate the emigrationist initiatives of other prominent Black Nationalists such as Martin Delany, Mary Shadd Cary, and Alexander Crummell of the 19th century; the anti-colonialism of the Pan-Africanist Congresses led by Du Bois, Joseph Ephraim Casely-Hayford, and later Kwame Nkrumah in the 20th century; and Marcus Garvey's UNIA & ACL, which was the largest international organization of Black peoples. It simply is ahistorical to attempt to suggest that Black Nationalism in the U.S. is somehow inherently contradictory to "internationalism"; or that "internationalism" represents an "expansion" beyond Black Nationalism. Moreover, internationalism is not an ideology but a strategic or tactical point of reference. It is meaningless as a political ideology, but serves mainly to describe one's conceptual or programmatic focus. Further, given that just about every major political ideology has an international focus—especially regarding war, peace, or human rights, where the term is logically employed it is often superfluous.

Nevertheless, it is this moniker that Marable uses to describe Malcolm's political orientation that presumably could no longer be subsumed under the rubric of Black Nationalism. The impetus for the change that Marable observes in Malcolm's political ideology is primarily Malcolm's time spent abroad—for which Marable has excellent access through Malcolm's diaries. Marable records Malcolm's reflections upon leaving Mecca: "My mind has been almost incapable of producing words and phrases lately and it has worried me" (p. 384). To this Marable adds his own supposition: "What [Malcolm] appears to be saying is that his Middle East and Africa experiences had greatly broadened his mind, yet his limited vocabulary of Black Nationalism was insufficient to address the challenges he so clearly saw confronting Africa. Malcolm sensed that he needed to create new theoretical tools and a different frame of reference beyond race" (p. 384). But the latter are not Malcolm's ruminations, but Marable's. As pointed out above, Malcolm had no difficulty describing himself or his organization, the OAAU, as Black Nationalist just three days prior to his death. This is well after Malcolm's initial articulation of the "world-wide revolution going on," therefore, his global focus did not preclude his conceptualization of his political ideology as Black Nationalism.

What had been "expanding" for Malcolm, conceptually—and what

Malcolm had been consciously reworking over the past two years—was not his ideological moorings away from Black Nationalism, but the specific emphasis of his Black Nationalism. That is, just as Du Bois modernized the classical version of Black Nationalism away from the emigrationism and Anglophilia that characterized so much of its 18th and 19th century versions to one rooted in a positive conception of African culture,[8] an African American culture garnered from African cultural retentions such as found in the Black church, and Black folk culture that endured the slave plantations; so too was Malcolm modernizing Black Nationalism even further. Building on those elements that Du Bois highlighted, Malcolm's Black Nationalism also emphasized the relevance of Black liberation theology (especially but not exclusively Sunni Islam), Third World solidarity rooted in the "spirit of Bandung," women's rights, and domestic colonialism.

In addition, his Black Nationalism noted that revolution in the U.S. should reflect the interests of the "field Negro," which was Malcolm's conception of the class differentiation apparent in Black America, which generated divergent interests among Black Americans across a variety of issues, including civil rights. It was clear that Malcolm's Black revolution would focus on liberation from racist, sexist, and class domination; and the breadth of this revolution influenced Malcolm X's view that political, economic, and cultural factors were often intimately tied together, thus the broad program of the OAAU; and his advocacy of a sweeping anthropological focus of culture in its materialist as well as its aesthetic sense, to encapsulate, inculcate, and direct important aspects of the revolutionary change that he sought. Accordingly, for Malcolm X, the "worldwide revolution" also represented a cultural reawakening of Black Americans.[9] To make it plain, Malcolm's modernized Black Nationalism compelled him to advocate Black cultural revolution, which was his major theoretical and programmatic focus in his last year; but Marable does not find space in a nearly 600 page book to even mention it. As a result, Marable does not address the novel contributions Malcolm makes as a political theorist. Marable, like other radical integrationists seems to have already made up his mind on what Black political theory should encompass and what goals it should address; and Malcolm's Black cultural revolution does not fit that model largely because it maintains its rootedness in the self determination of Black people, a clear articulation of Black culture, a castigation of white supremacy in all its forms, and its advocacy of armed revolution in the U.S. and abroad.

Consistent with his view of the dynamic quality of Black

Nationalism, Malcolm's incipient thesis of Black cultural revolution suggests a process of systemically transforming U.S. society through the projection and institutionalization of an affirming African American culture in order to fundamentally transform the major life-giving and life-sustaining institutions of the society and to create multiracial democracy—a clear corollary of such a revolution would be the wholesale rejection of white supremacy. This revolution could be violent, non-violent, or a combination of both. It is this multiple quality of cultural revolution that is implicit in Malcolm's articulation of the historical and contemporary relevance of violent revolution in the U.S. in his "Message to the Grassroots" (November 1963); and his argument on the prospect that the United States "is the first country on this earth that can have a bloodless revolution" in his "Black Revolution" (April 1964); and his focus on the prospects for both outcomes in his "The Ballot or the Bullet" thesis (April 1964).

Marable confuses and is confused by Malcolm's approach to revolution throughout his text. He notes that Malcolm "endorsed revolutionary violence" outside of the U.S. (p. 485); but inside, "as 'The Ballot or the Bullet' makes clear, the mature Malcolm believed that African Americans could use the electoral system and voting rights to achieve meaningful change" (p. 484). Marable is misleading here insofar as Malcolm does support Black electoral politics and even Black political parties; but, he also endorses revolutionary violence both outside and inside the U.S. What Marable seems to ignore is that Malcolm consistently included in his "The Ballot or the Bullet" speeches a discussion of the importance and utility of guerilla warfare in the U.S. The speech is called "The Ballot or The Bullet" because Malcolm is not simply advocating armed self-defense, but he is also advocating armed offensive operations—in this case, guerilla operations—in order to achieve the political objectives of Black Americans that cannot or will not be acquired through electoral means. Its rather ironic, given that Marable (1993) has little difficulty in recognizing and lauding Gramsci's neo-Marxist, dual conception of the war of position— which is largely an ideological struggle that facilitates the armed struggle, the war of maneuver; but Malcolm's articulation of the three salient options open to those pursuing Black liberation compels Marable to aver that Malcolm's revolutionary thesis is reducible to a singular advocacy of electoral reforms and a "politics of radical humanism" (p. 487). As a result, Marable leaves Malcolm's revolutionary thesis toothless, rootless, and hovering outside of its own history.

For Malcolm, the worldwide revolution proceeded in two stages: the first was a revolution against the Western imperialist powers and was evident in the anti-colonial struggles throughout the Third World; and the second was a cultural reawakening that galvanized Black Americans, in particular, to mobilize against white supremacy in the U.S., which would augur Black cultural revolution. The latter could take either of three forms: it could be violent, non-violent, or both, depending on the leverage exerted by a united front of Black revolutionists inside the U.S. and their allies in a united front operating through international links and coordinated through the OAAU. In a manner similar to that which Cruse (1968) evoked with respect to the impact of the Cuban Revolution on the revolutionary initiative of Black Americans, Malcolm argued that the revolutions in Africa and Asia were not only checking Western power in the periphery, they were also providing a model of resistance to those suffering under Western oppression within the Western states, themselves.

Malcolm X saw his cultural revolution as both a cause and a concomitant of the Black revolution that he observed throughout the world; and one that he hoped that Black Americans would embrace in their specific struggle for human rights in the U.S. Although he never proposed an actual theory of cultural revolution, he thought that the manner that it would be constructed would require an engagement with the "peculiar" history and circumstances of Black America that tied the political, economic, and cultural forces together in novel ways. Du Bois, Locke, as well as Cruse had made seminal contributions to this theorizing but Malcolm did not live to develop his revolutionary theory on these issues and to solidify his organization in his attempt to realize the political objectives implicit in them.[10] Nevertheless, his promotion of both Black Nationalism and Black cultural revolution would have the greatest impact on the Black liberation movement following his death—especially through its impact on RAM, SNCC, Us, the Black Panther Party, the League of Revolutionary Black Workers, CAP, the RNA, the Shrine of the Black Madonna, Third World Press/Institute of Positive Education, and many others (see Ahmad 2007; Brown 2003; Carson 1981; Cleage 1972; Henderson 1997; Madhubuti 1973; Obadele 1989; Woodard 1999). Marable focuses on none of these immediate and historic connections, opting instead to cast a much wider speculative net to conjecture on Malcolm's orientation towards Al Qaeda and the Obama administration more than four decades after Malcolm's death (p. 486).

In sum, while there are some laudable aspects of the book, such as the attempt to engage the historical development of Islam in the United States, the impact of Garveyism on Malcolm's parents, and the general discussion of Malcolm's family; there are many more areas of the book that are poorly thought out, lacking in evidentiary support, and generally unpersuasive. But, in this brief essay, I want to emphasize that it is Marable's neglect of these inherently political issues of Malcolm's important theorizing and advocacy of Black Nationalism and cultural revolution in the U.S. that undermine the work. These factors reflect the core of the politics of such an important political leader; and as such they deserve a much more serious and rigorous examination than what Marable—an often politically astute biographer—chose to or was able to provide.

Notes

1. Marable's word choice here is instructive insofar as he doesn't frame Malcolm's development as one of "transformation," which has a positive connotation; but of "re-invention" which suggests something more duplicitous.

2. Ironically, Dyson lauds Marable's book as a "magnum opus" and a "definitive work" and one of "extraordinary rigor and intellectual beauty that brims with startling insights and fresh revelations."

3. By comparison, in his slender though excellent social history of Us organization, which is about one third the size of Marable's work (227 pages), Brown (2003) references more than thirty individual interviews with Us members and associates over an eight year period—not including original source documents, archival materials, personal papers, government publications and documents.

4. Abdur-Razzaq made these claims during a symposium on Marable's book at the Schomburg Center in New York City on May 19, 2011.

5. In the 1964 "Statement of the Basic Aims and Objectives of the Organization of Afro-American Unity," Malcolm stated that "[w]e must launch a cultural revolution to unbrainwash an entire people." (Malcolm X 1970: 427). He insisted that "[a]rmed with the knowledge of the past, we can with confidence charter a course for our future." He emphasized that "[c]ulture is an indispensable weapon in the freedom struggle. We must take hold of it and forge the future with the past." (p. 427)

6. Interestingly, Marable refers to cultural revolution with respect to the Garvey movement (p. 18); and in a previous work, Marable (1998: 46) insisted that Du Bois' "Criteria of Negro Art" was the "clearest expression of Du Bois's objectives in promoting a permanent, cultural revolution among African Americans." So he is not unfamiliar with the concept (albeit, typically in a Gramscian rather than a black nationalist formulation), he simply ignored its relevance to Malcolm's political orientation and program.

7. Marable was the former Vice Chairman of the Democratic Socialists of America, and Chairman of the Movement for a Democratic Society, a latter day manifestation of SDS.

8. Du Bois appears to have coined the term "Afrocentric" in 1961 (Moses

1998).

9. One shortcoming of Malcolm's incipient thesis on black cultural revolution was its notion that black Americans needed to follow the lead of Africans who had already embarked on anti-colonial revolutionary change. Malcolm's "reverse civilizationism" correctly rejected the civilizationist theses of the pre-Du Boisian nationalists, but it failed to fully appreciate the novel, dynamic and transformative aspects of African American culture and black political development in the US. Such an appreciation of African American culture would demonstrate that the challenge for black Americans was not the replication of extant African culture forms, but a focus on the transformative elements of black culture in the US—largely African American urban culture, which was more relevant to—and practicable in—US society, which was/is dramatically different from Third World contexts that Malcolm—and many later theorists—would draw on for their models of revolutionary change (Henderson 2011).

10. See Henderson (2010, 2011).

References

Ahmad, Muhammad, 2007. *We Will Return in the Whirlwind: Black Radical Organizations 1960-1975*. Chicago: Charles Kerr.
Breitman, George, ed. 1990. *Malcolm X Speaks: Selected Speeches and Statements*. New York: Grove.
Brown, Scot, 2003. *Fighting For Us: Maulana Karenga, The Us Organization and Black Cultural Nationalism*. New York: New York University Press.
Carson, Clayborne, 1981. In *Struggle: SNCC and the Black Awakening of the 1960s*. Cambridge, MA: Harvard University Press.
Cleage, Albert, 1972. *Black Christian Nationalism: New Directions for the Black Church*. New York: Morrow Quill.
Collins, Rodnell, with A. Peter Bailey, 1998. *Seventh Child: A Family Memoir of Malcolm X*. New York: Kensington.
Cruse, Harold, 1968. *Rebellion or Revolution?* New York: William Morrow & Co.
Dyson, Michael, 1995. *Making Malcolm: The Myth and Meaning of Malcolm X*. New York: Oxford.
Evanzz, Karl, 1992. *The Judas Factor: The Plot to Kill Malcolm X*. New York: Thunder's Mouth.
—1999. *The Messenger: The Rise and Fall of Elijah Muhammad*. New York: Pantheon.
Franklin, V.P. 1992. *Black Self-Determination: A Cultural History of African-American Resistance*. Chicago: Lawrence-Hill.
Henderson, Errol 1997. "The Lumpenproletariat as Vanguard?" *Journal of Black Studies* 28, 2: 171-199.
—2010. "WEB Du Bois and the Evolution of Black Cultural Revolution," Dept. of Political Science, Pennsylvania State University. Typescript.
—2011. "Alain Locke and the Evolution of Cultural Revolution in Black America," Paper presented to the annual conference of the American Political Science Association, Washington, DC, September.
Karim, Benjamin, with Peter Skutches and David Gallen, 1992. *Remembering Malcolm*. New York: Carroll and Graf.
Kondo, Zak, 1993. *Conspiracys: Unraveling the Assassination of Malcolm X*. Washington, DC: Nubia Press.
Madhubuti, Haki, 1973. *From Plan to Planet: The Need for Afrikan Minds and Institutions*. Chicago: Third World Press.
Marable, Manning, 1993. *Blackwater*, Boulder, CO: University Press of Colorado.

——1998. *Black Leadership.* New York: Columbia University Press.
——2005. *W.E.B. Du Bois: Black Radical Democrat, 2nd ed.* Boulder, CO: Paradigm.
——2011. *Malcolm X: A Life of Reinvention.* New York: Viking.
Moses, Wilson, 1996. *Classical Black Nationalism: From the American Revolution to Marcus Garvey.* New York: New York University Press.
——1998. *Afrotopia: The Roots of African American Popular History.* Cambridge: Cambridge University Press.
Obadele, Imari, 1989. *America, The Nation-State,* Washington, DC: The House of Songhay.
Perry, Bruce, 1991. *Malcolm: The Life of a Man Who Changed Black America.* Barrytown, NY: Station Hill.
Sales, William, 1994. *From Civil Rights to Black Liberation: Malcolm X and the Organization of Afro-American Unity.* Boston: South End.
Strickland, William and Cheryll Greene, eds. 1994. *Malcolm X: Make It Plain.* New York: Viking.
Stuckey, Sterling, 1987. *Slave Culture: Nationalist Theory and the Foundations of Black America.* New York: Oxford University Press.
Wood, Joe, ed. 1992. *Malcolm X: In Our Own Image.* New York: St. Martin's.
Woodard, Komozi. 1999. *A Nation Within a Nation: Amiri Baraka (Leroi Jones) and Black Power Politics.* Chapel Hill, NC: University of North Carolina Press.
X, Malcolm with Alex Haley, 1964. *The Autobiography of Malcolm X.* New York: Grove Press.
X, Malcolm, [1964] 1970. "The Organization of Afro-American Unity: 'For Human Rights' [Statement of Basic Aims of the Organization of Afro-American Unity]," in John Bracey, August Meier, and Elliot Rudwick, eds. *Black Nationalism in America.* New York: Macmillan. pp. 421-427.

Malcolm X: The Man and Our Times
Fred Hord

In July 2011, the Chicago Council on Black Studies sponsored a day-long symposium at the Carter G. Woodson Branch of the Chicago Public Library on the book *Malcolm X: A Life of Reinvention* by Manning Marable. The morning keynoter, Haki R. Madhubuti, suggested two things that were absolutely critical to a viable African American future: integrity in leadership and the building/maintenance of Black institutions. The author connects those two ideas in this project to a classical criterion for practical action by Sonia Sanchez: "uh-huh, but how do it free us?"

The primary purpose of this brief essay is to engage the recent analysis of Malcolm X by the Black historian, Manning Marable, in a very specific manner: identifying ideas of Malcolm X in that analysis which seem to be useful for our times. The late, venerable historian, John Henrik Clarke, edited an extraordinary anthology by Blacks on Malcolm X shortly after his assassination, which appraised his views and place in his times. This project will focus essentially on those ideas in Marable's text that seem promising for the future liberation of African Americans. It will not explore several issues raised by earlier commentators such as reasons for Malcolm X's dismissal from the Nation of Islam, the debates about his assassination, or his sexuality. Rather, after giving some attention to Marable's theory of reinvention regarding Malcolm X, the author will attempt to isolate those ideas he privileges which appear to have the most resonance for an African American future that is unmistakably posted in race.

Marable claims Alex Haley was the revisionist of Malcolm X. Haley was a Republican, a liberal who was at odds with Malcolm X ideologically, and opposed to his views in the Nation of Islam. Yet, Haley seemed fascinated by Malcolm X's ascent from degradation. Marable argues that his "latter-day metamorphosis from angry Black militant into a multicultural American icon was the product of the extraordinary success of Haley's *The Autobiography of Malcolm X*" (7). He sees "the autobiography as a cautionary tale about human waste and the tragedies produced by racial segregation" (9). He also suggests Haley is a revisionist of Malcolm X by what he omits in the published version of *The Autobiography*. The missing chapters now held by attorney Greg Reed of Detroit apparently provide some information about the Organization of Afro-American Unity (OAAU), the secular organization Malcolm X formed in March of 1964. Marable disagrees with Haley's take on Malcolm X "as an integrationist and liberal reformer" (466). Additionally, in an essay Marable published in "Souls" six years before this book, he shares other concerns regarding Haley's perspective in co-writing *The Autobiography of Malcolm X*. He argues that Haley agreed with Mike Wallace's television series on the Nation of Islam (NOI) that it "was potentially a dangerous, racist cult, completely out of step with the lofty goals and aspirations of the civil rights movement" (*Beyond Boundaries*, 209). Finally, Marable expresses concern about Haley's late assertion that Malcolm X was on a decline before the assassination.

Marable also claims "that one of Haley's early articles about the NOI, co-authored by the white author Alfred Balk, had been written in collaboration with the FBI" (*Beyond Boundaries*, 229). That article was published in the January 26, 1963 issue of the *Saturday Evening Post*, entitled "Black Merchants of Hate." Later that year, Marable contends Haley was worried about Malcolm X's anti-Semitism, and censored "a number of negative statements about Jews in the book manuscript...without the co-author's knowledge or consent" (230). The upshot of Marable's 2005 piece on Haley's point of view that influenced *The Autobiography* is that there are both omissions and modifications which we should continue to explore.

Marable rejects not only Haley's revisionism but more broadly "the tendency of historical revisionism to interpret Malcolm X through the powerful lens of Dr. Martin Luther King Jr." (482). He writes rather that "Malcolm X perceived himself first and foremost as a Black man, a person of African descent who happened to be a United States citizen" (482). His statement at the end of the "Souls" article regarding the logic of the protection and censorship of certain information about Malcolm X is fiercely instructive: "the life and the man had the potential to become much more dangerous to white America than any other single individual had ever been.... Malcolm X, the real Malcolm X, was infinitely more remarkable than the personality presented in *The Autobiography*" (Souls, 231). Later he says:

> *Malcolm X also possessed the unique potential for uniting Black America in an unprecedented coalition with African, Asian, and Caribbean nations. He alone could have established unity between Negro integrationists and Black Nationalists inside the*

> United States. He possessed the personal charisma, the rhetorical genius, and the moral courage to inspire and motivate millions of Blacks into action. (Souls, 231)

A summary of Marable's views on Malcolm X after his ouster from the Nation of Islam can be found in both the prologue and the epilogue to the book:

> *He was a truly historical figure in the sense that, more than any of his contemporaries, he embodied the spirit, vitality, and political mood of an entire population—Black urban mid-twentieth century American....Even when I have disagreed with him, I deeply admire the strength and integrity of his character, and the love he obviously felt toward the African-American people and their culture* (13 and 14). *Malcolm linked his Black consciousness to the ideological imperative of self-determination.... Malcolm perceived Black Americans as an oppressed nation-within-a-nation, with its own culture, social institutions and group psychology....He realized that Blacks indeed could achieve representation and even power under America's constitutional system. But he always thought first and foremost about Blacks' interests.* (231)

Yet, even more central to the author's assessment of the Marable book is what he draws out as the Malcolm X legacy to African Americans, the strategies for our liberation he articulated near the end of his life. The agenda here is to extract and organize from the controversial Marable text on Malcolm X ideas that can be employed today to revive and sustain the Black Freedom Movement. After providing some contexts for his projected solutions, I'll focus on five areas which seem to reflect his vision: African American cultural revolution, Pan-Africanism, a science of politics, a shift toward socialism, a necessary re-evaluation of sexism, as well as the optimal roles of Whites.

Marable suggests five significant contexts for the above potential solutions of Malcolm X for our times: an international perspective, internal colonialism, institutions, human rights, and separation/ integration as finally only methods. First, he believes Malcolm X felt an international perspective was indispensible for Black struggle and progress. Round-the-blockism was fatal; even nationalism—though necessary—was insufficient. Second, he argues that Malcolm X saw clear connections between traditional colonialism and internal colonialism as a viable framework for African Americans to both make sense of their historical situation and plan liberation. Malcolm X's use of internal colonialism as a framework to understand the African American experience precedes that of the Black Panthers, early Black Nationalists and other intellectuals of the late 1960s and early 1970s. Third, central to internal colonialism are institutions; they not only drive the politics, economy, and education, but inherently are the engines of socialization. Structures, thus, are key to both the problems and solutions of a people. Fourth, Marable emphasizes Malcolm X's idea of moving from civil rights to human rights, both to broaden the forum of struggle to the international stage and to be clear about how struggling for human rights changes and shapes perspectives for securing civil rights. Finally, Marable makes sure the reader understands that Malcolm X saw integration and separation as just strategies for liberation rather than a permanent ideology for struggle.

As a father who brought Kwanzaa to his children in the late 1960s, started discussions of Black cultural revolution with college students in the 1970s, and who witnessed the mainstreaming of cultural values subsequent to that, it is notable that Marable gives substantial attention to their importance in Malcolm X's vision of a Black future. For the author, Marable was dead center on the mark when he explained that for Malcolm X, "the task of emancipating Black people from the effects of racial oppression... required a fundamental rejection of white values" (95). Or, as Marable quotes him later, "Our cultural roots must be restored before life (incentive) can flow into us; because just as a tree without roots is dead, a people without cultural roots are automatically dead" (211).

Malcolm X's belief that slavery decimated Black culture is certainly debatable, but the historical power of "dominant" institutions to set cultural norms is undeniable. So often, it seems, African Americans who led Black institutions and/or were called to leadership by the colonizers did succumb—whatever their personal beliefs were—to the oppressor's value system. Even today, Afrocentric leaders here too often demonstrate the colonial ethos of individualism and materialism in practice; witnessing that remains one of the most unsettling ongoing experiences of the author.

In two critical places, Marable underscores our witting or unwitting defection from the best Black values. He suggests Malcolm X believed that the process of identity confusion contributed to this defection and that "an appreciation of Black culture would liberate Blacks to advocate their own interests" (414). According to Marable, Malcolm X "encouraged Blacks to celebrate their culture and tales of resistance to European colonialism and white domination" (481). Drawing on the poet, Amiri Baraka, Marable points out that Malcolm X was an important contributor to the Black Arts Movement. "To Baraka, Malcolm represented a Black aesthetic, a set of values and criteria for cultural representations that affirmed the genius and creativity of people of African descent." (481).

Clearly, a return to Black culture and its roots must have Africa at its center. After the first few Marable references to Africa and Pan-Africanism, the author discovered more connections in these related areas to than any other single issue in the book. Marable points back and forward at once. African Americans must understand their relationships to historical Africa in order to rid themselves of hating Africa even as they learn historical legacies of the continent. Looking ahead, Marable maintains there are several reasons, in addition to racial ties, why Malcolm X thought African Americans must return to Africa culturally, philosophically, politically, and economically. Actually, before Malcolm X's dismissal from the Nation of Islam, he scrapped the Asiatic origins of African Americans and "affirmed the common cultural heritage that united Africans" (229) with them. Central to Marable's arguments for Malcolm X encouraging future connections to Africa are three points: (1) both of Malcolm X's visits to Africa resituated his thinking regarding the value of African American relationships with Africans; (2) those visits moved him to a Pan-Africanism encompassing Black Nationalism, broadening his citizenship to a global one, and his thinking to a global Black one; and (3) he came to believe that African Americans would never be truly free until Africa was a world power.

For Marable, Malcolm X took on the view that the relationship between African Americans and Africans was both an historical and a contemporary one. Malcolm X argued that the problems of each were inextricable; the problems in the United States could not be solved until Blacks here understood their inseparability to those on the continent. So the relationship was clearly more than one of blood.

Next, Marable is unclear about how Malcolm X's nationalism disappeared with his Pan-Africanism, how his thinking increasingly in global terms diminished his focus on African Americans. Marable cites Malcolm X's deep beliefs about how the psychological, cultural, political, economic dilemmas here must be addressed by an action program. But it is unclear how Malcolm X's views on human rights and the common African American goals of dignity and respect are inconsistent with nationalism (487). This author's view is that not only was Malcolm X's nationalism a part of his Pan-Africanism but that, for him, they became indivisible.

Third, Marable does suggest that Malcolm X believed African

Americans must look for and organize ways to contribute to Africa becoming a world power, and not in a patronizing way where we are the superiors and leaders. In addition to a cultural and psychological return to Africa, Blacks here must first learn the painful and promising truths about the continent and, in an unblinking way, begin the long, arduous process of becoming a real part of Africa's future. And, uncritical adulation will serve us no better than pessimism, cynicism, or despair.

Although Marable, a democratic socialist, does not invest as much time in discussing Malcolm X's shift toward socialism as on his deep-seated Pan-Africanism, he does give it some attention. At least three statements stand out: (1) "the Black Freedom Movement...would ultimately have to take aim at America's private enterprise system" (336); (2) Malcolm's Congo connection "for Black Americans had as much to do with the commonality of economic oppression as it did with race" (395); and (3) "when we look at the African continent... we find that the nations... are developing socialistic systems to solve their problems. ...You can't operate a capitalistic system unless you are vulturistic; you have to suck someone else's blood to be a capitalist" (400). Marable argues Malcolm X moved away from "the Garvey-endorsed virtues of entrepreneurial capitalism" (336). He supports his view of Malcolm X turning toward socialism by citing him: "I believe there will be a clash between those who want freedom, justice, and equality for everyone and those who want to continue the system of exploitation... but I don't think it will be based upon the color of skin" (407).

Marable also ties Malcolm X's focus on human rights in the United States more than civil rights to his being a global citizen, with Africa being a primary connection. Malcolm X saw the immense implications of working out racism on the international stage, broadening the forum and bringing the weight of Africans everywhere to bear on that international imperialism—with its African complicities—which embodies racism. Marable claims, and the author agrees, that Malcolm X believed that "we can never get civil rights in America until our HUMAN RIGHTS are first restored" (366). There must be respect and human rights first; civil rights without them are empty and keep Blacks in a second class position. Employing Frantz Fanon's argument, Malcolm X said that "the denial of HUMAN RIGHTS psychologically castrates the victim and makes him a mental and physical slave of the system" (366). In sum, the human status that is part and parcel of human rights necessarily informs civil rights, no matter the law.

Marable details Malcolm X's views on the use of civil rights as a route to Black power and so to self-determination. Although he gives some shrift to Malcolm X's notion of economic power, investing in the Black community for the sake of that community, more attention is given to the place of voting. In several places, he emphasizes the roles of voting. As early as 1957, Malcolm X was projecting that the Black vote could swing the balance of power in many elections and move forward the freedom struggle. This is roughly seven years before his famous "The Ballot or Bullet" speech that suggested the possibility of a bloodless revolution. Marable contends that Malcolm X's 1957 speech in Muhammad's Detroit Temple of Islam anticipates both the John F. Kennedy Presidential election and the 1965 Voting Rights Act; it was also before Dr. Martin Luther King's involvement in voting rights as key to Black progress. Also, Marable implies that the speech "proposes a broad-based coalition of civil rights organizations and other groups... to address the collective problems of Blacks" (133).

Elsewhere in Marable's book, there are additional references to Malcolm X's ideas about voting and equal rights. Malcolm X proposes an independent Black politics, indicating one week before he died that African Americans should be trained in the science of politics "so that we'll know what a vote is for and what a vote is supposed to produce, and also how to utilize this united voting power so that you can control the politics of your community, and the politicians that represent that community" (Final Speeches 106). In fact, Marable claims that politics broadly, including "civil rights demonstrations, Third World Revolution or Pan-Africanism...severed Malcolm's relationship with the Nation of Islam" (284).

If the five strategies above (cultural revolution, a Pan-African orientation, independent politics, a shift toward socialism, and a focus on human rights of Malcolm X for Black liberation that Marable stresses represent core ideas for our times, we must raise at least two questions regarding who Malcolm X thought should carry out these strategies other than Black men. More specifically, would Black women, who were principal organizers for all of the Civil Rights Movement, be led again by the men? And what, if any, would be the roles of Whites?

One of the most unsettling issues in reviews of Malcolm X's life has been his views of women. *The Autobiography* chronicles some of the sources, and suggests that women at best were to be sheltered, protected, and respected. Before that book concludes, however, we get two glimpses of his sentiments late in life. First, when it is clear there are plans to kill him, he expresses the strength he got from his wife, Betty, on which he learned to depend. Later, Malcolm X suggests there is a relationship between the moral strength/weakness of a country and the values internalized by its women, but there is no clear implication of leadership.

One statement Marable uses to indicate the change in Malcolm X's thinking about Black women sharing leadership in organizations refers to the controversy he stirred up in the Organization of Afro-American Unity by making clear that "women [should have an] equal position to the men" (374). Herman Ferguson, an Assistant Principal who joined forces with Malcolm X after his break from the NOI, admitted that former male members of that group wanted him "to approach [Malcolm] about the role of the women and how it was not sitting well with many of the brothers" (374).

In an essay by Black women historians, Barbara Ransby and Tracye Matthews, they cite a letter Malcolm X wrote to his cousin-in-law in 1965 that is consistent in a general way with his policy in the OAAU. He regrets contributing to keeping women in their places in the Nation of Islam, and pledges to change this patriarchal consigning. This author hopes that as more information is published about Malcolm's leadership of the OAAU, there will be more concrete evidence regarding his views on women near the close of his life, and so about his vision of Black women's participation in the two organizations that he formed in 1964.

There is more textual evidence about what Malcolm X felt were the roles of Whites in the Black liberation struggle. Essentially, Marable makes three points about those roles. First, Whites cannot join; among other matters, Malcolm X raised psychological issues both about Whites needing to join and their impacts on Blacks, even with the best motives. Second, Whites can assist financially. Third and referred to most often in Marable's assessment, is Malcolm's recommendation that Whites work in their own communities to understand and eradicate racism and all its ramifications. Malcolm X came to think of white as culture, regarding sickness in the ascendant value system in this society; that view has immense implications for the place of Blacks who have fallen victim to that system.

Perhaps no better way exists to bring full circle Malcolm X's legacy to African Americans today, to begin the institutionalization of his—in many ways—yet tentative solutions to our future but to cull pieces from the Basic Unity Program: Organization of Afro-American Unity. It had been planned for release on February 15, 1965, but was deferred to February 21, given the firebombing of his home. Here a launching of cultural revolution is proposed "which will provide the means for restoring our identity that we might rejoin our brothers and sisters on the African continent, culturally, psychologically, [and] economically...."(Final Speeches, 270). Here is proposed an action program with a coalition of Black Civil Rights organizations to address the psychological, political, economic, and social problems of African Americans. The two basic aims and objectives of the OAAU are self-determination and national unity. In the Basic Unity Program, it is suggested that African Americans must communicate both with Africans and each other to face the past and learn from it so there can be a future of freedom. African Americans must also reorient themselves to think globally and relinquish forever the destructive myth of being a minority. African Americans must not only free their people from economic slavery by, in part, maintaining a technical pool and technical bank, but also defend themselves physically by any means necessary. Those five practical pillars of strategy for the future Black Freedom Movement (restoration, reorientation, education, economic security, and self-defense) point yet today in real ways to institutional solutions for the malaise and confusion that have proceeded inherently from neither fully understanding nor practicing the ultimate extension of Malcolm X's legacy: resisting the Whiteness of culture and painfully, doggedly, systematically recovering the best of a Black value system.

In this essay, the author chose to stress the ideas of Malcolm X in Marable's book that seem to be useful for our times. He does not ignore other paramount issues that Marable addresses, some of which—at best—are unclear such as the sexuality of Malcolm X and the nature of his marriage with Betty Shabazz. The focus here highlights what Haki Madhubuti reminded us we need to move ahead—integrity in leadership and institutions, and prioritizes the question of Sonia Sanchez: "Uh-but how does it free us?" In that spirit, the following poem points up what Malcolm X might think about the use of his powerful legacy today.

EL-HAJJ MALIK EL-SHABAZZ: GOING THROUGH CHANGES

At eighty-six,
Malcolm would have sat down with us,
listening to lines of private freedom,
making it plain
that either we keep each other or die.

He would remind us now
how some thought
revolution was songs of overcoming,
a turning of precious cheeks,
a sharing of dollar signs,

and say again
from the main text of his life
that revolutionaries are lyrics of sweat,
are meek when credited with change,
and have no price.

In his strength,
Malcolm would cry at the small size
of our freedom,
our one wish with all candles lit,
the willingness to forget
to be remembered.

He would fall without new firing,
wondering why
his end of hustling
and beginning of passion for women
were yet not enough
for us to understand
community is our largest self.

Unearthing Meaning in Marable's Malcolm X
Peter James Hudson

Few figures have received plaudits from both the former New York City Mayor Rudolph Giuliani and the al-Qaida operative Ayman al-Zawahiri. Fewer still have found their likeness on the postage stamps of both the United States and the Islamic Republic of Iran. Such is the fate of Malcolm X. In the aftermath of his assassination in the Audubon Ballroom in Washington Heights on a cold February morning in 1965, the civil rights and Black Power icon has become an uncertain figure, lauded by most but little understood. The X of his surname, adopted to signify the obscure ancestry of the African American slave, now stands either as a cipher for the imprecise, befuddled meanings projected on to him—or, according to Manning Marable, as the emptying of meaning itself.

For Marable, who died just days before this biography was published, the myths and misinterpretations begin with the publication of Malcolm's *The Autobiography*. He argues that Malcolm's voice is smothered by his amanuensis; *Roots* author Alex Haley, and describes Haley as a "liberal Republican" and an "integrationist Republican" who was repulsed by Malcolm's radical politics. Haley, Marable writes, wanted to defang Malcolm and massage him into something marketable. Marable seeks to "deconstruct" *The Autobiography* to find some semblance of the "true" Malcolm. He follows the transformations through which Malcolm Little, a lanky, light-skinned black boy from Omaha, Nebraska became a globally known Black activist and spokesperson. Fastidiously researched, and with access to previously closed archives, *Malcolm X* documents how *The Autobiography* exaggerates some aspects of Malcolm's life – especially his early years as a hustler in New York and Boston – while omitting the details of others, such as those of Malcolm's engagement with the politics of pan-Africanism and pan-Islam in the final years of his life.

It is sex and death, however, not Pan-Africanism and Pan-Islam that promise the most spectacular revelations in Marable's book. He revisits the question of Malcolm's alleged homosexuality while offering compelling new evidence concerning the still-unresolved assassination. Marable only briefly addresses Malcolm's homosexual encounters during his hustling Detroit Red years. He confirms that the encounters happened, but adds nothing new to our understanding of them beyond what was already revealed, in a much more graphic fashion, in Bruce Perry's *Malcolm: The Life of the Man Who Changed Black America* (1991). More suggestive are Marable's accounts of Malcolm's inadequacies as a husband and a father. Malcolm admitted to Elijah Muhammad, his then-mentor and head of the Nation of Islam, that he was unable sexually to satisfy his wife, Betty Shabazz. Marable also has Malcolm literally running away from Betty after the birth of each of their children. Political focus encouraged parental neglect.

Marable unearths new information from FBI and NYPD surveillance files regarding Malcolm's assassination. Three men were originally convicted; only two of them were present during the shooting. Marable's research points to a conspiracy organized by members of the Nation of Islam's Newark, New Jersey mosque; some of the conspirators remain alive and unindicted. The assassination was tacitly endorsed by the Nation's leadership, and indirectly abetted by both the NYPD and the FBI. However, "the chief beneficiary of Malcolm's assassination," Marable asserts, "was Louis Farrakhan"—his former disciple. With Malcolm dead, Farrakhan was able to assume Malcolm's exalted position within the Nation before taking over the leadership of the organization after Elijah Muhammad's death.

Marable's reconstruction of Malcolm's engagement with Africa may be the most important and long-lasting aspect of this new biography. He shows how, from fairly early on in his political career, Malcolm looked to African American civil rights veterans such as A. Philip Randolph, Bayard Rustin and Adam Clayton Powell, Jr.; he privately admired their non-militant political tactics even as he publicly derided them as Uncle Toms. His appreciation and understanding of their work grew over the course of three trips to Africa, during which he discussed the anti-colonial struggle and postcolonial leadership with Kwame Nkrumah, Gamal Abdel Nasser, Ahmed Sékou Touré, Jomo Kenyatta and others.

During his final trip to the continent, he tried to persuade the Organization of African Unity to endorse a memorandum claiming that racism in the United States and South Africa were the same, as part of his efforts to demonstrate that the African American struggle was one of human, not civil, rights. (The OAU refused for fear of being lumped with the Soviets and China.)

Malcolm's pilgrimage to Mecca is well known. But Marable

demonstrates how Malcolm's experiences in Saudi Arabia slowly distanced him from the Nation of Islam's fantastical eschatology and its avowedly anti-white theology. While Malcolm's break from Elijah Muhammad was initially prompted by his recognition of the latter's earthly proclivities—in particular, his series of affairs with young women—it also came about because he realized the limited usefulness of Nation theology to the African American struggle.

One of the great shibboleths of American thought puts Martin Luther King and Malcolm X as reconciling opposites: Martin vs. Malcolm, the integrationist apostle of non-violence versus the separatist demagogue, coming to a dialectical synthesis near the end of their lives. Marable evokes this dualism while implicitly rejecting it. Malcolm X demonstrated that mere reconciliation would not suffice, especially within the insular political and spiritual worlds of the United States. By showing how Malcolm X had to look abroad fully to apprehend the condition of Blacks in the States, Marable suggests that American redemption may only come through the path that Malcolm took: through the political philosophy of Pan-Africanism and the theological ambit of Pan-Islam. It is, on Marable's part, a bold and radical move, but one of critical importance. "Malcolm X," Marable writes, "represented the most important bridge between the American people and more than one billion Muslims throughout the world."

Manning Marable's Regurgitation on the Life and Memory of Malcolm X

Ezra Hyland

> *i remember...*
> *january 1968*
> *it's snow,*
> *the desire that i had to build a black snowman*
> *and place him upon Malcolm's grave*
>   *(Jackson, 1968)*

April 4, 2011, marked the 43rd anniversary of the murder of Martin Luther King Jr. This day should have been a day of commemoration, celebration and rededication to the lives, sacrifices and struggles of all those who gave so much, to obtain human rights and dignity during the last half of the 20th century. Unfortunately much of the attention that should have gone to such a significant day was usurped by the release of Manning Marable's book *Malcolm X: A Life of Reinvention.* The release of this long awaited tome, even with its ill chosen release day should still have been a special occasion, if not for the tragic death of Dr. Marable two days earlier and because much of the early commentary and reportage on the book focused on the scandalous, sensational and poorly documented aspects of his final work, resulting in warring fronts between Malcolm's and Manning's defenders. It is important now to move beyond emotion and critically respond to Marable's text. This response is necessary, because too many people believe if something is in print it must be true.

    I will attempt to explore some of Dr. Marable's logical errors, and attempt to provide a framework through which to understand why Dr. Marable may have portrayed Malcolm the way he did. This essay will not vilify Manning Marable because he is too important a figure in African American letters to diss based on one text. Nor is the purpose of this essay to deify Malcolm X for in the words of Olaudah Equiano (1995), Malcolm was neither a saint, a hero, nor a tyrant, (p. 33) Malcolm X was a man—a human being, an ancestor. In African culture, to be considered an ancestor is to occupy a sacred space in our lives. Toni Morrison (Wright, 2006) states that our ancestors are not to be worshiped "slavishly, or uncritically, or without a sense of the need for revolutionary change," but to base what is possible in our lives upon the foundations they laid (p. 4). In that way the ancestors remain alive and connected to us as we live. Only when we turn ancestors into idols static and unchanging do they die.

> *I hope no white person ever has cause to write*
> *about me because they never understand...(Giovanni, 1968)*

Sometime in the late '90s, I saw Manning Marable give a talk and discuss his researching the life of Malcolm and his book project, from that point on I began to look for the final text. Finally, the life of Malcolm would be in the hands of someone Black who understood Black life and would apply the rigorous methodology of the historian, which would include, according to Manning (2005) complete archival investigation, of letters personal documents, criminal records, etc to demystify Malcolm and expose him warts and all. (p. 26) I was prepared for the demystification of my hero whom Marable (1995) described as the personification of an individual to overcome the worst circumstances to achieve personal integrity and leadership (p. 137). It is important to note myth does not mean lie. Myths according to John Campbell (1988) are necessary parts of all civilizations, they are "clues to the spiritual potentialities of the human life...myths are created so that we may experience meaning" (p. 5). When people become myths in the universal sense of the word they simply become models, touch stones to live our lives by. What happens to a people who their myths destroyed? People create their own morals, law and initiations, which leads to violence and disintegration (p. 8).

Dr. Marable argues *The Autobiography* as told to Alex Haley is flawed, but does not make that case powerfully, nor does he significantly contradict Haley's heavily truncated version of Malcolm's life. *The Autobiography*, criminal records, recollections of associates, speeches etc. are pieces of the man. To focus on any one of these as the soul truth is to destroy the wholeness of the one studied. A figure of the historic importance of El Hajj Malik El Shabazz can only be understood as, alive and though dead still in a constant process of change. Because each succeeding generation will interpret the life through its own cultural filters.

Manning says, Detroit Red as Malcolm constructed him...who used illegal drugs and engaged in illicit sex, who broke all the rules...upon close examination many elements of Detroit Red's narrative are fictive (p. 481). Fictive is defined by Merriam Webster as not genuine, as imaginary. Marable established Malcolm did use and sell illicit drugs, was involved in all manner of crime and vice and was a rule breaker, so what aspects of his life were a sham. What aspects of *The Autobiography* was fictive, names, dates and facts (p. 10), remember Malcolm was a one-time a junkie, how many junkies accurately remember dates and facts, years after events? If there were substantive factual errors, what were they? Manning, never gets around to telling us. This was an "as told to" biography, to record events as Malcolm relayed them. Were the "fictive" aspects because of Malcolm's faulty recollection or was that the deliberate work of Haley in cooperation with the editors, lawyers of the publisher and or his FBI mole writing partner?

To critique a text, we must understand the author's reason for writing. Dr. Marable (2005) stated his purposes for writing the book were to recount what actually happened in Malcolm's life. Marable states he originally had the idea to write a modest "political biography" in 1987 and a time in which there was a substantial body of literature about Malcolm. By 2002 when apparently he began in earnest, the corpus had grown to over 930 books, 350 recordings and another 360 films and internet resources (p. 26). By 2010 those numbers may have doubled. Instead of something new and corrective, much of the book is the regurgitation of past works.

He criticized most of the prior works about Malcolm X by saying almost none relied on serious research, and as being shallow and lacking original sources, yet his book contains more references to prior publications then original research itself. Goldman is referenced over 70 times, Decaro over 65. Chapter one is 23 pages and Strickland/Green are referenced over 20 times. Also many of the most sensational revelations about Malcolm's personal life and the name of his assassin seem to come from an interview with Abdur-Rahman Muhammad in October and November of 2010, even though the acknowledgments and research notes, usually completed after the book is completed are dated September 25, 2010 (p. 493).

Second, he wants to present facts that Malcolm could not have known, such as the extent of illegal law enforcement tactics against him. What he does not speculate about is how this knowledge might have caused Malcolm to act differently. Most glaringly he does not seem interested in how the knowledge Malcolm did have affected his functioning as a leader. Malcolm and Nation of Islam were extremely aware of the disruptive tactics employed by law enforcement local and national. The Nation of Islam knew it was under surveillance dating back to the 1930s. It is safe to assume,

Malcolm was well aware of the infiltration of the Nation of Islam and other Black organizations. A 1959 article in *U.S. News and World Report* ended with ominous words about law enforcement watching them. Malcolm also had a long relationship with Louis Lomax, who identified by name possible FBI agents within the Nation of Islam's leadership. Marable does not offer any new information, in the years since Malcolm's murder, most of the information in the book has been revealed. We have Cointelpro documents, and dozens of texts have been written detailing the FBI and CIA's role in the destruction of Black groups and nations including noted scholar Clayborne Carson's *FBI Files on Malcolm X*. Karl Evanzz's the *Judas Factor* are two of the best researched. Again, Manning is regurgitating info that his readers have had time to thoroughly digest.

He lists his third goal as identifying those responsible for Malcolm's assassination. Scooped again. In 1977, Talmadge Hayer gave the first of several detailed confessions naming his fellow killers and details of the plan that differed from the official governmental story. Marable writes on May 2010, Abdur-Rahman Muhammad directly accused William Bradley as the man who "delivered the first and deadliest shot" in an "internet publication" (p. 476). Marable, does not even bother to give the link to the article in the notes. It is inconceivable that Marable could claim one of his chief aims was to identify the killers of Malcolm X, and then cite the internet as the support for his claims is pitiful at best. At worse, to accuse someone of murder and expose that person and his family to harm based on an internet publication is criminal.

> *I stay cool, and dig all jive, that's the way I stay alive.*
> *My motto, as I live and learn, Is Dig and be dug in return.*
> *(Hughes, 1967)*

Marable uses the term reinvention to characterize the stages of Malcolm's life but he never makes it clear who is responsible for the reinvention. Code shifting is a term borrowed from linguistics which refers to fact that to survive in a society in which has defined Black people as other and denies the legitimacy of their vernacular traditions, Black people speak in a variety of dialects based on the expectations of the social setting. This does not imply the speaker is faking or acting white or reinventing herself etc. It reflects a fundamental aspect of Black life, the ability to be authentically yourself while wearing various masks. What he calls reinvention is in reality more an example of the cultural code shifting Black people experience rather than some conscious or cynical maneuver on his part. Malcolm's life rather than being one of reinvention is the quintessence of the lives of far too many Black children.

> *In an atmosphere where broken promises are daily*
> *realities, where deferred dreams are nightly facts,*
> *...disappointment produces despair and*
> *despair produces bitterness, ... Bitterness has not the*
> *capacity to make distinctions between some and all*
> *(King, 2001)*

At an early age Malcolm loses both his parents. Before they leave his life they plant the seed of Garveyism deep into their children. Later when Malcolm encounters the Nation of Islam and its teachings, it is more of a reawakening than a reinvention. Malcolm's father is murdered as Malcolm approaches adolescence. Marable does not seem to consider how that may have affected the young boy. His father, murdered by whites, prepares him for the Nation of Islam's doctrine of whites as devils. Malcolm's mother struggling to deal with the loss of her husband and the pressure of raising her family alone becomes pregnant by a boyfriend and eventually succumbs to mental illness and is placed in a mental hospital. How would her abandonment be interpreted by young Malcolm? Would a young child interpret her pregnancy as a betrayal of his beloved father? His father dead and feeling abandoned and betrayed by his weak mother, he gravitates toward the pimps, men who survive by encouraging and exploiting weak and vulnerable women or men. Rejected by the academy, Malcolm's higher learning institution becomes the streets. Marable provides us with the facts of these events, but fails to understand how these early childhood experiences work to shape the adult.

It's a thin line between Love and Hate

For at least two decades Dr. Marable promised to mine the mountains of documents from government files to uncover the smoking gun that would answer all the unknown questions. It had to be incredibly disappointing to finally realize that the years spent on this quest was wasted, leaving Marable to express his disappointment in attacks on Malcolm and his family.

A brief exploration of the concepts of negative transference and alienation may reveal the unconscious factors that shaped the final text.

Freud (Fromm, 1981) observed that patients tended to develop idolatric worship of their analyst caused one of three responses, they tended to fall in love with, to be afraid of, or hate (p 52). If we apply this concept to the biographer, Malcolm was certainly and idolatric figure in the life of Marable the self described "X man." As we read his writings about Malcolm over the years, hints of alienation creep up and eventually these feelings manifest themselves as hatred and utter contempt.

These attacks in the biography begin with Manning (2011) going after Malcolm's father Earl by stating he abandoned his family and never bothered to get a legal divorce (p 16). Marable never bothers to establish that Earl was legally married. But, in the arc of the narrative, this prepares us for his later attacks on Malcolm, after all "fruit does not fall far from the tree." Next Marble goes after Betty Shabazz.

Marable notes when Giuliani then mayor of New York was booed as he attempted to deliver his condolences at the funeral of her mother, Attallah Shabazz stepped up to thank the mayor for his kindness and criticized the audience for being rude. Marble (2011) dismisses her action as reflecting Betty's bourgeois politics, but not her father's (p. 475). There is no justification for a scholar of Dr. Marable's status to take such a cheap shot at the late Betty Shabazz and her oldest daughter for a spontaneous display of class and dignity.

Perhaps after so many years in search of the real Malcolm, he became an idol, causing Manning lose sight of the fact that to Betty, Attallah, Qubilah, Ilyasah, Gamilah Lumumba, Malikah and Malaak, he was husband and father. When Malcolm was murdered, there were no national and international political figures at the funeral. Even his obituary in *Time Magazine* featured his mug shot from 1944 with the caption "If ballots won't work..., the second photo was a close up of Malcolm on a stretcher, with the caption "... bullets will." The presence of Mayor Giuliani and other dignitaries at Betty's funeral reflected a level of acceptance and respect that eluded their father at his funeral.

Not only does Manning (2011) trash Betty Shabazz for the choice of speakers at her funeral, he sets out to absolutely destroy her in life by accusing her of having an affair with Charles 37X Kenyatta, her bodyguard. Marable based the accusation on the fact that Betty and Kenyatta were frequently traveling by car (p 380). This is almost too silly to challenge. If she was in a car with anyone it should have been her bodyguard. It is not like the old Flip Wilson line, where Geraldine says they were "in the booth in the back, in the corner in the dark." Marable does not seem to consider the possibility that these rumors were spread by government paid agents and provocateurs, or that the strained nature of the relationship between Ella and Betty regarding their roles in Malcolm's life, may have encouraged Ella to spread such gossip (p. 388). He almost offhandedly mentions James 67X may have encouraged such rumors and gossip because it would give him an advantage in future power struggles (p. 388). Marable accepts the most outlandish claims about Malcolm and Betty's personal lives without any reservation, but criticizes Rodnell Collins (Malcolm's nephew) and Peter Bailey with embellishing Ella Collins' narrative with their own speculations (p. 499). When the slander is directed at Malcolm or Betty it never occurs to Manning that some of the sources may have embellished their stories.

Marable's alienation seems to have made him vulnerable to fundamental errors. The first is failing to apply the proper historical context to the life of Malcolm X. Malcolm was shaped by the cultural norms of the 1940s and 1950s, if we are to understand Malcolm and critique his behavior, we must start there. Marable states Malcolm was his most caring while Betty was pregnant, yet, after the birth of the child Malcolm virtually disappeared (p. 148). Malcolm disappeared so thoroughly that Marable is able to tell us he spoke at NOI gatherings in Albany, Hartford, Newark and New Jersey. This is hardly disappearing, Malcolm went back to work. In the '50s, the wife was rushed to the delivery room while the husband sat in the waiting room passing out cigars. In most cases after he counted the fingers and toes he was back at work, the baby represented another mouth to feed.

His alienation also allows Marable to jump to the worst and most unsubstantiated claims. He accuses Malcolm of having an affair while in Geneva, because Malcolm wrote in his diary a woman with whom he worked in Cairo turned up at his hotel and said she was "madly in love...and seems willing to do anything." Marable then says on another occasion she joined him in his room and left a couple of hours later, (p 385) but again, Marable provides no proof in the notes that happened.

Marable does a good job detailing how the unpredictability of Malcolm's last weeks caused difficulty for the MMI and OAAU. Often business couldn't be done, because Malcolm couldn't be found. Malcolm frequently stayed in hotels and even traveled alone during his final weeks. In spite of these observations Marable states Malcolm *may have* spent the night with a young girl the night before his death, but once again he provides no proof (p. 423). In a concatenation worthy of a Walter Mosley novel, Marable has this same girl involved in a relationship with a man allegedly involved in the plot to kill Malcolm.

> *I didn't hit him. I should have but never did.*
> *...so I hated him instead...the hate is till there,*
> *today, over twenty years later.*
> *(Wideman, 1984)*

If Judas was alive today he would still have to say something bad about Jesus. Marable sets out to expose Malcolm warts and all to the harsh light of truth and expose the fictive and exaggerated nature of his biography. But, he does not seem to apply the same skepticism to Malcolm's enemies. Most bizarre perhaps is Marable's unquestioning reliance on the word of sworn enemies of Malcolm or those who were rivals of Betty. Marable asserts the true views of the Nation of Islam and its adherents, had not been adequately represented in the past (p. 12). The views of the Nation of Islam since Malcolm's leaving have always been absolutely clear. Elijah Muhammad condemned Malcolm as a hypocrite, Farrakhan said Malcolm was worthy of death. Marable writes the Mosque No. 7 FOI class was told "We should destroy Malcolm" (p. 374). The Minister of Mosque No. 24 declared "Malcolm X really should be killed." Marable accuses a NOI crew of attempting to "wound or kill" Benjamin 2X Malcolm's assistant. He accuses the Nation of Islam of firebombing Malcolm's home. All NOI faithful were obligated to denounce Malcolm as a "hypocrite and liar." The position of the Nation of Islam at the time is all too clear.

> *He made us so proud. A master player who faced death on his*
> *own terms. One who never faked the funk.*
> *One who never disgraced the game at anytime.*
> *(Hassan, 1996)*

Even with its flaws, and inconsistencies, hopefully this biography will inspire new efforts to interrogate and make meaning of Malcolm's life, and in reexamining his life cause us to reexamine ours. If we allow anger, fear and shame to cause us to shun the book and not reexamine our beliefs, to not become reacquainted with Malcolm or meet him for the first time, then the fault will be our own. Then and only then, when we transform Malcolm for a living force to an idol, will he die, and this time the blood will be on our hands.

References

Campbell, J. (1988). *The Power of Myth.* New York: Bantam Doubleday Publishing Group, Inc.

Equiano, O. (1995). *Interesting Narrative of the Life of Olaudah Equiano.* Massachusetts: Bedford Books.

Fromm, Erich, (1962) *beyond the chains of illusion*: My Encounter with Marx and Freud. New York: Simon & Schuster.

Fromm, Erich. (1981) *Greatness and Limitations of Freud's thought.* New York: Mentor. pp. 10 - 14

Giovanni. N (1968). *Nikki-Rosa. Black feeling Black talk Black Judgment.* (pp. 58 - 59) New York: William Morrow & Company, Inc.

Hasan, U. (1996). *On a Mission.* New York: Henry Holt.

Hughes, L. (1967). *Motto.* In *The Panther & the Lash* (p. 11). New York: Vintage Classics

Jackson, M. (1974). *I Remember,* In A. Adoff (Ed.), *My Black Me: A Beginning Book of Black Poetry* (p. 58). New York: D. P. Dutton & Co., Inc.

King, M., Carson, C. (Ed). (2001) *The Autobiography of Martin Luther King Jr.* New York: Grand Central Publishing.

Marable, M. (2005) *Rediscovering Malcolm's Life: A Historian's Adventures in Living History* in *Souls*, Winter 2005 (p. 26)

Marable, M. (1995) *Malcolm as Messiah: Cultural Myth versus Historical Reality* in *Beyond Black and White.* New York: Verso.

Marable, M. (2011) *Malcolm X: A Life of Reinvention.* New York: Viking.

Wideman, J. (1984) *Brothers and Keepers.* New York: Holt Rinehart and Winston.

Wright, J. (2010). *Shadowing Ralph Ellison.* Mississippi: University Press of Mississippi

X, Malcolm. (1967) *On Afro-American History.* New York: Merit Publishers.

Is Imitation Truly the Mother of Invention?
Regina Jennings

I am so disappointed in Manning Marable's supposed "magnum opus" *A Life of Reinvention: Malcolm X* (2011). If I wanted to read a kiss-and-tell-all text, I certainly would have selected another book. To be fair to Marable, however, I do appreciate the enormous amount of research and years involved in writing this text, and its detail in some areas: such as presenting a racist policeman eavesdropping on X and then becoming a proponent (355). Or, the plump particulars of Malcolm X's international travel in Egypt, hanging out with Shirley Graham Du Bois and her son David (364-5). Or the sampling of the culinary delights Malcolm X enjoyed in Alexandria and his consistency in legitimizing the Muslim Mosque Incorporated by officials in the Islamic world (366). As a Malcolm scholar, it is always a pleasure to reread how this amazing man crisscrossed the globe to change for the better the saga of African American people. In fact, Malcolm X urged the call for this new racial name "African American." When he walked the Earth, we were known as n/Negroes. Yet, my greatest disappointment in Marable's work is based on the salacious material he chose to expound and his overreaching interpretations.

Before I begin, I must ask two questions. What is the role of the Black historian/critic/biographer? How did such jobs occur in academia? Most reading this already know the answers, but they are worth revisiting. Black Studies happened in academia because of activism in the streets and on college campuses. Malcolm X was very much a part of that whirlwind of courage once young people and the not so young heard his powerfully persuasive African-centered voice. As Black courses were negotiated in higher education, those offerings were supposed to address not only edification standards but also the massive and diversified lack in the lives of Black people beyond college campuses. In spite of this, that mandate somehow disappeared among those fortunate enough to get university and college positions in departments or programs that study the Black world.

Beginning with his characterization of Betty, Malcolm's wife and the mother of his six daughters, Marable oversteps reasonableness with his rendition of her as an adulterous, ball-breaking bitch (my words not his) who caused and broadcasted Malcolm's weaknesses which forever colored her husband's decisions. In plainer language, according to Marable because of the flip of Betty's lip, Malcolm stayed on the road creating temples or mosques for Elijah Muhammad in order to avoid going home to her (148). Neither a Marcus Garvey heart nor a Martin Delany brain, neither a Harriet Tubman vision, nor a Queen Nzingha fierceness heightened Malcolm's life force to accomplish his mission. Instead, Betty's insult to her husband about his unsatisfactory, sexual performance overwhelmingly influenced his constant travel and oration to uplift the so-called Negro. That conclusion is unacceptable to me.

Manning Marable's book indeed harkens back to William Styron's racist fictional depiction of Nat Turner. Styron has Nat selecting to frontally attack the system of enslavement because of his arousal for a White woman. He has Nat Turner lusting after this image so engrossingly that in his dissatisfaction of not having her, he wages war on Whites. In Styron's imagination, slavery was not the culprit that spurred Nat Turner to kill White people. Turner's unrequited love for a woman, White, was the catalyst. In the literary imaginations of both Manning and Styron, each writing about revolutionary, selfless, brave thinking and doing Black men, women have a vast subordinating power.

With Styron being both White and male, I was alarmed by his fictitious rendering of Nat Turner, but I could understand his predilection. He is White and proud and believes that his people have the controlling image of Black male behavior and in some instances he is correct; just not when portraying a Black revolutionary who responded to the raping, selling, bartering, butchering, branding, killing, maiming, beating, whipping, pederasty, molestation, terrorizing, and all around abuse of his people by not just saying I will fight back, but doing it. To minimize the revolutionary potency of Nat Turner, Styron entered the Klan-like thinking that all Black men are obsessed with White women similar to Othello the Moor. William Shakespeare had this character so grateful and gratified with his White wife that when turning unsure of her faithfulness, Othello kills Desdemona and therefore destroys himself.

When Betty married Malcolm X, she was twenty-three years old, an orphan lucky enough to have had loving adoptive parents. Before joining the Nation of Islam, Betty was already in college studying nursing while listening to the ideology of Elijah Muhammad. She joined the Muslims, like most men and women who became members because she was disgusted with American racism and she delighted in finding a religious, family-oriented organization which was an alternative to a society that had legally and culturally dehumanized her people. The separatist formula inherent in the dogma of the Nation of Islam appealed to her fighting spirit and independence. It structured her life with race-centered purpose and meaning. In her own right, before Malcolm ever looked her way, her joining the NOI states clearly a Black Nationalist freedom fighting personal directive. In the NOI she could formulate that desire into a home and a spirituality that allowed the open expression of Marcus Garvey's inspired dictum: "race first." Her filling out the membership form shows her willingness to change religions from one where all of the images were opposite her own. Betty opted to reject the American lie so when she discovered the Nation of Islam—put together, maintained, and built by a son of sharecroppers—she joined.

Marable does give Betty her props (138-9) as an educated, self-motivated woman, but he also claims she was a nuisance to Malcolm (164) which kept the minister on the road to avoid her. Such a conclusion cripples Malcolm's selflessness and demeans this man who labored until his assassination to put together an international solution to address the so-called Negro's American trauma.

Louis X, now Louis Farrakhan undertook becoming a minister under Malcolm and Manning writes that it was Louis who told him that although Malcolm married Betty, he was still in love with a pre NOI lover named Evelyn who had also joined the Nation. This is mind boggling, unknowable and unnecessary information. Even more, what has this double female destiny to do with the back breaking work that Malcolm performed for his nation? If he so loved Evelyn who returned his affection, why didn't he marry her or even have two wives. Polygamy is allowed in Islam. For the sake of sensationalism, Marable offers up Malcolm uncertain in his decisions and henpecked at home his wife a biblical Eve and a dominatrix.

Betty was in an extraordinary position in the late 1950s and early '60s, living with a legend whose extraordinariness never ceased to grow. Certainly, there were strains. What she verbally lashed at her husband in the privacy of their home needed to rest there. Her comments became public because Malcolm wrote a letter to his spiritual father for marital advice; thus, Betty's taunt about her husband's unsatisfactory sexual performance was not a community matter. She may have wanted to disparage her husband, because she felt neglected and excluded from his mostly male and public life. All Malcolm scholars know how Malcolm gave everything that he had to build Muhammad's Nation: constantly travelling nationwide either starting new mosques or aiding their development, making speeches at universities, churches, and community organizations. In his absences and then meetings and responsibilities at Temple #7, Betty may have simply wanted to get his attention, desiring more time with him.

Even though she knew that she was marrying a legend in the making, after the rush and excitement of courtship, for all women (and men), daily life together can be anti-climatic, especially for a woman like Betty. Once married to Malcolm her independence was notably clipped and because of her new position as the wife of the national spokesman for the Nation, she was cordoned off by NOI security. Betty an educated woman prior to marriage had to feel cloistered in Malcolm's absences and to challenge his non-attention she verbally slapped him where it would hurt the most. However, when I consider the growing family that she provided for Malcolm, if there ever was a bedroom problem, more than likely it solved itself. Even though Marable claims that the couple was on the brink of divorce, they never did.

Marable's many mistakes rest upon using the mundane aspects of Malcolm's life as a catalyst for his daring, evolutionary precepts and activities. Sensationalism always is preferable for publishers than the truth of what Native American displacement and genocide and African enslavement has accomplished among the people Red and Black. Deciding to turn Malcolm's legacy into sketches of cultural and contemporary reality television, I fault Marable for not even considering the effect this would have on Malcolm and Betty's children and grandchildren. Many leaders have multi-generational bans on personal papers for these very reasons, and what's up with Minister Farrakhan?

The assault on Betty's character enlarges where Marable relies on the testimony of James 67X who in explicit terms said that Betty flirted with him during her husband's absence. Why would 67X say that to Marable? Perhaps, he wanted to unburden himself from a long held secret, especially now that Betty is dead and her daughters quite alive. Let's look closer at him as a person. First of all, Malcolm made him a lieutenant in the NOI, who was certainly taught the dictum of Black unity. If Betty flirted, why not get help for the sister. Why not go to the Big Mommas in the NOI or MGT and discuss Betty's inappropriate, youthful behavior? Instead, James 67X just split the scene, never telling Malcolm or anyone until Marable. He continued providing security for Malcolm and when Malcolm split with the Nation and formed the Muslim Mosque Incorporated, James 67X went with him and was in charge of communications and correspondence (306). Marable later reports that Betty disliked James 67X, yet she phoned him regularly when Malcolm travelled to Africa to find out and hold onto any messages he may have received from her husband (327). According to Marable people in the MMI found 67X "argumentative and notoriously secretive" (376) and he disliked independent women with authority. Lynne Shifflett often caught his wrath once Malcolm appointed her organizing secretary for the Organization for Afro-American Unity (374).

After Malcolm's assassination, James 67X escaped to Guyana where Bruce Perry hunted him down and purchased the tapes that became *Malcolm X: The Last Speeches* (1992) published by Pathfinder Press. Perry states in the introduction that he and 67X corresponded for "the better part of a year." In leaving America, James abandoned his wife and family. With broken Black families an American tradition, I wonder how they fared in his absence?

Manning had early in the text adopted an inside/outside Dante inferno, scenario for his characters beginning with Earl Little, Malcolm's father. For him, he equally compares domestic life with the unconscionable terror of lynching in Reynolds, Georgia. He says that Earl's home life was "slightly less tumultuous" (15) than the Nazism that Blacks endured in the outer world of Georgia. This is an obscene comparison. Also, by referring to Malcolm as a method actor, Marable sets us up to re-envision Malcolm as a puppet and deceiver. Most notably, he finds fault in the *Autobiography of Malcolm X* because Malcolm and Haley omitted such scenes as this: young conman Malcolm once stole his big sister Ella's coat and robbed a friend (65).

All of us who read *The Autobiography* recognize that every feature in Malcolm's life would not appear; that's implicit in the nature of any autobiography. In fact, when I read those silly omissions, that Marable provided, I recalled my Uncle Jim's behavior on Annin Street in South Philadelphia during the late 1950s when he stole my sister's and my Easter outfits. Uncle Jim was a drug user and my grandmother, mother and aunt were upset, but not completely surprised because they recognized the extent of his illness and most importantly, why he was ill. Marable says that Malcolm was shaping how his life should read, deceiving readers.

Marable continues with his Malcolm the deceiver line when he attempts and fails to prove that Malcolm was not genuinely hardcore. In my view, one does not have to be Vito Corleone, Al Capone or Bumpy Johnson to be a gangster. Readers of *The Autobiography* get the sense of Malcolm's unlawful behaviors, which finally lead him to the Nation of Islam. What Manning has forgotten is the role of hyperbole in Black culture, particularly the urban variety and more broadly in this lost memory he fails to enlighten and educate the readers who adored Malcolm most.

Black readers in particular need to learn exactly how a son of sharecroppers and an ex-con built an empire, legally, and independent of government support. Useful clarifications would illuminate why and how Elijah Muhammad gathered so many devoted followers who turned away from drinking alcohol, using drugs, thievery, sexual lewdness, and assumed moral, conservative deportment. What were the economic factors that Elijah mastered that enabled him to build an enterprise that employed thousands? How did he become first a small businessman and then CEO without a hedge fund? How did Elijah Muhammad create independent schools that taught the next generation from his perspective, not school board selected texts? How did this man layout a platform that encouraged maleness to soar independently from White America? Neither Malcolm nor Farrakhan had to submit to a company or corporation for a job. Marable judges Malcolm and Muhammad by a set of Christian rules and values based on and biased to Black revolutionaries.

When Malcolm was traveling abroad in Geneva to meet with the Muslim Brotherhood, Marable instead of explaining this organization which would have enlightened and educated readers about his international relationships, the author instead discusses that Malcolm "had a surprise encounter with a young woman named FiFi, a United Nations secretary and Swiss national who had worked with Malcolm in Cairo" (385). Again no information about the Muslim Brotherhood which is so well examined in Juan Cole's book, *Engaging the Muslim World* (2009) instead Marable goes for the gossipy, recording that Malcolm in his journal wrote that FiFi had surprised him by saying that she "is madly in love with [him] and seems willing to do *anything* to prove it." After Malcolm had dinner with an Islamic dignitary and guests (Brotherhood people?) the following evening and returned to his hotel room around 9 p.m., guess who knocked on his door? Marable says that FiFi spent a couple of hours in Malcolm's room and "uncharacteristically" Malcolm didn't record in his journal what "transpired" between the two.

Now, where does that take our imagination? Nevertheless, let's go where Marable implies. Suppose dear FiFi made Malcolm an offer he refused to refuse? Now what? Let's see: Malcolm the adulterer. An adulterer is terrible in the Christian tradition and normally is a liar, a theme that Marable built since the opening of the text. Next, let's examine another route of interpretation. Malcolm and FiFi talked of triviality that Malcolm would never record because of its unimportance. Now let's try this possibility: She made him an offer that he did refuse and as she cried to lessen the rejection, he held her for a couple of hours and talked to her about his wife and his mission as he let her talk about her personal life and morality. Or how about this prospect: for a couple of hours, this young woman made a travel-and-Black-people-champion-weary male feel special with her presence and banter. How would he have recorded that?

There are some moments in life unnecessary for words. That is what private means. Manning Marable, in his reach for recognition never considered Malcolm and Betty's very much alive family, as well as the lovers of Malcolm who grew richly from his legacy. To further enhance my position, Manning Marable additionally wrote in his afterward that scholars should examine the similarities between the Nazi Party and the Nation of Islam. Manning Marable, rest in peace.

Malcolm because you conjured Bobby and Huey you created me a forever worker for our people: Malcolm, who travelled the world for Black people; who took a barrage of bullets for us; who publicly demonized the White man; Malcolm the seeker to make the n/Negro whole; who is the reason we are African American; so willing to walk the hero's journey; who selected bravery instead of bile; who soared from Elijah Muhammad's runway; who lionized Black history and culture; who was the father of millions: the MMI, OAAU, Black Arts Movement, Third World Press, The Black Panther Party, Nguzo Saba, Revolutionary Action Movement, Republic of New Afrika, African American Studies; Afrocentricity; Africalogy; Africana Studies; Black Studies; charter schools; who fought the police in court and won; and who turned supplicating Negroes to independent African men; thank you for giving Black women, brothers worthy of admiration.

RIP.

Rescuing Malcolm X From His Calculated Myths
Peniel E. Joseph

Malcolm X bestrides the postwar age of decolonization alongside global icons like Martin Luther King Jr. and Mahatma Gandhi. If King and Gandhi evoked nonviolence and disciplined civil disobedience as a shield to protect the world from imperial wars, racism, and rampant materialism, Malcolm wielded the specter of self-defense, violence, and revolution as a sword to permanently alter power relations between the global North and South. In an epoch contoured by revolutions that connected local political struggles to national and international upheavals, he self-consciously brokered links among Africa, the Middle East, and America, setting the stage for political, religious, and cultural reverberations that would continue past his lifetime.

Almost a half-century after his death in 1965, Malcolm X continues to capture the global political imagination. His denunciations of white racism to packed Harlem crowds remain searing images that capture a specific style of Black radicalism while simultaneously serving as a template for political revolutions that go beyond race and established the Third World as a bracingly independent geopolitical force. His speeches, political activism, and religious beliefs achieved mythic proportions after his death, spurred by the huge success of *The Autobiography of Malcolm X,* written in collaboration with Alex Haley and published posthumously. It remains a classic memoir of the once wayward youth's transformation from juvenile delinquent and criminal into the Nation of Islam's fiery national spokesman and, following a messy divorce from the group that would ultimately lead to his death, a radical human-rights advocate and Pan-Africanist who candidly admitted that some of his past views had been politically shortsighted, even reckless.

Embraced by Black Power activists, hip-hop artists, socialists, and Black Nationalists, Malcolm's iconography had been successfully rehabilitated enough by the 1990s to merit a major motion picture, an official U.S. postage stamp, and mainstream identification as King's angry but eloquent counterpart. Recognition came at a high cost. Despite a plethora of popular and scholarly works—on Malcolm's political and religious views, his life as hipster and hustler, his embrace of Pan-African impulses, his break with the Nation of Islam—a definitive scholarly biography illuminating his singular importance as a dominant twentieth-century historical figure remained absent. For personal, financial, and political reasons, his widow and subsequently his estate restricted access to important archival material until 2008. His former associates were loath to give interviews, and the Nation of Islam remained mostly silent about the circumstances surrounding his death. The FBI and the New York City Police Department closed off thousands of pages of surveillance and wiretapping records. Then too, the success of *The Autobiography* as a literary memoir narrowed the opening for a scholarly biography.

Historical scholarship has focused on Malcolm's words of fire, depicting him more as a brilliant speaker than a community organizer. His supple intellect, burgeoning political ambitions, and organizing prowess have garnered far less attention. As have details of his private life. And no single volume has attempted to craft a cohesive portrait that stands outside *The Autobiography's* considerable shadow. In that celebrated book, Malcolm X outlined his views on the importance of producing an accurate history: "I've had enough of somebody else's propaganda," he proclaimed.

Malcolm X: A Life of Reinvention (Viking Press), by Dr. Manning Marable, a historian at Columbia University who died just days before publication of what is clearly his life's work, achieves the rare feat of rescuing a man from his own mythology with deep archival research and brilliant insight. Marable's untimely death adds a layer of poignancy to a biography that will stand as the most authoritative account of Malcolm's life that will be written for a long time.

Marable emerged as one of the leading scholars of Black Marxism and radicalism in the early 1980s. The founding director of Columbia's Institute for Research in African American Studies and a prolific scholar, his work charted the black-freedom movement's domestic and global reverberations. In books like *Race, Reform, and Rebellion: The Second Reconstruction in Black America, 1945-1990* (second edition, University Press of Mississippi, 1991), *African and Caribbean Politics: From Kwame Nkrumah to the Grenada Revolution* (Verso, 1987), and *The Great Wells of Democracy: The Meaning of Race in America* (Basic Books, 2002), he deftly explored the way postwar Black radicals helped transform American democracy in the service of a human rights movement that transcended borders and boundaries.

His commitment to Black political empowerment went beyond the confines of academe, however, as he established an international network of contacts with activists and scholars throughout Africa, the Caribbean, and the larger Third World. Building enduring intellectual and institutional links between Harlem and Columbia—a hard-fought achievement in an Ivy League institution that has at times had a fraught relationship with the historically Black neighborhood—he was the rare public intellectual willing to speak truth to power while using scholarship to transform society.

In *Malcolm X*, Marable found a perfect subject, one whose uncanny ability to reinvent himself during his prematurely short life and truncated public career touched upon themes of Black political self-determination, economic justice, internationalism, and radical democracy represented in the scholar's own intellectual corpus.

Marable's subtitle, *A Life of Reinvention,* succinctly captures his book's larger effort to recast the political and personal life of the Black Power icon in both subtle and surprising ways. The Malcolm X revealed in these pages is at once a larger-than-life figure and a scaled-down, even frail human being. Marable refuses to shy away from Malcolm's flaws, candidly discussing his sexism, errors in political and personal judgment, and occasional anti-Semitic utterances. Suggestions, albeit based on circumstantial evidence, that Malcolm may have engaged in homosexual encounters during his time as a hustler promise to unleash renewed controversy about the identity of a man who adopted almost a dozen different names.

For scholars, if not the general public, Marable's *Malcolm X* now joins *The Autobiography* as an indispensable resource in comprehending Malcolm's complicated life. It not only "illustrates that many elements of Detroit Red's narrative are fictive," as Marable notes, referring to an early alias. More important, the book also offers the first accurate and in-depth chronology of a turbulent journey from criminal to icon. It shows us a man possessed of an uncanny ability both to absorb and project the sights and sounds of his surroundings, an aptitude that helped him convey a political and personal sincerity that has made him, until this day, perhaps the single most authentic leader that the Black working class has produced.

Portions of the biography questioning Malcolm's sexuality and alleging an extramarital affair by his wife have already elicited controversy, including at least one critical review attacking Marable's research methods. Years in the making, *Malcolm X* is a thoroughly researched biography, mining a rich archive of primary sources (including many never accessed before) and collecting oral histories from Malcolm's associates and Nation of Islam officials (most notably Louis Farrakhan). Marable's discussion of Malcolm's at-times strained marriage relies on such oral histories and on personal correspondence from Malcolm to Elijah Muhammad, his mentor and the Nation's spiritual leader, which offer substantive evidence of a troubled union. That's also the kind of material undoubtedly painful for surviving family members. The even more controversial assertion that Malcolm may have participated in a homosexual business relationship with a white man who served as his sometimes benefactor rests on more slender evidence, which the author himself describes as "circumstantial." But such instances of interpretive overreach are scarce.

Racial politics formed part of Malcolm Little's birthright, an inheritance from his parents, Earl and Louise Little, two politically courageous supporters of Marcus Garvey—or, depending on your perspective, ill-fated pioneers of Black Nationalism—in the distant outpost of Omaha, Nebraska, where Malcolm was born on May 19, 1925. While Malcolm was still young, the family moved to Lansing, Michigan. His was a difficult childhood, plagued by bouts of domestic violence, harassment from the local Klan, and Earl's gruesomely suspicious death (he was cut nearly in two by what white authorities claimed was a streetcar accident, and Malcolm surmised was part of a lynching). Earl Little's death shattered his surviving family, hurling them into an emotionally fatiguing battle with state relief agencies that found the young Malcolm relying on foster care and eventually triggered Louise's mental breakdown and institutionalization. By 1941, Malcolm had moved to Boston to live with his older half-sister Ella. It was here that Malcolm Little first reinvented himself as a small-time hood whose crimes were at least partially inspired by Ella's own extralegal activities in pursuit of a middle-class lifestyle.

Marable deconstructs the Legend of Detroit Red outlined in *The Autobiography*, finding that Malcolm purposely exaggerated his criminal exploits as a way of obscuring painful and embarrassing memories and of emphasizing the importance of the Nation of Islam in his eventual transformation. Far from being aligned with major gangsters, in this period Malcolm alternated between part-time legal employment like selling food on railroads (where he was known as Sandwich Red), dealing small amounts of marijuana to jazz musicians, and engaging in largely amateurish holdups, at least one of which ended in an early arrest. Successfully evading the draft by feigning mental illness, Malcolm engaged in escalating drug abuse and petty crime that ended abruptly shortly after World War II. Arrested in 1946 for a series of burglaries, fooled by false promises of leniency, he turned in his whole crew. The interracial makeup of the burglary ring, which included Malcolm's white girlfriend, inspired a harsh sentence of eight to ten years.

Within the walls of Norfolk Prison Colony, in Massachusetts, Malcolm Little would reinvent himself again. Through letters from his brother Reginald, he was first introduced to the Nation of Islam, a religious nationalist sect whose emphasis on pride, self-respect, and discipline echoed his father's distant Garveyite preaching. Newly energized and clean and sober, Malcolm dove into a meticulous study of religion, history, and philosophy. Paroled in 1952, he quickly became a full-time Nation of Islam minister. Whereas Garvey resurrected ancient African kingdoms as proof of Black nobility and self-respect, the Nation of Islam touted religious prophesy through an imaginative blend of Islam, Black Nationalism, and religious mythology that identified whites as "devils" and predicted America's destruction even as it embraced a conservative economic vision of Black capitalism.

Reborn as Malcolm X, a surname that reflected Black people's loss of identity in America's racial wilderness, the former Detroit Red now embraced personal self-discipline and an ascetic lifestyle. "The trickster disappeared," writes Marable, "leaving the willful challenger to authority." The biography weaves in new details to flesh out the narrative of Malcolm's becoming a minister and his rise to power within the Nation of Islam. He was an indefatigable organizer whose remarkable ability to inspire new converts and recruits helped propel the Nation's tiny infrastructure into a formidable group with global ambitions.

But tensions cropped up early. One of the new biography's greatest strengths is in shaping a nuanced portrait of postwar Harlem as a city within a city, teeming with competing political, religious, and labor groups, self-appointed leaders, and deteriorating economic conditions, which helped the Nation of Islam tout itself as a haven for Black men and women. Malcolm's extraordinary talent for "fishing" for new recruits outside of his fast-growing Harlem Temple No. 7 and his ability to successfully establish new temples in the North, South, and the West Coast between 1952 and 1962 marked him as Elijah Muhammad's most indispensable minister. It also made him enemies within the organization, especially among those connected by blood or marriage to Muhammad. Ultimately, even Malcolm's handpicked protégés would side against him in the aftermath of his split from the group, unexpected circumstances that he found bitterly disappointing.

According to Marable, Malcolm's poor choice of political allies within the Nation extended to his personal life and the fateful decision in

1958 to marry Betty Sanders, later renamed Betty Shabazz. In contrast to the loving, dutiful wife characterized in *The Autobiography* and 1992 film, Betty is depicted here as a stubborn, willful spouse who challenged Malcolm's patriarchal views of marriage and even engaged in an extramarital affair with one of his closest lieutenants—revelations that have understandably upset the Shabazz family. The couple endured rather than enjoyed each other's company over the course of a seven-year marriage, and Malcolm went so far as complaining to Muhammad in private correspondence of their sex life: "At a time when I was going all out to keep her satisfied (sexually), one day she told me that we were incompatible sexually because I had never given her any real satisfaction. From then on, try as I may, I began to become very cool toward her."

That quote, taken from a March 1959 letter written barely a year after their wedding, powerfully illustrates that Malcolm's marriage to Betty was tense from almost the beginning; tensions were exacerbated by periods of prolonged absence, financial stress, and harassment from law enforcement and later the Nation of Islam. Despite sustained analysis of his personal life, the complex psychological reasons behind Malcolm's reticence toward emotional intimacy with Betty remain elusive, buried, it seems, beneath a disciplined exterior that Marable seems incapable of completely shattering. He makes an intriguing suggestion that Malcolm's past sexual history with prostitutes and fast women created a kind of emotional trauma that rendered him incapable of properly addressing Betty's "emotional and sexual needs"; it's only a hint, and it deserves more exploration.

All of the forces that had built Malcolm X seemed to speed up in the 1960s. Joint surveillance from the New York Police Department's Bureau of Special Services unit and the FBI added to Malcolm's increasingly complicated life, one that by 1960 included extensive speeches on the college lecture circuit, a popularity spurred by the previous year's documentary *The Hate That Hate Produced,* narrated by Mike Wallace. The film was dedicated more to sensationalism than journalism and characterized the Nation of Islam as akin to the Ku Klux Klan, but it cast Malcolm into the public eye.

Politics increasingly animated Malcolm's public speeches and organizing energies, a situation that created anxiety within the upper reaches of the Nation. His national notoriety announced Black Muslims as a kind of ghoulish counterpart to King and the Southern civil rights movement's nonviolent demonstrations—even though Muhammad strictly forbade his group from engaging in secular political activity. Moreover, both

Malcolm and Muhammad agreed that the Nation should be part of a global community of Islam, but the Messenger, as Muhammad was known, sought recognition from orthodox Muslims in the Middle East to reinforce his standing at home, while Malcolm hoped that the entire group might join in a secular civil rights movement.

While Marable shows that the Nation's internal decision-making process, including formalizing a nonaggression pact with the American Nazi Party and George Lincoln Rockwell, pained Malcolm, his portrait does not shy away from Malcolm's own culpability in constructing an elaborate and eventually deadly cult of personality around the Messenger that brooked no internal criticism and meted out violence to dissenters. By the early 1960s, the Fruit of Islam had emerged as a powerful arbiter of physical violence within the Nation, a group implicitly sanctioned by Malcolm that would emerge as a deadly adversary after his break from the Nation.

Malcolm's circle was changing. Against the backdrop of the civil rights movement, his radical call for Black political self-determination struck a chord in urban Black militants discontented with nonviolence yet skeptical of Muhammad's claim to divinity. A diverse network of activists, entertainers, and celebrities like Sidney Poitier, Ossie Davis, and Ruby Dee, and elected leaders like Adam Clayton Powell Jr., formed alliances with Malcolm. His secular ambitions found him balancing on an increasingly perilous tightrope: implicitly sponsoring the kind of robust political activity Muhammad considered taboo while maintaining a public, almost fawning fealty to a religious sect he was intellectually outgrowing. Zesty debates with the nonviolent guru Bayard Rustin, the writer James Baldwin, and the leader of the Congress of Racial Equality, James L. Farmer Jr., quickly turned into more-intimate friendships, a pattern replicated with journalists like Louis Lomax and Alex Haley. Collectively, such people first challenged and then helped propel Malcolm into a more activist posture. "He seemed more than ever of two minds" during the early years of the Kennedy administration, Marable writes, "pulled both by his loyalty to Muhammad and by a need to engage in the struggle."

In 1963, the year that civil rights demonstrations in Birmingham and the March on Washington captured the world's collective imagination—and the Nation of Islam was quashing scandalous accusations regarding the Messenger's sexual misconduct—Malcolm X became the Nation's national minister. On November 10, he delivered his famous Message to the Grassroots, brandishing revolution as the antidote to racial oppression to sympathetic militants in Detroit who imagined him the leader of an as-yet-unnamed movement that would both parallel and intersect the civil rights struggle.

Throughout the year, Malcolm had blasted President Kennedy's reluctance to defend Black citizenship in the face of German shepherds and fire hoses in Alabama, even as he recoiled at King's use of children in demonstrations that erupted into violence. Unwisely, in December, he continued his blistering criticism, in flagrant violation of Muhammad's explicit orders to remain silent. Malcolm's "chickens coming home to roost" sound bite in response to a reporter's question about Kennedy's death sought to illustrate the boomerang effect of American violence, but quickly became engulfed in conjecture as to whether the Nation rejoiced in the death of the president. Malcolm's enemies in the Nation pounced, prodding Muhammad to discipline his wayward prodigy. What began as a three-month suspension turned into an organizational rout and whispers of assassination plots.

Banished from the Nation, Malcolm reinvented himself once again, this time as an independent, radical political activist and religious apostate. Marable's biography offers the most detailed examination yet of the final, exhilaratingly frenetic year of Malcolm's life: one in which he founded two short-lived religious and political organizations; spent 24 weeks in Africa; reimagined his understanding of revolution; embraced orthodox Sunni Islam; and networked with African and Middle Eastern rulers in an effort to leverage revolutionary political struggles back home.

Shortly after his departure from the Nation, Malcolm delivered his famous "The Ballot or the Bullet" speech, in which he touted a vision of radical democracy. But he remained an unapologetic political combatant, offering the ballot as a rapprochement with politics, while reminding listeners that the bullet might well remain the ultimate arbiter of America's historical racial divide. The speech also emphasized his longstanding belief in racial solidarity and united-front politics, sentiments often obscured by impassioned polemics, Marable shows us.

Malcolm's hajj to the holy city of Mecca that April culminated in another transformation: The sectarian religious warrior now embraced a universal vision of Islam that transcended race, geography, and ideology in favor of what Marable calls a new "role as a kind of evangelist," capable of fusing revolutionary politics and religion as part of a global human rights effort. Malcolm's travel diaries, revealed for the first time in this biography, reflect the contemplative thoughts of a man of war who had at last found peace. "There is no greater serenity of mind," he wrote, "than when one can shut the hectic noise and pace of the materialistic outside world, and seek inner peace within oneself." Africa also offered festivities, including meetings with Nigeria's Azikiwe and Ghana's Nkrumah, before returning home for a scarcely two-month effort to put together the Organization of Afro-American Unity, a secular attempt to expand support beyond disgruntled Muslims and loyalists who formed Malcolm's relatively small political base.

By July he was off again for an extended stay in Africa, where he became intimately acquainted with the strengths and limitations of Pan-African politics, found small joys in sightseeing, and drinking alcohol for the first time in many years, and basked in the luxurious hospitality of being recognized as an official guest of state in many countries. That summer and fall, he experienced a sense of freedom, energy, and spiritual renewal that made this period one of the happiest in his life. Collectively, Malcolm's three trips to Africa and the Middle East represent a stunning level of international engagement that Marable argues produced tangible religious and political alliances that disturbed the State Department and outraged Nation of Islam officials. Politically, these trips provided a blueprint for a subsequent generation of radical activists, most notably Stokely Carmichael, who would (sometimes consciously) retrace Malcolm's itinerary, en route to fashioning their own global political identities.

Malcolm returned to the States under the threat of a death sentence by the Nation. Marable painstakingly dissects Malcolm's February 21, 1965, assassination, arguing that two of the three convicted assassins were absent from the Audubon Ballroom at the time of the murder and making a compelling and detailed case for the ways in which the New York police's botched investigation allowed four guilty conspirators (including Malcolm's main shooter) to go free. The person Marable names as the alleged assassin currently lives in Newark and denies any involvement in Malcolm's death. Marable accessed thousands of new FBI, CIA, and other surveillance and informant files under the Freedom of Information Act, but the issue will remain open until all the relevant files have been found and released.

Marable takes pains to illustrate that the iconography in Haley's *Autobiography* at times presumptuously crafted an image of Malcolm in line with Haley's own political views as a "liberal Republican"—and one apt to sell commercially. *The Autobiography* sanitized Malcolm's radical politics by tacking on an introduction by a *New York Times* writer and an epilogue by Haley himself, even as it excised three chapters originally designed to showcase Malcolm's new political philosophy.

A self-made political leader, Malcolm "keenly felt, and expressed, the varied emotions and frustrations of the Black poor and working class," Marable reminds us. In that he became the avatar of not only a domestic movement for racial justice, but a symbol of an international human rights movement, one that crossed religious and racial boundaries and transcended geographical and ideological restrictions. Yet for all of his efforts at reinvention, Malcolm X remained at his core "a Black man, a person of African descent who happened to be a United States citizen."

One of the many pleasures of Marable's *Malcolm X* is its ability to reveal the sights and sounds of Black America's postwar freedom surge, a time marked by the exhilarating sounds of bebop, the internal migration of rural Southern Blacks to the urban North, and escalating racial protest against Jim Crow. Tellingly, jazz musicians and entertainers were attracted to Malcolm and the Nation of Islam. Malcolm's own powerful rhetoric contained jazz flourishes and clipped, at times improvised, passages that attested to his time around musicians as a young man.

More than 45 years after his death, we now have a historical portrait of Malcolm X that goes beyond literary clichés and autobiographical fictions to reveal an all-too human man beset by personal trials and political tribulations that would have felled the less courageous. Stripped from the cocoon of his posthumous aura of invincibility, Malcolm X emerges from these pages an endlessly fascinating and protean figure whose shortcomings make his political accomplishments all the more remarkable. Against the backdrop of private disappointments and embarrassingly public betrayals, Marable reminds us that Malcolm X still managed to transform "the discourse and politics of race internationally," a final enduring reinvention that continues long after his death.

[First published in the *Chronicle of Higher Education*, May 1, 2011]

Malcolm, Charisma and Ancestry
Clyde Ledbetter Jr.

At the dawn of the much-anticipated release of Manning Marable's *Malcolm X: A Life of Reinvention*, a close male friend of mine of the same age called me on the phone. I mention his age because I believe the conversation that followed is to a greater or lesser extent typical for young Black men who have heard of or read the book. The conversation went something like this:

Me: Hel—

Friend: Did you hear about some (expletive) that's sayin' Malcolm was a (expletive denoting homosexual men)?

Me: —lo

Friend: Tell me that (expletive) ain't true, cuz?

Me: I haven't read the book yet, bro.

Friend: It can't be true. It can't! I mean, it would change the way I look at the dude. Man, this is (expletive) with me. This (expletive) ruined my day.

I spent the rest of the thirty-minute conversation calming down my friend, who at moments sounded like he was on the brink of tears. His universe seemed to have caved in on him. For him, Malcolm is greater than a hero. For him, Malcolm was the very epitome of African leadership and manhood. The very thought that Malcolm X, *his* Malcolm X could an anyway be a homosexual shook his soul. I told him to read the book before he completely gave up on Malcolm and his example. We hung up and I immediately ordered the book hoping probably just as hard as my friend that the claims within weren't true.

I cite this particular and rather extreme example because it shows how Marable's text has affected many of those who have either heard about it or read it. After reading the book, I was left with one question: why did Marable writes this? Marable himself states that the purpose of his writing the book was "to go beyond the legend: to recount what actually occurred in Malcolm's life."[1] Aside from the fact that much of what Marable "recounts" about Malcolm and others (including an implication of Amy Jacques Garvey as a murderer) does not go beyond the realm of legend or more accurately gossip, this is only a partial statement regarding the purpose of his writing of the book. With his death, Marable cannot answer as to his motivation in writing a text that although has many high points is peppered with tales of illicit behavior based on largely hearsay information. Many have argued that texts such as these seek to "humanize" historical figures such as Malcolm. But what exactly is the goal of the "humanizing" project as it is presented in Marable's book? Marable does a terrific job pointing out the implicit goals behind the now classic *The Autobiography of Malcolm X*. He posits that Malcolm's initial goal was to exalt Elijah Muhammad and his work as a prophet. Following his split from the Nation, the goal was then changed to explain his current political ideology although much of this did not make it into the final version as a result of the implicit goals of his collaborator Alex Haley who sought to use Malcolm's life as "a cautionary tale about human waste and the tragedies produced by racial segregation."[2] The implicit goals of Marable however remain remote at this time.

Marable writes that, "the historical Malcolm, the man with all his strengths and flaws, was being strangled by the iconic legend that had been constructed around him."[3] Had he presented a text that sought to display the flaws of Malcolm's political thought and some of the weaknesses of his efforts at organizing the African masses in order for contemporary and future organizers to learn from and not repeat his mistakes, then Marable would have been lauded by the community for his efforts. Instead, many are asking (quite angrily I might add) why Marable would put out a work that seemingly attempts to undermine the legacy of a man who had "come to embody the very ideal of Blackness for an entire generation"[4] and was and is considered "our living Black manhood" by attaching to his life a series of "strongly suggested" implications concerning his sexuality and illicit sexual behavior ranging from homosexual prostitution to extra-marital affairs. Although we may never know what Marable was really attempting to do by including these unfounded items within his book, we do know the effect it has had on many of those who have read it. It has been seen as an unprovoked attack on the character of a charismatic ancestor who still continues to influence African people the world over 56 years after his transition. An understanding of charisma and what ancestry means to African people demonstrates why such a work would elicit the response that it did from not only my friend but the majority of people of African descent who have engaged the text.

Malcolm X is often characterized as a charismatic figure. However, the words "charisma" and "charismatic" much like "revolution" and "revolutionary" are often misused in popular media and what results is a defamation of the word's original meaning. Today, reality TV stars are charismatic and new sneakers are revolutionary. Thus, the term charisma is often used as a synonym for popular without its true sociological foundation brought to the fore. Marable himself refers to Tupac Shakur as charismatic in his book's epilogue. Charisma is not simply a crude measure of "likeability" but is a theoretical concept that deals primarily with authority. Authority in this case being a dialectical relationship between the leader and the led with the led *voluntarily* giving the leader some measure of power over their being. Although a great poet and artist, Tupac's charisma, if authoritative at all, was limited in its ability to lead large numbers of people to make significant life changes.

The term charisma was coined by nineteenth century German sociologist Max Weber who wrote on among other things, this concept of authority. For Weber, authority came in three forms: traditional, rational-legalistic, and charismatic. Traditional authority rests on an established belief in the sanctity of immemorial traditions and the legitimacy of the status of those exercising authority under them. Examples of traditional would be any dynastic monarchy such as the rulers of Swaziland or the established clergy of the Catholic Church headed by the Pope. For the vast majority of human history, traditional authority held sway as the form of authority most people found themselves submitting to in one way or another. The relatively newest form of Weber's authority is rational-legalistic. Rational-legalistic authority rests on a belief in the legality of patterns of normative rules and the right of those elevated to authority under such rules to issue commands. Modern forms of government whether parliamentary democracies or even one-party states led by central committees are rational-legalistic forms of authority.

According to Weber, charismatic authority rests on the devotion of the polity to the specific and exceptional sanctity, heroism or exemplary character of an individual person and of the normative patterns or order revealed or ordained by him.[5] Charismatic authority according to Weber is said to exist when, "an individual's claim to 'specific gifts of body and mind' is acknowledged by others as a valid basis for their participation in an extraordinary programme of action."[6] This is an individual set apart from and above other men through some exceptionality. Charismatic leaders are thought by those who follow them to have exceptional gifts usually but not always of divine origin. Gifts could include physical strength, intelligence, or perceived miraculous abilities. In ancient times, charismatic authority presented itself in the form of prophets, leaders in the hunt, and heroes in war.[7] The charismatic leader also leads his followers outside the realm of the everyday routine. He/she repudiates the past, and is in this sense a specifically revolutionary force. The followers obtain " 'freedom' from the commonplace, the ordinary, the recurrent by surrendering to both the initiatives of the leader and the emotional centers of his own being."[8] The charismatic leader will continue to be followed until his/her favor from the divine source appears to run out.

Weber writes: "In China the charismatic quality of the monarch... was upheld so rigidly that any misfortune whatever, not only defeats in war but droughts, floods, or astronomical phenomena which were considered unlucky, forced him to do public penance and might even force his abdication. If such things occurred, it was a sign that he did not possess the requisite of charismatic virtue, he was thus not a legitimate 'Son of Heaven.'"[9]

Malcolm X was not only a charismatic leader in the Weberian sense but held the type of charismatic authority that Weber called "pure charisma." This pure charisma is not something that could be taught, learned, or inherited but comes naturally or more specifically in the eyes of the followers from supernatural sources to the leader. Malcolm's pure charisma was displayed early in his life when he was elected class president and given some measure of authority in a predominantly white middle school in suburban Mason, Michigan in the 1930s do to his "verbal and intellectual skills."[10] This same pure charismatic leadership would blossom years later and allow Malcolm to build off the work of the semi-charismatic Elijah Muhammad to take a fledging religious organization of a few hundred people and turn it into an organization that would number in the tens of thousands and affect the lives of millions. Malcolm's leadership as a minister and top recruiter for the Nation of Islam would truly lead his followers outside the realm of the everyday routine. The strictness of Nation's regulations for its members and the complete life changes that occurred for those who converted to its program could only be made attractive to those outside the organization through the medium of a charismatic figure which Malcolm was.

On the idea of pure charisma, Anton Allahar writes, "It is particularly disdainful of economic pursuits or economic gain and prefers instead to be supported by voluntary gifts and communal largesse."[11] Throughout Malcolm's time in the Nation, he sought no financial gain and lived an extremely modest life. Even with a wife and four young children Malcolm did not even own his own home. This pure charisma is what differentiated Malcolm's authority ultimately from that of Elijah Muhammad whose charisma was more traditional as the source of his authority rested in his position as prophet to Allah who members of the Nation believed came in the form of W.D. Fard. Malcolm's pure, and in relation to Elijah Muhammad, greater charisma would ultimately lead to his break with the Nation. His charismatic authority was so strong that even without a well-defined program he was followed out of the Nation by large numbers of the faithful who had hitherto structured their lives on the teachings of Elijah Muhammad. It was this pure charisma that made Malcolm's split from the Nation so dangerous for so many different groups. For those in leadership positions inside the Nation, Malcolm's charismatic authority would in all likelihood continue to lead people both away from and out of the organization. For the reactionaries of America, Malcolm's charismatic authority would influence a much larger audience and be coupled with an ever-sharpening revolutionary Pan-African political and economic ideology.

Understanding charisma as a type of authority and not a measure of "likeability," it is easy to see how Malcolm X was a charismatic leader in the purest sense of the term. The question becomes however, in the African worldview, does charismatic authority, in this case Malcolm's, stop at the end of physical life? Malcolm Jarvis in his memoir *The Other Malcolm—"Shorty" Jarvis* quotes Roy Wilkins as saying of Malcolm X, "He was a master spell binder. Even in death he cast a spell far and wide—and more disturbing than he cast in life."[12] Although Roy Wilkins was in no way an open advocate for or known believer in traditional African spiritual beliefs, his statement rings true to the growing number of those who are. As Asante and Nwadiora write, "the dead members of the community, watch what we say and do and can affect what happens on the earth."[13] These ancestors are "the ones who must be invoked and revered, because they are agents of transformation."[14] The authors go further by stating,

Everything must be approached through the ancestors. This means that in PTARE (Popular Traditional African Religions Everywhere) there is always ancestral priority, presence and power. The ancestral spirits are the most intimate divinities and must be consulted on important occasions. Africans regard the ancestors as the keepers of morality... Therefore, the living must do everything they can to avoid crossing the moral path laid down by the departed ancestors.[15]

As an ancestor, Malcolm X's presence most certainly can be felt in the African community the world over. Not only is Malcolm an ancestor, but he is revered as a great ancestor whose presence is invoked at countless libation pourings and other such spiritual communings by diverse groups of Africans professing different faiths yet untied by their desire to be influenced by his spirit. By invoking Malcolm's presence, African people are affirming the continuity of his pure charisma in that they are continuing to submit to his authority as both moral and revolutionary example par excellence. When Malcolm speaks to those who invoke his presence they listen and they respond. When Malcolm's voice tells us that "of all our studies, history is best qualified to reward our research," we study history. When he tells us to protect our women with our lives, we do. And when Malcolm tells us to fight for our human rights and for self-determination by any means necessary, we have no choice but to act.

Thus, the anger and confusion felt by my friend and large numbers of Africans who have engaged Marable's book. They see it not as an attack on a dead lifeless icon but one on a living, charismatic ancestral presence. As was mentioned earlier, charisma can only be maintained as long as the followers of the leader believe to be extraordinary. Thus, to take down a charismatic leader one must prove to his followers that he or she is only human or in some way flawed to the point that his ability to lead comes into question. Malcolm understood this. A short time after leaving the Nation, Malcolm sought to shatter the semi-charismatic authority of Elijah Muhammad by exposing his well-known and documented sexual misbehavior to the world. Malcolm attempted to "humanize" Elijah Muhammad in much the same way Marable was attempting to "humanize" Malcolm, only Malcolm was honest in his actions and factual in his information. With Marable seeking to save the historical Malcolm "with all his strengths and flaws" from being "strangled by the iconic legend that had been constructed around him" he was unknowingly (hopefully unknowingly) attacking Malcolm's authority to continue to lead African people with a handful of undocumented implications. Fortunately, the power of Malcolm's ancestral charisma is much greater than any baseless attack and continues to hold authority over the masses of African people.

Notes

1. Marable, Manning. *Malcolm X: A Life of Reinvention.* New York: Viking Press, 2011. (Kindle edition)
2. Ibid., Location 231
3. Ibid., Location 9272
4. Ibid.
5. Weber, Max. *On Charisma and Institution Building.* Chicago: University of Chicago, 1968. p., 46
6. Dow, Thomas E. "An Analysis of Weber's Work on Charisma." *The British Journal of Sociology*, 1978: 83-93. p.84
7. Weber, p. 48
8. Dow, p. 84
9. Weber, p. 50
10. Marable, Location 747
11. Allahar, Anton L. "Charisma and Populism: Theoretical Reflections on Leadership and Legitimacy." In *Caribbean Charisma Reflections on Leadership, Legitimacy and Populist Politics*, by Anton L. Allahar, 1-33. Kingston: Ian Randle, 2001
12. Jarvis, Malcolm. *The Other Malcolm—"Shorty" Jarvis: His Memoir.* Jefferson: McFarland, 2001. p. 144
13. Asante, Molefi K., and Ememka Nwadiora. *Spear masters: an introduction to African religion.* Lanham: University Press of America, 2007. p. 24
14. Ibid., p. 3
15. Ibid., p. 24

Reinforcing Barricades
Fred Logan

A decade ago on January 21, 2002, the late Dr. Manning Marable gave the keynote address for the annual Martin Luther King Day program at Carnegie Mellon University in Pittsburgh. Marable chastised the U.S. establishment for trying to distort and suppress the radical social democratic legacy of Dr. King. He charged the establishment was portraying Martin Luther King, Jr. as little more than a liberal icon of the status quo.

In his biography of W.E.B. Du Bois, Marable adamantly defends Du Bois's radical legacy as a social democrat, socialist, Marxist, and anti-imperialist scholar and activist. This tenacious defense of African American radicals on the left is a major theme in the career-long scholarship of Manning Marable.

For this reason, his last book, a long waited biography of Malcolm X, has stirred up quite a controversy with the combatants lining up on unanticipated sides of the barricades. It has been praised in various establishment journals, and criticized by many scholars and activists across the spectrum of the black left. Some Black people of various political orientations have praised it.

Some people may not understand. But the pitched adversaries on both sides of the barricades are acutely aware that far more than just another academic debate is at stake. The struggle over Malcolm's legacy—along with the legacies of Du Bois, King, and their peers—is a major political and ideological battle to define the meaning of the black freedom movement and to set its future course.

Had this book been written by a white author or a conservative Black author it would not have received the widespread level of praise it has enjoyed in mainstream white American. It also would not have aroused the fierce debate it has kindled in the Black community. Just suppose the conservative Black journalist Armstrong Williams had written a book with repeated rumors, allegations, and gossip about Malcolm's moral life. By now scholars and activists on the African American left would have read the book, cussed it out, and soon forgot it.

But over the last four decades, the late Manning Marable was a very prominent, widely published scholar on the black left. He was a persistent socialist critic of the race, class, and gender status quo. So, the author, Manning Marable and his subject, Malcolm X are equally at the center of the Black debate.

Malcolm X: A Life of Reinvention provides some interesting information on Malcolm's childhood and on his travels in Africa in the months immediately before he was assassinated. But Marable's main purpose is to strip Malcolm of his legacy as a radical Black Nationalist. Like many scholars on the U.S. left, Marable tends to denigrate Black Nationalism as reactionary. Like everything else in existence, African American nationalism has contradictions, both positive and negative tendencies. This is immediately evident in the numerous schools of Black Nationalist thought and practice.

Marable criticizes Malcolm's anti-white stance during his membership in the Nation of Islam. But Marable does not acknowledge the seminal and historic contribution the teachings of Minister Elijah Muhammad made to the demise of the domination of the white supremacy and Black inferiority complex on the collective African American psychic. The rise of "Black is Beautiful" and all that mind-set has contributed to the political, cultural, and social struggles and to the overall advancement of Black people in our time are forever indebted to the message of the Messenger.

For the collective African American psychic steeped, as it is, in religion, the negation of the religious mythology of white supremacy and Black inferiority demanded the open challenge and confrontation of its opposite in a period marked by mass Black social struggles against white domination and oppression. The religions of the oppressed quite often and quite logically demonize their oppressor as the incarnation of the devil. The Nation of Islam was by no means unique in this respect.

The progressive nationalism of an oppressed people struggling against oppression is not, in honesty, to be equated with the reactionary nationalism of an oppressor struggling to maintain domination.

By now we all are probably familiar with Malcolm's often quoted 1964 statements on his philosophy of Black Nationalism. You surely recall his statements, "The political philosophy of Black Nationalism mean that the Black man should control the politics and the politicians in the ghetto... The economic philosophy of Black Nationalism ... only means we should control the economy of our community... The social philosophy of Black

Nationalism only means we have to get together and remove the evil, the vices, alcoholism, drug addiction, and other vices that are destroying the moral fiber of our community. We ourselves have to lift the level of our community."[1]

And we also know Malcolm argued that the African American freedom struggle is part and parcel of the world-wide nationalist struggles of oppressed people against western domination.

Manning Marable argues Malcolm had discarded nationalism, and that the Malcolm X legacy can best been summed up as a nebulous "radical humanism" which offers the world the open-ended virtues and prospects of "hope" and "peace."[2]

The professional historian Manning Marable had studied the Federal Bureau of Investigation's relentless campaign to discredit King's moral authority, and thus discredit the moral and political authority of Black struggle. This moral propaganda offensive is a major weapon in the establishment's strategy to discredit the struggle. So Marable had to know full well that any allegations or rumors that impugned the morality of Malcolm X, an icon of the Black Movement, would be used by the establishment to discredit the movement both past and present.

For this reason, a radical scholar of the movement would, presumably, challenge and hold to the highest standards of research for verification any malicious rumors he encountered that slandered the moral reputation of Malcolm X. He would not, presumably, spread and embellish on any such allegations. Also, in his 2005 biography of W.E.B. Du Bois, Marble noted the criticism some scholars had made concerning the speculations on Du Bois's sexual life in David Lewis's two-volume biography of Du Bois. Marable wrote the historian Mark Higbee" felt...that Lewis's discussion of Du Bois sexuality were speculations." He also noted that historian David Garrow felt David Lewis's "repeated psychosexual speculations (of Du Bois) devoid of concrete evidence, according to Garrow, had undermined (Lewis') entire thesis."[3]

In contradiction to all of this, Marable goes on to claim, "Based on circumstantial but strong evidence, Malcolm was probably describing his own homosexual encounter with Paul Lennon" a white man born in 1888. Marable does not detail this "strong evidence."[4]

Further, Marable spreads what he admits is gossip that Betty Shabazz, Malcolm's wife, may have had an illicit affair with Charles 37X Morris (A.K.A. Charles Kenyatta). Marable writes, "This indeed was Betty Shabazz, who enjoyed going out of town with the handsome man." These "enjoyed," "out of town," and "handsome man" remarks are clearly intended to add a sexual favor to this speculation. Marable was not present for any of these alleged instances. So, how "indeed" would he know how she responded to Kenyatta?[5]

Marable makes 17 references to Kenyatta. It is not, however, until his final reference almost 500 pages into the book that Marable reveals the New York City police "considered (Kenyatta) a reliable informant and (had) developed a close working relationship with him." Kenyatta was a police-snitch. Marable tells us that Kenyatta's FBI files revealed he was also an agent provocateur.[6]

Obviously, the establishment would far rather see "Black-on-Black" rumors, allegations, and gossip spread by a prominent Black scholar than by the FBI, or Fox News.

In his long years of research, Manning Marable could not find any conclusive evidence to directly connect the police to Malcolm's murder. The state is thereby exonerated by Marable, and this gives the establishment a very important reason to praise this work by a Black scholar from the Black left.

Marable also could not find any conclusive evidence to directly connect Minister Elijah Muhammad or Minister Louis Farrakhan, leaders of the Nation of Islam, to Malcolm's death. But these findings obviously did not satisfy him. He was apparently disappointed. He must have wanted to find something, even if there was nothing to be found.

Why else did he engage in totally unwarranted speculation? "Years from now," he wrote, "it would not be entirely surprising if an FBI transcript surfaced documenting a telephone call from Elijah Muhammad to a subordinate authoring Malcolm's murder." In this vein, he adds, "And at present, the evidence suggests that Farrakhan ...was not personally involved and had no prior knowledge of the plot, however..." This "however" indicates he was not satisfied with his own research and is trying to cast ungrounded suspicious that he can not substantiate.[7]

Equally important here, he does not speculate about the police. He does not care to ask, what if "years from now"—or sooner—FBI transcripts surface that exonerates the NOI and conclusively prove the state was behind Malcolm's death. This speculation is equally as credible as his speculation on the NOI.

It is much more credible to speculate that if the FBI, the New York City police, the CIA, or the establishment at large had evidence that linked Minister Muhammad or Minister Farrakhan to Malcolm's assassination, they would have released that information years ago, not years from now. Just ponder how such information would play to the advantage of status quo and disrupt Black struggle. These are a few of Marable's allegations the U.S. establishment does not question, but Black people challenge and condemn: opposite reactions on opposite sides of the barricades.

Manning Marable's book does have some Black supporters. They apparently accept his rumors and allegations at face value. They do, however, criticize Marable's Black critics. Marable's defense argues that he makes Malcolm more human and reveals he was not perfect. They accuse Marable's critics of glorifying Malcolm X.

Throughout the African Diaspora, Black people observe Malcolm's birthday. They expound his message, and promote Malcolm X as a role model for the Black freedom movement. In this respect, these Black people are guilty of glorifying Malcolm X. But this glorification does not validate or substantiate even one of the allegations or rumors Marable raises.

Even if some confused Black people somewhere tried to deify Malcolm, this would be wrong, something Malcolm himself would surely oppose, but this kind of unwarranted glorification would not validate Marable.

Objectively, this glorification argument is a red herring. It defends rumor mongering and gossip that is detrimental to the liberation struggles of the Black community, and this is independent of the intentions of Black people who make this argument.

Malcolm emphasized repeatedly that he was always studying, learning more and trying relentlessly to improve himself, and never said he was perfect. And the critics of Marable's book have yet to argue that he was perfect.

And we must ask, very curiously, are there actually Black people in this world who believe that Malcolm X became more human because of the allegations Marable raised?

There is nothing in Marable's book to suggest his intent is to deliberately discredit Malcolm X to benefit the status quo. The book does strongly suggest, however, that Marable's radical left passions had ebbed considerably since the days of his self-published commentary, *Black Nationalism in the Seventies: through the Primes of Race and Class,* and other writings. In those days, he called for, among other things, a national Black convention of Black workers and a Black Nationalist party, and the socialist transformation of the U.S. political economy.[8]

This is diametrically opposed a very revealing question on the future course of Black struggle Marable proposes near the conclusion of his last book. He asks, "Given the election of Barack Obama, it now raises the question of whether Blacks have a separate political destiny from their white fellow citizens. If legal racial segregation is permanently in America's past,

Malcolm's vision would have to radically redefine self-determination and the meaning of Black power in a political environment that appear to many to be 'post-racial.'" Here Marable does not call for interracial class-based alliances, just black people and their class-neutral "white fellow citizens."[9]

This suggests Obama's election has liquidated the domination of race and class. It reads like the yearnings of a radical turned mainstream liberal.

Now back to the barricades. Marable's Black critics do not share his rosy optimism about any prospects for a post-racial and post-class American political arena for the on-going Black freedom struggle. On the other side of the barricades, however, the guardians of the status quo cheer him on.

Manning Marable as a career-long partisan in this ideological battle had to be fully aware of how his book would be received on both side of the barricades.

Notes

1. See www.edchange.org/multicultural/speeches/Malcolm_X_ballot.html

2. Marable, Manning, *Malcolm X: A Life of Reinvention* (New York, Viking, 2011) p. 487

3. Marable, Manning, *W.E.B. Du Bois, Black Radical Democrat* (Boston, 2005) pp. xxv-xxvi

4. Marable, *Malcolm X*, p. 66.

5. Op cit. p. 386

6. Op. cit p. 467

7. Op. cit p. 478

8. C.f. Marable, Manning, *Black Nationalism in the Seventies:* through the prism of race and class (Dayton, Black Research Associate, Inc. 1980); Marable, Manning, *How Capitalism Underdeveloped Black America: problems in race, political economy, and society* (Cambridge, Mass, 2000).

9. Op. cit. p. 468

Our Malcolm, Ourselves
Kevin McGruder

Manning Marable, author of the biography *Malcolm X: A Life of Reinvention* did not live to see the flurry of criticism that met his recently published work. He died three days before the book was available. While this twist of fate or history is truly tragic, Marable's passing spared him the sometimes vitriolic critiques that have dominated on-line forums, radio broadcasts, and panel discussions since the book's publication. Many of the criticisms tell us more about African Americans' perspectives on sexuality than they do about the accuracy or value of this new depiction of Malcolm X.

In *Malcolm X,* Marable proposes to breathe life into the icon and restore his humanity by demonstrating the complexity of his life or lives. He succeeds in this task by retelling Malcolm's well-known transformation from wayward youth to criminal to religious figure, illustrating the range of influences that inspired the various transformations. As in his life, Malcolm's work with the Nation of Islam is central to the story. The Nation was critical to his transformation from convict to national and eventually international figure. His stormy departure from the Nation occurred in the midst of, and led to additional reinventions as Marable chronicles. While Malcolm's work with the Nation is the centerpiece of the biography, some of the heated criticism of the book has focused on an issue related to Malcolm X as a person rather than as a political or religious figure. Marable's suggestion that before joining the Nation, Malcolm Little was involved in a sexual arrangement for pay with an older white man has generated heated criticism.

Marable quotes from *The Autobiography of Malcolm X* in which Malcolm describes a hustle that a friend "Rudy" had in which he was paid to undress an older white man and himself "then pick up the old man like a baby, lay him on his bed, then stand over him and sprinkle him all over with talcum powder." Marable suggests that "Based on circumstantial but strong evidence, Malcolm was probably describing his own homosexual encounters with Paul Lennon" a wealthy white man in whose home he worked. Later in the book when Malcolm is imprisoned in Massachusetts,

Marable notes that Malcolm continued to communicate with Lennon, hoping that he could assist in his release. As his release became more of a reality, even though he had by then joined the Nation of Islam, he wrote to his brother that a wealthy white man who had visited him "can give me a home and a job..." upon his release. Instead, when Malcolm left prison in 1952 he went to live with his brother in Detroit, and Marable suggests that communication with Lennon seems to have ended at that point.

Critics of this depiction have suggested that Marable took a great leap of logic in reaching his conclusion. He does note that the evidence he considered was "circumstantial, " using the qualifier "probably" in assuming that the encounters described in *The Autobiography of Malcolm X* were really Malcolm's encounters. We may never know why Marable felt confident enough to suggest the existence of a relationship of some sort, but he notes that in addition to the continued communication with Lennon after Malcolm's imprisonment, including a visit, that Malcolm's reference to Lennon's ability to provide him with a "home" "implies more than a business association."

One could argue that without definitive information on a matter as sensitive as this, the author should have declined to speculate. The process of attempting to reconstruct and provide an interpretation of a person's life or of events is as much an art as a science. For many situations definitive information is not available or does not exist. Historians look at the weight of evidence, the context of an event, and the likelihood that their interpretations are accurate in reaching conclusions. They may make hundreds of decisions such as this in the course of writing a book. Marable undoubtedly did in writing *Malcolm X*. It is natural that people will question some of those decisions. But the fact that critiques of Malcolm X have been dominated by severe criticisms of Marable's suggestion that Malcolm at one point participated in homosexual activity confirms the iconic stature of Malcolm X but also illustrates the fragile nature of our image of Black masculinity. Some critics have suggested that Marable's agenda was to destroy the image of Malcolm X. Others have suggested "What could be expected from an African American scholar practiced in the Eurocentric tradition?" implying that an African American willing to make such a suggestion could not really be part of the race.

These responses are painful but understandable. In his famous eulogy at Malcolm X's funeral, actor Ossie Davis described what Malcolm X represented to Black people: "Malcolm was our manhood, our living Black manhood!" Malcolm X transformed his life to become the symbol described by Davis. In *The Autobiography of Malcolm X* he described his previous activity with drugs, steering prostitutes, and burglary, all activities that he left behind when he joined the Nation of Islam, which was respected for its ability to inspire similar transformations in others. But while these pursuits were viewed negatively by many, they were all pursuits identified with masculinity, and even celebrated by segments of the African American community then and now. Homosexuality activity does not fit into this calculation of either masculinity or transformation.

Until recently Americans adhered to the "one drop rule" to determine racial identity: anyone with one drop of Black blood was considered Black. We have adopted an equivalent to the "one drop rule" when it comes to homosexuality. We believe that anyone who engages in homosexual activity is a homosexual. Sexuality is much more complicated than this rule suggests. The use of the term sexual orientation over the last thirty years was meant to acknowledge the gender to which a person's attraction is primarily oriented regardless of the behavior that person might engage in at a given time. Sex research has concluded that there is a spectrum of sexual orientations ranging from people who are only attracted to the opposite sex, people who are predominantly attracted to the opposite sex, people who are attracted to both sexes, people who are predominantly attracted to the same sex, and people who are only attracted to the same sex. Even given this spectrum, people may occasionally or frequently engage in sexual activity with someone of the gender different from their sexual orientation, often motivated by what is sometimes called "situational sex." A heterosexually oriented man engaging in homosexual activity in prison because he does not have access to women is an example of situational sex. A homosexually oriented man engaging in sex with a woman in order to maintain a marriage is another example. In this construct the homosexual activity that Manning Marable suggests that Malcolm X engaged in during his years of criminal activity would be described as situational sex, in this case for pay, by a person whose previous and later known sexual activities suggest that he was predominantly heterosexual.

Because the concept of sexuality in popular culture does not accommodate the complexity of sexuality that really exists, we come to the conclusion that the suggestion that someone engaged in homosexual activity is a suggestion that the person is homosexual. This is what Marable's critics imply he was saying about Malcolm X, which he did not say. He noted that after his release from prison Malcolm X did not seem to have further communication with Paul Lennon the man for whom he had worked. Marable's later references to Malcolm's sexual relationships all involve women.

But the fragile status of Black masculinity, the result of centuries of limited power during slavery, oppression in the decades following, assaults on the Black male's image ranging from depictions as creatures of lust to characterizations as criminals, has resulted in a belief that homosexuality is another assault on the image of the Black man. This belief has led to a hyper vigilance of the definition of Blackness and Black masculinity that requires an exclusion of homosexuality. In addition to confirming Malcolm X's iconic stature, the visceral responses to Marable's brief suggestion of homosexual activity in Malcolm X provide us with a gauge of the opinions regarding Black, male homosexuals by at least one fairly vocal segment of the African American community. To suggest that Malcolm engaged in such activity is clearly considered the ultimate insult. Why is this opinion regarding the activity of a man who has been dead for over forty-five years important to African Americans living today? The opinions expressed regarding Malcolm X do tell us something about our opinions today. If we believe that a suggestion of homosexuality was an insult when applied to Malcolm, does that mean that we believe it is also an insult when applied to Black men today? Derogatory terms suggesting that a Black man is a homosexual are still the ultimate insult on the basketball court or in the street.

While Malcolm was the image of "our manhood" we can learn about ourselves from our responses to Manning Marable's account of his life. The unwillingness of some African Americans to find an acknowledged place in the definition of Black manhood and within the Black community for men who are not heterosexual is weakening us as a people and as a community. It is not a coincidence that lesbian, gay, bisexual, and transgender African American youth are over-represented among homeless youth. Many are cast out of their homes by parents who sincerely believe they are protecting the image of Black manhood or Black womanhood as well as the Black family. Other segments of the population have been able to dramatically reduce the impact of HIV and AIDS, through provision of support, but Black men who have sex with men continue to be over-represented among those infected with HIV and those living with AIDS. Although some resources such as funding and social services have improved for this group, many continue to lack the family and community support as individuals that is essential to developing a mindset that would enable them to value their health and futures enough to protect themselves to prevent infection.

If Malcolm X were still living, he would have turned eighty-six years old in May of this year. One of the most fascinating elements of *Malcolm X: A Life of Reinvention* is the realization that with so many things pulling him in various directions over his life, in the last years of his life Malcolm X was so successful at maintaining his focus on improving the status of people of African descent, and that in his thirty-nine years of life he made substantial progress at least in highlighting the important issues and strategies to be followed.

If Marable is correct in his conclusion, Malcolm probably would have preferred that the nature of his relationship with Paul Lennon were not mentioned in his biography. On the broader issue of homosexuality and Black masculinity it would be interesting to know what he would have said. He would have continued to read, to question, to debate, and this topic may have been a subject on which he would have had something to say. During his years in prison, Marable notes that Malcolm made disparaging comments regarding fellow inmates who engaged in homosexual activity. But a few years later as Malcolm X he was cordial with civil rights activist and known homosexual, Bayard Rustin, with whom he debated the value of integration. He was also friendly to James Baldwin whose 1956 novel *Giovanni's Room*, about a homosexual relationship made clear for some Baldwin's own sexual orientation. Perhaps this was just a matter of common courtesy between public figures. While we will never know whether his opinion of homosexuals would have changed, that should not prevent African Americans from examining our own conceptions of Black masculinity and questioning whether they are really resulting in stronger men and a stronger Black community.

A Response
Starla Muhammad

For decades, *The Autobiography of Malcolm X* has been viewed by many as a complete look inside the heart and mind of a man who for years was hated and criticized in life by some of the same entities that have named streets and schools for him after his death.

Whereas Malcolm X was called a bigot, anti-Semite and anti-White during his tenure in the Nation of Islam as a student, minister and follower of the Honorable Elijah Muhammad, his image is now available on postage stamps.

Pictures of him on posters now adorn the walls of libraries, dorm rooms and T-shirts. *The Autobiography of Malcolm X* as told to Alex Haley is required reading in high schools and college campuses all over the country and his life was further immortalized in the 1992 movie Malcolm X, based on the book, by filmmaker Spike Lee. Myths, misconceptions and unanswered questions about the circumstances surrounding his 1965 assassination continue to be raised. This includes inquiries about any involvement or knowledge of his death by law enforcement agencies.

A new biography, released April 4, *Malcolm X: A Life of Reinvention*, authored by Dr. Manning Marable delves into this and more. Twenty years in the making, Marable spent much of the last decade intensely researching the life and history of Malcolm X and was a history and political science professor at Columbia University. He died at age 60, three days before the book's release.

Zaheer Ali, a doctoral candidate at Columbia University in New York and lead researcher on Marable's book, says the well-known autobiography written by Alex Haley is a powerful story of transformation and inspiration that has affected millions of people but it is a literary text not a historical text.

"It is a literary text because it is a very powerful story but it's not a story that is completely grounded in evidence; so as a historical text you have to look at it with a critical eye," Ali told *The Final Call*. However, he explains that it is the nature of memoirs that when people tell their own stories things may have been forgotten, omitted, exaggerated or blended together. *The Autobiography* was also presented through the prism of Alex Haley, he added.

Marable's book explores the fact that Malcolm X was not fully aware of the extent undercover law enforcement were in his presence, notes Ali. "In his autobiography, he isn't fully aware of the degree to which the federal and state law enforcement agencies are surveilling him," says Ali. Malcolm did not know the degree to which his organization as well as the Nation of Islam had been infiltrated by agents and informants, he added.

Marable's research uncovers the fact that as early as the 1950s Malcolm was helping the Honorable Elijah Muhammad establish Temples around the country and Boston was a city he helped set up a meeting place in a private home. "Maybe 10 or 12 people were in attendance at this first meeting in January of 1954 and one of those people was an informant and that gives you a sense of how deeply embedded intelligence services were in the Nation of Islam," Ali told *The Final Call.*

According to the book, undercover agents and informants also infiltrated Muslim Mosque, Inc., (MMI) and the Organization of Afro-American Unity, two groups Malcolm formed after he left the Nation of Islam. Gene Roberts, who was one Malcolm X's chief bodyguards, and at the Audubon Ballroom when he was shot, was an undercover agent in the Bureau of Special Services. In the book, Marable says Roberts' first assignment was to infiltrate the newly formed MMI.

It is important to understand the forces that were acting upon Malcolm and the way he responded to hopefully gain a deeper understanding of him as well as to address unanswered questions about his assassination says, Ali. "One of the things Dr. Marable was really hoping to do with this book was to raise those questions and the volume of those questions to the point where people would see that the case needed to be reopened." says Ali.

The Honorable Minister Louis Farrakhan has repeatedly called for reopening and investigating the case and releasing government files. On May 6, 1995 at Harlem's legendary Apollo Theatre, Farrakhan along with Malcolm's widow, the late Dr. Betty Shabazz, met publically to begin a process of healing and reconciliation between the Nation of Islam and Malcolm's family. The meeting was sparked by the arrest of Qubilah Shabazz, daughter of Malcolm X and Betty Shabazz.

Qubilah Shabazz had been accused of trying to hire an assassin to kill Farrakhan. The alleged hit man, Michael Summers Fitzpatrick, a member of the Jewish community was also an informant for the federal government. He would have been the chief witness against Qubilah Shabazz, who was described as a troubled young woman who knew

Fitzpatrick in high school.

Farrakhan responded to an explosion of news about the plot by challenging the federal government's role and motivation, calling for no harm to come to the Shabazz family and calling Qubilah the "smallest part" of any conspiracy against him. The Minister's strong response led to government squelching the charges against Qubilah but no action on his call for the release of all government files on Malcolm X was taken.

"We want the truth to be made known so that we as a people can be made free of suspicion and doubt and let the truth condemn whomever truth would condemn. But the people must go free and we, the Nation of Islam, as well as those outside the Nation of Islam, need to know all of the truth as it relates to the assassination of Brother Malcolm X," Farrakhan said at the historic gathering. Five months later, Betty Shabazz addressed the crowd at the Million Man March called by Farrakhan. She died in 1997 as the result of injuries in a fire set by grandson Malcolm Shabazz, Qubilah's son.

Farrakhan, speaking recently to Muslims, again challenged any rumor that he had any part in the knowledge, planning or carrying out of Malcolm's death. If the government had evidence, legal action would have been taken, said the Minister. They have nothing, he said.

Abdul Akbar Muhammad knew and worked with Malcolm X in the 1960s and is the international representative of Farrakhan. The reason this book is different from other books written about Malcolm is the number of years of research Marable conducted, he says.

As a member of the Nation of Islam for over 50 years, Akbar Muhammad says though there are aspects of the book he does not agree with and differs with, he can appreciate the tremendous research that went into the book.

"I would hope, agree or disagree with Dr. Manning that Muslims who want an insight to this period, you know Malcolm is an enigma and in the American landscape especially in the Black American community, people want to know and this book gives them a base of knowledge about Malcolm," says Akbar Muhammad.

[Published in *Final Call*, 2011]

Revising Perspectives on Malcolm X
Nell Irvin Painter

Violence begets anger, the two a tragic combination in African American life. Until relatively recently, non-Black Americans ignored the facts of racially motivated violence, from the beatings essential to the preservation of slavery to the lynchings and rapes that preserved white supremacy. As late as 2000, for example, "Without Sanctuary," an exhibition of postcards of lynchings, took masses of Americans utterly by surprise.

More than racial violence went largely unseen. African Americans were rarely visible in American culture until the mid-twentieth century, and when a Black face appeared, it had better be grinning—a happy darky, or at least a comforting Louis Armstrong. The fact of violence and the prohibition against anger warped African American life until things began to change when Malcolm X burst into view.

Malcolm first appeared in the 1950s as an angry Black man equally proud of his anger and his Blackness. His was a singular presence in the era of "Satchmo." Instead of comforting white people, Malcolm faced them down, decried police brutality, and demanded Black men's right to armed self-defense. Whether attraction to his outspokenness outweighed the weirdness of his religion, thousands flocked to his message of Black Nationalism and nascent Black power and pride.

Since his death in 1965, Malcolm has become a cultural icon, defined largely by *The Autobiography of Malcolm X*, which was published in the same year. While many an author has probed the phenomenon of Malcolm X, his own version of his life, expressed in his own words, has dominated his bibliography.

That is until now. With the publication of *Malcolm X: A Life of Reinvention*, Manning Marable offers a fuller portrait of the minister, the activist, and the man, beautifully advancing our understanding of the accomplishments of this pioneering leader within his own time.

Malcolm Little was born in 1925 in Omaha, Nebraska, to a couple united by Marcus Garvey's Black Nationalism, a source of inspiration throughout Malcolm's life. After his father's death his mother tried but failed to provide for the family and was committed to an insane asylum in 1939. Ella Little, Malcolm's half-sister, brought the children emotional and financial support, and remained Malcolm's sustainer throughout his life.

Ella Little lived in Boston in 1941, where nearly sixteen-year-old Malcolm joined her. City life became a life of crime, landing Malcolm behind bars in 1946. There he educated himself in the prison library and, under the influence of his siblings, converted to the Nation of Islam.

After his release in 1952, Malcolm visited Elijah Muhammad, leader of the religious movement, and, as Malcolm X, began the evangelical career that made him famous. By 1953 he was working for the organization full time, and the FBI had begun its surveillance. By 1954 he was leading Harlem's Temple No. 7, sparking a remarkable expansion.

During Malcolm's 12 years as the religion's most prominent minister, he came to question its founding beliefs that African Americans were the "original Asiatic Black man," that all white people were "devils" created by the evil Black genius Yacub, that Blacks should separate from whites, that an imminent racial apocalypse would end "the white man's" reign, and that in the meanwhile, Nation members should refuse to vote or undertake political action.

That apolitical creed might have worked during the 1950s, when antiracist protest attracted little attention nationally, but not later, when an overwhelming number of Black people favored demanding the right to vote. With Blacks on the move with notable white support, Malcolm found it difficult to remain apolitical and implacably anti-white.

It was only a matter of time before his surging popularity and departure from Nation of Islam doctrine cost him his position. The organization first attempted to silence him and later expelled him.

But much more determined the break. Malcolm's travel outside the United States during the Third World ferment in the era of postcolonial Pan-Africanism helped him conclude that the group's race-obsessed parochialism was out of touch.

Malcolm visited Egypt and Saudi Arabia in 1959, a trip that spurred the international orientation and orthodox Islam that marked the last years of his life. Although the trip was a turning point intellectually, it is not mentioned in *The Autobiography*. Marable, however, presents a full description of the journey as part of his thorough examination of both the Nation of Islam's and Malcolm's changing relations to orthodox Islam.

The fruit of decades of careful research in older and newly opened archives, Marable's magisterial work provides a more complete view of Malcolm X within broader historical contexts. Marable describes a life unfolding and the people and institutions around Malcolm who counted in his life, for good and for ill.

His religion's financial support and organizational infrastructure facilitated Malcolm's rise to prominence, just as its increasing reliance on violence as a disciplinary tool cost him his life. Marable investigates the planning and execution of Malcolm's assassination, naming the Newark killers and following their lives after the attack. Malcolm's wife, Betty Shabazz, receives sensitive treatment throughout, as a dutiful (if independent-minded) Muslim wife trapped in a miserable marriage, a widow embracing new opportunities, and, ultimately, the victim of a fatal family tragedy. Malcolm's right-hand man, James 67X Warden (Abdur-Razzaq), emerges as the worker who makes it possible for Malcolm to function publicly.

Given the fervor of Malcolm X's fans, Marable's biography is an exceedingly brave as well as a major intellectual accomplishment. Scholarly biography demands detachment, and Marable (who died on April 1, 2011) was a scholar (politically engaged, yes, but a distinguished scholar). Marable's thorough, sensitive, deeply researched biography admires Malcolm X's commitment to his people without diminishing his humanity. Like the *The Autobiography* it supersedes, *Malcolm X: A Life of Reinvention* is deservedly a bestseller, one that helps us understand the development of a leading American struck down before he could help us understand our world in which Islam plays so crucial a role.

[First published in the *Boston Globe*, May 8, 2011]

A Review of Manning Marable's *Malcolm X*
Imani Perry

In the early 1990s, it was popular for African American teenagers and young adults to wear T-shirts with images of Malcolm X that read, "Our own Black shining prince," a reference to Ossie Davis' poignant eulogy of the slain leader. At that time, the embrace of Malcolm X, particularly by young hip-hop fans, seemed a deliberate counterpoint to the sanitized, mainstream and universally celebrated image of Martin Luther King Jr.

Malcolm X was, in our iconic rendering, the unapologetic Black radical voice for freedom and justice. He served an important symbolic role for a post-civil rights generation of African Americans who faced the devastating long-term effects of deindustrialization, poverty, educational inequality and mass incarceration.

Now, some 20 years later, with the publication of Manning Marable's *Malcolm X: A Life of Reinvention*, the public is being challenged to dismantle the iconography of the "Black shining prince" and confront Malcolm X as an incredibly complex and at times deeply conflicted figure.

Impassioned conflicts have arisen over the content of the biography. Salacious interest in whether Malcolm had homosexual encounters; whether he and his wife, Betty, were unfaithful to each other; whether he and Alex Haley misrepresented his story in *The Autobiography of Malcolm X*; and whether the convicted parties were actually the ones responsible for his murder have been matched with outrage at the manner in which Marable unflinchingly presents Malcolm X as a fallible human being.

Marable's death, just a few days before his book's release, feels like a last gasp of herculean effort, a final, noble offering from a path-breaking historian and political scientist. While the author's absence facilitates some of the melodramatic reaction to his magnum opus, we are forced to defend or decry without his input.

But in truth, although the conflict over the content has probably driven sales and attention to the book, the brilliance of this biography has little if anything to do with its apparently shocking revelations. Marable has crafted an extraordinary portrait of a man and his time. Malcolm moves through the social and intellectual history of mid-twentieth century Black America, and his periods of growth and stagnation mirror the tides of Black life.

In depicting the young Malcolm Little's participation, with his father, in meetings of Marcus Garvey's Universal Negro Improvement Association and African Communities League, Marable gives us the long view of Black politics devoted to a belief in a linked fate for Black people across the Diaspora, laying the foundation for the Pan-Africanist philosophy Malcolm would embrace at the end of his life.

Marable describes Malcolm's descent into street life in light of the ghettoization of Blacks in the urban North. Later, as we witness the birth of Malcolm X as a minister in the Nation of Islam, Marable contextualizes Malcolm in the broad and diverse world of Black activism and political thought.

As Malcolm develops his voice, and chafes against the Nation of Islam's rejection of political engagement and Elijah Muhammad's control, he finds footing in the midst of a complex landscape. This portrait of a thinker becomes particularly compelling in the period after Malcolm breaks from the Nation of Islam and travels through Africa and the Middle East. We witness Malcolm develop a politics that connects him to independence movements across the globe, a philosophy of freedom that no longer depicts white people as devils, a religion that is closer to orthodox Islam. And yet he sustains a deep and abiding commitment to addressing the particular suffering of black people in the United States.

However, this is no idealized image. As Malcolm struggles through this process, we see him flailing and failing, at the same time that he is growing and blossoming, until his assassination on Feb. 21, 1965. Our last picture of Malcolm is of a man who is caught between socialists and fundamentalists in the Islamic world, between the mosque he founded and the Organization of Afro-American Unity, and between a raceless and a race-based politics.

Marable's central theme, that Malcolm was a man who reinvented himself, also provides the critical tension of the book: Marable reveals how Malcolm could never peaceably remain in any of his invented selves because he never ceased seeking.

Although recounting the details of a subject's death is the biographer's responsibility, the conclusion of Marable's book is less powerful than the whole. It moves from illuminating to speculative, from epic to mystery, and then finally to a somewhat more academic-sounding assessment of Malcolm's legacy. Notwithstanding this departure from the richly woven prose of the main parts of the text, the book is a masterpiece of meticulous detail and powerful social history.

Ultimately, the Malcolm that Marable offers us serves an important purpose for the twenty-first century. This book arrives in a moment of petty partisan politics and a sound-bite-driven culture, and gives us a glimpse into a past of rich debate and impassioned struggle. Marable's Malcolm assists us in understanding the current wildfire of resistance and revolution through Africa, the Midwest and the Middle East. Most of all, in this book, Malcolm is reimagined as an intellectual and political role model for us all, a man who possessed the courage to put himself at risk consistently in order to better understand the world, in order to make the world better.

[First published in the *San Francisco Chronicle*]

By Any Means
Gregory J. Reed and Bryonn Bain

For millions around the world, the most critical and controversial human rights leader of the last century was Malcolm X. During a life spanning just shy of four decades, the outspoken revolutionary, christened Malcolm Little was in a perpetual state of evolution. From class president to porter, from pusher and pimp to prisoner and disciplined disciple of Islamized Black pride and power, one thread remained throughout his adult life. Whether hustling in Harlem or lecturing at Harvard, virtually everyone within the reach of his voice was transformed. Nearly half a century after his assassination, FBI files and other previously unreleased documents have finally surfaced to fierce debate from scholarly halls to neighborhood barber shops, from talk shows and street corners to backyard brawls across the nation.

One of the twentieth century's most important books, according to *Time* magazine, the impact of *The Autobiography of Malcolm X* is undeniable. However, several key essays intended for publication in 1965 were censored. In the words of Alex Haley, Malcolm's social program and political agenda included his economic blueprint and were "The most impactive material of the book, some of it rather lava-like." Nevertheless, the three chapters Haley boasted of, "The Negro," "The End of Christianity," and "Twenty Million Black Muslims," were not included in the manuscript published after Malcolm's death. Columbia University historian Manning Marable, the author of a recently released and rigorously debated 594-page biography on Malcolm, had only a glimpse of these omitted pages when he wrote: "These three chapters represent a blueprint for where Malcolm at that moment believed Black America should be moving" and the leadership he envisioned for "the construction of a united front" (Pg. 330).

These critical chapters censored from *The Autobiography of Malcolm X* have been completely inaccessible to the public, and we are glad to present here a glimpse of their importance. A former campaign strategist with Rosa Parks and Nelson Mandela, Gregory Reed will soon publish

Malcolm X: The Lost Chapters—"Best Interests of Humanity," A Poetic Anthology.

Finally making these writings public, Reed is the Detroit attorney and cultural activist who rescued the documents at auction in 1992. The censored words of El Hajj Malik El Shabazz include discoveries made during his final days and the missing pages of his most influential work. These previously unpublished documents are also the basis for a new, theatrical production including unreleased passages by Malcolm, his handwritten notes, politically charged but little known poetry, and the breathtaking verse of his Black Power Movement contemporaries and torch bearers: Amiri Baraka, Nikki Giovanni, Sonia Sanchez, Haki Madhubuti, the Last Poets and noteworthy others inspired by Malcolm.

Unhindered by the blind spots of all other previous works, Reed is now releasing excerpts of the previously "lost" chapters for the world to see the life and legacy of Malcolm X as never before.

1. Freedom Fighters?

BAIN: Not only were you responsible for bringing the legendary Last Poets back together, but you have also worked with South African freedom fighter and political prisoner-turned president Nelson Mandela. You were the chief curator for the first U.S./South Africa international exhibit, and were appointed to escort Mr. Mandela during the exhibit premiere at his 90th birthday. After serving as attorney and guardian for civil rights legend Rosa Parks, you then played a pivotal role in securing the Congressional and Presidential Medals of Freedom on Parks' behalf.

How have these experiences helped prepare you for your work honoring the legacy of Malcolm X? How does the human rights work of El Hajj Malik El Shabazz relate to the campaigns of Ms. Parks and Mr. Mandela?

REED: The distinction I can see in understanding these figures is that Ms. Parks role was more of a catalyst that stimulated a movement in America. I see the role in working with Nelson Mandela as one of transforming South Africa and getting them ready for freedom and self-determination. I recognize Malcolm X had a global role in launching our people as well as all human beings onto the international stage of human rights. I saw that he was more prepared for that by utilizing experiences of Ms. Parks and Mr. Mandela.

It should be noted that Ms. Parks's family members were part of the Garvey movement. A lot of people did not know that her fight for freedom began at such an early stage of her life. She deeply admired Malcolm X as a role model and his philosophy both were a product of the Garvey movement. We cannot overlook that some of Elijah Muhammad's philosophies were derived from Garveyism through Master Fard's teachings. I have been very blessed and fortunate to be a curator who is involved with the archival artifacts of the Nation of Islam and Malcolm X that connected this history through Alex Haley's writings.

Malcolm saw things from a global perspective. Along with Dr. King, he was one of the first African Americans of his time to travel internationally and develop this insight to relate to all persons. This has helped many of us to recognize that we have the ability to relate to all persons from a global perspective. If you look at Nelson Mandela, he set the example for South Africa to seek freedom and self-determination on various levels internally. We can credit Malcolm with waking us up on an international plane to see that we are all connected. We are still struggling with that today, but he set the foundation for what is yet to come. This is why he was seeking to take the African American plight to the United Nations—which is still overdue.

2. Auction Block?

BAIN: African people in the Americas have had a long, painful history of being bought and sold on the auction block. When Alex Haley passed in 1992, Malcolm X's eldest daughter, Attallah Shabazz, wrote that she was "greatly disappointed" that the original manuscript of her father's autobiography, with handwritten notes by Malcolm himself, was sold at auction without the permission or participation of his family. His daughter, Ilyasah, however, recently agreed to write the foreword for your forthcoming publication of writings omitted from her father's influential book.

How were the Shabazz family's initial concerns about the release of this material reconciled? What impact did our legacy of dehumanization at auction have on your decision to purchase these unpublished works?

REED: Before we get to that, we have to look at the sentiments of Ms. Attallah Shabazz. Ms. Shabazz's thought are the precursor to my thoughts on where I am with the legacies of Malcolm and Alex Haley. We so often overlook our history, and she has made a very profound point. Ms. Shabazz lost her godfather Alex Haley and saw her father's legacy and Alex Haley's papers being auctioned off so her feelings were intertwined with the archives being sold off at the auction block. So we have to look at the chickens coming home to roost from an archival and preservation standpoint. If we don't take care of our own history, it will come back to haunt us.

We find that today in urban America when we don't preserve our history, violence comes home to roost. When we do not learn to preserve anything that is an extension of ourselves, then others do not respect us. To have this material auctioned off was to have our selves auctioned off as well.

Malcolm X and the book of *Roots'* words and passages are like our Declaration of Independence. Words can be used over and over again to liberate our people. The words of Malcolm X and Roots are actually linked to our self-determination. As long as others take our words and alter our writings, they can keep us from our self-determination and maintain us in a state of darkness. I was afraid the words of Malcolm and Alex would be suppressed and used to keep us in an unconscious state. I did not know what the manuscript actually contained, or the omitted chapters, but I knew it was something of value that needed to be preserved and protected for all humanity. It was good to see and hear Ilyasah informed me that she wanted to meet the man who used whatever resources he had to preserve the legacy of her father and Alex Haley for all humanity. It is important that we all take a stand to protect our own history and culture and heritage as opposed to just talking about it. Many people would speak in this light, but would not risk their own resources to protect it.

3. Detroit Red?

BAIN: A firestorm of controversy surrounding Manning Marable's new biography *Malcolm X: A Life of Reinvention* has emerged since its release in April. Although it is well documented that Malcolm was sentenced to "four concurrent eight-to-ten-year sentences" in prison (Pg. 68), Marable argues that his life as a criminal was largely inflated.

What insight, if any, do the omitted chapters offer into the impact of the life Malcolm led just before being incarcerated? Was the life of a hustler described by "Detroit Red" in the autobiography essentially "fictive" as Marable claims?

REED: *The Autobiography* itself was not fictive. The part that was modified, which I have insight on are the early years, notably, the chapter on Laura. The reason why it was fictive, and I have two original versions of it, is because the publisher put pressure on Malcolm because they thought they would be attacked by libel lawsuits. Malcolm tells that in a chapter that is unpublished on Laura.

There are actually five unpublished chapters. "The Negro," "Twenty Million Muslims," and "The End of Christianity" are the most noted. The others are the chapter on Laura and the Introduction by Malcolm X—which I read at Malcolm's 85th birthday celebration at the (former) Audubon Ballroom last year. The intro published with *The Autobiography* is by M.S. Handler, not his own which he (Malcolm) wrote. Malcolm wanted readers to know, in the chapter on the character "Laura," who these people were because he was concerned about their privacy and the "truth." That Laura's name was Gloria Strother. That "Shorty" was really five-foot-eleven and his name was Malcolm Jarvis. Professor Marable was able to detect the actual characters' names in most cases. He did an excellent job in tracing some of these names that matched up with the unpublished materials. I saw these names in Malcolm and Alex's own handwriting, but the publisher insisted they make changes to the details of the Laura chapter to protect against invasion of privacy lawsuits. Malcolm states in the unpublished chapters that names were changed and details were altered to protect certain people, but what he states happened is factual.

The chapter on Laura/Gloria is the only one in the original materials noted as being fictive. His relationship with Laura wasn't one of intimacy, but one of a companion and friend. Malcolm felt that he could have supported that friendship in ways that he regretted because her life went into an irreversible tailspin. She went into prostitution, became a heroin addict and ended up in a mental asylum prison, but the book and movie only portrayed her indulging in prostitution. Malcolm protected her by not exposing her name or the condition that she ended up in. The unpublished chapters described the details of those who were in his life at that time. Now we can reconcile the circumstantial remarks that were made by Mr. Marable. He did not have access to the actual manuscript. Some of the Marable's remarks should have been omitted.

4. *Grassroots Messenger?*

BAIN: Malcolm's genius was evident in the powerful metaphors he gave the world for thinking about our condition. One which still resonates and is referenced today is the allegory of the "house negro" and the "field negro."

Harry Belafonte recently invoked this analogy calling out the support Colin Powell and Condoleezza Rice gave George Bush in his declaration of War on Iraq. Violating international law and human rights, this "pre-emptive strike" in the name of post 9/11 counter-terrorism caused the death and injury of thousands of innocent men, women, and children.

Malcolm's provocative plantation story has been referenced by everyone from conservatives defending elite access as the fruits of their labor to progressives arguing that those in the house were best suited to poison slave traders, or let field slaves know when to escape or revolt as slavers slept. Why do you think this paradigm remains so poignant today?

REED: There's a reason why that is so relevant today. The fact of it is this ties into the suppression of *The Autobiography* manuscript, the omitted chapters and the unpublished writings. "The Negro" is one of the key suppressed chapters of the book and his introduction. The importance of a non-supportive person of humanity suppressing "The Negro" chapter is to maintain the Negro in a state of not knowing who he is. One can alter another's behavior when you don't know who you are. When we recognize who we are, any human being regardless of race, creed, or color, regardless of your station, you will conduct yourself in accordance with who you are.

We have people of African descent who have been taught to align themselves with their own heritage, their own culture, their own intellect. As long as anyone is misaligned with their own heritage, culture and intellect, they can be used for another's purposes. The reason people suppress who you are is to exploit you for their own economic purposes. That's why the suppression paradigm of history still exists. Those who look like us don't always have our own best interests. We are weakened by others who use our own kind as gatekeepers. We get caught up on the imagery and not the substance.

We should always question and look to the substance of anything we do. As Malcolm said, "...judge people by their deeds and not by their race." He had evolved beyond a civil rights to a human rights perspective. It should be noted that the civil rights perspective means your rights are defined by law rather than that you were born with them as a human being. The civil rights perspective marginalizes your birthright because it is being legislated. That's not just something cliché being spoken by him, but he had evolved after recognizing that there were those who looked like him who were out to marginalize the African American plight and were out to do him in! This became more understood by Malcolm during his trip to Mecca when he saw those who were light and white skinned and saw him as their brother. Until African Americans free their minds on the basis of human rights we will not reach our full potential.

5. Plantations Turned Penitentiaries?

BAIN: Between prisons, probation and parole, more Black folks are reportedly caught in the criminal justice system today than once enslaved on American plantations. The mass incarceration crisis in the U.S. has led prisons to be seen by countless youth as an American rite of passage.

Brooklyn comic Chris Rock even suggested recently that if you come from a small apartment in the projects, a prison cell might be somewhat of an upgrade. Without glorifying prisons as popular culture often does today, what inspiring lesson can young folks draw from Malcolm X's transformation from angry inmate to international human rights activist?

REED: One of the roots of Malcolm's metamorphosis was having a solid self education of himself. He addressed that in his letters during the last years of his life. He said he would have studied more languages. He might've become a lawyer as one of his teachers said he could not be one. Education was Malcolm's bedrock.

Malcolm was self-educated, but so much more than many who are college graduates. Still he recognized that his mind had so much more infinite space in what he could learn. In essence, he did not place any limits on his ability, and we should not as well. A psychoanalysis that Alex Haley had done on Malcolm X, initially done secretly and presented to Malcolm, is part of the censored epilogue (Pg. 454). It showed how curious his mind was. It was noted by the psychologist when Malcolm went to the zoo to look something up because he was so dedicated to learning. She was able to connect this love affair he had with learning to his love of his people and advancing their plight.

6. Revolutionary Theater?

BAIN: After the release of his influential film "X" in 1992, legendary director Spike Lee was critiqued by Black Arts pioneer Amiri Baraka for portraying Blackness as little more than "Black faces on the wall of a pizzeria." One of Baraka's criticisms of the film was not only that it with Lee as the sidekick character "Shorty," but also that Malcolm's life as a street hustler, who conked his hair to look like a white man, was its centerpiece. Others attacked Lee for spending more time on Malcolm and his white girlfriend and crime partner than with his daughters and wife, Dr. Betty Shabazz.

How do you see the theatrical production you are producing based on the omitted chapters from the autobiography as different from the film? While Broadway has historically been called "The Great White Way," even its discriminating history could not deny the extraordinary talent of giants like Paul Robeson, August Wilson and Angela Basset, to name a few of the legendary writers and thespians who have brought color and breathed life to its stages. When the theatrical production of the lost chapters that is currently in development hits Broadway, who do you envision playing Malcolm?

REED: The unpublished writings and omitted chapters can educate and enlighten people, but also culturally entertain and create a transformative experience. It will be a bridge to what people are dealing with today. It will be transformative and different from others productions you are co-developing. This is one of those theatrical pieces that is being developed from the unpublished writings to prepare future generations and be used over and over as a classic.

There are many great actors to consider and others who have yet to come. Some of those I could see in the role have often been overlooked like Jeffrey Wright. He played Martin Luther King once and I think he has something to offer in this role. We know how awesome Denzel Washington is, and of course he has something to offer. Then there's Laurence Fishburne who could carry the role well. He has put on a little weight lately, but he would be committed enough if he desired the role to slim down.

Another great actor who no one would have thought of in his early years, but lately people have seen him in a different light, and he has taken on very serious roles, is Will Smith. Those are some of the individuals that I have taken note of who could do justice to the theatrical work. There is another actor who has committed his life to the theatrical portrayal of Malcolm and that is Duane Shepard. He has committed his life to playing Malcolm as a solo character for years.

7. *Chickens Come Home?*

BAIN: Malcolm's split with the Nation of Islam is portrayed in his autobiography as a response to evidence of sexual relationships and children he learned Elijah Muhammad fathered with several of his secretaries, as well as Malcolm X's hajj experience with Muslims of diverse ethnicities. Yet prior to these revelations, Malcolm was already moving in another direction. During the last year of his life, his close study of the burgeoning civil rights movement and anti-colonial politics throughout the "Third World" brought him to urge followers towards a Black United Front bringing human rights violations against African people in the Americas before the United Nations. His expanding view of empire increasingly brought him into greater alignment with the Pan-Africanism of the Garvey movement followed by his parents.

What insights do the documents you have acquired from being suppressed and lost offer about his evolution?

REED: During Malcolm's evolution, he came to realize where we were as a people at that time. Malcolm had three deep loves. He loved Elijah Muhammad to the point that it was earth shattering to him when Elijah Muhammad's affairs were revealed; he had a deep profound love of his wife, and family and for his people.

One of the things that came to light in these documents is Malcolm's 14-point economic plan. Elijah Muhammad gave him the floor or the foundation for the progress of the African American people, but Malcolm began to build a house for moving the African American plight beyond the civil rights movement. Malcolm had a plan that exceeded Elijah Muhammad's plan—beyond the separation philosophy. And it really is more evolutionary than what the President or our public officials think. He had an economic plan for how Black people could bring about their own progress. They did not want to release the unpublished writings that address this economic plan because it was just too informative, too transformative and highly educational, which the masses could not grasp, but Malcolm had a plan.

Part of that plan addressed: what good is housing when you have unemployment? What good is integrating a restaurant when you do not have the economic power to purchase a cup of coffee? Just as well, what good is it to have a house if you cannot take care of it? Malcolm had all of these things connected. You need housing. You also need access to capital and financing. I have never seen any economic plan that addressed the points that Malcolm has integrated such as education, museums, social services, policing, and other essential points. Why would you need a museum? Because then you know who you are. He said you need policing. Not the police, but you need to be self-policing. The people need to protect themselves so they can rid the community of whatever can harm that community. He saw these points that could be self-supporting in the system that is in place. We must have social services, not welfare, but people need to support one another so we can learn to support ourselves.

As long as you keep a people mentally imbalanced and not knowing who they are, no one is going to respect them. The Garvey movement, the Du Bois and the Niagara movement, Malcolm learned to integrate them as a part of his infrastructure and philosophy, and went beyond those great leaders into a world stage leader. And that is the evolution that Malcolm went through. Militants who only see pieces of who he is, resist seeing him holistically. Even with the great work of Dr. King, Malcolm and King saw many important facets, but when King began to look at things from an economic perspective as Malcolm and that's when he was assassinated.

Malcolm was already there in terms of the insight that he had developed according to the documents that have been censored and unpublished.

8. Reinvention of a Life?

BAIN: Manning Marable's new biography depicts Malcolm X's relationship with his wife, Dr. Betty Shabazz, as one he entered into reluctantly out of obligation to the Nation of Islam. Not only is their intimate life exposed by letters and conversations claiming their incompatibility in the bedroom, but both are alleged to have violated each other's trust in extramarital affairs. Not unlike other public figures in American politics, such claims have been made about Dr. Martin Luther King in recent years as well.

What is the significance of such revelations? Is it inappropriate to make such indiscretions public based on "circumstantial" evidence? Or does assessing both their virtues and alleged vices pay homage to their full humanity? What light is shed on their relationship by the censored chapters? Are these personal matters even relevant?

REED: I can speak to Malcolm X and Dr. Betty Shabazz' relationship by reporting the facts beyond *The Autobiography* manuscript hand written notations and based upon the unpublished writings. One thing is misaligned...in terms of the materials that were recorded in Malcolm's own handwriting vs. what was reported by Marable's book and others who sought to report things based on circumstantial information, but not direct sources. What I read is a misrepresentation: that Malcolm was forced into marrying Betty out of obligation based on the Nation of Islam's practices. It is false. It is a lie. Malcolm was celibate for twelve years according to his handwritten documents. He had committed himself to a greater cause for humanity and to cleaning himself up, as well as to be more fitting for a woman of great virtue. That became his beloved wife, Betty Shabazz.

According to Malcolm's handwritten notations in *The Autobiography*, Elijah Muhammad did not want him to get married. That is in red ink. Regarding Betty, he deeply admired her, because of her intellect, and he deeply desired her based on the lady he wanted in his life. Not out of obligation. Elijah Muhammad did not want him to be married possibly because Malcolm might be divided in his duties in building the Nation of Islam. There were assignments Muhammad wanted Malcolm to carry out on his behalf.

As the end result, in the end and as noted, the results were that Betty Shabazz gave him greater stability, and Malcolm worked even harder and expanded the Nation of Islam's influences more than it ever was. He expanded it from hundreds to thousands. In a letter to Alex Haley, sent during his hajj to Mecca (and its parts omitted from *The Autobiography*), Malcolm wrote to Betty: "Please call my wife tonight. Tell her that I love her. Without her high morale, I could never take my place in history." He knew he could never impact humanity in the way that he did without Betty Shabazz. (The text also omitted George Sims' name, Haley's researcher of *Roots* and *Autobiography*).

This is what Malcolm said in his own handwriting. That letter is being preserved at Syracuse University where I have been allowed to review it in their Library's Rare Documents section. Are these personal facts relevant? Yes, because it shows how one should conduct oneself with one's family. He set the standard for us and maybe some of us will work just as hard. That is a family and relationship standard we should all adopt, and maybe many of us will take our place in history.

9. Ancestors Watching?

BAIN: As Malcolm looks down on us today, do you think he would he agree with those who argue we are living in a "Post-Racial" America? Do you agree with Marable's assessment that Malcolm X's meeting with the KKK was "despicable" given their violence against Blacks and diverse civil rights activists?

REED: I don't agree that it was despicable, especially in this context. What we have to learn is that we must learn in order to move ahead, we must be able to dialogue with the devil to understand where the devil is coming from. We have to learn from our enemies. MLK was practicing that all the time. You can never judge nor prejudge a person without communication taking place because you don't know what their experiences are or where they're coming from. It's not despicable. We understand what the KKK represents, but there is something to be learned from them. We can learn from all people of all walks of life. That's one reason why we have the UN. They never all agree with each other, but communication and conversation are so powerful when actually employed.

We are not in a post-racial America. We are still in a racial state in America and it's evident in prisons, in urban and rural communities, even in the education system. We think we have progress, but when you look at the sociological (evidence) and get down underneath it, you find out it's the same thing going on in another form. The root of it is still here and has to be dealt with. That's why communication is so important.

Many of us are still hiding behind our masks, and many around the world are still suffering. The world is still controlled by the four to five percent who controls the wealth and keeps us boxed in. The racial state is what keeps us divided, but Malcolm saw past that and recognized it's a human rights game that is needed and not a segregation game that needs to be employed.

10. By Any Means?

BAIN: What does Malcolm's call to fight racism and colonization "by any means necessary" mean for us in the twenty-first century? Does this position support anti-racist and anti-imperialist action through both armed rebellion and non-violent civil disobedience? Would our efforts today be better spent demanding reparations from Congress? Or human rights enforcement by the United Nations? ...or pursuing some other path to self-determination?

REED: So many people get this incorrect: by any means necessary. People like to put it in a violent state. One thing I have learned from *The Autobiography* manuscript is that we look at things from a conclusive point and not in their broader context.

This ties into the missing chapters, and especially "The Negro" and "Twenty Million Muslims" and also Malcolm's introduction. In order for the Negro to move forward, we have to act as one body "by any means necessary." Twenty million was the number of African Americans in the population in the country at that time, and Malcolm wanted to build and educate his people by any means necessary. The chapter entitled "The End of Christianity" is misunderstood. Yes, Malcolm identified with Jesus Christ. He was not against him, but we have been miseducated and Christianity has been misaligned and improperly taught to African Americans.

We were taught that to get our just rewards it would be in heaven and not on earth. That it should be deferred. So many of us have to unlearn what we have been taught. We were taught that in order to enjoy the fruit of the land and our labor, we must defer ourselves from being prosperous and supporting one another. It has taken years to correct this misconception and we must prosper while we are here *and* get our just due afterwards. We can have both, here and now, as Malcolm recognized. By any means necessary.

I look at it from Malcolm's life and understand from a greater depth. Malcolm was brought up on that phrase from his early years as a child. His family survived because they understood they had to survive by any means necessary: When they did not have any food; when they took care of his mother. When he moved to Boston and he had to survive. When he was hustling and had to survive by any means. In prison, when he read at night to educate himself by any means; to protect his family, even holding a gun by the window. By any means necessary. In building the Nation of Islam, "by any means necessary." It was a universal connecting thread of his life. We have applied the words in a limiting context. To understand it we must move humanity forward, by any means necessary.

Note: *This material cannot be used by any party without authorization in writing or licensed only through the Keeper of the Word Foundation. All rights are reserved by the Foundation. This contribution is granted to Herb Boyd, and humanity to help Third World Press in its evolutionary state. All rights and responses are reserved by the Keeper of the Word Foundation and the family of Alex Haley.*

We Declare Our Right To Be A Human Being: Malcolm X, "A Life of Reclamation"

Michael Simanga

"By Any Means Necessary" is the most widely known and quoted phrase of Malcolm X. In popular mass market culture it could be considered the branding tag line of Malcolm's revolutionary voice and work. In that way it also functions as a condensed message to differentiating Malcolm's revolutionary philosophy from others in the civil rights movement, especially Dr. Martin Luther King. Too often the complexity of the struggle and the critical understanding of differing approaches is reduced to the simplistic, "King Non-Violence, Malcolm By Any Means Necessary."

While, "by any means necessary" may be useful in introducing many to Malcolm X, unfortunately it has overshadowed the more important content that proceeds it, "We declare our right on this earth...to be a human being, to be respected as a human being, to be given the rights of a human being in this society, on this earth, in this day, which we intend to bring into existence by any means necessary." That statement was made in a speech by Malcolm on June 28, 1964 at a founding rally of the Organization of Afro-American Unity (OAAU). By any means necessary is the tactical "how" to the strategic "what" our right to be a human being.

It is Malcolm's unique authentic voice expressing the what and the how of the African American struggle that defines the power of his presence and leadership in our movement and history. His life was our voice and his voice was our life. His life was our voice because we heard our history in his sound, struggling to survive and surviving to struggle for freedom. His life was our voice because he was never defeated no matter how much abuse and pain was heaped on him. Like us, wearing the scars of our ancestors and experience, he continued to rise from the deepest most downtrodden condition. He continued to grow more true to himself, to us, to his capacity as a human being by reclaiming his right to be. Like us.

His voice was our life because he was able to gather our pain and the pride peering out from the broken pieces of our story and speak it. Like the music full of memory and vision that has continued to erupt in our people's throats, the rhythms and the tones, the intelligence and humor, the honesty and love were all present in Malcolm's oratory. His voice was our life and when he spoke it, from the moment we heard him, we were different, transformed. Our movement became organized in a different way, our people were inspired in a different way, our sense of Africa and our place in the history of the world, our place in the human family were all understood in ways we had not envisioned, even with all we'd seen and done before the period of Malcolm's leadership.

It was his voice, his articulation of us in thought and movement, a sound still resonating today that makes Malcolm X important. It was his voice, one of two dominating voices of our movement and the historical period of the 1950-60s that has also generated years of debate, scholarship and examination of Malcolm X the political phenomenon. Dr. Manning Marable's book, *Malcolm X: A Life of Reinvention* is a work that seems to be inspired by that sound, that voice too.

Marable was a respected progressive historian who led a dedicated life researching, writing, teaching and working to contribute to the body of knowledge and the on-going conversation about liberation politics. As it should be, there are occasions where the community of liberation fighters and scholars disagreed with some of his ideas and conclusions. That disagreement is not a bad thing; it is an important part of our struggle. We must be able to disagree and have open discussion and critique of our ideas and our work in order to come to greater theoretical knowledge and practical unity. Again, that is part of the how, but we must not lose sight of the what. The open debate must not prevent us from finding common ground for organizing together to fight our enemies and continue to move our struggle forward. The discussion cannot deteriorate into destructive and paralyzing posturing and personal attacks.

Marable's biography of Malcolm X emerged out of the progressive scholars' life he lived. As it should be, it has ignited a national conversation and debate about the book, but more importantly how we access, understand and learn from the critical essence of Malcolm X as a historical figure key to the Black Liberation Movement of the last part of the twentieth century and the beginning decades of the twenty-first century. The national discussion that has ensued since the publication of the book and Marable's untimely death just before its release will help us focus on our tasks today. It is unfortunate that Marable is not here to participate in this discussion. However, we are obligated to critique and exam its content and impact.

For all oppressed people, the salient and necessary feature of subjugation is the imposition of an identity of inferiority by the subjugator. This identity of inferiority is imposed by law, custom, tradition, violence, culture, education, religion and every other tool and weapon available to the oppressor. This imposed identity is meant to make the oppressed subservient and docile in order to facilitate their exploitation. It is also meant to kill the voice, the articulation of self, of the oppressed because it carries the basis of resistance. This process has been seen all over the world where people have been colonized and/or enslaved. It is India being forced to behave as if it were British, or African Americans who continue to believe we are inferior to white people. To subjugate you must destroy the peoples' sense of self and replace it with the inferior self-created by the oppressor.

At the core of the struggle for freedom is the necessity to maintain an identity that is in opposition to the oppressor imposed identity. This oppositional identity resists the imposed identity by holding on to and claiming elements of its pre-subjugation history, culture, religion, family, language and stories of resistance. But that oppositional identity is not enough. It is an identity of resistance but not yet of liberation.

By necessity, the transformation of the resistance movement into a successful liberation movement requires the construction of an identity that is not just in opposition, but an identity that asserts vision of a liberated people asserting their right to be free. This asserted identity is constructed from the history of ancestors before the subjugation, the history of resistance during subjugation and a distinct vision of the people's collective life free from the oppressor. It is an identity that projects a distinct vision of the future with a political, social, cultural and economic program that is drastically different from the life under the imposed identity. It is the movement for National Liberation that swept Africa, Asia and Latin America. The people of those places constructed and asserted their national identities to unify the struggle to defeat the imposed identity of colonial subjugation and exploitation and project themselves into the future.

Malcolm X expressed a revolutionary vision of the African American people, not because he used revolutionary rhetoric, but because he used his personal life and our collective life to reclaim our humanity. His life was not one of reinvention as Marable asserts. While Marable seems to admire Malcolm's accomplishments, the book also suggests that Malcolm was constantly reinventing himself to adapt to new conditions for personal gain. This assertion demonstrates a lack of understanding of both Malcolm X and the African American struggle.

When I say Malcolm used his personal life and our collective life to reclaim our humanity it is because the ideas, the ideology, the conceptualization of a liberated people is a process of emerging and developing consciousness that requires critical self-examination and a willful search for the truth. In this process of self-examination we discover who we are in the context of where we are. In order for our ancestors who were second or third generation enslaved Africans born in the United States, held in captivity in South Carolina, living under the imposed identity of slavery to liberate themselves, they had to reach before and beyond the condition they were in. They must reach before that condition to capture a sense of who they were prior to the enslavement, and they must reach beyond it to see themselves as other than slaves. The most powerful element of our people's history is that though we endured hundreds of years of slavery and another hundred years of Jim Crow, every generation understood enslavement and degradation was our condition not our destiny. To get to the asserted identity of liberated people, they had to understand who they are, not just who they are in the system of slavery.

Who are we? I am a woman, a man, a father, a mother, a daughter, a son. I am Black, African, human. These acknowledgements are small steps in reclaiming full humanity. If we accept that I am a man or woman, what now must be done to uphold that, to reclaim that? What must be done to resist the imposed identity that does everything it can to deny us that claim?

This process of reclamation is acutely evident in Malcolm's life as a reflection of our own collective black life. Malcolm's family was shattered and dispersed. Malcolm was denied education that would allow him to fully realize his potential. Malcolm lived in African American communities of poverty that had rich cultural lives, but also had conditions that fostered crime, despair, drug addiction, and death. Malcolm's imprisonment was commonplace and still is amongst African American men. Malcolm sought salvation in religion and spiritual redemption. Malcolm sought freedom from those conditions, that power that continued to impose and identity of inferiority upon him and his people.

For each one of these and other personal life experiences for Malcolm, it was the small, consistent steps to reclaim his and ultimately our humanity that led him to his public ministry and national leadership as the voice of a new nation of Black people. This reclamation, this gathering of bits and pieces of our humanity, claiming them as a birthright is the evidence of his and our struggle for freedom. Marable's book talks about some of these reclamations, but illuminates them in a strange light. They are referred to as reinventions presented as if they were contrived and not the milestones that are achieved in the course of struggle.

From a child denied a quality education to a globally respected intellectual, thinker and theorist was a journey Malcolm undertook as an act of resistance against the imposed identity of our oppressors. His turn to religion that did not revere or worship the God of our oppressor was necessary as an act of reclaiming the right to decide one's own ontology. His relentless drive to create organizations and institutions capable of both resistance and construction of the new asserted identity to project us into the future was also reclamation as he grew to understand that a people without its own instruments of culture, politics and power cannot sustain itself or build its own future. At each one of these steps, each stage of his own personal development he was discovering, digesting and adapting to new information, new truth. And as Malcolm made those discoveries he was able to reclaim more of himself and lead us in reclaiming more of ourselves. His entire life was a series of acts of reclamation that led to his greatest and most influential contribution to our struggle, contextualizing as a human rights struggle.

Meticulously researched and written in a narrative style that should allow non-scholars to access it, Marable' book also helps to understand some of the inner workings of some aspects of the movement in the 1960s especially the Nation of Islam. This is important because it holds lessons for us as we attempt to build the necessary political instruments required of our struggle today. However, there are two important areas where brother Marable fails in his book, *Malcolm X: A Life of Reinvention.*

First, is the failure to recognize that Malcolm's life and work as both example and metaphor for the African American experience, is the process of reclamation I spoke of previously. In this process, the process of all peoples struggle against oppression, we are constantly adapting to and transforming ourselves and our reality as we gain strength through the affirmation of our human capacity through reclamation and construction of a historically based and visionary identity that we assert as free self-determining people. This lack of focus on Malcolm's life and work, with its victories and mistakes, minimizes what is important for us to understand. We need the process of reclamation to understand the trajectory of the struggle and to differentiate the what and the how.

The second failure is a result of the first. Marable's book is consistent with the current American bourgeois trend in popular culture, praising a public figure while also degrading them through innuendo and the spreading of rumors to undermine their character and influence. There has been repeated discussion about Marable's attempt to humanize

Malcolm, to remove him from the pedestal so we can examine him as a man. But this examination does nothing more to humanize him. There are passages about Malcolm's personal life that include speculation that he may have prostituted himself as a homosexual when he was hustling in his criminal past. Or that he may have had a relationship with a young Muslim woman and he may have spent the night with her the evening before he was murdered. He might have purposely made himself unavailable to his children. Perhaps he was not really changing ideologically but was making calculated decisions to present his program after the split with the Muslims to get white support.

These passages undermine the credibility of the book not only because they are unsubstantiated but more importantly because they do not further our understanding. We need great scholarship, especially on the intense period of Black Power/Black Liberation during the 1960-70s. We need research, study and writing on the communities that gave rise to the movements, organizations and people of the Black Liberation Movement. We need information that helps us understand our mistakes and our victories. We need to record our history, to tell our own stories so generations behind us will know what happen and why.

To understand Malcolm X, a person like all of us, fragile, flawed, searching, causing harm and trying to do some good, full of contradiction and trying to reconcile them, we must weigh the result of a life of reclamation. We must follow the process that brought him to stand on the world stage for us and with us and: "declare our right on this earth...to be a human being, to be respected as a human being, to be given the rights of a human being in this society, on this earth, in this day, which we intend to bring into existence by any means necessary."

Let the work continue.

Malcolm X: Reinvention or African-centered Service and Sacrifice

Diane D. Turner and Aslaku Berhanu

I believe in a society in which people can live like human beings on the basis of equality.
—Malcolm X, January 1965

In Malcolm X's last television interview with Pierre Berton, he made the preceding remarks (Gallen, 1991, p. 186). Malcolm spent nineteen of his thirty-nine years searching for truth to acquire wisdom and understanding for solutions to eradicate white supremacy, first at the national level then globally. At every juncture, his journey as an African-centered Black man in America was very painful.

Through his African-centeredness, he expanded his knowledge recognizing the importance—first Blacks then Africans—knowing their history and culture to affirm their role as actors in their struggles against white supremacy. During his lifelong learning process, Malcolm underwent personal resurrection, transformation and renewal. Ultimately, Malcolm X, as a race-conscious Black man, committed himself to a life of African-centered service and sacrifice because of his deep love for his people. Once he arrived with a vision to achieve freedom, justice and equality for Black and Brown people globally, Malcolm called for self-affirmation and self-determination. His untimely death at the hands of assassins elevated him to the status of a martyr.

A number of books and anthologies have been written to offer a deeper understanding of Malcolm, the man, some fact and some fiction. The legacy of Malcolm X and his importance as a freedom fighter to a majority of people of African descent continues. In fact, Denzel Washington who played Malcolm X in Lee's screenplay named his son Malcolm in honor of Malcolm X. Marlon Riggs in Joe Wood's edited book titled *Malcolm X: In Our Own Image* stated that: "[Malcolm's] His life, even after death, can remain heroic because its spirit of survival, of defiance, of self-assertion and self-determination, still lives" (p. 153).

If Malcolm X were alive today, he would be eighty-six years old. In reconstructing the life and character of an African-centered intellectual activist like Malcolm X, the scholar must be sensitive to and cautious about the use of methodology and interpretation. Serious considerations to the influences of race in America are paramount. More importantly, interpretations must examine the pathological nature of white supremacy that impacts almost every aspect of Black life on a daily basis. As actors in their history, Black people also have used numerous and diverse methods to respond to white supremacy. As Malcolm states in *Malcolm X Speaks*, 1965, "Regardless of where or when one attends school in America, he receives along with legitimate educational experiences, a dose of pure, unadulterated racism." More than twenty years later, Toni Morrison concurred with Malcolm X in an article in *Essence*, December 1987 when she stated, "Racism is a scholarly pursuit, it's taught, it's institutionalized."

The scholar has a responsibility not only to avoid the traps of sensationalism and gossip that have developed around Black heroes to denigrate their contributions to history but also provide facts and interpretations on how they overcome against great odds. This is not to say that they should be portrayed as virtual saints. However, this is especially crucial when one tries to understand Malcolm X and Toni Morrison critique of racism provided in the preceding paragraph. The researcher also must check and re-check secondary and primary sources for their accuracy and truth. This is critical because there have been recent revisionists' attempts to discredit the contributions of courageous black men and women like Harriet Tubman, W.E.B. Du Bois, Paul Robeson, Martin Luther King Jr. and Malcolm X who struggled to liberate Black people. In their undertakings, they have sought to replace first person accounts about these men and women given by them. Betty Shabazz writes in *Malcolm X The Man and His Times* edited by John Henrik Clarke that, "how things in this country are so designed to break the back of a Black man. Any Black man today who strives to be a man among men is singled out and accused of everything except what he is trying to do" (Clarke, 1990, pp. 136-137).

The legacy of Malcolm X has endured not only because of *The Autobiography of Malcolm X* but also for his sincere African-centered service and sacrifice which inspired many blacks, especially youth, to take pride in their Blackness—Black History and culture—from civil rights activists to Black Power advocates and activists to leaders and participants of the Black Arts Movement. Ten years after Malcolm's assassination, sales of his autobiography amounted to over 6 million copies. Manning Marable states in *Malcolm X: A Life of Reinvention* that *The Autobiography* was "A best seller in its initial years of publication, the book soon established itself as a standard text in hundreds of college and university curricula. By the late 1960s, an entire generation of African American poets and writers were producing a seemingly endless body of work paying homage to their fallen idol" (7-8).

Manning Marable's biography of Malcolm X attempts to disassemble some of the stories that have been told and written about Malcolm for some time now; this includes the widely read and studied *The Autobiography of Malcolm X* that Malcolm produced with journalist Alex Haley. More than forty years after the initial publication of *The Autobiography of Malcolm X*, the present study of Malcolm X attempts to brings to fore new insight gleaned from a number of archival material, interviews, and government documents. The reception of Marable's biography—*Malcolm X: A Life of Reinvention*—has been met with mixed reviews from both within the academy and from without (the general public). On one hand the scholarship is praised for its rigorous pursuit of primary sources for a retelling of the story that many have previously been aware of since the publication of *The Autobiography*. Then there are the naysayers who question the analysis applied to the evidence he cites, as well as "the evidence of things unseen." It is here where most of the criticism rests because of presumptions unsubstantiated by the archival sources of which most of the text rests; then, too, there is the issue with the interviews from persons who were believed to be Malcolm's enemies (Baraka 2011). These objections strike fundamentally at the base of the scholarship, meaning its intention and method. Even more, other readers dismiss the text altogether saying that Marable offers nothing new in his portrayal of Malcolm in this fashion. Marable's students and other scholars do see the merits of the work and suggest, like Professor Imani Perry (2011) of Princeton University, that "the book is a masterpiece of meticulous detail and powerful social history." Marable states,

> The great temptation for the biographer of an iconic figure is to portray him or her as a virtual saint, without the normal contradictions and blemishes that all human beings have. I have devoted so many years in the effort to understand the interior personality and mind of Malcolm that this temptation disappeared long ago. (13)

One might ask the questions: Did Marable take liberties to include presumptions about Malcolm X without substantial evidence because of what he saw as his task to include the "normal contradictions and blemishes that all human beings have?" Did he go too far without considering the factor of race? For example, Marable includes circumstantial evidence about Malcolm Little's sex life prior to his conversion to Islam.

During his perilous life, Malcolm X is catapulted into a segregated American society that is a violent world of poverty and white supremacy. In Marable's biography, he documents Malcolm's paranoia, self-doubt, criminality, drug addiction, prostitution, and incarceration. Yet, he does not place Malcolm's human fragility and flaws within the context of white supremacy. Malcolm embraces the Nation of Islam to liberate himself and Black people and, in the process, was often misunderstood. Here Marable had an opportunity to offer insight into these gray areas but does not. He does not offer a depthful analysis of the importance of Islam in Malcolm's life. Marable states, "One of the greatest challenges I encountered in reconstructing his life was the attempt to examine his activities inside the Nation of Islam" (12). Marable explains, "Part of the problem in unearthing his earlier speeches and letters from the 1950s was the current NOI leadership, headed by the former Louis X Walcott, known today as Louis Farrakhan, had never permitted scholars to examine the sect's archives" (12). Louis Farrakhan and other Nation of Islam members who were enemies of Malcolm X became main informants in the biography. How accurate is the information? Malcolm was called a racist, a separatist and a hater. But Malcolm did not remain static in time, he was constantly changing. During his transformation, he raised critical questions about the society he lived in and the injustices and inequalities that blacks faced on a daily basis. In spite of the uncertainty of his early years, the mistakes that resulted in his incarceration, the threats and attacks by the Nation of Islam and surveillance and harassment by the FBI, NYPD and CIA he becomes El-Hajj Malik El-Shabazz.

In an attempt to shed more light on Malcolm's life during a turbulent period of American history, Marable's study was intended to take us deep into the lived experiences of Malcolm X to learn more about who made Malcolm, what made Malcolm, and the many spaces and places that bore witness to Malcolm's transformations (reinventions). Marable attempts to bring together a narrative that is full of ideas, constructions, questions, and doubts useful to the continued study and teaching about Malcolm X and African American social and political struggle in the United States. He tries to move away from canonizing Haley's *Autobiography* in which Marable argues that "Malcolm died in February 1965, he had no opportunity to revise major elements of what would become known as his political testament" (p. 9).

There are sixty-three pages of footnotes in the biography. Prior to this particular writing of Malcolm, access to the records that Marable used were inaccessible. The FBI records reveal the ways in which Malcolm was not privy to many of the things that were happening around him, not to mention the many decisions that were made which would ultimately affect his life in many ways. In addition to the FBI and NYPD records, Marable had access to other materials including the archives of the Nation of Islam, and interviews with persons who were very close to Malcolm at points in his transformation. To be sure, FBI, NYPD and NOI records might pose a problem as sources: Malcolm was basically viewed in an antagonistic way as the enemy.

It is true that the Nation of Islam and the theology of Elijah Muhammad's ideology had a great impact on Malcolm. However, Malcolm's development as a human being begins with his parents as a child when he was introduced to the teachings of Marcus Garvey. He was instilled with values of Black pride, which continued after the death of his father and his mother's nervous breakdown. There were many instances in Malcolm's life where he had the chance to observe the philosophy and practices of orthodox Islam first hand. Once he was encouraged to convert to the Nation of Islam by his siblings, it was there, coupled with his ability to consume a great deal of literature while incarcerated, that Malcolm was able to develop more nuanced thoughts and ideas about the world of Islam. Malcolm's travels to Africa and the Middle East allowed him to witness the ways in which orthodox Islam is practiced throughout the Muslim world. On each occasion, as told in the text, Malcolm engaged in conversations which ultimately forced him to grapple with the central tenets of the version of Islam as practiced by the Nation of Islam. For instance, Marable writes about Malcolm's exchange with Prince Faisal where he realizes that he would have to rethink Elijah Muhammad's theology. In the end, as Marable reported, Malcolm, "In taking the necessary steps to become a true Muslim he had regained the certainty that had abandoned him with each new revelation of Elijah Muhammad's perfidy or infidelity. He could also now see the role Islam would play not just in his spiritual life, but in his work" (p. 311). Malcolm's sojourns abroad expanded and broadened his spiritual and intellectual consciousness.

Marable includes information about the fissures that ultimately led to the split between Malcolm and Muhammad. Marable reveals that much of this split is the result of the fears and jealousies belonging to the Nation of Islam's national leadership and some constituents regarding Malcolm's increasing high profile and growing popularity among people in the United States and abroad. Malcolm developed critical insight and leadership skills, which were seen as a threat. As a result, Elijah Muhammad was more restrictive and authoritative towards Malcolm's every move. Muhammad limited Malcolm's speaking engagements and censored his talks even though Malcolm praised him and defended the Nation of Islam's philosophy sometimes to his own detriment. Malcolm was also instrumental in the growth of the Nation of Islam but he was not one of the monetary benefactors.

In the chapter titled "Brother, a Minister Has to be Married," Marable presents a picture of two people who wedded because of Malcolm's role and status in the Nation: he had to fulfill an obligation of selecting a wife. Marable writes that Malcolm and Betty Shabazz were not particularly in love with one another. However, Betty Shabazz in her essay "Malcolm X As Husband and Father" which appeared in Clarke's anthology writes, "I too had concluded that Malcolm wanted to marry me" (Clarke, 1990, p. 133). Shabazz admitted that he had apprehensions about marriage because of his father and mother's relationship and their arguments. However, Shabazz stated, "I could see that his apprehension lessened as our marriage continued and we began to have children" (Clarke, p. 134). Marable suggests that they had many issues not the least of which was sex, finances, life styles, and children. In this text, Marable points to Betty Shabazz as the one who engages in an extramarital affair with another NOI member. It must be noted here that even the cited FBI records seem to be mere speculation, and largely hearsay. Also, in the case of Malcolm, it is revealed that Malcolm considered having an affair with someone from his past. Again, this was largely hearsay. Shabazz reflected on Malcolm as husband, stating that, "He also used to do tender, little things that I suppose every woman looks for in her husband. When he was gone for long intervals he used to leave money in different places around the house." Marable includes circumstantial evidence about marital problems between Malcolm X and Betty Shabazz. However, he does not offer facts to prove the allegations. In David Gallen's edited volume *Malcolm As They Knew Him*, Maya Angelou stated that while in Ghana, "he would talk at length about Betty and about the children. He really was a family man. In other circumstances, if racism and other kinds of cruelties were not operating against him, he would have been the typical family man, having the job and looking after the wife and children, and, being a religious man, being in a church or a temple, whatever..." (p. 36-37). In the same edited volume, former staff reporter for *Amsterdam News,* James Booker, affirmed that Malcolm, "He was very loving toward his family; that stood out the most with me" (p. 37). Including interviews with women like Maya Angelou, Ruby Dee and Malcolm's daughters might have resulted in a balanced and richer narrative related to his family life.

One aspect of Malcolm's transformation not explored in depth in Marable's biography is his changing views on gender issues. Marable documents that: Another source of conflict was the role of women in the organization. Former Black Muslims believed that "women played secondary role to the men. The men were out front, the protectors, the warriors.... Malcolm tried to break this patriarchy, insisting that in the OAAU "women [should have an] equal position to the men." His new commitment to gender equality confused and even outraged many members.

Among the many struggles throughout Malcolm's life that he had to deal with was his thoughts of women and the varying degrees of patriarchy embedded in the cultural logics of Islam. Women in the NOI had to adhere to a stricter code of conduct compared to men. This code that they had to follow was consistent with conservative values regulating women's behavior. The rationale, of course, for such regulations, was because of the gender ideology upheld by the organization, which devalued women much in the same way that women were debased in the larger society. Women were primarily taught how to be domestics who were required to maintain a proper home and take care of their husbands and children. Not only did these codes dictate the women's conduct, but it also provided a guide for how men in the NOI should also respond to and interact with women. Malcolm surely did not escape such teachings. Although we have been led to believe, in part, that he valued women and treated them properly, Marable presents a version of Malcolm who did not see women as being equal to men in comportment or mental prowess.

As noted in the text, Malcolm's perceptions of women originated during his childhood, observing the relations between his mother and father. After the murder of his father, the social strains stemming from various social service agencies took its toll on his mother—she suffered from the onset of depression and mental illness. This was the first instance where Malcolm began to harbor negative views of women. The notion that women are weaker to men would become a staple in his beliefs about women. Eventually, he would incorporate other negative perceptions that women are untrustworthy and deceptive, selfish, opportunistic, and that women were "inherently inferior and subordinate to males" (p. 142). All of such perceptions were only enhanced and confirmed by the specific type of patriarchy offered to women in the organization. Nonetheless, ultimately this kind of thinking affected his relations with his wife and other women around him. Marable quoted him saying that "The true nature of a man is to be strong, and a woman's true nature is to be weak . . . [a man] must control her if he expects to get her respect" (p. 142).

Marable's documentation provides him with an excellent opportunity to examine Malcolm X in new ways. How does Malcolm move from the views that he had about women while in the Nation of Islam to commitments to gender equality? In George Breitman, edited, *By Any Means Necessary: Speeches, Interviews and a Letter by Malcolm X*, 1987, the following remarks were made by Malcolm in a Paris interview, November 1964:

> One thing that I became aware of in my traveling recently through Africa and the Middle East, in every country you go to, usually the degree of progress can never be separated from the woman. If you're in a country that's progressive, the woman is progressive. If you're in a country that reflects the consciousness toward the importance of education, it's because the woman is aware of the importance of education. (179)

During his last year, Malcolm's views were changing with regards to the role and place of women. He also said in the Paris interview that, "one of the things I became thoroughly convinced of in my recent travel is the importance of giving freedom to the woman, giving her education, and giving her the incentive to get out there and put that same spirit and understanding in her children" (179). This is a different Malcolm than the minister controlled by Elijah Muhammad in the Nation of Islam. Malcolm concludes by stating that, "And I frankly am proud of the contributions that our women have made in the struggle for freedom and I'm one person who's for giving them all the leeway possible because they've made a greater contribution than many of us men" (179). What might have Marable revealed to readers by investigating Malcolm's changing views on questions of gender?

Marable offers many reasons why the case of the assassination of Malcolm X should be re-opened and investigated in light of the interview and trial transcripts, FBI documents, and police records. Marable's opinion and many other *Malcolmites* are that the true murderers remain at-large. Marable writes that, "Malcolm was not fully aware, until too late, of the deep hostilities he had provoked inside the Nation of Islam that led a coterie of officials around Muhammad to call for his murder. He placed his trust in a bodyguard who may have planned and helped to carry out his public execution" (p. 479).

Malcolm had the ability to transform himself because of his convictions to raise Black consciousness about the importance of one's own making and re-making which may be attributed to his African-centered service and sacrifice. This earned him respect as well as ability to recruit diverse followers. His Black consciousness and critique of white supremacy in America lead to his ending. As much as the text is about overcoming obstacles that makes a life complete, it is also about the fantastic moment that keeps us tuned into this never ending story of Malcolm. Marable opens and closes the text at the site and discussion of Malcolm's assassination, which peaks curiosity for a continued search for the truth about not only Malcolm's death, but his life of African-centered service and sacrifice.

We respect Manning Marable's contributions to African American history. However, his biography of Malcolm is flawed with presumptions, insupportable facts and questionable sources from organizations that viewed Malcolm X as the enemy. Still, Marable's biography provides the opportunity to revisit the life and contributions of Malcolm X while opening up a space for more serious dialogue and research around the life and times of an African American hero. Struggle for humanity, self-reliance, self-determination and transformation was a major theme in Malcolm's life story, but his life was also about African-centered service and sacrifice because of his love for his people.

Marable's work does not go far enough to examine the painful process that Malcolm experienced in his lifelong learning to obtain a consciousness of liberation not only to eradicate the shackles of white supremacy but also the structures and barriers placed on him by members of the National of Islam who he had mentored and worked for. These were the same people that one could place into the personality category that Frantz Fanon critiques in his work *The Wretched of the Earth* where he documents the pathology of oppression which results in self and group hatred perpetuating Black on Black crime. The same people Malcolm fought for and dedicated his life of African-centered service and sacrifice to betrayed him, resulting in his ultimate sacrifice. What role did the U.S. government play in Malcolm's assassination? This is an important question that needs to be addressed.

References

Baraka, Amiri (2011). Manning Marable's Malcolm X Book. downloaded August 25, 2011: http://panafricannews.blogspot.com/2011/05/amiri-baraka-on-manning-marable-malcolm_10.html

Breitman, George, edited. (1967) *Malcolm X Speaks: Selected Speeches and Statements.* New York, NY: Grove Press, Inc.

———. (1987) *By Any Means Necessary: Speeches, Interviews and a Letter by Malcolm X.* New York, NY: Pathfinder Press

Clarke, John Henrik, edited. (1990) *Malcolm X The Man and His Times.* Trenton, NJ: Africa World Press, Inc.

Collins, Rodnell P. with A. Peter Bailey. (1998) *Seventh Child: A Family Memoir of Malcolm X.* Secaucus, NJ: A Birch Lane Press Book, Carol Publishing Group

Gallen, David, edited. (1992) *Malcolm X As They Knew Him.* New York, NY: Carroll & Graf Publishers, Inc.

Perry, Imani (2011). Malcolm X, by Manning Marable. downloaded August 25, 2011:http://www.sfgate.com/cgi-bin/article.cgi?f=/c/a/2011/04/23/RV611J2B0B.DTL

Wood, Joe, edited. (1992) *Malcolm X: In Our Own Image.* New York, NY: St. Martin's Press, Inc.

LAST WORD

On My Father
Ilyasah Shabazz

The following remarks were delivered by Ms. Shabazz at a forum hosted by the Institute of the Black World 21st Century at Mother AMEZ Church in Harlem on Saturday, May 7, 2011.

I would like to thank Dr. Ron Daniels for his continuous commitment to the cause of human rights. And for the extraordinary panels he's assembled this afternoon: Sister Monifa Bandele, Sister Viola Plummer, Brother Herb Boyd, Brother Imam Talib Abdur-Rashid, and Brother James Small. I thank each of you for your diligence, your compassion, and, most of all, for your scholarship.

Introduction

People often ask me what it's like to be the daughter of Malcolm X and Dr. Betty Shabazz. I could not be more proud of my parents. When my father was killed, he was younger than I am today, and likely younger than many of us here this afternoon.

Both Malcolm and Betty, as many of the people in the Civil Rights era, were young activists committed to a cause. They dedicated themselves to the struggle for social justice—because they saw themselves in us—a people of African ancestry "troubled" by generations of institutional and systemic oppression—and a "nation" troubled by miseducation.

The struggle cannot die with Brother Malcolm. The struggle cannot die with Dr. King. Those is us present understand that the struggle...the Movement is far from over. Too many of our young men are shackled within the confines of jails and prisons throughout this country. Many of our babies are giving birth to babies. Many of our children are scoring in the lowest percentile on National Achievement tests. Many of grown folk are unable to find work and cannot afford decent housing. Certainly, we must understand that the Movement is not over, ladies and gentlemen. And it is our duty to remind every living being that the Struggle is NOT over.

Betty

I was fortunate enough to observe my mother's efforts towards the cause of human rights; and empowering women, particular. Writing my book, *Growing UP X*, afforded me an opportunity to reflect on her life as a source of inspiration and empowerment.

My mother was just a young woman in her twenties when she witnessed the assassination of her husband. She struggle through raising six daughters...alone. She continued to educate herself while she educated her daughters. With so much going on in her life, my mother saw the need to continue her husband's work, and she was relentless in her efforts. Dr. Betty Shabazz did not allow adversaries to write El Hajj Malik El-Shabazz, Malcolm X, out of history. Dr. Shabazz refused to allow the legacy of her husband to fade out of America's history and world history.

Malcolm X

Malcolm X was only in his twenties when he joined the Civil Rights movement. He campaigned for every breathing human being. He campaigned against institutional racism. He challenged a government that continued political violence against its own citizens. And, in the twelve short years immediately preceding my father's martyrdom, El Hajj Malik El-Shabazz, (1) rose to the defense of African Americans brutalized by discrimination, (2) he challenged white supremacy and racial injustice, (3) redefined the American Civil Rights movement to include human rights agenda, and (4) he worked tirelessly to unite Africa and the Diaspora towards a singular international struggle for freedom and independence.

El Hajj Malik El Shabazz, Malcolm X, accepted the mantle of leadership in the human rights struggle because he understood the oneness of humanity—that we are all brothers and sisters in the family of God. He awakened us with information of our heritage; with information to provide us with a healthy identity as persons of African ancestry—as we navigated through the challenges of institutional racism. Malcolm X was a man of impeccable integrity. Malcolm X is a testament to our ancestors; Malcolm X will continue to be a role model for generations following him. Thus, we cannot sit by and allow "speculative historians" to strip away his influence, his motives, his integrity, his love for humankind and the true history of who El Hajj Malik El Shabazz is.

We have been conditioned to think that we are singular, insular, individuals who must strive and accomplish alone; that we must pull our individual selves up by our own bootstraps. But if we take an honest look around, we must admit... "It isn't working!"

Brother Malcolm helped us to understand the importance of that African proverb: "That it indeed it takes a village to raise a child." And, that each one of us must play our part in that village. I am very encouraged by people like you who are refusing to have our history diluted or reduced to speculation and personal hypothesis.

Our Responsibility

This is our history! And we cannot allow any one person or any one group of people to continue to rewrite any portion of our history without "substantiated" competent, evidentiary proof.

This topic of discussion should teach all of us that we must be consistently diligent in our demands that any historian not be allowed to reduce "history" to speculation. I believe that, at this juncture, our purpose has been defined for us, and I am encouraged by all of you who have gathered here today with the knowledge that this is not a dilemma, predicament or difficulty that we can afford to ignore. All history must be as factual, as humanly possible. Truth must always prevail and we must be able to separate truth from sensationalism.

Conclusion

I do not stand in defense of my father. El Hajj Malik El Shabazz...stands on his own! It was Brother Malcolm's personal journey and self-discovery that led him towards peace. His short life was a continuous search for truth—for us! And the least we can do for our beloved Malcolm is to demand that those who claim to define him bring us his truths.

Contributors

Herb Boyd is an activist, journalist, author, and a teacher of African American history for four decades. He is the author and editor of 22 books, most recently *Civil Rights: Yesterday and Today* with Todd Steven Burroughs. Among his most popular books are *Baldwin's Harlem—The Biography of James Baldwin*; *We Shall Overcome: The History of the Civil Rights Movement As It Happened*; and *Simeon's Story: An Eyewitness Account of the Kidnapping of Emmett Till* with Simeon Wright.

Ron Daniels is President of the Institute of the Black World 21st Century, Founder of the Haiti Support Project and Distinguished Lecturer at York College City University of New York. He previously served as Executive Director of the Center for Constitutional Rights, Executive Director of the National Rainbow Coalition and Deputy Campaign Manager of Rev. Jesse L. Jackson's 1988 Campaign for President. In 1990, along with Dr. James Turner, Dr. Daniels served as Co-Chairman of the National Malcolm X Commemoration Commission which proclaimed May 19, the birthday of Malcolm X, a National African American Day of Commemoration.

Maulana Karenga is Professor and chair of Africana Studies at California State University, Long Beach. An activist-scholar who has played a major role in Black intellectual and political culture since the 60s, he is the creator of the pan-African cultural holiday Kwanzaa and the author of several books including the forthcoming novel *The Liberation Ethics of Malcolm X: An Emancipatory Critique and Corrective*, a study of the social and ethical philosophy of Malcolm X.

Haki R. Madhubuti is a renowned poet, author and educator and has published more than 30 books, and founded Third World Press, an African American book-publishing house, in 1967. He is also a founder of the Institute of Positive Education/New Concept School, co-founder of Betty Shabazz International Charter School, Barbara A. Sizemore Middle School, and DuSable Leadership Academy. In 2010, Madhubuti was awarded the Hurston/Wright Legacy Poetry Prize for his book, *Liberation Narratives*.

CONTRIBUTORS

Imam Al-Hajj Talib Abdur-Rashid is the religious and spiritual leader (imam) of the Mosque of Islamic Brotherhood Inc. in Harlem, New York City. He also serves as both the Vice-President (Deputy Amir) of the Majilis Ash-Shura (Islamic Leadership Council) of New York and the Deputy Amir of The Muslim Alliance in North America.

Mumia Abu-Jamal was among the founding members of the Black Panther Party (Philadelphia branch), which was deeply Malcolmist in its original orientation. With a B.A. in Psychology and M.A. in Humanities, he has authored seven books and written several articles and commentaries that have appeared in several publications including the *Yale Law Review* and *Black Scholar*. Today, Mumia Abu-Jamal is being held on death row in Pennsylvania following a nearly 28 years trial that has evoked both national and international concern and protest.

Abdul Alkalimat is a Professor at the University of Illinois in the Department of African American Studies and the Graduate School of Library and Information Science. He is the editor of the listserv H-Afro-Am and maintains several websites including Brother Malcolm.net and eBlack Studies.org.

Molefi Kete Asante is a Professor in the Department of African-American Studies at Temple University. He is also president of the Molefi Kete Asante Institute for Afrocentric Studies and is credited for founding the theory of Afrocentricity. He has authored 72 books on various aspects of African culture and politics including *Maulana Karenga: An Intellectual Portrait* and *An Afrocentric Manifesto*.

Rick Ayers is a Professor of Education at the University of San Francisco in the Urban Education and Social Justice department. Possessing a doctorate from the UC Berkeley Graduate School of Education, he has written several books including *Teaching the Taboo: Courage and Imagination in the Classroom*, which he co-authored with his brother William Ayers.

Bryonn Bain is the author of the hip hop generation remix of a classic *The Prophet Returns*, and the internationally-acclaimed theatrical production *Lyrics from Lockdown*. His work has been featured by *The Amsterdam News, The Village Voice, The New York Times, The Boston Globe, Variety*

Magazine, Harvard Law Record, on BET, C-SPAN and 60 Minutes. The past decade of his critical essays and provocative interviews will be published later this year in The Ugly Side of Beautiful: Rethinking Race and Prisons.

Amiri Baraka is one of the worlds most prolific and versatile writers and artists. Having excelled in practically every literary genre, his most recent publication is DIGGING: The Afro American Soul of American Classical Music (Music of the African Diaspora) and his upcoming collection of essays RAZOR is due from Third World Press in 2011.

Aslaku Berhanu is Librarian of the Charles L. Blockson Afro-American Collection, Temple University Libraries. Her publications include "An Annotated Bibliography of Reference Sources on African American Women, Journal of Black Studies, November 1998, and her latest article on Dr. Caroline Still Wiley Anderson forthcoming in the Journal of Black Studies.

Amir Bey is a mixed media sculptor who has worked as a curator for over 100 exhibitions and performances including the Bronx River Art Center and Gallery, he has also exhibited in Japan, Turkey, Germany, Spain and Martinique. In addition to working as an artist, Amir Bey is a professional astrologer who has worked on thousands of charts, and has written several articles on astrology including The Astrology of Malcolm X, which was published by American Astrology, in 1995.

Todd Steven Burroughs is a Lecturer in the Department of Communication Studies at Morgan State University, a historically Black university in Baltimore, Maryland. A former National Correspondent, Columnist and News Editor of the NNPA News Service (nnpa.org; BlackPressUSA.com), he is the co-author of Civil Rights: Yesterday and Today with award-winning journalist and historian Herb Boyd. He is writing a journalistic biography of Death Row journalist Mumia Abu-Jamal.

Ta-Nehisi Coates is a senior editor at The Atlantic where he writes about culture, politics and social issues. He is the author of the memoir, The Beautiful Struggle, an autobiography that chronicles his coming of age in West Baltimore, Maryland.

CONTRIBUTORS

William Jelani Cobb is an Associate Professor of History at Spelman College. He specializes in post-Civil War African American history, 20th century American politics and the history of the Cold War.

Karl Evanzz is the author of three books, including *The Judas Factor: The Plot to Kill Malcolm X,* which is an investigative look at the assassination of Malcolm X. He is the coauthor of *Dancing with the Devil* with hip-hop artist Mark Curry.

Iyaluua and Herman Ferguson Iyaluua spent many years on the ramparts as a human rights activist, too many of those years without her devoted and equally revolutionary husband, Herman, dedicated colleague of Malcolm X a founding member of Malcolm X's Organization of Afro-American Unity (OAAU) and an eyewitness to his leader's assassination in Harlem's Audubon Ballroom, who spent 19 years in exile in Guyana. Their recent book, *The Unlikely Warrior: The Autobiography of Herman Ferguson* is a compilation of their combined fight against injustice and to free the land.

Bill Fletcher Jr. is an Editorial Board member of BlackCommentator.com and a Senior Scholar with the Institute for Policy Studies. Having served as the immediate past president of TransAfricaForum, Fletcher is also the co-author of *Solidarity Divided: The Crisis in Organized Labor and a New Path Toward Social Justice* which examines the crisis of organized labor in the United States of America.

Glen Ford is a veteran of more than 40 years in broadcast, print and Internet journalism. A former Washington Bureau Chief and White House, Capitol Hill, and State Department correspondent, Ford co-founded and hosted "America's Black Forum," the first nationally syndicated Black news interview program on commercial television. He also launched and owned the radio syndications "Black World Report," "Black Agenda Reports," and "Rap It Up," the first national hip hop music show.

Rhone Fraser is host of the radio talk show Freedom Readers, on WPEB 88.1FM in West Philadelphia. A Ph.D candidate in the Department of African American Studies at Temple University, Fraser is writing a dissertation on influential African American editors of the first half of the twentieth century. Having written several works including a biographical play on Fannie Lou Hamer, Fraser's work has been published in the *Journal of African American Studies* and the *College Language Association Journal.*

Kelly Harris is an assistant professor and coordinator of African American Studies at Chicago State University. His areas of concentration include African American politics, African politics, Black political thought, and the history of social science. His current research involves an interrogation of the correlation between abstract violence and African development, and a critical analysis of Black scholars' protracted attempt at developing Black social science.

Wil Haygood is a writer for the *Washington Post.* In addition to authoring a book on his life growing up in Columbus, Ohio; *The Haygoods of Columbus: A Love Story*, he has written biographies on several historic figures including Adam Clayton Powell Jr., Sammy Davis Jr. and, most recently, Sugar Ray Robinson.

Errol A. Henderson is Associate Professor of Political Science at Pennsylvania State University where he teaches International Relations. His research focuses on the analysis of war; the impact of cultural factors, such as religion, ethnicity, and language, on war and peace; African politics; and Africana Studies. Henderson is the author of nearly thirty publications including two books: *Democracy and War* and *Afrocentrism and World Politics.*

Fred Hord is a Professor and Director of the Africana Studies Program at Knox College. In addition to being the Founder and present Director of the Association for Black Cultural Centers, He is the editor of "Nommo," the bi-annual newsletter published by ABCC. Hord has written and edited several books and articles and is a long-standing member of the Board of the National Council for Black Studies.

Peter James Hudson is an Assistant Professor of History at Vanderbilt University in Nashville, Tennessee. He is currently working on a manuscript titled *Dark Finance: Wall Street and the West Indies, 1893-1933.* Hudson is the former editor of *North: New African Canadian Writing*, a special issue of the Vancouver-based literary journal *West Coast Line* and he is a co-founder and co-editor of the digital history resource, *The Public Archive: History beyond the headlines.*

CONTRIBUTORS

Ezra Hyland is a Teaching Specialist in the Department of Postsecondary Teaching and Learning (PSTL) at the University of Minnesota. In addition to teaching, Hyland is responsible for the African American Read-In, a national effort sponsored by the Black Caucus of the National Council of Teachers of English.

Regina Jennings teaches African American literature and culture at Rutgers University. As a scholarly writer and poet, her books include *Malcolm X and the Poetics of Haki Madhubuti* which won the Cheikh Anta Diop International Award; *Race, Rage, and Roses*; and *Midnight Morning Musings: Poems of an American African.* Her current work in progress is *Poetry of the Black Panther Party: Metaphors of Militancy.*

Peniel E. Joseph is a professor of history at Tufts University. His most recent book is *Dark Days, Bright Nights: From Black Power to Barack Obama.*

Clyde Ledbetter Jr. graduated from Lincoln University with a degree in Political Science in 2007 and earned his M.A. in African American Studies from Temple University in 2010. He is currently pursuing his Ph.D. at Temple University in African American Studies. His research interests include African political theory and human rights in Africa.

Fred Logan is a member of the Pittsburgh chapter of Black Voices for Peace. His commentaries have appeared in the *Pittsburgh Post Gazette, New Pittsburgh Courier, Review of Black Political Economy, New York Amsterdam News*, and other journals.

Kevin McGruder is Adjunct Assistant Professor of African and African American Studies at Lehman College (CUNY). From 1997 to 2001 he was Executive Director of Gay Men of African Descent.

Starla Muhammad is a staff writer for the influential independent Black-owned weekly, *The Final Call.* Her works have appeared in numerous print and online publications.

Nell Irvin Painter is the Edwards Professor of American History-Emerita at Princeton University. A leading historian in the United States, she is the author of *The History of White People.*

CONTRIBUTORS

Imani Perry is a Professor at the Center for African American Studies at Princeton University. She has authored several works including *Righteous Hope, Prophets of the Hood: Politics and Poetics in Hip Hop* and the notes and introduction to the Barnes and Noble Classics edition of the *Narrative of Sojourner Truth*.

Gregory J. Reed is an active practitioner and activist in the legal profession. He specializes in legalities involving entertainment, intellectual properties, and corporate and tax laws. Reed has worked with Rosa Parks, Malcolm X's legacy, Dr. Betty Shabazz, Nelson Mandela, Coretta Scott King, and has published sixteen books.

Sonia Sanchez is an award-winning poet, mother, activist, professor, and international lecturer on Black culture and literature, women's liberation, peace and racial justice. A sponsor of the Women's International League for Peace and Freedom, she has written over 16 books, including: *Homecoming*; *We a BadddDD People*; *Love Poems*; *I've Been a Woman: New and Selected Poems*; *A Sound Investment and Other Stories*; *Homegirls and Handgrenades*; *Under A Soprano Sky*; *Wounded in the House of a Friend*; *Does Your House Have Lions?*, *Like the Singing Coming off the Drums*; and most recently, *Shake Loose My Skin*.

Ilyasah Shabazz holds a Master of Science degree in education and human resource development from Fordham University. For many years she was director of Public Affairs and Special Events for the city of Mount Vernon, New York. In 2002, she, along with Kim McLarin, completed her memoir *Growing Up X*.

Michael Simanga is a poet, music producer, essaysist and the author of the critically acclaimed novel, *In the Shadow of the Son*. He is Director of Arts and Culture for Fulton County, Georgia and is currently completing a book on the Congress of African People.

Diane D. Turner is Curator of the Charles L. Blockson Afro-American Collection, Temple University Libraries. Her areas of teaching and research include Black history, film and music and she is the author of the children's book, *My Name is Oney Judge*, illustrated by Cal Massey, and *Feeding the Soul: Black Music, Black Thought*.

"We declare our right on this earth...to be a human being, to be respected as a human being, to be given the rights of a human being in this society, on this earth, in this day, which we intend to bring into existence by any means necessary."